Constitutional Law in Israel

Constitutional Law in Israel

Second Edition

Suzie Navot

This book was originally published as a monograph in the International Encyclopaedia of Laws/Constitutional Law.

General Editors: Roger Blanpain, Frank Hendrickx
Volume Editors: André Alen, David Haljan

Wolters Kluwer

Published by:
Kluwer Law International B.V.
PO Box 316
2400 AH Alphen aan den Rijn
The Netherlands
Website: www.wklawbusiness.com

Sold and distributed in North, Central and South America by:
Wolters Kluwer Legal & Regulatory U.S.
7201 McKinney Circle
Frederick, MD 21704
United States of America
Email: customer.service@wolterskluwer.com

Sold and distributed in all other countries by:
Turpin Distribution Services Ltd.
Stratton Business Park
Pegasus Drive, Biggleswade
Bedfordshire SG18 8TQ
United Kingdom
Email: kluwerlaw@turpin-distribution.com

ISBN 978-90-411-6943-3

e-Book: ISBN 978-90-411-6959-4
web-PDF: ISBN 978-90-411-6982-2

This title is available on www.kluwerlawonline.com

The Author

Prof. Dr Suzie Navot was born in Montevideo, Uruguay. She has an LL.B (Bachelor of Laws) (Cum Laude) from the Faculty of Law at the Tel Aviv University; an M.A. (Cum Laude) in Public Policy from the Faculty of Social Sciences at the Tel Aviv University and an LL.D. (Doctor of Laws) from the Hebrew University in Jerusalem. Her doctorate dissertation (on Parliamentary Immunities) was awarded the 1999 Prize of the Israeli Association for Parliamentarism.

Prof. Navot teaches Constitutional Law at the Striks School of Law at the College of Management Academic Studies (COMAS) in Rishon Lezion.

Professor Navot has written many articles, chapters of books as well as books on the Constitutional Law of Israel. Her last book, '*The Constitution of Israel- a Contextual Analysis*' (Hart Publishing) was published in 2014.

Prof. Navot's main fields of research are Constitutional and Parliamentary Law, and Comparative Constitutional and Parliamentary Law. Navot speaks fluent Hebrew, English, French and Spanish.

The Author

Table of Contents

List of Abbreviations

AAD	Appeal Administrative Detention
CA	Civil Appeal
CC	Civil case
CCPR	Covenant on Civil and Political Rights
CF (Jer.)	Civil File Jerusalem
CFH	Criminal Further Hearing (a special procedure that allows a special hearing by a bench of a large number of judges in a matter already adjudged by the Supreme Court by a small bench of judges, i.e., three judges)
CLA	Civil Leave to Appeal
Cr. A	Criminal Appeal
Cr. Req. A	Criminal request to appeal
EA	Election Appeal
GSS	General Security Service
HCJ	High Court of Justice (The Supreme Court of Israel serves also as the High Court of Judges, therefore the two terms are used without differentiating between them in the text)
IDF	Israeli Defence Forces (the Israeli Army)
MK	Member of Knesset (the Israeli Parliament)
PD	*Piske'i Din* – Judgments of the Supreme Court of Israel. The first number indicates the tome (beginning in 1948 with tome 1). The second number in brackets indicates the volume
SC	Severe Criminal case
Sec.	Section
Tak-El	*Takdin-Elion* – another source for Judgments of the Supreme Court

List of Abbreviations

Preface

This is an updated monograph on Israeli Constitutional Law submitted to the World Encyclopaedia of Laws.

Israel has no one official document known as 'The Constitution', but is, in fact since the 1990s, a constitutional democracy. The supreme norms are expressed in its basic laws; the powers of the legislative branch are limited; and laws are subject to judicial review. This situation is the result of a historical compromise, the enactment of two basic laws dealing with human rights in the 1990s – generally referred to as the 'constitutional revolution' – and of a judicial decision of monumental significance. Many argue that Israel has a 'judicial' constitution that lacks many elements that characterize more complete constitutions found in other countries. Certain fundamental constitutional issues do not appear in Israel's basic laws and their legal status remains unclear. Yet, though the constitution is incomplete, the Israeli Courts have acknowledged certain principles that may not be modified – primarily the constitutional principle that refers to the Jewish and democratic nature of the State of Israel.

The narrative of Israel's constitutional history is the narrative of Israeli society: a Jewish and democratic state that since its establishment in 1948 has found itself in a state of emergency; a society in need of establishing a *modus operandi* for the harmonious coexistence of different nations and religions, and in need of a balance between a plethora of conflicting interests; a society in need of a balance between the fact of the State being the national state of the Jewish people, and its democratic character; and in need of a balance between the imperatives of human rights and the dictates of security requirements in times of war. In all of these constitutional conflicts, the role of the Israeli Supreme Court has been crucial.

In this monograph, I have traced the relevant constitutional developments until August 2015, and the constitutional texts are updated until June 2015.

Acknowledgements

I would like to thank Dr Sheila –Susan Hattis Rolef for the translation of all constitutional texts.

Thanks to the Striks Law School at the College of Management Academic Studies, for financially supporting the preparation of this monograph, as well for granting valuable assistance to my research. I would also like to thank Prof. Claude Klein, former author of the Israeli Monograph on Constitutional Law, for encouraging the project all along.

Special thanks to Breony Allen for her meticulous editorial work.

Last but not least, thanks to my wonderful and supporting family, my husband and my daughters. This monograph is dedicated to them.

Suzie Navot
August 2015

Acknowledgements

General Introduction

§1. Constitutional History

1. The State of Israel was officially established and proclaimed in May 1948. The land which became Israel – a narrow stretch of land on the eastern shore of the Mediterranean Sea – was ruled for most of the modern era, until 1917, by the Turks as part of the Ottoman Empire. British troops conquered the land in 1917, and it was granted to England in 1922 by the League of Nations as a Mandatory Territory.[1] The purpose of the Mandate, as explicitly provided in its terms, was to establish in Palestine 'a national home for the Jewish people'.[2]

1. *See* Art. 22 of the Covenant of the League of Nations which states:

   '1. To those colonies and territories which as a consequence of the late war have ceased to be under the sovereignty of the States which formerly governed them and which are inhabited by peoples not yet able to stand by themselves under the strenuous conditions of the modern world, there should be applied the principle that the wellbeing and development of such peoples from a sacred trust of civilization and that securities for the development of this trust should be embodied in this Covenant.
   2. The best method of giving practical effect to this principle is that the tutelage of such peoples should be entrusted to advanced nations which, by reasons of their resources, their experience or their geographical position, can best undertake this responsibility and who are willing to accept it, and that this tutelage should be exercised by them as Mandatories on behalf of the League.
   3. The character of the mandate must differ according to the stage of development of the people, the geographical situation of the territory, its economic conditions and other similar circumstances.
   4. Certain communities formerly belonging to the Turkish Empire have reached a stage of development where their existence as independent nations can be provisionally recognized subject to the rendering of administrative advice and assistance by a Mandatory until such time as they are able to stand alone. The wish of these communities must be a principal consideration in the selection of the Mandatory.'

   The latter category of mandates was called 'A', and included Syria, Lebanon, Palestine etc. The 'B' mandates included Togo and Cameroun, and the 'C' mandate applied solely to Southwest Africa (Namibia).

2. The Mandate included the exact wording of the Balfour Declaration of 2 Nov. 1917, issued by the British Government: 'His Majesty's Government view with favour the establishment in Palestine of a national home for the Jewish people, and will use their best endeavours to facilitate the achievement of this object, it being clearly understood that nothing shall be done which may prejudice the civil and religious rights of existing non-Jewish communities in Palestine, or the rights and political status enjoyed by Jews in any other country'.

2. Palestine was governed by Ottoman Law for over four hundred years. The Mandatory period lasted for only thirty years, but left a lasting mark on the law and government in Israel. Most of the Ottoman heritage has not survived, and only a few sections remain today, most of them insignificant. One of the long-term influences of the Ottoman legal culture on Israel's law and politics was the extensive autonomy it granted to religious minorities in most family matters. When the British assumed the Mandate over Palestine, they were enjoined by the League of Nations from interfering with this autonomy. The same idea was adopted by the State of Israel, mostly to avoid inter-communal tensions. Because of this background, Israel has become the only modern state in the world lacking a domestic civil law of marriage and divorce. This idea is one of the inheritances of the Ottoman period. The British legal heritage was much deeper, and in many ways, it determined the basic structure and principles of Israel's constitutional law.

3. Following the United Nations debate over the future of Palestine, the General Assembly of the UN adopted, on 29 November 1947, a decision for the partition of Palestine into a Jewish and an Arab state. The Arabs rejected the partition plan, which was approved by the Jewish population in Palestine. On 14 May 1948, the Jewish authorities proclaimed the new Jewish state, through the first constitutional document: the Declaration of Independence.[3] The Declaration of Independence created temporary central institutions of government, in the anticipation that these would be replaced by permanent authorities, among them a 'constituent assembly', to be elected no later than 1 October 1948. However, due to the first Arab-Israeli war, which began almost immediately after the Declaration of Independence, the elections were postponed until the end of January 1949. A constituent assembly was indeed elected, with the purpose of enacting a constitution for the state of Israel. In its first legislative act,[4] the constituent assembly changed its name to the First Knesset, and stated that the legislative body would be known as the 'Knesset'. The first Knesset failed to adopt a constitution. Instead, on 13 June 1950, it decided to adopt a resolution called the 'Harari Resolution',[5] which states that the future constitution would be enacted 'chapter by chapter', each of them constituting a 'basic law'. The intention was that, following the enactment of all the basic laws, together these would form the Israeli constitution. The Harari Resolution was vague as to the status of these basic laws. It was unclear whether they were to have a higher status than regular legislation, from the very moment of their enactment, or whether they

3. A body of thirty-seven members, representing the various political groups among the Jewish population, adopted the Declaration. It is two pages long, and is divided into three parts. The first part describes the historical background of the Jewish people and their connection with the land of Israel. The second part is known as the 'operative' part (starting with the words: 'We hereby proclaim the establishment of a Jewish State in the land of Israel: the State of Israel … '). The third part affirms some of the basic principles of the new State ('it will maintain complete equality of social and political rights for all its citizens, without distinction of religion, race or sex. It will guarantee freedom of religion and conscience, of language, education and culture … '). This latter part of the Declaration raises the question of its constitutional value, which will be dealt with in Part I (Sources of Constitutional Law).
4. The Transition Law 1949 3 L.S.I. 3 (1949).
5. Named after the Member of Knesset who was the sponsor of this resolution.

would have the same normative status as regular legislation, and become constitutional only after the completion of all basic laws and their unification into a single document. This question raised an intense controversy in the academic field, as to whether the '*pouvoir constituent*' – the authority to enact a constitution – which was held by the constituent assembly (the First Knesset) – was indeed passed on to the second Knesset and the subsequent Knessets, or whether it expired with the termination of the First Knesset. This dispute would be resolved de facto by the Supreme Court in 1995,[6] following the enactment of two basic laws dealing with human rights; namely Basic Law: Human Dignity and Liberty, and Basic Law: Freedom of Occupation.

4. With the establishment of the State of Israel in 1948, the existing combination of Ottoman and British Mandatory law was preserved, subject to the changes necessitated by the need to adjust the law to the establishment of the new state and its authorities, and to Israeli legislation.[7] Until the enactment of the last two basic laws on human rights in 1992, the Israeli constitutional system was rooted deeply in the British model. With the failure to enact a constitution following the establishment of the State, Israel became a parliamentary democracy, based on the principle of parliamentary supremacy. The Israeli Knesset thus enjoyed almost unlimited legislative powers.

I. Israel: A Unique Mixed System

5. Under the powerful influence of its English legacy, Israeli law shares many features with the common law tradition. Until 1980, by force of Article 46 of the Palestine Order in Council, Israeli Courts were bound to follow English judge-made law. This article was abolished in 1980, but even so, the custom of following English and American traditions still prevails. The status of almost all members of the legal profession – of judges, advocates and legal scholars – is still far more similar to their counterparts in England or America than to those in Germany or France. Legal process and legislation is based on common law roots, despite the civil law influence behind the codification of private law.

6. Major fields of law still echo concepts and rules from the corresponding fields of English law. The Israeli system of government is a prime example of this phenomenon. The structure of the legal system and its legal institutions is undoubtedly influenced by common law tradition. Judicial decisions are considered a source of

6. In the monumental case of *Mizrachi Bank v. Migdal*, delivered in 1995 (CA 6821/93 *Mizrachi Bank Ltd. v. Migdal Cooperative Village*, 49(4) PD 221, to be discussed in the following chapters), the Supreme Court of Israel declared that it had the power to judicially revoke ordinary legislation that infringed the Basic Law: Human Dignity and Liberty and Basic Law: Freedom of Occupation, enacted in 1992. These Basic Laws were referred to as the 'constitutional revolution'. The new Basic Laws include a 'limitation' clause, similar to the clause found in the Canadian Charter of Rights and Freedoms.
7. Law and Administration Ordinance, 1948, s. 11.

law, often referred to as 'the Israeli common law', and the principle of binding precedent governs the creation of judge-made law. The structure of the judiciary, its inner hierarchy, rules of evidence and procedure, and the status of judges all bear similarities to their corresponding systems in common law countries. Case-by-case analysis and casuistic legal thinking are widespread.

7. The Israeli contribution to its own legal system, starting in 1948, has been quite peculiar, being focused not only on filling the gaps left by former rulers. There has, for example, been a great effort to build two new systems of law, one governing private relations between individuals, and the other governing the rights of individuals in a democratic system, finding expression in the ongoing efforts to concisely codify the private law, and to codify and reform the public law mechanisms and the substance of public law. Both of these branches of law are influenced by different sources. The codification of public law has often relied on European legal concepts. The emergence of a new constitution has been heavily influenced by the reasoning and wisdom of American judges. Furthermore, the basic laws dealing with human rights have been heavily influenced by the Canadian model.[8]

8. The mixture of all of these influences has created a mixed jurisdiction, although it is much closer to the common law family than to continental traditions. It has particular characteristics. Legal thinking in Israel is less casuistic and tends more to generalizations than its common law counterparts. It also appears that Israeli law is more liberal with regard to procedural and formal requirements. The major role that academics play in shaping the law is inconsistent with the common law tradition, as are the continental concepts that have been adopted in Israel's private law, such as the principle of 'good faith'.

9. However, Israeli law is also clearly not a member of the continental law family and cannot be identified with the Roman tradition. Despite the adoption of some continental law concepts and the ongoing process of codification, the Anglo-American common law characteristics of Israeli law remain significant. Moreover, English-speaking countries remain the major source for comparative law since most members of the legal profession in Israel are not fluent in continental European languages, which make it difficult to follow developments in continental law, unless they are translated.

10. To conclude, it is apparent that Israeli law belongs to a family of mixed legal systems. At this stage of its development, it is located between the common law and continental law traditions, although it maintains a closer link to the former. It has many unique features, given the varied history and culture of Israel and the internal and external challenges it regularly faces, and it may be said that the search for the most suitable combination of influences is ongoing.

---

8. These Basic Laws include a 'limitation' clause, that is, a substantive limitation allowing the legislator to infringe a human right, but only in accordance with a proportionality test. This 'limitation' clause was adopted from the Canadian Charter of Rights and Freedoms.

§2. Profile of the Form of Government

11. England has also had a pronounced influence on the structure of Israel's government. Israel maintains a parliamentary regime, in which the Prime Minister enjoys the confidence of the Knesset. Following elections, the president imposes the task of forming the government on the most suitable candidate, who in most cases is the leader of the party which has the greatest number of representatives in the Knesset. The adopted structure according to which parliament is supreme, the government relies on the confidence of parliament, and the president is symbolic, was the natural outcome of the influence exerted by the British regime. At the same time, a number of distinctions remain between the Israeli and English parliaments. First, whereas the English parliament is composed of two dominant parties, the Israeli parliamentary system is characterized by multiple parties. Second, England is commonly partitioned into constituencies, each of which sends a representative to parliament in a 'first past the post' system. Israel operates a unique system which is nationwide and proportional; in other words, the elected candidate lists are represented in the Knesset, which is the house of representatives of the country, in accordance with the percentage of people who have voted for it. In contrast to the majority of western parliamentary democracies, Israel follows this system zealously, subject to a threshold quota, which currently stands at 3.25%. The number of seats which each party receives in the Knesset (there are 120 MKs in total) is relative to the number of voters who cast ballots for it. According to this system, the electorate votes for a list and not for a particular person on the list. Some of the parties conduct preliminary elections, known as primaries, to determine which party members will become the party's candidates for the Knesset. The candidates of the Orthodox parties are selected by their spiritual leaders. Elections to the Knesset take place once every four years; however, the Knesset or the Prime Minister may decide to hold earlier elections. In very special circumstances, the Knesset may even extend its session for more than four years.

12. Between the years 1996 and 2001, Israel modified its governmental system from a parliamentary system to a 'Prime Ministerial' system or presidential parliamentary system, in which the Prime Minister was elected by direct election.[9] Three elections were conducted in pursuance of this system: the elections of 1996, to the

9. The Knesset elections of 1984 had already indicated the existence of a stalemate between the two political blocks (the 'right' and the 'left'), and that their leaders would not be able to form a government without bringing in representatives of the other block, thereby giving rise to the establishment of a 'unity government' and the rotation of the office of Prime Minister. Towards the end of the 1980s, the Israeli public's sense of dissatisfaction with the National Unity Government increased. The Direct Election to Prime Minister Law was the outcome of a series of private members' bills in March 1990, tabled a few days after the National Unity Government collapsed following a vote of no-confidence. The legislative process accelerated as a result of vocal protests by large public movements incensed by the intrigues prevailing in the party and parliamentary systems.

Fourteenth Knesset;[10] the elections of 1999, to the Fifteenth Knesset;[11] and the elections of 2001, solely for the office of Prime Minister.[12]

I. The 'Prime Ministerial' Regime

13. The direct elections for the Prime Minister – enacted by the Knesset as an amendment to the Basic Law: The Government in 1992 and repealed in 2001 – introduced a new electoral system, namely, a direct election to the office of Prime Minister. The law was the outcome of difficulties in governance paralyzing the Prime Minister, ensuing from divisions within the Knesset and the inability to reach crucial decisions when forming the government. The direct election system was a unique model; a parliamentary system characterized by a number of aspects of the presidential system. Under this structure, the Prime Minister was elected directly by the public; however, in his relations with the executive authority, the system of 'checks and balances' was preserved by the fact that each of the authorities could remove the other. Formally, the executive authority of the State continued to be the government; however, the basis of power shifted to the Prime Minister. He formed the government and was entitled to dismantle it. The Prime Minister was also entitled to resign from his office, a step which would lead to special elections for that post only, as indeed occurred in February 2001.[13] Likewise, the Prime Minister could send his resignation to the President of the State, and thereby bring about the dispersal of the Knesset. The Knesset for its part could bring down the government and bring about general elections to the Knesset and to the office of Prime Minister, by passing a vote of no confidence in the government with a majority of 61 MKs.

14. The primary goal of the new system was to increase the sense of stability of the government and to cause the electorate to feel closer to their representatives. When discussions were held in relation to the election bills, one option considered was to introduce regional elections. It was thought that this would focus the elected representative's personal responsibility towards his constituency. However, ultimately, the reform was restricted and dealt only with the executive authority. The Direct Elections Law was designed to greatly improve the representative aspect of

10. Benjamin Netanyahu, as Chairman of the *Likud* Party, obtained a majority of 50.8% of votes and defeated the leader of the *Labour* Party, Shimon Peres. The *Likud* received thirty-two mandates compared to Labour's thirty-five mandates.
11. Ehud Barak, as Chairman of *One Israel* (the *Labour* Party), obtained a majority of 56.08% of votes and defeated Benjamin Netanyahu. *One Israel* received twenty-six mandates compared to the nineteen mandates received by the *Likud*.
12. Ariel Sharon, as Chairman of the *Likud*, obtained a majority of 62.39% of votes and defeated Ehud Barak, the leader of the *Labour* Party.
13. The elections in 2001 followed the failure of the Camp David talks, and the amassing of a majority in the Knesset to bring down the government. Prime Minister Ehud Barak declared his agreement to hold early elections and resigned from his office as Prime Minister, in order to enable elections to be held for the office of Prime Minister only.

Israeli democracy and to constrict the power of extortion of the small parties and individual MKs. Three electoral processes were carried out in accordance with the direct election system over a period of five years. This fact, more than anything else, testified to the weaknesses of the system, and led to the repeal of direct elections and the return of the old system with a few minor changes, in 2001.[14] The direct election to the office of Prime Minister, which was intended to provide an answer to the increasing difficulties of governance in Israel, in fact achieved the opposite result.[15] The repeal of the law created a new opportunity to rehabilitate the parties and the Israeli parliamentary democracy. The selection of the Prime Minister was again the result of the electoral system, and once more, the fate of the Prime Minister was bound up with the fate of the legislative authority and the fate of the parties.

15. The direct election system was based, *inter alia*, on the experience of other countries, in particular the United States and France; however, the system was adopted without these models having been adequately studied. On the one hand, the new law did not create a presidential system in Israel, while on the other hand it distanced it from the parliamentary system. History shows that it is not possible to change a political culture within short periods of time by means of legislative measures. It probably would have been preferable to refrain from such change in circumstances in which the full ramifications of such change had not been comprehensively calculated. The direct election system was put in place without supplementing it with the necessary modifications to other elements of government, and it consequently failed to present a comprehensive, integrated concept of governance. This failure contributed considerably to its collapse.

---

14. For example, the adoption of the idea of 'constructive no-confidence', which compels the Knesset – as a condition for bringing down the government – to unite, with a majority of sixty-one MKs, over the candidacy of another person for the office of Prime Minister. This idea of 'constructive no-confidence' has even been improved, making it much more difficult for the Knesset to bring down the government. As from 2015, in order to dismiss the government, the Knesset needs to pass a decision to form a new government, by a majority of sixty-one MKs. This means that not only does another member needs to have a majority of sixty-one votes in order to become Prime Minister, but he/she also needs to present the Knesset with a full government, including all ministers and Government guidelines.
15. The reform in the system of government contributed to the erosion of the electoral force of the two big parties, the *Labour* Party and the *Likud* Party, and greater divisions within the Knesset. Netanyahu and Barak failed to preserve the coalition which they had created, and consequently were forced to hold early elections. The first elections were held after three years of office, and the second after only a year and a half. Thus, the primary goal of the Direct Elections Law to govern in a stable and effective manner was not achieved. Both Netanyahu and Barak were forced to exert enormous effort to coordinate the policies of a fractured coalition, the divisions of which had been augmented as a result of the dual ballot, and to invest additional time and energy in order to maintain their respective coalitions. In practice, the 1996 elections created a contentious and multi-party Knesset in which the two big parties were significantly reduced, and excessive expression was given to the narrow interests of new immigrants and the orthodox parties.

§3. State Territory and Non-self-governing Territories

16. The total area of Israel is 22,145 square kilometres.[16] This area includes East Jerusalem[17] and the Golan Heights, the area of which is 1,154 square kilometres.[18] The total land area is 21,671 square kilometres. According to the formal administrative partition of the State of Israel, there are six Districts which are distributed into 15 regions: the Jerusalem District possessing an area of 652 square kilometres; the northern District possessing an area of 4,478 square kilometres; the Haifa District possessing an area of 863 square kilometres; the central District possessing an area of 1,276 square kilometres; the Tel Aviv District possessing an area of 141 square kilometres; and the southern District possessing an area of 14,231 square kilometres.

17. Apart from these areas, Israel holds an additional territory[19] – the West Bank[20] – known also as Judea and Samaria, possessing a total area of 5,651 square kilometres.

---

16. The area of Israel – comprising its land and sea – according to the administrative boundaries of the territory of the state, include East Jerusalem and the Golan Heights. In consequence of the Peace Treaty between Israel and Jordan on 26 Oct. 1994, an exchange of territory was carried out in 1995 in the area of the southern Arava and the Bet She'an Valley.
17. East Jerusalem was annexed in 1967 following the Six Day War. From that year onwards, this territory has been included in the formal administrative boundaries of the State of Israel. In June 1967, immediately after the Six Day War, the government of Israel annexed 70,000 dunam (one dunam = 1,000 square metres) east of West Jerusalem and subjected it to Israeli law. This annexation, which included 6,000 dunam of Jordanian Jerusalem and additional territory from twenty-eight cities and villages in the West Bank, increased the area of the city threefold, and transformed it into the largest city in Israel. In addition to the annexation of territory, 69,000 Palestinian residents were added to Israel with the status of residents without full national rights. They have been allowed to vote in the Palestinian parliamentary elections, in 1996 and 2006.
18. The Golan Heights were attached to Israel in the formal administrative division of the State of Israel in 1981, by virtue of the Golan Heights Law which was enacted on 14 Dec. 1981. Prior to 1967, the Golan Heights formed part of Syrian territory. In 1973, certain parts of the Golan Heights were returned to Syrian control.
19. Following the Six Day War (in June 1967), Israel held Judea, Samaria and the Gaza Strip, as well as the Golan Heights and the Sinai. The United Nations adopted Resolution 242 which calls upon Israel to retreat from territories which it conquered in return for peace. Contrary to the situation in 1949, when the UN recognized all the territories conquered by Israel as sovereign territory, Resolution 242 declared 'the territory' conquered in 1967 as occupied territory. Consequently, the UN demanded that Israel deal with them in accordance with international law concerning occupied territory, namely, in accordance with the prohibition against making any changes in the occupied territory (including building settlements or paving roads); the prohibition on exploiting the natural resources of the occupied territories; the prohibition on imposing collective punishments on the population of the occupied territories and more. In August 2005, Israel decided to withdraw from the Gaza Strip, and in a unilateral move, vacated the settlements in the Strip and ended the military government which had been imposed on the Strip in 1967. The area of the Gaza Strip, which was under the control of Israel between 1967 and 2005, was 362 square kilometres.
20. An interesting phenomenon relating to the territory of Israel concerns the names which were given to certain tracts of land following the Six Day War. The first of these names – the West Bank – was a technical term used by the Jordanian Kingdom in the nineteen years which elapsed between the time the Hashemite regime in Amman and the East Bank of the Jordan River conquered these areas of the West Bank of the river. This term enabled the Jordanian occupier to draw a distinction, for its own purposes, between the two banks of the Jordan River. The adoption of this term by the Israeli

§4. State Population and Demographic Data

18. By the end of 2014, the population of the State of Israel totalled 8,297,000 people.[21] The distribution of the population according to religion (as of the end of 2013) is as follows:

Jews	6,104,500 people
Muslims	1,420,300 people
Christians	160,900 people
Druze	133,400 people

government was carried out at the height of the battle of June 1967, without due consideration being given to the lack of significance of the name from the perspective of observers on the Israeli side of the river; after all, the Galilee too occupies the west side of the river, it too is inhabited by an Arab majority which is not enthusiastic about Jewish settlement, and so on. The only difference between the Galilee and Judea and Samaria relates to the years 1948–1967, during which there was a gap between Israeli control of the northern section of the 'West Bank' and the control of the more southern tracts of mountainous land.

21. The Jewish population and others (including Christians and those without religious affiliation) comprise 6,576,700 and Arabs 1,720.200. All the data has been taken from the *Israel Statistical Yearbook*, the Central Bureau of Statistics (2013 and 2015).

Part I. Sources of Constitutional Law

Chapter 1. Treaties

19. Israeli law does not clearly prescribe the manner in which customs and treaties are enacted into domestic law, nor does it establish which of the governmental branches – legislative, executive or the presidency – is empowered to bind Israel in international treaties. From an historical perspective, questions concerning the status of international law in Israeli law arose primarily after the Six Day War in 1967. In the aftermath of the war, Israel was left in control of two territorial units: Judea and Samaria, which had previously been under Jordanian rule; and the Gaza Strip, which had previously been under Egyptian rule (hereinafter collectively referred to as 'the Territories'). In accordance with the requirements of international law, Israel established a military government in the Occupied Territories, and in legal terms, they are viewed as being under belligerent occupation. Insofar as the Territories are not under Israeli jurisdiction, and Israeli civil law is not applicable therein,[22] their status is determined in accordance with the sources of international law, both by force of the 1907 Regulations annexed to the Hague Convention (Respecting the Laws and Customs of War on Land), and the 1949 Geneva Convention Relative to the Protection of Civilian Persons in Time of War.[23] It should be remembered that in August 2005, Israel decided to withdraw from the Gaza Strip, and in a unilateral move, vacated the settlements in the Strip and ended the military government.

20. As stated, the occupation of the Territories was followed by the establishment of a military government, which functioned both as the executive and as the legislative authority within the Territories. The Israeli Supreme Court ruled that the military governor – in his aforementioned capacities – was subject to the judicial review of the High Court of Justice (HCJ).[24] The doors of the Supreme Court, sitting as the HCJ, were thus opened to the residents of the Territories. They could petition the Court against acts of the military governor, claiming that his actions contravened the international conventions which regulate the laws of war and human rights, meaning that rules drawn from international law feature in almost

22. Israel has unequivocally declared that these Occupied Territories are not within the boundaries of its jurisdiction. *See* Israel's report to the Human Rights Committee: CCPR/C/2001/2/4 December 2001, p. 5, para. 8.
23. Y. Zilbershatz, *The Adoption of International Law into Israeli Law – The Real is Ideal*, 25 Israel Yearbook on Human Rights, 243–279; *see also*: A. Roberts & R. Guelft, *Documents on the Laws of War*, 43 (Oxford, 2nd ed., 1989).
24. HCJ 302/72 *Sheich Solomon Hassain Oda Abu v. Government of Israel*, 27(2) PD 169, pp. 176–177.

every HCJ verdict that addresses activities associated with the Territories. In the legal literature, attempts have been made to establish a thesis whereby the Fourth Geneva Convention is indeed binding on Israel and the Israeli Courts should enforce its provisions,[25] but all of these attempts were rejected by the HCJ during the first years of Territories-related adjudication.

At the same time, HCJ rulings greatly contributed to the use of international law in Israel. It was adjudication that established that the humanitarian provisions of the Fourth Geneva Convention may be viewed as binding norms – if only partially – because they were part of the Israeli government's instructions to the local military commander. A large part of the international law that addresses the rules of war and occupation is customary and was absorbed into Israeli law without requiring domestic legislation, while another part was ratified by the government alone.

While in the early years, discussions mainly addressed the application of international law, the prominent phenomenon in recent verdicts is that judges have increasingly relied upon international law norms without discussing the problem of their applicability to Israel.

21. Towards the end of the twentieth century, and especially after October 2000, there was a resurgence of terrorist actions against Israel, both within its borders and in the Occupied Territories. This prompted a corresponding increase in preventative Israeli military operations. As a result, the Supreme Court was repeatedly required to rule on the legality of Israeli Defence Forces (IDF) actions in the Territories.[26] The Supreme Court also conducts ongoing judicial review of the security forces' actions in the Territories,[27] in addition to its review of the acts of the military governor.

---

25. Amnon Rubinstein, *The Changing Status of the Occupied Territories: From a Held Deposit to a Judicial Hybrid*, 11 Iyuney Mishpat 439 (Hebrew) (1986); see also Meron Theodor, *Human Rights and Humanitarian Norms as Customary Law*, 25–37 (Claredon Press, 1989).
26. The topic of the Supreme Court and the war against terror will be discussed below in the framework of the chapter dealing with human rights (Part IV, Ch. 2). For an example of the Supreme Court's approach in its examination of the legality of State actions in the light of international law, *see Barghouti*, SCC 1158/02 *State of Israel v. Barghouti.* Tel Aviv District Court, Jan. 19, 2003. In 2002, Marwan Khatib Bargouti, a member of the Palestinian Parliament, was captured in the Territories and transferred to Israel's jurisdiction in order to stand trial in an Israeli Court (and not in a military Court). He was accused *inter alia* of participating in the organization of terrorist acts committed within the borders of Israel, in which dozens of Israelis had been killed. In the sessions following the filing of the indictment, it was claimed that the Court lacked criminal jurisdiction over Barghouti in view of the Third Geneva Convention, under the terms of which he was considered to be a 'prisoner-of-war', and the Court therefore lacked jurisdiction to try him. The Court accepted the general proposition that international law prohibits the criminal indictment of a 'prisoner-of-war' but rejected the contention that Barghouti was entitled to immunity from criminal indictment. In explaining its decision, the Court stated that in view of the acts imputed to the accused in the indictment – even without ruling on whether or not he had committed them – the accused could not be regarded as a 'prisoner-of-war'. For not only did he not satisfy the conditions stipulated in s. 4 of the Third Geneva Convention, but also he had acted in flagrant violation of the laws of war and the provisions of section 48 of the Convention.
27. For an analysis of the Supreme Court's judgments dealing with military actions in the Territories, *see* by author: S. Navot, *The Supreme Court of Israel and the War on Terrorism*, 9(3) European Public Law (2003). *See also* in Part 4, Ch. 2 and Part 5, Ch. 3 on Emergency Laws.

22. As Israeli law does not clearly establish the particular branch empowered to bind Israel under treaties, it was the Supreme Court that ruled that this was a presidential prerogative. Nevertheless, the Court added that only under special circumstances, when the government requested the Knesset's ratification of a treaty, was the presidential signature actually required. This ruling represented a judicial confirmation of the constitutional practice that had been followed since the State's establishment, by which the Israeli government itself was fully authorized to negotiate, sign and ratify treaties, without the need for additional Knesset and presidential approval. The use of international law suggests the importance of 'custom' as a constitutional source in Israel. Customarily, Israeli governments presented the Knesset with peace accords they had signed before finally committing the State to the terms of the agreement or treaty. These agreements were acknowledged as being of particular importance and were expected to greatly impact on the nation's life. Thus, the executive decided, of its own accord and while it was free of any such obligation, to obtain the approval of the legislature before making political commitments.[28]

§1. The Legal Status of International Law in Israeli Domestic Law

23. The incorporation of international law into the Israeli legal system differs according to the normative source of the international legal rule, that is, customary law or treaty law. The position formulated and developed by the Supreme Court over the years is that international custom is automatically incorporated into domestic law, requiring no further legislative act by the Knesset. However, if there is a conflict between the customary norm and the Israeli law, the latter prevails.[29]

24. The incorporation of treaty law into Israeli law differs according to the nature of the treaty. Declaratory treaties, including treaties to which Israel is not a party (such as the 1907 Hague Conventions), which effectively restate and confirm an international custom, are automatically incorporated into Israeli law, but do not enjoy priority over conflicting Israeli laws. Constitutive treaties, however, do not become part of Israeli law without an incorporative legislative act. The reason for this distinction lies in the separation of powers doctrine: the government is empowered to sign and ratify treaties without the need for parliamentary approval (though over the past few years it has become customary to bring important international agreements, such as peace agreements, before the Knesset). In relation to constitutive treaties and any part of a declaratory treaty not anchored in existing custom, the Israeli Court has ruled that they cannot be relied upon in an Israeli Court as an independent, self-executing source of law.[30]

---

28. For further discussion *see* Part V, Ch. 1.
29. For example in the case of Adolf Eichman's kidnapping and being brought to trial in Israel, it was argued that the Nazi and Nazi Collaborators (Punishment) Law, having been enacted after the Holocaust, was therefore a law of retroactive application, in contravention of customary international law. The Court ruled that international customary law is powerless to supersede a provision of domestic law. Cr. A 36/91 *Eichmann v. Attorney General*, 16 PD 2033.
30. CA 25/55 *Guardian of Absentee Assets v. Abd al-Latif Samra*, 10(2) PD 1828.

In an attempt to achieve greater harmonization between Israeli law and international law, the Courts rely upon an interpretative presumption according to which 'the purpose of the law is to realize the provisions of international law and not to be in conflict with them'.

25. As a member of the United Nations, the State of Israel has agreed to be bound by numerous international treaties, and is a party to the major international humanitarian (1949 Geneva Conventions) and human rights conventions.[31] However, the fact that international law has no independent standing in Israel has evoked criticism, the thrust of which is that Israel should either formally legislate conventions into domestic law, or alter the manner in which international law is absorbed into the domestic law.[32]

In view of the process of globalization and the Israeli-Arab conflict, the Courts are frequently compelled to review the legality of governmental actions in accordance with the principles of international law, and to interpret them in a manner that harmonizes them with the international law. The ever-growing importance of the human rights discourse, and, in particular, the principle of the universality of human rights, have generated both international and domestic criticism with respect to Israel's failure to incorporate its international legal obligations into its domestic law.

26. The status of international law may therefore be summed up according to the following principles:

(1) Customary law and declaratory treaties are part of the domestic law as a normative source, provided that they do not contradict existing domestic law;
(2) Constitutive treaties (consensual [constitutive] treaties) are not a part of domestic law unless enacted into domestic legislation;
(3) Customary, declarative and conventional international laws have interpretative standing in Israeli domestic law, by virtue of the interpretative presumption of harmony.

---

31. The International Covenant on Civil and Political Rights (ICCPR) and International Covenant on Economic, Social and Cultural Rights (the ICESR), the Geneva Convention (1949) Relative to the Protection of Civilian Persons in Time of War, the Convention on the Rights of the Child (CRC), the Convention on the Elimination of all Forms of Discrimination against Women (CEDAW), the Convention on the Elimination of Racial Discrimination (CERD) and the Convention against Torture (CAT).
32. For a critique of this view, *see* Y. Zilbershatz, *The Adoption of International Law into Israeli Law: The Real is Ideal, supra* n. 23. *See also* Report of Supervisory Committee on the Convention for Economic, Social and Cultural Rights (E/C.12.1/Add.90) dated 23 May 2003, para. 12. The Committee reiterates its concern that the Convention has not been incorporated in the domestic legal order, and can therefore not be directly invoked before the Courts. Paragraph 29 states: 'The Committee urges the State party to undertake steps towards the incorporation of the Covenant and its provisions in the domestic legal order.'

Chapter 2. Constitution

§1. Introduction

27. Israel has no one official document known as 'The Constitution'. Even so, by virtue of the enactment of the basic laws concerning human rights in 1992 (Basic Law – Human Dignity and Liberty, and Basic Law – Freedom of Occupation), it has been argued that Israel thereby adopted a constitution.[33] In fact, since the 1990s, the Israeli governmental-judicial structure has been conducted in a manner consistent with a constitutional democracy. There are supreme norms, expressed in the basic laws; the powers of the legislative branch are limited; and laws are subject to judicial review. Israel's new 'constitution' is not complete, for it still lacks the chapters dealing with basic human rights such as freedom of expression and the principle of equality. It is often referred to as a fragile constitution, due to the fact that no special legislative requirements are required in order to amend the majority of its provisions. This situation is the result of an historical compromise, and of a judicial decision of monumental significance, as we shall presently observe.

§2. Historical Survey

28. After the termination of the British Mandate, on 14 May 1948, the members of the people's council[34] convened and declared the establishment of the State of Israel. The people's council then became the 'Provisional Council of State', which was the supreme organ of the State. The Declaration of Independence included a provision regarding the election of a 'constituent assembly' which was to frame a constitution. Following the election of the constituent assembly, the Provisional Council of State dispersed and its legislative powers were transferred to the elected constituent assembly, which in effect possessed both legislative and constituent authority. In its first session, on 17 February 1949, the constituent assembly enacted the Transition Law, 1949, by force of which the constituent assembly turned itself into 'the First Knesset'.

29. It is undisputed that the First Knesset, having been elected as a constituent assembly, was empowered to frame a constitution for the State of Israel, but due to political disputes between the various parties regarding the political character of the State, the Knesset was unable to decide upon an acceptable version of a constitution. Finally, in 1951 the compromise proposal of MK Harari (known as the Harari Decision) was adopted, under which:

33. Barak, *The Israeli Constitution: Past, Present, and Future,* 43 Hapraklit (1997) (In Hebrew) (iss. 1–2) p. 24.
34. A group comprising thirty-three members who represented the Jewish Community in Palestine, in all its political activities.

> The First Knesset charges the Constitution, Law and Justice Committee with preparing a draft of the State constitution. The constitution will consist of separate chapters, each chapter constituting a basic law in its own. The chapters will be presented to the Knesset ... and all of the chapters shall be consolidated into the State constitution.

This decision of the Knesset did not have the force of law, and as such was not legally binding.

30. Before the First Knesset's term was over, it enacted the Second Knesset (Transition) Law, 1951, under which the 'The Second Knesset and its members shall have all the powers which the First Knesset and its members had'.

The Law also stated that 'This law shall also apply *mutatis mutandis* to the transition to the Third Knesset and any subsequent Knesset'. The aim of this law was to ensure that with the transition from the first to the second Knesset and to every subsequent Knesset, constitutional continuity would be maintained.[35]

31. What emerges is that the First Knesset dispersed without having framed a constitution. The First Knesset decided to avoid the enactment of a formal constitution with the compromise of enacting basic laws in the future. This was a breach of the obligation imposed upon it by the Declaration of Independence, and prompted a plethora of academic debates over the years, primarily regarding the question of whether the First Knesset's power to frame a constitution (i.e., the *pouvoir constituent*) was actually transferred to all subsequent Knessets. Over the years however, and based on the Harrari Decision, the Knesset enacted a number of basic laws, and in many senses, this perpetuated the presumption that when the Knesset exercises its 'constituent power' and enacts a 'basic law' – it is not adopting a regular law.[36]

---

35. CA 6821/93 *Mizrachi Bank Ltd. v. Migdal Cooperative Village*, 49(4) PD 221 (hereinafter '*Mizrachi Bank*'). The issue of 'constitutional continuity' was disputed until the *Mizrachi Bank*, when Justices Shamgar and Barak ruled in the majority opinion (against the dissenting opinion of Justice Heshin) that the constitutional continuity had not been severed. According to Justice Shamgar, 'The powers of the Constituent Assembly were concentrated and consolidated in powers of the Knesset as the legislative authority. I unreservedly recognize the continuing power of the Knesset to enact constitutional legislation.' According to Justice Barak: 'There is no doubt in my mind that today we must adopt a single, unequivocal decision: The constitutional continuity was not severed. The Second Knesset was vested with the powers of the Constituent Assembly. Indeed, any other conclusion would be inconsonant with our national experience.' *See Mizrachi Bank*, pp. 367–368. In Justice Heshin's dissenting opinion, he contended that the authority of the Constituent Assembly did not include the 'inherent authority' to transfer its constituent authority to another, and nor did it acquire the authority to transfer its authorities. *See Mizrachi Bank*, p. 486. For an English short version of this case, see *Mizrachi Bank v. Migdal (the Gal Amendment) – translated extracts with commentary* in 31 *Israel Law Review* (1997) 754.
36. Rubinstein & B. Medina, *The Constitutional Law of the State of Israel* (6th. ed. 2005) (In Hebrew) p. 22. *See also* R. Gavison, *The Constitutional Revolution: Description of Reality or Self-Fulfilling Prophecy?*, 28 Mishpatim (1997) (In Hebrew) 21, 70. *See also* Justice Heshin's position in the *Mizrachi Bank* judgment. In his view 'deviation (from the fundamental principle of majority rule) can only be done by an appropriate procedure for the enactment of a constitution ... we speak of 'national consensus', 'the root conceptions of Israeli society', 'a social covenant' (*ibid.*, at pp. 524–525). 'The day on which the constitution is granted is a day of festivity. All are aware that the

32. Following are the twelve basic laws which have been enacted by the Knesset since 1958, by virtue of the Harari Decision:

> Basic Law: The Knesset (1958); Basic Law: The Israeli Lands (1960); Basic Law: The President of the State (1964); Basic Law: The Government (1968, replaced in 1992 and in 2001); Basic Law: The State Economy (1975); Basic Law: The Army (1976); Basic Law: Jerusalem, the Capital of Israel (1980); Basic Law: The Judiciary (1984); Basic Law: The State Comptroller (1986); Basic Law: Freedom of Occupation (1992, replaced in 1994); Basic Law: Human Dignity and Liberty (1992, amended in 1994); Basic Law: the Referendum (2014). In 2011, a Basic Law was enacted by way of a temporary provision in order to determine that the State budget would become a biannual judgment: Basic Law: State Budget (Special Provisions) (Temporary Provision) (Amendment 2011).

33. The common denominator of all twelve basic laws was the addition of the word 'basic' to their names, and the decision not to mention the year of enactment. This is indicative of the intention to place them above regular acts of legislation. The legislative intent was to enact a 'constitution in stages'. In other words – each chapter of the future Israeli constitution would consist of a basic law. Even so, the Knesset failed to make a clear distinction between a basic law and a regular law. On occasion, the term 'basic law' is used even though in terms of its content, the law does not belong in the framework of a constitution. Most of the basic laws were adopted in accordance with the procedure for adopting regular legislation, and most of them are highly detailed, in a format similar to the regular legislation, as opposed to constitutional legislation.

34. In terms of the institution-based topics of the constitution dealing with separation of powers, and the structure and powers of the sovereign authorities, the task of enacting basic laws is almost complete. Apparently, the one basic law still missing is the one dealing with legislative procedures, which is also supposed to deal with the power for judicial review of laws. The missing basic law, known as Basic Law: The Legislature, is also intended to regulate the normative status of basic laws, the manner of their enactment, and to confer the power for judicial review of a regular law that contradicts the provisions of the basic laws, as is known in most constitutional states. In terms of the chapter dealing with human rights, the Knesset to date has only enacted two basic laws, and numerous important rights have yet to merit constitutional anchorage in Israel. A significant portion of the work regarding constitutional recognition of human rights is therefore still at the Knesset's doorstep.

35. One of the interesting questions that arose following the Harari Decision and the enactment of the basic laws concerns the normative status of the basic laws. Arguably, from the moment of their enactment, the intention was that they be

---

authorized power is about to enact a constitution … a constitution is given in complete awareness …, with the nation's willingness to accept the burden of a constitution (*id.* 475).'

located at the apex of the Kelsian pyramid of norms, that is, above the regular laws, by virtue of their being the chapters of Israel's future constitution. The counter-argument is that, essentially, they still have the status of regular laws, and supreme normative status will only be conferred on them with the completion of all of the basic laws, when all of the chapters are consolidated into the State constitution. The question is highly significant, both in terms of the relationship between a regular law and a basic law, and naturally, from the perspective of the possibility of judicial review of legislation. The Knesset may have been expected to guarantee the entrenchment of all basic laws even before the completion of the constitution, in a manner that would prevent the adoption of amendments or contradictory legislation by any regular Knesset majority. Despite these expectations, none of the basic laws adopted until 1992 were entrenched by the Knesset, which means that the Knesset did not view basic laws as having special status or as being normatively superior to regular legislation. One of the central hallmarks of a constitution is stability and rigidity, specifically, the difficulty of amending its provisions. This feature is absent from Israel's basic laws.

§3. The Status of the Basic Laws Before 1992

36. The status of the basic laws has been discussed extensively in Israeli academic circles over the years, as the Harari Decision, which introduced the concept of basic laws, was silent on this issue.

One of the hallmarks of a constitution is of course the fact of it being a stable document with a special procedure for its amendment. The search for these features in the Israeli basic laws reveals an interesting phenomenon; the vast majority of the basic laws were passed without any 'entrenchment' provision i.e., a provision stating that the basic law can only be amended by a special majority of members of the Knesset. Hence, basic laws in Israel can be either revoked or amended by the same process required for the revocation or amendment of regular Knesset legislation.[37] The absence of an entrenchment provision may tip the scales in favour of the view that the basic laws have no superior normative status, and are in fact regular laws, designated for incorporation within the State constitution at the appointed time. The title 'basic law' may indicate that once all basic laws are introduced, they will become the building blocks to form a constitution, but as long as the constitutional project is incomplete, a basic law is no different from regular legislation in terms of its vulnerability to amendment. In operative terms, this means that a regular law enacted by a regular majority of Knesset members (Israel does not have a quorum requirement for legislation) can alter, revoke or override the provisions of a basic law.

However, Basic Law: the Knesset of 1958 established three entrenched provisions requiring a special majority for their amendment (a majority of 61 of 120 members of the Knesset). Even here, these provisions comprise three sections only out of the 46 sections included in the original Basic Law: The Knesset.

---

37. As we will observe below – a vote by way of a regular majority of those present, in three readings, suffices.

The question of the status of the basic laws in Israel arose precisely in the context of one of the entrenched provisions of Basic Law: The Knesset, which deals with the electoral system.

37. Section 4 of the Basic Law: the Knesset provides:

> The Knesset shall be elected by general, country-wide, direct, equal, secret and proportional elections, in accordance with the Knesset Elections Law; this section shall not be amended, save by a majority of the members of the Knesset.

This article actually protects the Israeli electoral system and its entrenchment may be considered to be the minimum of all possible entrenchments, meaning that there must be at least 61 positives votes out of 120 in order to amend the article.[38] In 1969, the Supreme Court had to deal with the status of this entrenched article in view of a regular law that appeared to contradict its provisions.

38. Before the Knesset election in 1969, the Knesset adopted a law providing financing from public funds for the coming elections. The fund allocation was based upon party representation in the outgoing Knesset, meaning that new parties, not represented in the outgoing Knesset, would be deprived of any funding under the law. The law was passed by an ordinary majority. A petitioner, Dr Bergman, questioned the compatibility of the new law with the entrenched section 4 of the Basic Law: the Knesset. According to this section, 'the Knesset shall be elected by general, country-wide ... equal ... and proportional elections'. The petitioner maintained that the financing law infringed upon the principle of equality included in section 4.[39] The Supreme Court accepted the petitioner's argument and decided that the allocation system constituted a grave violation of the principle of equality, mentioned in section 4. However, the Court failed to deal with the most important questions arising in the case, namely the status of the basic laws and the power of the Court to judicially review a regular law contravening the basic laws. These questions remained unanswered until 1995.

39. Despite the *Bergman* ruling, the Supreme Court refused – until 1995 – to recognize the normative supremacy of basic laws. For example in the *Negev* case,[40] the Court ruled that section 21 of the Standards Law, 1953, was not invalid by reason of its contravention of section 31(b) of the Basic Law: the Government, which is not entrenched. Justice Berenzon even ruled that the Basic Law has no special status, and added that, in fact, it was quite the opposite: The Standards Law is *lex*

---

38. The other entrenched provisions in those days were Arts 44 and 45 of the Basic Law: the Knesset and Art. 42 of the Basic Law: the Government of 1968. These provisions established a special protection for those basic laws against emergency ordinances. *See further* discussion of this matter in Part 5, Ch. 3: (Emergency Laws). Today Israel has three Basic Laws which are completely entrenched: Basic Law: the Government, Basic Law: Freedom of Occupation and Basic Law: Referendum.
39. HCJ 98/69 *Bergman v. Minister of Finance*, 23(1) PD 693. For an English translation of the Bergman case *see* 4 (1969) *Israel Law Review* 559.
40. HCJ 107/73 *Negev Automobile Service Station Ltd. v. State of Israel*, 28(1) PD 640.

specialis as distinct from the Basic Law: the Government, which is a general law, and the rule is that the specific law prevails over the general law.

40. At the same time, where a general law contravened an 'entrenched provision' of a basic law, it was determined that the Court is entitled to interfere with the legislative act, and to declare it to be invalid. Thus in the *Laor* judgment, the Court wrote:

> A law of the Knesset – whether a 'regular law' or a basic law – which purports to alter an 'entrenched' provision (the requirement of a special majority – meaning a formal entrenchment), without attaining a majority of the Knesset, contradicts the entrenchment provision of the basic law. Due to the legal status of the 'entrenched provision' it takes precedence. Where there is a conflict between the entrenched provision and a provision purporting to alter it without having attained the required majority, the normal rules do not apply, according to which a posterior law supersedes earlier law. This conflict is governed by the principle of the normative supremacy of the entrenched basic law.[41]

41. However, the theory of judicial review of legislation had yet to be adjudicated and provided with a sound foundation in Israeli law. The financing law in *Bergman* was thus invalidated without any theoretical basis or justification. Justice Landau, who wrote the judgment, expressly stated that he was not discussing the constitutional issues raised by the judgment; for example, the possibility of declaring the invalidity of a statute and the Court's power to do so. Despite the supposed normative supremacy of the entrenched section, in fact the Knesset could overcome the special majority requirement of section 4 of the Basic Law: The Knesset, quite easily. It needed to pass a law that infringed the principle of equality, ensuring its adoption by a majority of sixty-one votes. In such a case, the Supreme Court, naturally, would be powerless to declare the invalidity of the law.[42]

42. Until 1992, the Supreme Court had recognized the supremacy of a 'formal' (request for a majority) entrenched provision in a basic law, but had not yet invested the basic laws themselves with normative supremacy. This meant that, in the absence of entrenched provisions, a regular law could alter and even violate every arrangement prescribed in any basic law. In a number of cases, the Court specifically stated that the basic laws were not normatively superior to 'regular Knesset' legislation. This meant that the Knesset did not automatically limit its legislative power by passing the basic laws. The Knesset was still sovereign and had unlimited power to pass any legislation it chose. The basic laws did not harm the supremacy

41. HCJ 142/89 *Laor Movement v. the Knesset Speaker*, 44(3) PD 529, at 539.
42. In fact, laws concerning the principle of equality in the elections were passed by a majority of sixty-one, clearly indicating the Knesset's intention to infringe the principle of equality. For example, the amendment of the Basic Law: The Knesset, which permits the disqualification of parties by reason of the contents of their platform. This amendment, which will be dealt with in depth further on, was passed by a majority of sixty-one Knesset members. The assumption was that the denial of a party's candidacy for the elections violates the principle of equality in elections, guaranteed by s. 4 of the Basic Law: The Knesset.

of the Knesset. With relative ease, the Knesset could still overcome the formal entrenchment provisions. The Court itself was not required to discuss the normative status of the basic laws, or the constituent power of the Knesset, until the adoption of the basic laws concerning human rights in 1992.

§4. The Normative Status of Basic Laws After 1992

43. The constitutional dealing with human rights in Israel was the result of a political compromise. The draft version of Basic Law: Human and Citizen Rights had been discussed in the Knesset for years, but did not crystallize into a basic law. In a State in which there is no clear division between religion and state, the recognition of a bill of rights in the format adopted in the constitutional democratic states was a particularly controversial issue. The establishment of the State as a 'Jewish State' in accordance with the Declaration of Independence provoked a host of questions as to many basic freedoms. After a few unproductive decades of deliberations over a draft of a basic law, a compromise emerged in the spirit of the aforementioned Harari Decision. The Basic Law: Human and Citizen Rights would be divided into chapters and compilations of rights, each of which would be adopted as a basic law. Just as the State constitution was to emerge 'chapter by chapter' by the ongoing enactment of basic laws, so too, the bill of human rights would crystallize in stages, by the enactment of a basic law for each right or collection of rights. This compromise was intended to allow the enactment of basic laws for human rights, and to leave pending the discussion of the 'problematic' rights such as freedom of religion, conscience, equality etc. This original idea enabled the Knesset to overcome the opposition of various members, paving the way for the enactment of the two basic laws: Basic Law: Freedom of Occupation and Basic Law: Human Dignity and Liberty.

44. The enactment of the basic laws on human rights in 1992 was accompanied by a significant change in the meaning of constitutional 'entrenchment'. Until then, the concept of 'entrenchment' in the Israeli Legislature connoted 'structural' or 'formal' entrenchment. The idea was that only a Knesset majority had the power to amend a provision of a basic law. Basic Law: Freedom of Occupation reiterated this idea when it included a section that entrenched the entire law, conditioning any amendment upon mustering a majority of sixty-one Knesset members.

45. This formal requirement of a majority in order to amend the new basic law was not the only entrenchment to be included. The basic laws embody the idea of the inherent relativity of human rights. Infringement of human rights is therefore permitted where committed for worthy purposes in accordance with the rules prescribed in the basic law itself. In this context, the Israeli legislator adopted a criterion similar to the criterion prescribed by the Canadian legislator, called the 'limitation clause'. Accordingly, a 'regular' law that 'violates' any one of the human rights expressly stipulated in the basic law is valid only if it satisfies the cumulative conditions stipulated in the limitation clause, which states as follows:

> The rights according to this Basic Law shall not be infringed except by a law befitting the values of the State of Israel, enacted for a proper purpose, and to an extent no greater than is required.[43]

The limitation clause defines the conditions under which it is permitted to infringe the right to human dignity and liberty and the freedom of occupation. Its function is twofold: it limits the power of a law to violate human rights on the one hand, and it limits the protection conferred upon those rights on the other hand.

46. The limitation clause was an innovation in the Israeli legislature, establishing a 'substantive entrenchment' or 'substantive limitation' – and not just a formal 'majority' entrenchment – of the Knesset's power to enact a law that contradicted a basic law. It was now clear that if the Knesset attempted to enact a law infringing the rights enumerated in the Basic Law: Human Dignity and Liberty, in divergence from the conditions prescribed in the limitation clause, such a law would be invalid, even if passed by a majority of the Knesset members. The substantive limitation on the Knesset's power to infringe basic laws engendered a radical change in the overall structure of Israeli constitutional law, a change in the status of all basic laws, and led to the recognition of the power for judicial review of laws. Being nothing less than a transformation of the entire system, this development has been termed 'the constitutional revolution'.

§5. The Constitutional Revolution[44]

47. Despite the absence of formal entrenchment in the Basic Law: Human Dignity and Liberty, in the *Mizrachi Bank*[45] judgment of 1995, the Supreme Court ruled that the limitation clause is in fact intended to limit the Knesset's powers as the legislative authority. In an opinion with far reaching consequences, to be discussed below, the justices of the Supreme Court addressed the question of the validity of a law enacted by the Knesset, which infringed one of the fundamental rights enumerated in the basic law, and which – as argued – did not satisfy the requirements of the limitation clause. Basic Law: Human Dignity and Liberty lacked any formal entrenchment provision with respect to the majority necessary in order to amend it, and thus for the purposes of the question before it, the size of the majority that adopted the infringing law was immaterial. In its judgment, the Court ruled that under these circumstances, irrespective of the majority by which it was passed, an infringing law could be declared void. Following this argument, the Supreme Court finally gave judicial recognition to the principle of judicial review of laws, not only in the formal sense of examining whether the required majority was mustered, but

43. Section 8 of the Basic Law: Human Dignity and Liberty. A similar provision appears in the Basic Law: Freedom of Occupation.
44. This topic will be further elaborated upon in Part 2, Ch. 5, on judicial review.
45. *Mizrachi Bank, ibid.* This judgment is one of the most significant constitutional judgments in the history of the State of Israel.

also in the substantive sense, that is, the possibility of invalidating a law that contradicted the substantive provisions established in the basic law. Generally referred to as the 'constitutional revolution', this judgment established the constitutional guidelines for the supremacy of the basic laws, judicial review of legislation and the principle of a limited Knesset. The State of Israel underwent a constitutional metamorphosis: from being a state based on the English model of parliamentary sovereignty, it became a constitutional state.

I. The *Mizrachi Bank* Judgment

48. In this case, in an expanded panel of nine judges, the Supreme Court considered the question of whether a law passed after the adoption of the basic laws of 1992 violated the right to property guaranteed in the Basic Law: Human Dignity and Liberty, and if so, whether it satisfied the conditions of the limitation clause. The appeal was rejected on the merits, and the law was declared to be consistent with the limitation clause. But this time, unlike in the *Bergman* case, the Court chose to adjudicate all of the constitutional aspects raised by the petition, including questions such as:

- Which body is empowered to frame a constitution? – What is the status of the basic laws in Israel? and
- What changes occurred in the legal system following the enactment of the basic laws in Israel concerning human rights in 1992?

The main thrust of the judgment focused on the status of the basic laws. In the introduction to his ruling, Justice Barak, President of the Supreme Court, (hereinafter: 'President Barak'), wrote that:

> In March 1992 the Basic Law: Freedom of Occupation and Basic Law: Human Dignity and Liberty were adopted. Their adoption heralded a fundamental change in the status of human rights in Israel. They became constitutional rights. The constitutional revolution took place in the Knesset in March 1992. The Knesset granted the State of Israel a constitutional Bill of Rights.[46]

President Barak stated that the basic laws are the product of the *pouvoir constituent* of the Knesset, an authority that it has possessed since the days of the First Knesset, and which was transferred to each subsequent Knesset. His approach is based on the concept of constitutional continuity;[47] the Knesset has possessed constituent authority since the First Knesset, meaning that whenever the Knesset passed

46. *Mizrachi Bank*, Justice Barak, *ibid.*, at p. 352.
47. According to his approach, the Knesset's *pouvoir constituent* was based on the creation of the State on 15 May 1948. The first norm of the positive Israeli law was the legal determination that the Provisional Council of State is the supreme legislative organ of the State. The Provisional Council of State dispersed and transferred its powers to the Constituent Assembly. The Constituent Assembly enacted the Transition Law, 5709–1949, which transferred all of the powers of the Constituent Assembly to the First Knesset. This Knesset enacted the Second Knesset (Transition) Law,

a 'basic law', it was actually exercising its constituent power.[48] Accordingly, the Knesset has the formal legal authority to frame a constitution and the basic laws have constitutional status.

49. Justice Heshin took a different approach, maintaining that the Knesset is not authorized to frame a constitution, because it does not possess constituent power. According to Heshin, the chain of constitutional continuity was altered; the chain of continuity broken. The First Knesset was not authorized to transfer its constituent power to the Second Knesset and what began as a 'one time mission' will always retain its 'unique' character. However, Justice Heshin's view was not the majority view of the Supreme Court judges.

50. Some of the judges sitting in the panel in the *Mizrachi Bank* case, and particularly President Barak, considered that the supreme status of basic laws resulted from their being the product of the Knesset's *pouvoir constituent*. The doctrine of constituent power provides the best explanation of the social and legal history of the State of Israel, and in their opinion, it also reflects the ideal; that is, the Knesset should have constitutional power. Vesting the basic laws with 'constitutional' status compelled the Israeli Supreme Court to recognize the Knesset's constituent authority. Both President Shamgar[49] and President Barak expressly noted that the result they had arrived at was a desirable one. 'In my view, the Knesset's power is not limited to the enactment of basic laws and extends to the framing of an entire constitution. I also think that it should do so and give it my full support'.[50]

51. In the wake of the *Mizrachi Bank* case, the accepted view today is that the Knesset is vested with two 'crowns'; it is both the legislative power and the constituent power. When the Knesset establishes norms as a constituent power (basic laws), they are endowed with 'constitutional' status, i.e., they are at the apex of the normative pyramid. It follows therefore that the norms enacted by the Knesset in its legislative capacity are regular laws, and hence subordinate to the norms established by the constituent power. The sovereignty of the Knesset is therefore limited by the norms established by the Knesset itself, in its constituent capacity.

52. Naturally, the conclusions of this approach also affect the issue of judicial review of laws that infringe a basic law. In the footsteps of the American tradition, the Israeli Supreme Court established that the exercise of judicial review does not

5711–1951, which provided that the Second Knesset and the Third Knesset, and all subsequent Knessets, would have all the powers, rights and duties which the First Knesset had. From this, he inferred the principle of constitutional continuity, which ensured the transmission of 'all the powers', which also included the transmission of the *pouvoir constituent*.

48. For further discussion, *see* C. Klein, *Théorie et pratique du pouvoir constituent* (PUF Paris 1996).
49. In this judgment, there were two 'Presidents' serving in the Supreme Court: the departing president Shamgar, and the incoming president Barak. Accordingly, they both bore the title 'President'.
50. Justice Shamgar in *Mizrachi Bank*, *ibid.*, at p. 286.

require explicit authorization. Much like in the American case, *Madbury v. Madison*,[51] the Israeli Supreme Court arrogated to itself the power to invalidate the Knesset's legislation, despite the absence of any constitutional provision authorizing it to do so.

53. The identification of a basic law is based on a 'formal' criterion – its title. The twelve laws bearing the title 'basic law' are the products of the exercise of constituent power. 'The Knesset exercises its constituent authority ... when it gives it external expression in the form of a norm, and views it as a "basic law" (with no indication of the year of its legislation)'.[52]

§6. The Outcome of the Constitutional Revolution

54. The *Mizrachi Bank* ruling marked a change in the Israeli constitutional conception. The normative supremacy of the basic laws means that in any case of contradiction between a provision established in a basic law and a principle established in a 'regular' law, the principle determined in the basic law prevails.[53] The 1995 ruling in *Mizrachi Bank* thus endowed all the basic laws in Israel with constitutional status. Notably, the constituent act is described in the past tense. According to the Court, the Knesset had already 'enacted a constitution for Israel' – it was a *fait accompli.* Thus, the *Mizrachi Bank* judgment retroactively changed the normative status of all basic laws – whether or not they were (formally or substantively) entrenched. According to the judgment, all basic laws, the designated 'chapters' of the future constitution, have a constitutional status from the date of their enactment, even before being consolidated into a state constitution under the Harari Resolution. This recognition of the status of basic laws had two main results: first, the recognition of the normative primacy of arrangements prescribed in basic laws over regular legislation (the idea of supremacy); and, second, the recognition of the validity of the entrenchment provisions included in basic laws (the idea of rigidity). Since the *Mizrachi Bank* judgment, the accepted view is that a legislative provision that purports to limit the power of the Knesset is valid only if the 'limiting' provision is the product of the Knesset exercising its '*pouvoir constituent*'. The Knesset may, as a legislative authority, enact any law without being limited by a previous Knesset and if it seeks to limit its power by a later law, it must do so by exercising its constituent authority.

51. 5 US (1803) 137.

52. *Mizrachi Bank*, *supra* n. 6, p. 403, by President Barak. According to this test, which is now the only test, the question arises as to whether the Knesset is liable to misuse its constitutive power in order to enact inappropriate Basic Laws. This question will be discussed in Part 2, Ch. 5, on judicial review.

53. *Ibid.*, at p. 406, by President Barak: In the enactment of a basic law we find ourselves at the highest normative level. This dictates the conclusion that a basic law, or any of its provisions, can only be changed by another basic law. A basic law can be changed by a regular law only if the basic law contains an express provision to that effect.

55. Not only did the Court recognize the normative supremacy of the basic laws, but it also recognized the Court's right to judicial review of a law, which is an accepted practice in the majority of constitutional democratic states. Though the judgment was criticized, in practice the Knesset accepted it and acted accordingly. For example, one of the consequences of the constitutional move was that the Knesset was forced to amend the Basic Law: Freedom of Occupation when it enacted a law that prima facie did not meet the requirements of the limitation clause.[54] In the amendment to the basic law (adopted in the framework of a basic law, by a majority of sixty-one), a clause was added that enabled the Knesset to 'override' the limitation clause. This section, referred to as the 'override clause', was influenced by the parallel provision of the Canadian Charter of Rights and Freedoms.

The override clause stipulates that:

> A provision of a law that violates freedom of occupation shall be of effect, even though not in accordance with Section 4, [the Limitation Clause – S.N.] if it has been included in a law passed by a majority of the members of the Knesset [61 MK's – S.N.] which expressly states that it shall be of effect, notwithstanding the provisions of this Basic Law; such law shall expire four years from the date of its commencement.[55]

56. This clause effectively permits the Knesset to adopt legislation that violates the freedom of occupation, without satisfying the requirements of the limitation clause, provided that the law was adopted by an absolute majority of the MKs and expressly stipulates that it is effective 'notwithstanding' the provisions of the basic law. However, since its enactment, the Knesset has only once had recourse to the override section – to enact a law permitting the import of '*unkosher*' meat.

57. Since 1995, the Supreme Court has conducted judicial review of Knesset legislation that contradicts the entrenched rights of the basic laws on human rights, but the review has been cautious and measured, and to date, only a dozen laws have been invalidated.

The constitutional revolution also affected the status of the basic laws adopted before 1992. While the limitation clause was not included in the pre-1992 basic laws, several Supreme Court justices suggested that the Court 'lend' the limitation clause to the old basic laws, if they include rights, on the basis of an analogy with the new basic laws.[56] This view may indicate the future direction of Supreme Court decisions.

---

54. In the framework of the coalition agreement with the Ultra-Orthodox parties, the government undertook to pass a law prohibiting the importing of meat that had not received a '*Hecsher* certificate'. The Court hinted that the adoption of such a law would violate the Basic Law: Human Dignity and Liberty without fulfilling the requirements of the limitation provision.
55. Section 8, Basic Law: Freedom of Occupation.
56. Justice Zamir in the *Hoffnung* case, HCJ 3434/96 *Dr. Menachem Hoffnung v. the Knesset Speaker* 50(3) 70–73. See also HCJ 3166/14 *Gutmann v. Attorney General*, dealing with the constitutionality of changing the election threshold from 2% to 3.25%

58. The *Mizrachi Bank* judgment also engendered a transformation in the public perception of the importance attached to basic laws. Recent years attest to a growing awareness – in the Knesset and among the public at large – that the enactment of basic laws was an act of groundbreaking importance. Awareness of the need to evaluate legislation in terms of its compliance with the provisions of the basic laws[57] has become a cornerstone of the legislative process. Today the Knesset evaluates the constitutionality of any bill tabled for debate or voting, ensuring compliance with the principles established in the *Mizrachi Bank* decision. Still, since 1992, the Knesset quite easily passed a growing number of amendments to the basic laws, sometimes for very specific needs. For example, Basic Law: The Knesset was enacted in 1958 and until 1992 – some thirty-four years – was amended fifteen times, whereas from 1992 onwards, it was amended another twenty-four times. Similarly, Basic Law: The President of the State was enacted in 1964 and until 1992 – over twenty-eight years – was amended twice, and between 1992 and 2011 – some eighteen years – it was amended on five additional occasions.

There is also an enhanced understanding of the importance of the stability of the basic laws and the need to avoid amendments of basic laws based on narrow, temporal and partisan considerations. For example: The amendment to the basic law that accompanied the instalment of Ehud Barak's government in 1999 and Biniamin Netaniahu's Government in 2015 was subjected to scathing public criticism, when the Knesset approved the amendment of section 33 of the Basic Law: The Government, which enlarged the number of members in the government. The amendment was 'necessitated' by the 'need' to enable the appointment of a larger number of ministers.[58] Furthermore, almost all of the coalition agreements signed when governments are established have included a clause according to which basic laws would not be amended without the consent of all the coalition members. These facts indicate that basic laws have taken hold in Israel's judicial culture, and politicians and the public normatively view them as parts of the state's 'constitution'. However, the fact that it is rather easy to amend Israel's basic laws contradicts their status as a 'formal' constitution. Supreme Court President Dorit Beinisch asserted that a constitution needs some stability:

> A constitution presents society with a normative standard. The complex process of amending a constitution keeps this standard solid and stable even at times of social turmoil and alternating regimes. The situation in Israel is not like that. Most of its basic laws are not entrenched and thus may be amended

57. A. Rubinstein, *The Knesset and the Basic Laws Concerning Human Rights*, 5 Mishpat U' Mimshal (2000) (In Hebrew) 339.
58. *See* HCJ 5160/99 *The Movement for the Quality of Government in Israel v. Constitution, Law and Justice Committee of the Knesset*, 53(4) PD 481. Recently a new amendment to Basic Law: the Government actually postponed the implementation of a section that restricts the number of Cabinet members to eighteen. Prime Minister Netaniahu, who was elected to form Government in March 2015, decided he needed more than eighteen Ministers in order to form his new Government; therefore, a quick amendment was passed (by a Majority of sixty-one MKs) postponing this restriction to the next Knesset. This initiative drew severe public criticism, both from public figures and from leading jurists.

by a regular majority of the Knesset members and through routine legislative processes.[59]

It appears, therefore, that Israel is still far from having a stable constitutional situation.

59. Moreover, the *Mizrachi Bank* ruling and the basic laws concerning human rights lead to the constitutionalization of Israeli law. These rights pulse through the arteries of all areas of the law, influencing their contents. Every legal realm and legal norm must now adapt itself to the new constitutional 'regime'. Consequently, although the Basic Law: Human Dignity and Liberty includes a section that prevents the invalidation of laws enacted prior to its enactment, the Israeli Supreme Court interprets the prior legislation 'in the light of' the basic law and under its influence. Indeed, the basic laws also ushered in the 'interpretative revolution', wherein the Court must interpret every legislative act, regulation, order or even contract in a manner that harmonizes them with the new basic laws.

60. The 'constitutional revolution' caused a prodigious quantity of academic writing in Israel, and scathing criticism as well – its main target being the phenomenon of 'judicial activism' manifested in the initiative, spearheaded primarily by the Supreme Court. It was claimed that the Supreme Court had arrogated to itself the authority to grant a constitution to the State of Israel, by way of a judicial decision.[60] However, despite the criticism, the constitutional revolution was thoroughly internalized by the Israeli legislature. Moreover, it has been argued that the emerging constitution is an enterprise promoted mainly by the secular Jewish majority in Israel, which is culturally and politically associated with Western culture and ideals. The religious parties argued that they failed to comprehend the meaning of the 1992 basic laws and resented the Supreme Court's judicial review prerogative. It was not long before their opposition to the constitutional revolution turned into an open struggle against the Supreme Court, which, religious parties claimed, 'assumed' the power to judicially review laws without being explicitly authorized to do so by the Knesset.

61. Since 1995, the Supreme Court has had the power to judicially review any Knesset legislation violating protected human rights. But it is important to remark that the Knesset intentionally prevented the judicial review of laws enacted prior to the commencement of the Basic Law: Human Dignity and Freedom. Section 10 of the Basic Law provides: 'This Basic Law shall not affect the validity of any law in force prior to the commencement of the Basic Law.' This means that all laws that were in force in March 1992 will remain in force, and a contravention of the provisions of this basic law will not expose the offending section to invalidation. Laws enacted in Israel since 1948 until 1992 are thereby entrenched against constitutional judicial review. The arrangement itself was the product of a political compromise,

59. HCJ 4908/10 *Bar-On, MK v. The Knesset* (rendered on April 2011), President Beinisch's opinion at [21].
60. For example, this was the view of the Justice Landau, a previous President of the Supreme Court.

creating, in the words of Prof. Barak, 'a constitutional anomaly'.[61] Nevertheless, the interpretation of the old law is influenced by the enactment of the basic law and is conducted 'in the spirit' of the provisions of the basic law.

62. Summing up, the basic laws of 1992 and the *Mizrachi Bank* judgment represent the most impressive constitutional developments since the establishment of the State. Today, Israel is a constitutional state like most world countries. The significance of the occasion was eloquently expressed by President Barak in the first paragraph of the *Mizrachi Bank* decision, while festively declaring that the State of Israel had joined the other constitutional states:

> In March 1992 the Basic Law: Freedom of Occupation and Basic Law: Human Dignity and Liberty were adopted. Their adoption signalled a fundamental change in the status of human rights in Israel. They became constitutional rights … . A 'regular' law of the Knesset cannot alter them. A regular law cannot infringe protected human rights unless it satisfies the requirements established in the basic laws. Failure to fulfil these constitutional requirements transforms a regular law into an unconstitutional law. It is a law flawed by a constitutional defect, and the Court is liable to declare it invalid. Israel is a constitutional democracy. We have joined the community of constitutional states (including the United States, Canada, Germany, Italy, and South Africa) who have a constitutional bill of rights. We became part of the revolution of human rights that characterizes the second half of the twentieth century … judicial review of the constitutionality of laws that infringe human rights became the legacy of the vast majority of states. This revolution did not pass over us either. We joined it in March 1992.[62]

63. The State of Israel can now be said to have a formal constitution, but it must be remembered that this constitution is not complete and has even been referred to as a 'lame constitution'. Not all of the basic laws are entrenched, thus exposing them to amendment with relative facility; and the framing of the constitution awaits completion by the enactment of additional basic laws.

The constitutional revolution itself is a *'fait accompli'*. The authority for judicial review of laws contravening the basic law concerning human rights is undisputed. It would seem, however, that apart from acknowledging, and even internalizing the Supreme Court's move, the Knesset has yet to recover from that move to the extent of becoming an active partner in the constitutional enterprise. Paradoxically, it seems that the constitutional revolution actually discontinued the process of creating the Israeli constitution. Since 1992, only one basic law has been enacted by the Knesset (dealing with the possibility of having a referendum in Israel). The reason is that the constitutional revolution produced tremendous tension between the authorities, that is, the Supreme Court and the Knesset, the later having eventually halted the constitutional process. From a political perspective as well, it is doubtful whether there is majority support in the Knesset for the constitution's completion.

61. A. Barak, *Constitutional Interpretation* (1994) (in Hebrew), p. 562.
62. *Mizrachi Bank, ibid.*, at p. 352.

The constitutional revolution impacted on the political as well as on the legal spheres in several ways. On the one hand, the years following this ruling were characterized by politicians' increasing awareness and understanding of the special status attached to the enactment of basic laws. Accepting the concept of judicial review of legislation, the Knesset actually pledged to verify the compliance of Knesset legislation with the provisions of the basic laws and to examine their constitutionality in accordance with them. Judicial review has been conducted with circumspection and restraint, but even so, the Supreme Court has consistently ruled that there is judicial review available in Israel, which is a position that follows from the supremacy of the basic laws. On the other hand, the Knesset, which was supposed to resolve the pending questions in the *Mizrachi Bank* case, has in fact completely abandoned the task of completing the constitution – apparently in response to the constitutional revolution.

§7. Characteristics of Basic Laws

64. The common denominator of all twelve basic laws lies in the addition of their formal identification – i.e., the word 'basic' – to the title of the law, and the intentional non-stipulation of the year of their adoption. Prima facie, according to the Harari Decision, this suffices for the establishment of the presumption that the law is a basic law, namely – a chapter of the Israeli constitution. The import of this approach is that the basic law is identified by one factor only – the 'formal' aspect: A basic law is a law bearing the title 'basic law'. Proponents of this approach concede that the formal criterion is somewhat arbitrary, but that it is preferable for the purposes of legal certainty.[63]

65. However, Israeli academics have generally rejected the formal aspect as the sole and conclusive characteristic. According to Professor Zamir, a former judge of the Supreme Court, the basic law is characterized as belonging to the constitution by virtue of the style of its 'formulation': that is, a constitution should establish fundamental principles, of general applicability, and be succinct in language and majestic in formulation. A broad formulation of general principles affords the Court flexibility in interpretation, as is required in order to adapt the constitutional provisions to changing exigencies without having to frequently amend it, thereby diminishing its stature.

66. Proponents of this 'stylistic' or 'formulation' characterization base their approach on the provisions appearing in the existing Basic Laws, such as the provisions of Basic Law: The Knesset, on the subject of immunity, which state: 'The members of the Knesset shall have immunity; particulars shall be prescribed by law;' 'The building of the Knesset shall have immunity; particulars shall be prescribed by law'; and the provisions of Basic Law: The State Economy, which state:

63. I. Zamir, *The Basic Laws: Towards the Constitution* (Preface to book: *Basic Law: The Knesset*) (1993) (in Hebrew) 13.

'The State Budget shall be prescribed by law', etc. In this way, the supremacy of the basic laws is manifested in the manner of their formulation.

67. The difficulty with this approach is that, empirically, significant portions of the existing basic laws are formulated in a highly detailed manner, bearing precisely the same format as regular legislation. In the *Mizrachi Bank* case, there was a proposal for a material or substantive examination. In other words, it was proposed that consideration be given to whether the contents of the basic law belonged to the matters customarily dealt with in a constitution. A basic law is characterized as such if it has 'constitutional content', if it deals with fundamental principles, the structure of the regime, human rights, etc. The problem with this approach is that it grants broad discretion to the Court, thereby promoting legal uncertainty. For example, if a basic law can be identified by its material content, the Court could rule that a regular law has 'constitutional character', and endow it with normative supremacy.[64] In the absence of a basic law to regulate the legislative process and the enactment of basic laws, the approach today refers to all three aspects, the most prominent of which is the formal aspect, which is the most expressive of the Knesset's desire. To date, the Supreme Court has refrained from expressly conferring constitutional status to a law just by virtue of its constitutional content.[65]

§8. Procedures for Amending the Basic Laws

68. In the wake of the *Mizrachi Bank* case and the ensuing decisions, the basic laws adopted were conferred supreme normative status, meaning that their amendment is conditional upon the Knesset exercising its 'constituent authority'. In terms of the normative hierarchy, the basic laws are positioned above the regular laws.

69. This rule applies even where the basic law does not include an entrenchment provision. The upshot is that until *Mizrachi Bank*, the amendment of a basic law or a section thereof could be done by a regular law. Nowadays, a basic law can only be amended by way of another basic law. To amend a basic law, the Knesset must exercise the same authority that it exercised in its enactment, namely, its constituent authority. Accordingly, a basic law can only be amended by way of a basic law:

> There was a change in the Knesset's legislative policy, manifested by these two basic laws; and by anchoring the new and appropriate conception of the normative hierarchy, it is now possible to adopt a uniform legislative criterion,

---

64. Hints of this approach can be found in the decisions of the Supreme Court, for example, in relation to the constitutional status of the Law of Return and of the Equal Opportunities for Women Law. The question of the normative status of these laws was left unsolved and requiring further examination.
65. Despite the comments made by judges on various occasions regarding the 'constitutional' character of regular laws such as the Law of Return (a law entitling every Jew to immigrate to Israel and receive automatic citizenship, by virtue of his being Jewish) and the Equal Opportunities for Women Law. To date, these laws are characterized as regular laws.

according to which an amendment of any basic law can only be done by way of a basic law.[66]

Nonetheless, the majority of the basic laws lack an entrenchment provision prescribing the need for a majority of Knesset members to support their amendment. The result is that, theoretically, a non-entrenched basic law can be changed and even repealed by a simple majority of two Knesset members. This is the main weakness of the Israeli constitution, which does not require an unequivocal, special majority even for purposes of its amendment.

70. Frequent amendments of basic laws are not the only signs of their weakness. Another inadequacy of the Israeli constitution may be discerned from the *Bar-On* case of 2011.[67] In this case, the Supreme Court was asked to annul and judicially review a 'provisional' basic law (or *Pouvoir Constituant*) or, rather, a new basic law that 'amends' Basic Law: The State's Economy, but does so 'temporarily'. Each year, as in many other states, Israel regularly introduces an Annual State Budget Act, but in 2009, the Knesset decided to irregularly introduce a two-year budget, which it then decided to anchor in a provisional order of a basic law. A year after this provisional basic law was enacted, the government decided that the biennial budget was preferable and decided to extend the Act by another two years to cover 2011 and 2012. This amendment was unique because it was an extension of a provisional measure that was meant to be 'temporary' in nature.

Addressing a petition against this 'provisional constitutional amendment', the Supreme Court was faced with numerous constitutional issues. A seven-judge panel unanimously rejected a petition that challenged the constitutionality of amending a basic law. Their ruling, however, contained harsh remarks about the procedure chosen by the Knesset for this move. President Beinisch repeatedly stated that such legislation gives rise to serious difficulties and stressed that even in an ideal world, where states have special rules for amending their constitutions, it is not certain that a constitution can be amended temporarily. The situation in Israel is not ideal and therefore a basic law cannot be nullified only because it was introduced as a provisional instruction.

Another interesting argument made in the *Bar-On* petition referred to the boundaries of judicial review and the option of revoking a constitutional amendment. The petitioners argued that the amendment impairs a constitutional principle because, in Israel's parliamentary regime, the annual state budget is one of the tools that the Knesset uses to supervise government actions. In this respect, the Supreme Court addressed – for the first time in the history of Israel's constitutional adjudication – the 'unconstitutional constitutional amendment' doctrine and its potential application to Israeli law. The Supreme Court established that the question of whether a basic law may be disqualified for conflicting with the fundamental principles of a

66. *Ibid.*, per Shamgar, at 272, s. 26.
67. HCJ 4908/10 *Bar-On, MK v. The Knesset* (delivered on April 2011), President Beinisch's opinion at [21].

regime is a rather complicated issue that addresses the very legitimacy of the constituent authority and the root of the Court's authority to judicially review laws. In this case, the judges held that the fact that the biennial state budget impaired the Knesset's ability to monitor government expenses was not so grave as to justify the annulment of a basic law.

Chapter 3. Legislation and Equivalent Legislative Rules

71. The establishment of the State of Israel on 14 May 1948 was accompanied by the establishment of the Provisional Council of State – the legislative authority of the nascent State. The Provisional Council of State published the proclamation, which was intended to determine the initial arrangements for the new State's activities. Among other things the proclamation determined was that the law, which was in force on the eve of the State's establishment, would remain in force (subject to some exceptions) and that the provisional council would be the legislative authority. On 19 May 1948, the council enacted the Law and Administration Ordinance, which prescribed more detailed arrangements.

72. The Law and Administration Ordinance was intended to serve as a temporary, urgent arrangement, but due to the non-completion of the constitutional legislation, most of its sections have remained in force until this very day.

One of the most prominent subjects regulated by the Ordinance concerned the adoption of the Mandate law and its adaptation to the conditions of the country. The termination of the British Mandate led to the potential creation of a legal vacuum. Therefore, the enactment of a provision for the absorption of Mandate law was indispensable as a temporary measure, until the creation of an independent Israeli law was completed. This need was addressed by section 3 of the proclamation and subsequently, by section 11 of the Law and Administration Ordinance.[68]

§1. Legislation as a Source of Law

73. The parliament – the Knesset – is the primary legislator in Israel. Its legislative acts are laws, which constitute a dominant source in the creation of Israel's law. Laws enacted by the Knesset are 'primary legislation'.

In view of the fact that since the 1950 Harari Decision, the Knesset also enacted the basic laws, the primary legislation in Israel consists both of 'constitutional legislation' and 'regular legislation'.

74. Primary legislation also comprises 'ordinances' – the remnants of Mandate legislation. The term 'ordinance' refers to pre-State legislation enacted by the provisional council of State, as distinct from the post-State legislation (laws) of the Knesset, in its capacity as the elected legislative authority. Knesset laws and those ordinances that retained their validity share identical normative status. The term 'ordinance' was retained in the Israeli Book of Laws (Sefer Ha-Hukkim) in order to underscore the fact that the legislation referred to as 'ordinance' originated during

68. Section 11 of the Law and Administration Ordinance provides that: 'The law which existed in Palestine on the 5th Iyar 5708 (14 May 1948), shall remain in force, insofar as there is nothing therein that contradicts this Ordinance or other laws which may be enacted by or on behalf of the Provisional Council of State, and subject to such modifications as may result from the establishment of the State and its authorities.'

the Mandate period, even if the ordinance itself underwent various changes during the years of the State's existence.

75. There are three categories of ordinances:

(a) Ordinances enacted by the provisional council of State, from immediately after the State's establishment until the establishment of the First Knesset, for example: The Law and Administration Ordinance;
(b) Ordinances enacted by the British High Commissioner in Council for Palestine (the official name given to the *Erez Yisrael* by the British) reformulated by the Knesset as a 'New Version'; and
(c) Ordinances of the High Commissioner which, as stated, have not been repealed, and the original wording of which has been retained.

76. Essentially, ordinances enacted by the provisional council of State have the normative standing of Knesset laws. However, the ordinances of the Mandate government in Palestine draw their force in the State of Israel from section 11 of the Law and Administration Ordinance, 1948. More precisely, the words 'shall remain in force' refer to the entire Mandate 'law' and not just its 'ordinances'. However, the validity of both the ordinances and the remaining part of the Mandate law are subject to 'modifications as may result from the establishment of the State and its authorities', meaning that provisions inconsistent with the existence of a Jewish State in Israel and its democratic, independent institutions, cannot remain in force in Israel.[69] It therefore emerges that the ordinances from the Mandate period remain in force in Israel unless formally repealed or amended by implication due to their non-conformity with the nature or character of the State or its governmental structure.

77. It must be noted that the ordinances from the Mandate period that remained in force were originally written and legislated in the English language. However, section 16 of the original Law and Administration Ordinance authorized the Minister of Justice to issue a new version of any law which existed in Palestine, and which was still in force in the State. Over the years, this section underwent numerous changes and amendments, and what was initially the exclusive function of the Minister of Justice has now become a function executed by committees of experts, whose proposals must be examined and approved by the Constitution, Law and Justice Committee of the Knesset.

78. The distinction between Mandate ordinances reformulated in a new version and those that were not, is also addressed in Section 24 of the Interpretation Law,

69. *See* for example, the Mandatory Press Ordinance which empowered the High Commissioner to order the closing down of a newspaper at his own discretion. In 1953, the Court ruled that this abridgement of the freedom of expression was inconsistent with the establishment of a democratic state. At the same time, it did not regard itself as being empowered to invalidate the Ordinance, and therefore limited the authority to close the paper – currently in the hands of the Minister of the Interior- exclusively to cases in which the publication created a 'certain and imminent danger to public peace'.

which provides that the binding text of any law is the text in the language in which it was enacted. However, in the case of a law enacted in English before the establishment of the State, of which a new version has been introduced under section 16 of the Law and Administration Ordinance, 1948, the new version shall be the binding text.[70] In addition to the 'new version' of ordinances from the Mandate period, the Israeli Book of Laws also includes the 'consolidated version' of particular laws or ordinances. These are the legislative acts which underwent numerous changes or amendments over the years. The act of consolidating the law refers to the amalgamation of all its amendments, interspersed both in the original law and in other laws, into a single, unified and consolidated version. This facilitates the search for any particular provision of the law.

79. The primary legislation is supplemented by secondary legislation, which occupies a lower normative level. While the government is the executive authority, operating in accordance with the provisions of the law prescribed by the legislative authority, it is also involved in legislation, in its capacity as the secondary legislator. The government has direct control over the establishment of the legally binding norms, and it discharges this power through the agency of its ministries, which function as administrative authorities. The administrative (governmental) authorities use their legislative power extensively, in two central formats:

(a) The power to enact secondary legislation, in accordance with the empowering provisions included in the primary legislation; and
(b) Legislative power in times of emergency.

80. The government gives a particularly broad construction to its legislative power, and it regulates an extensive and varied spectrum of subjects. Nevertheless, the powers of the secondary legislator are limited, and the rule is that where the secondary legislator exceeds the boundaries of the power conferred upon him, the secondary legislation may be declared voidable by the Courts. On occasion, legislative authority is transferred to bodies that are not part of the governmental authorities. In this context, the Supreme Court ruled that no transfer of legislative powers to non-governmental bodies is allowed, unless it is specifically authorized by the legislative authority.[71] As opposed to the English parliament, where the supervisory process over secondary legislation is broadly regulated in extensive detail, the Knesset has no special supervisory tools, apart from the cases in which the need for its approval is expressly stipulated in the empowering law.

81. At the highest level of secondary legislation are the 'Defense Regulations for Times of Emergency'. The reason is that these acts of secondary legislation are the only ones that have the power to alter any law, to temporarily suspend its effect, or

70. Numerous ordinances merited reformulation in a new version. In some cases, the Knesset deemed it proper to upgrade the status of a New Version of an Ordinance, to that of a Law. *See* e.g., the Penal Law, 1973, most of which is a new version of the English Criminal Code Ordinance, 1936.
71. CA 825/88 *Association of Israeli Football Players v. Israel Football Association*, 45(5) PD 89, 103–104.

subject it to conditions, as well as to impose or increase taxes or other compulsory payments.[72] The general rule is that only a law enacted by the Knesset can change another law. Emergency regulations however are not regarded as Knesset legislation – hence their appellation as 'regulations' as opposed to 'law'. The minister's authority to issue emergency regulations is subject to the condition that the provisional council of State (or the Knesset) has declared the existence of a state of emergency. However, on the 19 May 1948, the provisional council of State declared a state of emergency and that declaration has remained in force until today.

§2. EFFECT OF A LAW

82. A law commences operation upon its publication in the Official Gazette (Reshumot), unless an alternate effective date is stated in the publication.[73] The same applies to a regulation with the force of legislation. Official publication ensures the publicity of the law, and publicity is a precondition for the law to take effect. Apart from the importance attaching to the publicity of the law, the date on which it takes effect is essential. The legislature can determine the effective date of the law in the law itself, but should it fail to do so, the law takes effect concurrently with its official publication, and not on the date of its adoption by the Knesset. Even where the law focuses exclusively on a future action, one cannot prevent its influence on existing interests, expectations and long-established customs. In many laws, the legislature explicitly provided that the law would not affect existing rights and obligations. There is only one category of laws where the presumption is that they are of retrospective effect, namely – the laws of procedure, which determine the procedures governing the conduct of judicial proceedings. The legislature is presumed to have intended these laws to apply to currently pending proceedings, and not just to proceedings beginning after the adoption of the law.

83. The amendment or repeal of a law is not a practical ruling, but rather a distinct act of legislation in its own right. As such, the procedure employed by the legislature to amend a law, or even repeal it, must be identical to the procedure by which it was originally enacted. The difference is that the amendment is generally introduced by the addition of a section to the law, or an amendment in the wording of one of its sections, by way of an amendment law, which is added to the original law. The word 'amendment' is added in parenthesis to the name of the original law, occasionally with an additional word or phrase indicating the content of the amendment. With respect to some laws, if the quantity of amendments introduced becomes unwieldy, the Minister of Justice can publish the law and all its amendments in a 'consolidated version'. The repeal of a law is generally effected in the form of a new law that replaces the old law, or in rare cases, by a special law that repeals the old law and does not replace its provisions with new ones. It should be noted that until

72. *See* s. 9 of Law and Administration Ordinance, 1948. For a detailed discussion on emergency laws *see* Part V, Ch. 3.
73. Section 10(a) of original Law and Administration Ordinance, 1948. The authority to enact Emergency Regulations is currently found in the Basic Law: The Government.

a piece of legislation is repealed either explicitly or implicitly by the legislature, it remains in effect. However, this rule is subject to certain exceptions.

84. The repeal of the Mandate legislation may serve as an instructive example of why the repeal of a law is an act of no less consequence than its adoption. A legislature that leaves antiquated laws in effect, and fails to replace them with laws suited to the times, betrays the confidence of those who elected it. The legislature must therefore be constantly sensitive to public opinion, and ideally, the legislature should uproot laws that are no longer commensurate with contemporary needs and that are repugnant to the concepts of justice and prevailing norms. Nevertheless, there are various Mandate ordinances that have remained in force until today, despite their being incongruent with the spirit of democratic states. Examples of this are the Cinematograph Films Ordinance of 1937 which established a public committee charged with granting permits for the public screening of movies, and authorized to prohibit the screening of a film, and the Mandatory Press Ordinance of 1933, which required the licensing of newspapers, and others. Notably, the Supreme Court has given a particularly narrow construction to these ordinances.

§3. The Hierarchy of Norms

85. The various legal norms operating in the State of Israel are generally classified in terms of their location on the normative pyramid, which is determined in accordance with their importance and legal status. As stated, the constitutional norms (basic laws) are at the apex of the pyramid. Further down on the normative scale are the regular laws, and secondary legislation is at the lowest level.

86. In cases of conflict between norms, the higher norm will invariably prevail over a lower level norm. A regular law is subordinate to a basic law and similarly regulations cannot alter constitutional norms. As a rule, constitutional provisions can only be altered in the manner prescribed in the basic law itself. Thus, for example, Knesset legislation can violate the provisions of Basic Law: Human Dignity and Liberty if the law conforms to the requirements of the limitation clause.

87. The regular laws – whose status is lower than the constitutional norms – consist of numerous norms that regulate individual conduct in far greater detail than their regulation in constitutional provisions. The provisions of regular laws may be altered by another law, with the later law taking precedence.

88. Secondary legislation – at the lowest level of the normative pyramid – is enacted by the various bodies of the executive branch. Almost every law establishes a specific authority that is empowered to enact such regulations necessary for the implementation of the law. The secondary legislation consists of the relevant, practical details, which the legislature is unable to include in the wording of primary legislation, and accordingly leaves for the determination of the secondary legislator. Another standard form of secondary legislation is the by-laws. For example, municipal by-laws are enacted by force of an empowering provision in the primary law authorizing a municipality to enact by-laws. Notably, every municipality enacts its own by-laws.

89. Binding legal norms can also be established between individuals in the realm of private law. For example, the provisions of a will establish a legal norm. Where a contract is concluded between two individuals the provisions of the contract establish a legal norm to be complied with, and the breach of which is regarded as a breach of contract.

Chapter 4. Jurisprudence

§1. Introduction

90. The judicial branch enforces the limitations imposed on governmental powers, and is charged with the resolution of disputes. Trial Courts establish facts and the relevant law, and determine the legal conclusion dictated by application of the law to the facts. An appellate Court's task is to evaluate the trial Court's decision, and to assess whether its decision was mistaken, although the scope of its examination is generally limited to an examination of the legal conclusions drawn from the facts established. Together with the resolution of individual disputes, the Court also engages in the creation of law and the formulation of general norms. This is primarily the task of the Supreme Court, whose judgments enjoy the status of binding precedent, applicable to all lower Courts and the various governmental and executive authorities. While in a democratic state, the principal source for the creation of the law is the legislature, it has neither a monopoly nor exclusivity in the creation of the law. In Israel, the Supreme Court is regarded as the legislature's 'senior partner' in the creation of legal norms.

§2. The Judiciary as a Source of Law

91. The judiciary has the power to 'create' the law in three different ways. The first is by interpreting enacted legal norms created by other authorities. The second is by the development of Israeli 'common law'. The third is by filling in lacunae in legislation.

92. Where the law is anchored in a statutory norm, the author of the norm is the creator of the law. Nonetheless, judicial interpretation is also a form of creating law. This is obvious when the statutory text is vague or ambiguous, and where regular rules of interpretation fail to produce an unequivocal solution. In these cases, the judge is required to choose a specific interpretation from among a number of interpretative possibilities allowed by the text, without the system itself having prescribed rules for selection. The absence of mandatory rules of interpretation paves the path for judicial discretion, which in effect is 'judicial legislation'. According to this conception, any act of legislation necessarily involves conferring power to interpret such legislation, which includes the exercise of judicial discretion.

93. Both the Anglo-American tradition and Israeli law legitimize the phenomenon of judicially created 'common law'. In Israel, it is the source of major parts of the administrative law, the laws of evidence and the laws of remedies. By delivering a judgment in a particular case, the judge creates a new general norm for the entire system. Here there is no enacted law being interpreted, and thus it differs from interpretation as explained above. In addition to these two forms of creating law, the Israeli judge is also empowered to fill in a legislative lacunae, which implies an auxiliary power of determining that the arrangement provided by a particular law is incomplete. Section 1 of the Foundations of the Law Act, 1980 directs the Court to fill in lacunae by way of an analogy to a similar law, and absent an appropriate analogy, the Court is directed to decide it 'in the light of the principles of freedom, justice, equity and peace of Israel's heritage'. Consequently, the role of the Courts in filling legislative lacunae generally involves judicial creativity, thus creating new law.

94. While any judge adjudicating a case is involved in the creation of law, such judicial creation in private cases is made on an individual basis, being binding exclusively on the disputing parties. The justices of the Supreme Court operate on the general level, their rulings being binding on society at large.

§3. THE LEGAL PRECEDENT: STARE DECISIS

95. Section 20 of Basic Law: The Judiciary provides as follows:

(a) A rule laid down by a Court shall guide any lower Court.
(b) A rule laid down by the Supreme Court shall bind any Court other than the Supreme Court.

This section provided the Supreme Court with the basis for creating constitutional rules as well as major parts of different fields of law. An example of this process may be seen in the *Kol Ha'am* decision in 1953, which was one of the most important cases decided in the early years of the State.[74]

96. This case dealt with the power granted by the Mandatory Press Ordinance to the Minister of Interior to suspend the publication of a newspaper if 'any matter appearing in a newspaper is, in the opinion of the minister, likely to endanger the public peace'. In this case, the minister had ordered the suspension of the publication of a communist paper, 'Kol Ha'am'. The Court was clearly confronted with a major constitutional question, in relation to which sound democratic and liberal principles clashed with the Mandatory Press Ordinance. After having discussed the importance of freedom of expression in a democratic regime, as established in Israel by virtue of the Declaration of Independence, Justice Agranat explained that the power to suspend the publication of a newspaper was inconsistent with all democratic-liberal principles. The only way to justify the existence of the ordinance in Israeli law was to 'balance' the importance of freedom of expression with the need to keep public peace. Justice Agranat therefore read the words 'likely to endanger public peace' in the Press Ordinance as containing a 'probability test', similar to the 'clear and present danger test' in American jurisprudence. This resulted in the suspension order being cancelled. Agranat's decision was greatly influenced by American law, and the available interpretation of the US Constitution's First

74. HCJ *Kol Ha'am v. Minister of Interior* (1953) 7(2) PD 871*r*. A complete translation of this case may be found in Selected Judgments of the Supreme Court of Israel, Vol. 1 (Jerusalem 1962), p. 90.

Amendment in the 1950s.[75] The new balancing test was therefore established as the binding test for the limitation of freedom of speech.

97. In Israel, the statutory rule of binding precedent raised the question of whether in all cases the ruling must comply with past precedent, or whether the principle of legal stability should prevail. In responding to this question, the Supreme Court answered that when deciding between 'truth and stability', truth was preferable. Basic Law: The Judiciary endorsed this approach. The Supreme Court is not bound by precedents established in its own rulings, but these rulings are binding upon all other Courts, which are obliged to rule in accordance with precedents laid down by the Supreme Court. The effect of this statutory obligation is to ensure the stability and uniformity of the law. In exempting the Supreme Court from ruling in accordance with its own precedents, the legislature expressed its anticipation and expectation of judicial innovation, and perhaps even assented to 'judge-made law'. Nonetheless, the binding nature of the precedent on inferior Courts was limited to the *ratio decidendi*, and does not apply to obiter dictum.

98. While the judgments delivered by the Supreme Court are binding upon all other Courts, rulings given by other Courts have the status of non-binding guidelines, applying only to Courts of a lower normative standing than the Court that issued the ruling. Rulings issued by the District Court 'guide' the Magistrate's Courts, but District Courts cannot bind each other, and are certainly not bound by the precedents established by the Magistrate's Court.

99. As for the Supreme Court, while it is not bound by its own rulings, it usually abides by them, in recognition of the importance of legal stability as an indispensable value. Hence, as a rule, the Supreme Court does not readily deviate from its own precedents, even though it is statutorily empowered to do so. However, if the Supreme Court considers that a past ruling is liable to give rise to injustice, it regards itself as not only permitted, but also duty bound to deviate from what it regards as an antiquated norm, which no longer realizes the legislative purpose in the light of contemporary reality.

§4. The Judges' Discretion in the Creation of Law

100. There are four primary criteria to which judges tend to in the creation of the law:

The first criterion is giving expression to the fundamental values of the system.[76] These values primarily relate to morality and justice, which the judge draws from

75. *See* Pnina Lahav, *Judgment in Jerusalem: Chief Justice Simon Agranat and the Zionist Century*, 108–109 (University of California Press 1997); Pnina Lahav, *American Influence on Israel Jurisprudence of Free Speech*, 9 Hastings Constitutional Law Quarterly 21 (1981).
76. This subject is dealt with at length in an article by Supreme Court President, Professor Aharon Barak, *see*: Barak, Forward, *A Judge on Judging: The Role of a Supreme Court in a Democracy*, 116 Harvard L. Rev. 16 (2002).

constitutive documents such as the Declaration of Independence and basic laws, and from the essential nature of the democratic regime.

101. The second criterion is the ongoing aspiration to close the gaps between 'law and life', through the exercise of judicial discretion. The judge balances the need for change and the preservation of the current situation. His mandate is to adjust the law to the exigencies of practical life and reality, in a manner that ensures 'dynamic stability'. Societal changes lead to changes in the function and essence of norms, and the judge is occasionally required to straddle the gap between the law and the social reality, by giving a new and modern interpretation to an old law.

102. Third, the judge attempts to maintain the democratic nature of the state and the protection of its constitution and values. The Supreme Court's task is to protect the material or formal constitution, and to protect the existence of the state and its laws, to give expression to its democratic character, which is based on majority rule and the protection of human rights.

103. Fourth, the judge strictly insists upon preservation of the rule of law and the separation of powers, both of which are uniquely important when evaluating the importance of the system's various fundamental values. The judiciary as a whole, and particularly the Supreme Court, is charged with the supervision of the rule of law in the state. This ensures that each of the branches of governmental authority operates within the framework of its statutory powers, and ensures that nobody is above or beyond the law. In addition to maintaining the rule of law, the Supreme Court must also promote the principle of separation of powers in the framework of checks and balances.

§5. Trends in Case Law: The Past and the Present

104. During the first years following the State's establishment, in the 1950s and 1960s, the Israeli legal system was characterized by legal formalism. Cardinal importance was given to legal norms, which were regarded as promoting legal certainty. The written word reigned supreme, and the solution to legal problems was found primarily in the language of the law.[77] The legal system advocated strict separation of powers, especially as to the relations between the judiciary and the Knesset. The absence of a formal constitution prevented the judiciary from conducting judicial review of laws, and the Court's role was limited to the interpretation of existing legislation, in accordance with the principles of the Declaration of Independence. Court decisions of that period differentiated between distinct legal categories, and the Court dealt mainly with the classification of legal situations into

77. HCJ 287/51 *Re'em et al. v. Minister of Finance*, 8(1) PD. Justice Goitein ruled that a new State required not only a law that was clear but also a stable and certain interpretation of that law. If the Supreme Court was to be permitted to give alternating interpretations to the same law, the result would be the confusion of the average citizen, who would be under the misconception that the law was fundamentally flexible, and that Court decisions were essentially the product of the legal dispute between the parties' attorneys, without any fixed principles guiding its decisions.

legal rubrics. In the field of administrative law, the Court's consideration was limited exclusively to the question of whether those exercising power had acted within the parameters of their powers.

105. Despite these defining characteristics, Israeli case law has been neither static nor uniform since the establishment of the state, and even during that period, the Supreme Court displayed sensitivity to fundamental values and human rights. The decision in the *Kol-Ha'am* case, discussed above, is a prime example of this.

106. In contrast to the first period, the case law of the 1980s was characterized by a decrease in the weight attaching to formalistic argumentation, and increased reliance upon value-laden arguments and considerations. These changes have their source, among other things, in the political and social transitions, and not only in the approach of the Supreme Court itself. In many ways, the change in the case law reflected the Court's response to the changes in the political system, which had become increasingly unstable. A hallmark of this period was the struggle over the character of the state in a cultural sense: the increasing power of extremist forces, the struggle regarding the status of women, the awakening of the Arab minority, in addition to other factors. These changes resulted in increased judicial involvement in societal changes, due to the need for an objective forum which could resolve these disputes. The change has also been attributed to an imminent, internal development within the legal system itself, a change in the orientation of the judges, from the traditional English-Mandatory approach to an increasingly American approach.[78] Israel came under the direct influence of US culture in the 1970s and 1980s, and social values such as individualism and liberalism started to have an impact on the world of law as well. Since the 1980s, Israeli legal education has been greatly Americanized. This American influence was eventually reflected in academic papers authored in Israel and in the adjudication of the HCJ.

107. One of the striking changes in the case law was the increasing prominence of fundamental values as normative considerations in the judge's rulings. The importance attached to the language of the law receded, gradually being supplanted by new terminology, comprising such terms as 'the purpose of the law', 'the spirit of the law' and the 'legislative intention'. The judges highlighted the creative aspect of adjudication. They felt free to search for creative solutions in order to arrive at a result which was just, moral and value-based. The same period also witnessed a

78. Justice Zamir, CA 6821/93 *Mizrachi Bank Ltd. v. Migdal Cooperative Village*, 49(4) 221, at 259–260, when writing about the constitutional revolution, cites American Law: 'And nonetheless, the revolution [the Israeli Constitutional Revolution SN] succeeded. The revolution succeeded because, as with other revolutions, it occurred when the time was ripe … because it was carried out using correct tactics, which enabled the sovereign to attain its goals … and perhaps also because it circumvented the controversy over weighty constitutional questions. In these aspects it resembles the successful revolution that took place in America, about 200 years ago, which was also in the realm of the relations between the judiciary and the legislature, in the famous case of *Marbury v. Madison*, 5 U.S. 137 (1803).'

decrease in the importance of procedural requirements in the judicial system, meaning that from that period on, Courts have tended to attach less importance to procedural questions, and greater importance to substantive matters.

108. All the same, the salient hallmark of this period was without a doubt the role played by the Supreme Court in the formulation of the Israeli constitution. With the enactment of the basic laws concerning human rights, the Supreme Court was confronted with the question of the relationship between the basic laws and regular laws which violate human rights – an issue which was adjudicated in the *Mizrachi Bank* case. In this case, the Supreme Court declared that basic laws have the status of a constitution, and that the Court is empowered to invalidate Knesset legislation that contravenes the provisions of the basic law. This declaration constitutes the pinnacle of the Supreme Court's activist period.

109. By virtue of their inclusive, general and broad wording, the basic laws provide ample opportunity for creative interpretation. The Supreme Court declared that it would endorse an expansive approach with respect to rights included within the ambit of these basic laws. Accordingly, even where rights were not explicitly mentioned in the law, such as the principle of equality, where Knesset legislation permitted discrimination against a particular group, the Court would interpret the term 'human dignity' as including the right to equality. This would enable it to invalidate a discriminatory law on the grounds of its violation of human dignity, which is a protected right under the Basic Law: Human Dignity and Liberty.

§6. Judicial 'Activism'

110. Over the last few years, the Israeli Supreme Court has been regarded as being an activist Court. Especially since the 1980s, the Court has developed a number of powerful tools for intervening in government actions, even in areas that in many states are considered to be 'unjusticiable', such as the army and politics. By way of a gradual process, case law has expanded the scope of judicial review, and the judges now regard themselves as a supervisory and review authority. Here are some examples that illustrate the Court's degree of intervention in the decisions and activities of different authorities:

(a) *Judicial review of the internal proceedings of the Knesset.* Quite a few legal systems have endorsed the concept that the internal acts and decisions of the legislature are beyond the reach of the Courts. Not only did the Supreme Court of Israel reject this approach, but also in fact it has been prepared to review almost all aspects of the Knesset's activities.[79]
(b) *Enforcement of ethical norms regarding public figures.* The realm of public ethics is one in which Supreme Court intervention has been particularly striking. During a period in which political culture gave rise to undesirable norms of conduct, the Supreme Court enforced rules of ethics even in the absence of a clear

79. *See* discussion below, on Part 2.

law. The Supreme Court developed a doctrine according to which 'a public figure is a trustee of the public'. Hence in the case of a minister against whom an indictment was filed,[80] the Supreme Court instructed the Prime Minister to remove him from his position, even in the absence of an explicit statutory obligation to do so. The Supreme Court similarly concluded that the rules of public law, and especially the fundamental principles of democracy, compelled the publication of coalition agreements.[81]

(c) *Supervision of the religious establishment* and intervention in its application of religious-halakhic considerations. As observed below, there is no separation between religion and state in Israel and on a number of occasions over the years, the Court has intervened in decisions that were influenced by religious considerations. For example, the Court disqualified municipal by-laws that restricted the operation of businesses on the Sabbath[82] and intervened to prevent the harassment of non-kosher butcheries and of shops selling sex products.[83] To a certain degree, the Court even limited the monopoly granted by the Knesset to the religious establishment over matters of marriage and divorce of Jews.

(d) *Judicial Review of state security issues* – Notwithstanding that the subject of state security is widely regarded as sacred, the Supreme Court did not hesitate to intervene in this field too. The classic example of this is *Shnitzer v. Military Censor*[84] in which the Court invalidated the military censor's decision to withhold publication of an article criticizing the actions of the head of the Mossad [Israeli Intelligence] and the timing of his replacement. Since the 1990s, the Supreme Court has judicially reviewed numerous military operations, even during the course of battle.[85]

111. Over the years, the Supreme Court has become a highly dominant and influential factor in Israeli society. Nonetheless, its intervention in the decisions and activities of the sovereign authorities and its decisive role in the creation of legal norms has been criticized both in the public domain and in academic circles. Among the central critiques of the Supreme Court's role are the claims that appointed judges should not be involved in legislation, which is and should be the role of the democratically elected legislator. Further, it is alleged that judicial legislation violates the principle of separation of powers. However, these critiques confront the counterclaim that the modern conception of separation of powers is not a dichotomous one, and accepts the notion of the judge being at least a minor partner in the legislative enterprise. The executive authority creates law without it being regarded as a violation of the principle of separation of powers, and under the modern view, the same rule applies to judge-made law. Notwithstanding the criticism, it is undisputed that the Supreme Court's contribution to the creation of Israeli constitutional law has been a unique one. In its decisions, it has enforced and established the rule of law

---

80. HCJ 3094/93 *The Movement for the Quality of Government v. Government of Israel*, 45(5) PD 404.
81. HCJ 1601/90 *Adv. Meshulam Shalit v. Shimon Peres*, 44(3) PD 353.
82. HCJ 39/82 *Elazar Hanpling et al. v. Tzvi Tzikler, et al.*, 36(2) PD 537.
83. HCJ 230/73 *STM Ltd. v. Head of Jerusalem Municipality*, 28(2) PD 113.
84. HCJ 680/88 *Meir Shnitzer v. Chief Military Censor, et al.*, 42(4) 617.
85. *See below* in Part 4, Ch. 2 and Part 5, Ch. 4, dealing with the Supreme Court and the war against terror.

and the separation of powers and in so doing has given expression to democratic values and protected fundamental constitutional principles. Furthermore, notwithstanding the Supreme Court's rhetoric affirming its power to intervene in the actions of other authorities, on a practical level, its decisions over the years reflect a policy of caution and self-restraint.

Chapter 5. Customary Law, Unwritten Law, General Principles of Law

§1. Custom

112. Custom plays a key role in Israeli public law. Some customs may actually replace legislation but in the majority of cases, they complete and supplement legislation where legislative arrangements are seen as being deficient, and in the absence of guidance based on Israeli common law. Imprints of custom-based law can be seen in all aspects of Israeli public law, *inter alia*, with respect to the reciprocal relations between the sovereign authorities – the government, the president, and the Knesset; central and local government, enforcement or non-enforcement of statutes, the formulation of conventions of conduct applicable to holders of official positions, appointments to positions in sovereign offices, and to sovereign bodies.

113. In numerous statutes, custom is recognized as a binding source of law. The legislature understood the need to recognize and give legal force to customs and conventions as part of the formalization of a system of rules which efficiently regulates legal relations. Following are just some of the many examples of this phenomenon:

(1) Section 17 of the State Service (Discipline) Law, 1963 provides that a state employee is guilty of a disciplinary offence where he failed to carry out or was negligent in the performance of any duty imposed on him as a State employee, having its sources in custom, law, regulation or in a validly issued general or special direction;
(2) Section 133(2) of the Military Justice Law, 1955 defines an offence as the non-compliance with a standing or routine order, or other general orders published in accordance with the military directives or military custom; and
(3) Section 9(2) of the Local Authorities (Discipline) Law, 1978 defines a disciplinary offence as the non-fulfilment or negligent fulfilment of a duty imposed on the employee of a local authority according to any law, regulation, or custom, or any general or special direction validly issued to him.
(4) Custom also appears in Israeli basic laws. For example, section 19 of Basic Law: The Knesset empowers the Knesset to prescribe its working procedures and provides that insofar as such procedures have not been prescribed by law, the Knesset will prescribe them by rules. As long as such procedures have not been prescribed, the Knesset is directed to follow its accepted custom and routine.

114. Notwithstanding a plethora of statutory references to custom as a source of law, in the sphere of public law, only rarely does Israeli law rely on claims and argumentation based on custom. Two possible explanations present themselves: first, the difficulty of proving the existence of a custom; and second, awareness of the importance of the custom is low among advocates and judges.

§2. Crystallization of Custom into Law

115. A custom firmly rooted in daily practice over a long period may receive the force of law by its incorporation into existing primary legislation. A few examples of this include:

(1) The subordination of the chief of general staff to the Minister of Defence and the government was accepted practice for many years, and enacted as law at a much later stage in section 3 of the Basic Law: The Army. Similarly, the appointment of the chief of general staff by the government upon the recommendation of the Minister of Defence was accepted practice until given legal standing by the legislature in the form of section 3(c) of Basic Law: The Army.
(2) The submission of the annual budget in the form of a law, as well the custom of submission of interim budgets and additional budgets was crystallized in section 3 of Basic Law: State Economy.

116. It should further be noted that the incorporation of custom into law may be effected in a partial manner only, and that laws are sometimes enacted exclusively in order to restrict or qualify deeply rooted customs. For example, the Administrative Procedure Amendment (Statement of Reasons) Law, 1959, terminated the case law development of a custom which extensively broadened the citizen's right to receive the reasons from authorities for their decisions. The law established clear limitations on the authority's duty to give reasons for its decisions.

117. Custom and practice may similarly serve as an important interpretative tool in the interpretation of laws. In the case of *Ein Harod v. Lugasi*, Justice Witkon wrote the following:

> This does not mean that an entrenched and accepted practice is not likely to influence the Court's decision. The very fact that judges and attorneys adopted a certain approach over a period of time … is significant proof that this approach was indeed the right one, but this only applies when the judge has a doubt, and is required to decide whether a particular approach is correct or not.[86]

§3. Conflict Between Law and Custom

118. Where a statute conflicts with custom, the statute prevails. A previously accepted custom can influence the interpretation of a statute, but not if the judge concludes that the custom was based on a mistaken interpretation. Occasionally, this type of conflict may be prevented by statutory interpretation that is consistent with the custom. In other words, where a particular statute can be constructed in a number of ways, the chosen construction may be the one that conforms to the custom.

86. CA 29/59 *Ein Harod v. Lugasi*, 13 PD 1883, 1899.

In his ruling in the *Of Haemek v. Ramat Yishai Local Authority* case,[87] Justice Barak ruled that: 'If the previously accepted custom was based on a mistaken interpretation of the statute then it is of no significance, regardless of the severity of the result … as is well known, a custom cannot legitimate a mistaken interpretation of the law. The judge is duty bound to uproot the mistake. This is a fundamental duty, imposed on the judge by force of his duty to uphold the law. This is not the case when the previously accepted custom is based on a possible and legal interpretation of the law, even if not regarded by the Court as the best possible interpretation. In that situation, the Court must have consideration for the factual reality created in the past, as one of the factors to be considered in deciding whether to deviate from past custom by giving a new interpretation.'[88]

§4. An Example of a Constitutional Custom in Public Law: The Process of Ratifying and Absorbing International Conventions and Treaties

119. The procedure for ratifying and adopting international conventions and treaties in Israel is an outstanding example of the existence of a constitutional custom. This procedure is not regulated by a statute that clearly prescribes how international customs, treaties and conventions Israel become part of the domestic law, and which of the governmental branches – legislative or executive or the presidency – is empowered to bind the State of Israel.

120. In the past, the Supreme Court opined that the presidency was the most appropriate branch for ratification and adoption of treaties as part of Israeli domestic law. However, over the years, practice has indicated that there was a constitutional custom which required the government to sign and ratify treaties. In Cr. A 131/67 *Kamiar v. State of Israel*, the Supreme Court gave its legal approval to this custom, accepting the government's position that it alone was empowered to sign and ratify treaties without the Knesset's participation. The Court established the legal basis for the government's power to conclude treaties by force of its general power to conduct foreign policy, and having consideration for the constitutional custom whereby all treaties requiring ratification were ratified exclusively by the government without Knesset participation. One of the questions arising in that particular case concerned the interpretation of section 11(a)(5) of Basic Law: President of the State, which provides that the president's powers include the power to conclude treaties with foreign states that have been verified by the Knesset. The appellant argued that the section's reference to the Knesset's power as opposed to the government's power indicates that the Knesset is the empowered body. The Court rejected the appellant's interpretation, and accepted the government's

87. HCJ 547/84 *Of Haemek v. Ramat Yishai Local Authority*, 40(1) PD 113, 145–147.
88. *Ibid.*, at pp. 145–147.

interpretation of the section, according to which Knesset approval and a presidential signature are only required in special circumstances, in which the government specifically requests Knesset ratification of a treaty.[89]

121. In 1983, the difficulty which arose in *Kamiar v. State of Israel* was resolved when a government decision was adopted, along with an explicit guideline of the attorney general, stating that treaties were to be tabled in the Knesset before their ratification by the Knesset. As a matter of practice however, and despite the decision of the government and the attorney general, only treaties of exceptional importance are in fact tabled for Knesset approval, for example, matters involving territorial concessions, security issues and human rights.

122. It should be stressed that this custom is valid with respect to international treaties and international conventions of which Israel is a signatory, such as peace agreements and ceasefire agreements. Among the more outstanding of these is Israel's joining of the United Nations, in 1948; the General Armistice Agreements signed in 1949 between Israel and Lebanon, Egypt, Jordan and Syria, respectively; the Convention on the Prevention and Punishment of the Crime of Genocide; the Camp David Accords (1978); Peace Agreements with Egypt (1979); Israel – Lebanon Peace Agreements (1983), and others.[90]

§5. The Basic Principles of the Legal System[91]

I. General

123. The Israeli legal system is not based on any single, central document which consolidates the basic principles of Israeli law. Rather, these principles must be gleaned from the judgments of the Supreme Court.[92] In Cr. A 677/83 *Borochov v. Yefet*, Justice Barak discussed the contents of the system's basic principles, noting that these general principles include the principles of equality, justice and morality. They encompass the social goals of separation of powers, the rule of law, freedom of expression, freedom of assembly, worship, occupation, human dignity, independence of adjudication, public peace and security, and the democratic values and existence of the state. These principles include good faith, natural justice, fairness and reasonability ... the list of these principles can never be 'closed'. These principles often all gravitate in the same direction; however, they occasionally pull in different, conflicting directions. In these situations, the Court must take account of

89. Y. Zilbershatz, *The Adoption of International Law into Israeli Law – The Real is Ideal*, 25 Israel Yearbook on Human Rights, 243–279; *see also*: *Documents on the laws of war* (Oxford, 2nd ed. By A. Roberts & R. Guelft (1989), 43; Motion 21/59 *Shimshon v. Attorney General*, 4 PD 143; H.J. 610/78 *Oyev v. Minister of Defence*, 33(2) PD 113, 120.
90. *See* discussion in Part V, Ch. 1.
91. A. Barak, *Interpretation in Law*, (In Hebrew) vol. 2 – *Statutory Interpretation*, p. 422.
92. 39(1) PD 205.

all of the principles, line them up side by side and give each of them a commensurate weight in the particular circumstances. Having done so, it must aim to strike a balance between the different values.

II. Fundamental Principles

124. The Declaration of Independence provides that the State of Israel will be based on the precepts of liberty, justice and peace as envisaged by the prophets of Israel. It further provides that the State of Israel 'will uphold the full social and political equality' of all its citizens, without distinction of race, creed or sex, and that it will guarantee 'full freedom of conscience, worship, education and culture'. While the Declaration of Independence has no independent legal force, the Supreme Court has ruled on a number of occasions that the Declaration of Independence may well serve as a normative source from which the rights can be derived and that its provisions constitute a legal norm that expresses the 'charter of the nation's values'. In the *Mizrachi Bank* case, Justice Levine espoused a unique doctrine which was even prepared to regard the Declaration of Independence as an independent source for giving force to rights not included in the basic laws on human rights:

> This declaration was not put into written form for decorative, symbolic purposes; rather it expresses ... fundamental and basic constitutional principles and values ... these basic laws produced a dramatic change in the status of the Declaration of Independence and the intensity of the power emanating therefrom. It is no longer to be regarded a reliable and appropriate source for interpretation of the law, for its power has been augmented and it can henceforth be viewed, in an appropriate degree, as an independent source of human rights.[93]

It must be remarked that this view has not been adopted as such by the Supreme Court.

§6. Israel as a Democratic State

125. The basic elements of democracy have been repeated in many of the Supreme Court's decisions. The democratic nature of the State of Israel has been embedded in it since the day of its establishment. It clearly and openly emerges from the text of the Declaration of Independence, which expresses the fundamental concepts that have been a part of the state since that day. The democratic perception and its practical implementation are reflected in the governmental structure, in the practical and legal status of the state's citizens and residents and, among other things, in the principles of the rule of law and equality before the law. In *Neiman v. Chairman, Central Elections Committee*, President Barak wrote that:

93. CA 6821/93 *Mizrachi Bank v. Migdal Collective Village*, 49(4) PD 221, 482–483.

> It appears to me that just as the existence of the state is a fundamental tenet in our legal system, so is its existence as a democratic state. The Declaration of Independence – in the light of which our legislation is construed – indicates that Israel rests 'upon foundations of liberty, justice and peace as envisioned by the Prophets of Israel' and that it will ensure 'complete equality of social and political rights for all its citizens, without distinction of creed, race and sex'. All this presupposes not only the actual existence of the state but also its democratic essence, for it is impossible to ensure equality, liberty and justice without maintaining a democratic regime under which these principles will be realized.[94]

§7. Separation of Powers

126. One of the most prominent characteristics of a democratic regime is its separation of the sovereign powers between three main branches – legislative, executive and judicial – and this indeed characterizes the system in the State of Israel. The separation of powers doctrine finds expression in two fundamental features. The first is the division of powers between various authorities. Hence there is a legislative branch, which is empowered to resolve and decide on central issues affecting society as a whole, individual relations between citizens, and relations between citizens and the administration, and to give its decisions legislative expression by determining general and specific arrangements; the executive branch, which is empowered to implement the various arrangements established by the legislative branch; and the judicial branch, which is empowered to resolve individual disputes and disputes concerning the manner in which the other branches exercise their powers.

127. A second fundamental characteristic of the separation of powers is the reciprocal oversight which each of these authorities has over the others, and the establishment of mechanisms for balancing between them. Prime examples of this include the judicial review of the decisions of other sovereign branches, and the Knesset supervision of the actions of the executive branch. As stated by President Barak:

> Separation of powers does not mean dictatorship [of each authority in its areas of power – SN]. Separation of powers means balancing and reciprocal supervision between the various branches. The authorities are not separated by walls, but rather connected by balancing and supervisory bridges. Indeed, this is the root of the conception that a judicial declaration of the invalidity of a statute is not a violation of the principle of separation of powers but rather its realization.

94. EA 2/84 *Neiman v. Chairman, Central Elections Committee*, 39(2) PD 225, 314.

§8. Independence of the Judiciary

128. The judicial branch is entrusted with the enforcement of restrictions imposed on the other sovereign authorities. It can only discharge this task if it is guaranteed independence from the political system. This gives rise to the concept that 'the existence of an independent network of Courts, adjudicating without external influences, is one of the basic values of the state'.[95] Indeed, to a large degree the judiciary in Israel exists and operates independently of the other sovereign authorities; it constitutes an independent sovereign authority and is not part of the political network.

§9. The Rule of Law

129. The rule of law is a fundamental principle in all democratic legal systems, and it consists of two foundations, the formal and the substantive. In its formal sense, the rule of law requires that all persons and bodies in the State – individuals, associations and governmental agencies – act in accordance with the law, and that any act in conflict with the law must be met by society's organized sanction. In this formal sense, the principle of the rule of law means the subjection of all the sovereign powers to the provisions of the law. In that sense, this principle expresses the philosophy that power does not belong to those who hold positions but rather, it is a part of a comprehensive network of norms, binding upon all. The law is the source of the power vesting in all sovereign authorities, and it determines the limitations of their powers. One of the central features of the rule of law is the circumscription of the power of the legislature by virtue of constitutional provisions. Another aspect is the principle of the legality of administration, ensuring that the executive branch may only act in accordance with the powers conferred upon it by law.

130. However, the rule of law also means the substantive rule of law. Here, the key concern relates to ensuring that, from a substantive perspective, all sovereign decisions comply with certain basic requirements. These requirements consist of the generality and consistency of legal norms; the prohibition of imposing sanctions of any kind absent legal authorization (including the duty to publish laws, and the prohibition of the retroactive amendment of the law; the prohibition on ambiguity in legislation and others); and the duty to litigate in accordance with 'the rules of natural justice'.

§10. Israel as a Jewish State

131. The State of Israel is a Jewish State. The Jewish character of the State receives expression both in its legislation and its case law. The 'purpose' sections of the Basic Laws: Human Dignity and Liberty, and Basic Law: Freedom of Occupation, both state explicitly that their purpose is to protect … [human dignity and

95. HCJ 14/86 *Laor v. Council for Film Censorship* 41(1) PD 421, 433.

liberty/freedom of occupation, respectively] … 'in order to establish in a Basic Law the values of the State of Israel as a Jewish and democratic state'.

132. The State of Israel was established by virtue of the natural and historical right of the Jewish people to live like all other nations in their own sovereign state.[96] The State of Israel is the realization of the desire of the Jewish people for countless generations, to renew their national life as in days of yore and the actualization of the Zionist vision.[97] The notion that the State of Israel is a Jewish state constitutes and functions as a basic principle of the Israeli legal system, receiving expression in a number of aspects relating to the rights of Jews to immigrate to Israel, its language, its festivals and the day of rest, which according to the Jewish religion is the Sabbath. The official languages of the State of Israel are Hebrew and Arabic. With respect to the basic values of Judaism being a part of the Jewish State, these values are not necessarily the entire suite of Jewish religious values. The State of Israel is not a Jewish State in the religious-halakhic sense, but rather in the sense that its basic values, such as the sanctity of life, social justice etc., are principles that are identified with Judaism. Establishing the Jewish nature of the State in the light of those principles is one of the purposes of its legal system along with the establishment of the democratic nature of the State. Regarding the Jewish and democratic nature of the State, Justice Menachem Elon wrote that, by force of the Basic Law: Human Dignity and Liberty:

> we are instructed to arrive at a synthesis that will achieve the dual-value goal of the Basic Law: Human Dignity and Liberty – to anchor in the laws of the State of Israel its values as a Jewish and democratic state. The natural way of achieving this synthesis is to find the common ground between the Jewish democratic systems – the principles that they share, or at least those that can be used to integrate the two systems.[98]

133. Another law giving expression to the Jewish nature of the State, and directly affecting the status of Jewish law in the State of Israel, is the Foundations of the Law Act, 1980. This statute was enacted in order to revoke the connection to and reliance upon English common law in cases of a gap in Israeli legislation. This statute provides that 'Where the Court, faced with a legal question requiring decision, finds no answer to it in statute law or case law or by analogy, it shall decide the issue in the light of the principles of freedom, justice, equity and peace of the Jewish heritage'.[99] In the *Jereczewski* case, Justice Elon wrote that:

> The purpose of the Foundations of the Law Act is cultural and nationalistic. Its aims are to create a link between the law of the Jewish State and the legal heritage of the Jewish people, throughout its generations and diasporas, and to

96. Declaration of Independence.
97. EA 2/84 *Neiman, ibid.*, at p. 230.
98. CA 506/88, *Yael Shefer, Minor represented by her mother v. State of Israel*, 48(1) PD 87, 96–97. This subject is discussed extensively in Part 5 of Ch. 5, with respect to the nature of the State of Israel as a Jewish state.
99. Section 1 of the Foundations of the Law Act, 1980.

implement the principles of justice, equity, freedom and peace that Jews have fostered throughout the generations and that have been expressed in the rich literature of the Jewish heritage in every generation.[100]

100. HCJ 1635/90 *Joseph Jerecezwski v. Prime Minister*, 45(1) PD 749. Justice Barak's interpretation of the scope of this law and the cases in which a judge is bound to rule in accordance with its provisions, was disputed by Justice Menachem Elon, *see*: FH 13/80, *Hendeles et al.v. Kupat Am Bank Ltd.*, PD 35(2), 785.

Chapter 6. Administrative Regulations and Orders

§1. Introduction

134. Under the principle of legality, an administrative authority is permitted to act exclusively in accordance with, and within the limits established by, its statutorily conferred powers, by comparison with the citizen, for whom the point of departure is that he can act as he pleases, unless his activity is statutorily proscribed.

135. The principle of legality requires that all administrative actions be based upon and must derive their authority from Knesset legislation. This applies equally to individual acts or the establishment of general norms of secondary legislation, both of which must be anchored in Knesset legislation. The law creates the administrative power, and the administrative authority draws its authority exclusively from the law. Any administrative actions performed in the absence of an enabling law are unauthorized, of no effect, and invalid.[101] Every citizen is entitled to know that any administrative action is performed by force of the authority's statutorily conferred power, and that legal administrative discretion was exercised in that context.

136. The principle of administrative legality applies first and foremost to the exercise of power that potentially violates human rights. This principle was declared immediately upon the establishment of the state, in the *Bezerano* decision.[102] At that time, however, the principle was not statutorily anchored, whereas today it is both legally and constitutionally entrenched in the restrictive clause of the Basic Law: Human Dignity and Liberty, which prohibits any violation of human rights 'except by law … or express authorization in such law'.

137. Administrative power is only conferred on the particular body of the executive authority specified for that purpose by statute, meaning that an executive authority is not allowed to 'delegate' its powers to another body, unless specifically authorized to do so by law or if, in the circumstances, there is a justification for it. In exercising its powers, the administrative authority will, on occasion, explicitly state the source of the power, for example a specific section in a specific statute. Nonetheless, there are numerous instances in which administrative authority is exercised without specification of the specific source of power. Failure to stipulate the

101. In a long series of judgments, the Supreme Court declared the ability to annul an administrative act performed without an express empowering provision in primary legislation. In certain cases, the Court ruled that the issue should be resolved by the legislature, and that absent an express pronouncement by the legislature, the administration has no authority to act. *See* HCJ 355/79 *Katalan v. Prison Authority*, 34(3) PD 294.

102. HCJ 1/49 *Bezerano v. Minister of the Police*, 2 PD 80. The Court ruled that absent express empowerment in the law, the Police Minister was not permitted to prevent persons filing applications for vehicle licenses on behalf of the vehicle owners.

source of power does not detract from the legality or validity of the exercise of powers in the absence of any positive statutory requirement to do so. Compliance with the principle of legality is strictly adhered to in all matters involving the exercise of judicial or quasi-judicial powers by administrative authorities.

§2. Administrative Legality and the Rule of 'Legislative Guidelines'

138. Knesset legislation determines not only the powers and the identity of the administrative bodies authorized to exercise it, but also the criteria governing the manner in which those powers are exercised. In its legislative capacity, the Knesset cannot restrict itself to determining the existence of a sovereign power in any particular area; its legislation must stipulate the central arrangements for exercising the power (legislative guidelines). A general directive of the legislature which fails to prescribe legislative guidelines for its implementation is much like the legislature divesting itself of its legislative power by transferring it to another body.

139. The specificity required in the legislative guidelines will inevitably vary from case to case, in accordance with the nature of the power concerned. The Supreme Court ruled that to the extent that the regulation of a particular field requires fundamental decisions, such decisions must be made within the framework of the principal legislation. The extent of violation of human rights occasioned by legislation determines the extent of specificity required in the primary guidelines established by such legislation: The greater the violation of individual freedom or other protected rights, the greater the degree of specificity required and the less tolerance there is for general and abstract legislation. In the past, however, this rule governing legislative guidelines expressed the 'ideal law' and lacked practical implementation.[103]

140. Over the last few years, however, the Israeli Supreme Court has broadened the duty of prescribing legislative guidelines, precisely in order to limit the powers of the executive branch. The Court established an 'interpretative presumption' whereby the legislature was presumed not to have enabled the executive authority to establish primary orders. One example is the power to grant an exemption from military service. Under section 36 of the Defence Service [Consolidated Version] 1986, the Minister of Defence is permitted to defer a person's duty of military service 'for reasons connected with the requirements of education … or for family or other reasons'. The Minister of Defence attempted to base his authority to exempt Yeshiva students from their duty of military service on a general authorization to grant exemptions for 'other reasons'. During the 1980s in the *Ressler* decision,[104] the Court ruled that this provision empowers the Minister of Defence to defer

103. *See* e.g., D. Schoenbrod, *Politics and the Principle that the Elected Legislators Should Make the Law*, 26 Harv Journ of L. & Public Policy, 239 (2003).
104. HCJ 910/86 *Ressler v. Minister of Defence*, 42(2) PD 441 (Justice Barak).

military service; 'the legislature, having determined that "other reasons" may serve as grounds for exemption of military service, obviously thus empowered the Minister of Defence to determine what those other reasons are and that they include "religious reasons" as well'. However, a decade later the Court changed this ruling in the *Rubinstein* decision,[105] stating that:

> We are therefore confronted with an extreme case of delegation of power to the executive branch, without the primary legislation containing any kind of guidelines for the Minister of Defence with respect to the primary arrangements ... [A]s a matter of principle the Minister of Defence is entitled to exempt Yeshiva students. Even so, the discretion must be exercised having consideration for the basic rule concerning legislative guidelines ... . He is authorized to grant an exemption to full time Yeshiva students, but this decision must be as part of a fundamental decision adopted by the Knesset ... . Hence, the Knesset cannot 'pass the buck' to the Minister of Defence – it must resolve the issue in the law. This is how a legal system faithful to the principle of separation of powers operates, within the rule of law.

141. The Court therefore ruled that the Minister of Defence was not empowered to grant a blanket exemption to all full time Yeshiva students, in the absence of legislative guidelines for such exemption in the primary legislation. The *Rubinstein* ruling determined that the exemption of Yeshiva students was an issue requiring resolution within the framework of primary Knesset legislation. The existing arrangement, made by the Minister of Defence, was illegal, having been adopted without the requisite empowerment in primary legislation. The Supreme Court has ruled more recently on the constitutionality of the legislative amendment (the '*Tal*' Law) concerning the exemption of full time Yeshiva students from military service, enacted in the wake of the *Rubinstein* decision. This amendment was challenged in the HCJ on the grounds of being discriminatory. The Court, sitting in an expanded panel of nine judges, decided that, although the *Tal* Law infringed the principle of equality, it was nevertheless 'constitutional'.[106] The appeal was dismissed, with Justice Heshin dissenting. The judges argued that the *Tal* Law had proper purposes, such as to diminish the discrimination existing in the exemption of the Yeshiva students, but that the measures taken in order to arrange for the Yeshiva students to integrate into Israeli society and in the army were lacking. Therefore, at that stage it was too early to properly evaluate the *Tal* Law. A few years later, in 2012, the HCJ determined that the right to dignity, as it appears in Basic Law: Human Dignity and Liberty, includes several aspects of the right to equality, and eventually decided to nullify the *Tal* Law because it disproportionately harmed the right to equality.[107]

---

105. HCJ 3627/97 *Rubinstein v. Minister of Defence*, 52(5) PD 481.
106. HCJ 6427/02 *The Movement for Quality Government in Israel v. the Knesset* PD r 61(1), 619 (2006).
107. HCJ 6298/07 *Ressler v. The Knesset* (published by Nevo on 21 Dec. 2012).

§3. Regulations

142. Usually administrative power is established by statute, but on occasion it is set out in regulations. The legislature may expressly state that a certain authority is entitled to vest powers in another authority by regulations. In such a case, the regulation is the principal source of power. According to the principle of the legality, it is insufficient for an administrative authority to act within the framework of the powers vested in it by the regulation; rather, it is necessary to examine whether the regulation itself was promulgated within the framework of the power established by statute. Section 37 of Basic Law: the Government provides that the minister charged with the implementation of a law is empowered to promulgate regulations for its implementation. This is the general empowerment section applicable to all ministers which enables them to promulgate regulations for the implementation of statutes.

By way of example, section 70 of the Traffic Ordinance provides that the Minister of Transport is entitled to make regulations regarding a variety of matters. *Inter alia*, he is entitled, by regulations, to empower the inspector of traffic to prohibit or restrict, by traffic signs, the driving of any vehicle.

143. According to the basic laws on human rights, a new law cannot vest in an administrative authority the power to violate protected rights, save if the power meets the conditions of the limitation clause; and this is *a fortiori* the case when the power is vested by regulations. True, the basic law enables a violation of basic rights not only in a law, but also under law, i.e., in regulations. However, it is clear that the regulations must meet the conditions of the limitation clause.

144. Section 10 of the Law and Administration Ordinance, 1948, section 17 of the Interpretation Ordinance [New Version] and section 3 of the Interpretation Law, 1981, outline the normative infrastructure of the duty to publish statutes and regulations. Publication is an essential precondition for the validity of a regulation. It is possible to identify a regulation by identifying three cumulative features: it is a provision by virtue of law which has 'legislative effect'; it is general – that is, the regulation must be directed at a non-specific public; and the normative requirement, namely, that the regulation must create change in prevailing law.

§4. Administrative Directive

145. In the same way as it is possible to vest administrative powers by regulations, and not necessarily by statute, it is also possible to vest powers in an administrative directive. A decision by a minister to empower a local authority is an administrative directive.[108] This directive is the source of the power of the administrative authority. It follows that the administrative directive is the primary source of the power.

---

108. *See*, for example, s. 22(2) of the Land (Acquisition for Public Purposes) Ordinance, 1943. The section provides that the Minister of Finance is entitled, subject to certain conditions, to empower a local authority or a particular person to confiscate land for public purposes.

146. It should be pointed out that administrative directives are numerous and vary widely. They are called directive or circulars, procedures or guidelines. Often they are set out in writing, but there is no requirement that this be the case. An oral directive may also comprise a source of power.[109] Administrative directives generally establish rules of policy, and the criteria which must be observed by the authority in order to exercise its powers. Directives have great practical importance. They translate the principles set out in legislation and case law into the language of the daily work of the authority. Such directives are not in the nature of regulations having legislative effect. First, they are not directives by virtue of law, as no statute empowers the authority to perform such an activity. Second, administrative directives do not establish a legal norm but an informal administrative norm possessing legal consequences. With regard to the question of publication, until the judgment in the case of *Ephrati v. Ostfeld*,[110] the prevailing law was that administrative directives were not subject to the duty of publication, whether in Reshumot or in some other way. The Court pointed out the positive aspects of such publication in this case, but did not make it a binding legal obligation.

147. One example of interesting directives are those issued by the attorney general in his capacity as the legal adviser of the government. Besides issuing legal opinions when required by the government, the attorney general also issues more general directives for the various branches of the executive. These opinions are now widely published and may be found in any legal library, as well as on the internet.

§5. General Governmental Powers

148. In the Israeli system of government, there are entire areas of governmental activity which are not regulated by an empowering statute, and which are not regulated by law. The legislature is unable to regulate all the activities of government or to expressly state which powers are required in each and every area. These areas of activity fall within the framework of 'general governmental powers' which are granted to government by virtue of section 32 of Basic Law: the Government. This section provides:

> The government is authorized to perform in the name of the State and subject to any law, all actions which are not legally incumbent on another authority.

It is noteworthy that the power vested in the government is exclusively 'residual', i.e., this section does not vest powers in the government if the power has been

109. *See*, for example, s. 22(2) of the Land (Acquisition for Public Purposes) Ordinance, 1943. The section provides that the Minister of Finance is entitled, subject to certain conditions, to empower a local authority or a particular person to confiscate land for public purposes.

110. HCJ 5537/91 *Ephrati v. Ostfeld*, 46(3) PD 501 – the duty to publish established by this ruling is limited. It refers only to directives having ramifications for individual rights. In addition, it established that the source of the duty of publication is not statutory.

lawfully vested in another authority.[111] Likewise, where the section empowers the government to act, it requires it to do so subject to law. In other words, the section prohibits the government from violating basic human rights. The power is also subject to the duty to act on the basis of relevant considerations and within the boundaries of reasonableness. Notwithstanding the scope of the section, in practice, its declared use has been confined to few cases. The Court has regarded this section as a source of power of the government to deal with such issues as the Holy Places, the grant of allocations, and foreign relations activities, including the provision of overseas aid.

§6. Auxiliary Powers

149. In addition to the general powers of government, every administrative authority is vested with general auxiliary powers. This rule was formulated in Israel in a statutory provision, section 17 of the Interpretation Law, 1981. Auxiliary powers under this section are intended to supplement the primary powers of the administrative authority. The section is generally applied for preliminary activities, including visits and tours, publication of notifications, consultations and the like. Auxiliary powers are subject to two qualifications. First, an auxiliary power cannot expand the range of powers and apply them to new areas. Second, the section provides that auxiliary powers are vested in an authority only so far 'as reasonably necessary' to enable the exercise of a primary power, i.e., they are subject to the test of reasonableness.

§7. Orders

150. The power to issue 'orders' enables administrative authorities to impose prohibitions and duties. Administrative orders may be divided into two main classes – general and personal.

A general order is, in effect, a regulation. The regulation is directed at the general public or at a non-specific part of it. Accordingly, this type of provision is also known as 'secondary legislation' or 'administrative legislation'. Orders are required because the primary legislature does not have either the time or expertise required to enact all the necessary legislation. The relevant statute empowers the minister in charge to promulgate regulations in order to carry out the law, and these regulations are intended to establish secondary provisions which will implement the legislative guidelines. The legislative authority grants the administrative authorities a further power, to promulgate regulations which 'contravene the law', such as emergency regulations.[112] The power to promulgate regulations is the most important power of the public administration. From the point of view of its legal status in the hierarchy,

111. In HCJ 2918/93 *Municipality of Kiryat Gat v. State of Israel*, 47(5) PD 832, 844. Justice Goldberg held that 'as there is a law which establishes an arrangement, the power of the government retreats and it cannot establish an alternative arrangement'.
112. This issue will be further elaborated upon in Part V, Ch. 3 on Emergency Law.

it is located between a statute and a personal order. Nonetheless, the power to promulgate regulations is essentially an administrative power. Accordingly, it is subject to all the principles applicable to this area. *Inter alia*, the regulating authority is under a duty to exercise its powers on the basis of relevant considerations only, and like every administrative authority, the promulgating authority is subject to judicial review.

151. A personal order is issued by an administrative authority in every area and at every level. Occasionally it is issued directly by virtue of statute or by virtue of regulations, and occasionally it is issued by virtue of a personal order which derives its force from a statute or regulation. A personal order may progress in the hierarchy from order to order, such as a personal order issued by the chief inspector of police, which may roll over and eventually reach the police officer who implements it; a hospitalization order which is issued by the District psychiatrist; a restraining order against building which is issued by the city engineer; or an order to disclose documents which is issued by a committee of inquiry. There are personal orders which the law requires to be issued in writing,[113] although, in general, the power to issue a personal order is not dependent on any formalities.[114] Statutes customarily vest the power to issue personal orders in broad language, i.e., they allow broad discretion regarding whether and how to exercise the power.

113. For example, an order of arrest under the Emergency Powers (Arrest) Law, 1979.
114. For example, s. 28 of the Traffic Ordinance [New Version] provides that a police officer is entitled, in certain circumstances, to arrest a driver without an arrest warrant.

Chapter 7. Codification, Interpretation and Publication

§1. The Interpretation of the Law

152. Interpretation is one of three types of 'judicial legislation' alongside filling lacunae and the development of the law. The significance of interpretation – writes the President of the Supreme Court Aharon Barak[115] – is that it is an intellectual activity which gives meaning to a legal text. When engaging in interpretation, the judge considers a text and his function is to determine its meaning. The text which is the subject of the interpretation may be general (such as a constitution, statute, precedent or custom) or individual (such as a contract or will). The interpretation is a process by means of which the legal significance of the text is 'extracted' from its linguistic significance. When the judge encounters vague or ambivalent language, which raises a number of possible linguistic meanings, the judge must decide – using his judgment – which linguistic meaning may be reconciled with the purpose which the language of the law seeks to achieve.

153. The purpose of the text is a normative concept, and is not part of the text itself. By the process of interpretation, the judge decides the meaning of the text. The interpreter formulates the purpose according to the will of the creator of the text – the subjective purpose, and according to the principles of the legal system – the objective purpose. Purposive interpretation is based on the presumption that every legal norm has more than one purpose, where the function of the interpreter is to identify these purposes, analyse them and draw a balance between goals and aspirations. Often all the purposes may be reconciled with each other. On occasion, the purposes contradict each other and the interpreter is required to reconcile the contradictions and seek synthesis and unity between the various purposes. Judicial creativity is also expressed, as noted, in the judge's development of the law. This involves the reconciling of contradictions between legal norms, and the correction of mistakes in existing norms. The judge creates a new legal norm, which is required by the necessities of life, without in fact interpreting the existing normative text, or creates a new normative text in order to fill a lacuna in an existing normative text. In Israel, considerable portions of administrative law, the laws of remedies and laws of evidence are the product of judicial activity in developing the law.

154. The power of a judge to engage in interpretive activities is no longer a matter of doubt. All modern legal systems recognize this power, even when the interpretation is creative. The function of the judge in a democratic society is to protect the democratic regime and create a bridge between the law and the necessities of life. For this purpose, he must give expression to both the supremacy of legislation and the supremacy of principles protected by the constitution. He must give the law a meaning which will provide a solution to the inevitable gap between the legal norm and social reality.

115. Professor Barak wrote a monumental series of five books on 'interpretation in law'.

§2. Codification

155. Professor Aharon Barak has set out five signs by which a 'codex' may be recognized, when analysing Israeli law.[116] (a) Wholeness: the codex is designed to provide a whole regulation, with the aim of providing a solution for questions relating to a particular issue. (b) Methodic: the codex is due to provide an organized, reasonable and scientific order in the system. (c) Simplicity: a codex should establish general principles which provide a key to the resolution of concrete problems by way of deriving the particular from the general. (d) Scope of application: a codex should embrace a broad area of law. (e) Novelty: the codex is intended to replace old law.

156. In Israel, apart from the 'constitutional revolution' (expressed in the formulation of a material constitution based on the basic laws), a second revolution took place in the area of private law. Whereas in the area of public law, statutory activities were fairly limited, in the area of private law considerable legislative work took place repealing the majority of remaining Ottoman laws, and replacing them with a modern legal system embracing the principal institutions of civil law. Currently, a new and whole private law codex is about to be submitted as a draft law in the Knesset, after years of preparation.

157. It would seem that in accordance with these criteria, the new civil legislation indeed reflects – from an objective point of view – the principal characteristics of codification. As noted, these concepts do not apply to constitutional law. So far, no real attempt has been made to formulate all the basic laws needed for the constitution of the State, as decided by the Harari Decision of 1950. Numerous questions dealing with the status of the basic laws remain unanswered. The Knesset has sought to formulate a draft constitution for the State of Israel which will be tabled for a first reading and the approval of the Knesset; however, this effort is still at its earliest stages. Consequently, at this stage of its development, the State of Israel does not maintain a codified regime of constitutional law.

§3. Publication

158. In Israel, the State is under an obligation to publish statutes, regulations and orders. The principle of the duty to publish is particularly important in the field of criminal law, which is based on the concept that 'no person is punished unless he has first been warned'. In one of the first judgments dealing with the duty to publish, HCJ 220/51 *Aslan v. Military Governor of the Galilee*, Nazareth,[117] Justice Sharshevsky held:

> There is no law unless it has been brought to the knowledge of the public in a way which the law itself has determined, since otherwise a state of chaos will

116. A. Barak, *Towards the Codification of Civil Law*, C Y'une'I Mishpat (1973) (In Hebrew) 5.
117. HCJ 220/51 *Aslan v. Military Governor of the Galilee, Nazareth*, 5(2) PD 1480 at 1486–1487.

arise and no man will know what is permissible and what forbidden, and accordingly it will not be possible to demand of him that he abide by the law and refrain from performing unlawful acts.

159. Publication is an expression of publicity. Administrative publicity is a basic principle of a democratic regime. It enables the public not only to plan its actions but also to develop a dialogue with the administration, as well as to review the latter's acts. In the words of Justice Heshin:

> The principle draws its strength from the nature and values of the proper social order: publicity of government and its appropriate procedures – in the light and not in concealment. A proper government operates in the light of the sun, in the open, and thus exposes itself to continuous review as well as to the rectification of flawed modes of action.[118]

160. Both the duty to publish and its scope are determined in the law itself and there many ways to publish. The official form of publication adopted by the State of Israel is publication in Reshumot. Documents published in Reshumot include legislation, regulations, treaties and other official papers. On occasion, publication is not carried out through Reshumot but through notice boards, newspapers and other such means. The duty to publish primary legislation is set out in two principal pieces of legislation, section 10 of the Law and Administration Ordinance, 1948,[119] and section 13 of the Transition Law, 1949.

161. There is also a duty to publish regulations. Section 17 of the Interpretation Ordinance [New Version], states that regulations having legislative effect shall come into effect on the date of publication, unless otherwise provided. This duty to publish applies to regulations 'having legislative effect'. The case law has held that such a regulation is characterized by being issued by virtue of law, by being normative and by its general application.

162. As to the duty to publish general guidelines, administrative guidelines embrace all the internal rules and directives which an authority sets for itself as a policy tool and as criteria for the purpose of exercising its powers. These guidelines

---

118. Cr. Req. A. 1127/93 *State of Israel v. Klein*, 48(3) PD 485. *See also* I. Zamir, *Administrative Power* (In Hebrew, 1996, Vol. 2) at 924.

119. Section 10 of the Law and Administration Ordinance, 1948, provides:

> (a) Every Ordinance shall come into force on the date of its publication in the Official Gazette, unless it has been provided therein that it shall come into force on an earlier or a later date than the date of publication.
> (b) The publication of an Ordinance in the Official Gazette shall be evidence that such Ordinance has been duly enacted and signed.
> (c) The provisions of this section shall also apply to regulations within the meaning of Section 8 and emergency regulations within the meaning of Section 9.

Section 13 of the Transition Law, 1949 provides that 'Everything required by law to be published in *Iton Rishmi* shall henceforward be published in *Reshumot*; every reference in the law to *Iton Rishmi* shall henceforward be deemed to be a reference to *Reshumot*.'

are not regulations having legislative effect for two primary reasons. First, they are not issued by virtue of law – as the law does not mandate their being issued. Second, a guideline is not defined as a legal norm. It is an informal norm possessing legal consequences.[120]

163. Until the beginning of the 1990s, the prevailing rule was that administrative guidelines were not subject to the duty of publication, whether in Reshumot or otherwise. The Court indeed pointed out that it was desirable for the authority to publish guidelines generally but that this was not a mandatory rule.[121] In recent years, the trend of the Supreme Court has been to require the publication of general guidelines. Thus, for example, Justice Zamir held that administrative guidelines, which case law requires to be published, should be brought to the knowledge of those concerned:

> When the case law requires the publication of guidelines, it does not require their publication in Reshumot. The duty is to give reasonable publicity to guidelines in a way which will cause them to reach the knowledge of those interested ... Such publicity may be achieved through a notice in a daily newspaper, or a notice on a notice board, or publication in professional literature, and the like.[122]

164. Notwithstanding the existence of a duty to publish administrative guidelines, Justice Zamir refrained from establishing a definitive rule. In his view, the administrative guideline under discussion must be examined as there are many significant differences between different types of guidelines, and these differences must also have consequences as to the duty to publish the guidelines.

165. In 1998, the Freedom of Information Law was enacted in Israel. This law adopted the position of the case law regarding the duty to publish administrative guidelines and auxiliary regulations, and provided in section 6(a) that: 'A public authority shall provide for public perusal the written administrative guidelines under which it operates, and which affect, or are of importance to, the public.'

---

120. HCJ 80/54 *Nochimovsky v. Minister of Justice*, 8(2) PD 1491, 1496.
121. HCJ 80/54 *Nochimovsky v. Minister of Justice*, 8(2) PD 1491, 1496. Justice Berenzon held: 'We *see* no obstacle to a public body, which by virtue of law performs judicial functions which involve discretion, setting its own policy and providing its own standards and considerations when performing these functions. Likewise, we wish to praise the committee, which did not make its policy a secret but thought it right to publish it widely for the benefit of those needing it. And we would add: if only other public bodies followed this example.'
122. HCJ 3081/95 *Romeo v. Scientific Council of the Medical Federation in Israel*, 50(2) PD 177 at 194–195.

Part II. Form of Government

Chapter 1. General

§1. Introduction

166. Israel is a parliamentary system in which the people elect the parliament. Following the elections and after consulting with the heads of the political parties, the President imposes the task of forming the government upon the most suitable candidate. This is generally the leader of the party with the greatest representation in the Knesset.

167. The adoption of a parliamentary system whereby government depends on the confidence of parliament, with a 'figurehead President', was the natural outcome of the influence of the British regime on the emerging state; particularly in view of the great admiration felt by David Ben-Gurion for the British system of government.[123] Yet a number of important distinctions exist between the Israeli and British parliaments. First, whereas two parties (Labour and Conservative) dominate the British parliament, the Israeli parliament is composed of multiple factions. Second, England is divided into constituencies, each of which elects a representative to parliament, in a personal system. Israel operates an electoral system known as 'nationwide proportional representation'; in other words, the elected lists are represented in the Knesset, which is the house of representatives of the State, in accordance with the percentage of ballots cast for each list. In contrast to most Western parliamentary democracies, Israel adheres to this system in an extreme manner, the only limitation being the threshold percentage of votes cast, which currently stands at 3.25%.

168. The number of seats each list obtains in the Knesset (there are 120 seats in total) is proportionate to the number of ballots cast. Under this system, the electorate votes for a list and not for a particular individual on that list. In some parties, preliminary elections ('primaries') are held, in which candidates are elected to the Knesset by members of the party in a direct process. Elections to the Knesset are conducted once every four years; however, the Knesset or the Prime Minister may call for elections at an earlier time, and in special circumstances, the Knesset may function for more than four years. For the last two decades, governments have lasted

123. David Ben-Gurion, the first Prime Minister of Israel, declared the establishment of the State of Israel in 1948 and acted both as interim Prime Minister and as Minister of Defence.

less than four years, motivating new proposals to change the system of government in order to stabilize it.

169. It is noteworthy that between the years 1996 and 2001, Israel ceased to be a pure parliamentary democracy and switched to a Prime Ministerial system or 'presidential parliamentary system' in accordance with an amendment to Basic Law: The Government. Three elections were held under this system, in 1996, 1999 and the election in 2001 for the Prime Minister only. This was a revolution not only in relation to the system of government but also in relation to the system for forming political coalitions and conducting political bargaining.

I. The Changes in the System of Government: Background

170. Towards the end of the 1980s during the period of the national unity government,[124] there was an increasing sense of dissatisfaction among the Israeli public which ensued *inter alia* from the political stalemate and the inter-party and intra-party impasse, primarily in relation to issues of security and the future of the Arab-Israeli conflict. In March 1990, an amendment to the Basic Law: The government was initiated, with the aim of introducing direct elections for Prime Minister. The initiative was launched a few days after the national unity government was brought down in a vote of no confidence. The legislative process followed protests by large segments of the public who were frustrated with the party and parliamentary systems. The culmination of the process came in 1990, when MKs deserted their parties ('crossed the floor') in return for political gain. The government became dependent on a number of individual MKs, certain political deserters and small Orthodox parties which obtained power disproportionate to their size. The grave political crisis was a trigger for a change in the governmental and electoral systems. Yet, notwithstanding the very real need for reform in the system of government, the two-year struggle resulted in only a limited proposal for modifying the electoral system by introducing the principle of direct elections for the Prime Minister. The amendment to Basic Law: The Government passed by a majority of 55 to 32.[125]

II. The 'Prime Minister of Israel' Regime

171. Basic Law: The Government, which was adopted by the Knesset in 1992, introduced direct elections for the Prime Minister, commencing with the elections to the 14th Knesset. This system first operated in May 1996. It involved a unique

124. During the period of the formation of the government for the 11th Knesset, following the 1984 elections, it became clear that in fact the two large political camps ('left' and 'right') were of equal strength even though the *Labour* Party led by Shimon Peres had won the most votes. The option whereby Shimon Peres and Itzhak Shamir, head of the *Likud* Party, would rotate as Prime Minister was preferred over new elections.

125. There was not even a majority of sixty-one Knesset members to approve the law, even though it could reasonably have been expected that broad consensus would be required for such a significant change to the system of government.

merger between the parliamentary system and a number of features of the presidential system. The Prime Minister was to be elected directly by the public; however, his relations with the legislative branch were to be characterized by a process of 'threat balancing'; that is, each of the branches would be able to disband the others. Formally, the executive branch of the State was still the government; however, the power would shift to the Prime Minister. He was to form the government and it is he who would be entitled to shorten its tenure. In special circumstances, he would also be entitled to terminate the period of office of the Knesset. The Prime Minister could resign from office, a step which would precipitate special elections for the office of Prime Minister only, an event that actually occurred in February 2001.[126] As in the previous parliamentary system, the decisions of the government would be made by majority vote and the Prime Minister could theoretically be in a minority within his own government.

172. The legislative process concerning this amendment to the Basic Law: the Government (usually called the 'Direct Elections Law') was accompanied by heavy political pressure which led to a law differing from the original bill. The primary purpose of the new system was to increase the stability of the government. However, it soon became clear that embedded within the law itself were mechanisms which would lead to instability and inefficiency.[127]

173. Even though the Prime Minister was directly elected, he remained dependent on the Knesset. One of the dangers posed by this situation was the potential for the country to be dragged into frequent elections. As the elections did not change the social distribution in the country, it was possible to fall into repeated rounds of non-determinative elections. The only sanction, which the Prime Minister was able to impose on the Knesset, was to dismiss the government and thereby cause the Knesset to dissolve, forcing new elections. In fact, these provisions weakened the independence of the Prime Minister so that if the purpose of the law was to strengthen the leadership of the Prime Minister this objective was not attained. An additional objective of the Direct Elections Law was to bring the electorate closer to its representatives. When debating the various proposals for reform of the election laws, one possibility considered was the integration of regional elections. However, the reform was confined to the executive branch, and the process of electing representatives to the Knesset was left unchanged. Another goal was to limit the power of smaller parties or individual Knesset members to make extortionate demands. In the period prior to the reform, small parties had a degree of influence

126. The 2001 elections: following the collapse of the Camp David talks, the continued uprising in the Territories – which had broken out at the end of September – and the creation of a majority in the Knesset to bring down the government, Prime Minister Ehud Barak announced his agreement to early elections and resigned from his office as Prime Minister in order to allow elections to this position alone.

127. Thus, for example, the law provided that the Knesset was obliged to pass the Budget Law within three months of the beginning of the fiscal year, in the absence of which the Knesset would be deemed to have resolved to dissolve and hold new elections for the Knesset and for the Prime Minister's office. This provision granted the party which lost the elections the power to bring about early new elections by frustrating the Budget Law.

which was disproportionate to their relative strength in the public. The Direct Elections Law did not resolve this problem and perhaps made it even more acute. The choice given to voters to use two voting slips – one for the Prime Minister and the second for a party – enabled greater fragmentation of the Knesset – a large quantity of small parties – a process which made it more difficult for the Prime Minister to form a coalition. Thus, for example, the 1996 elections created a divided multi-partied Knesset in which the two major parties were significantly weakened.

III. Repeal of Direct Elections and Return to the Parliamentary Model

174. Direct elections to the office of Prime Minister were intended to provide an answer to the increasing difficulty of governing encountered by the regime in Israel. In fact, the reform achieved the opposite result from that sought by its proponents. The reform contributed to the erosion of the electoral power of the two main parties – Labour and Likud – and increased divisions within the Knesset. History teaches us that it is not possible to modify a political culture within a short period of time by purely legislative processes. The lesson to be learned from the changes in the system of government in Israel is that it is best to avoid changes which have not been thoroughly studied and understood. The new system was applied without complementary modifications to other components of the system of government. The reform did not present a comprehensive and integrated concept of governance. Various issues were left unaddressed. As evidence of this, three elections were held over a period of five years illustrating the flaws in the system. The large parties became even more dependent on the smaller ones, which were then able to exercise political leverage in exchange for their coalition membership. At the same time, the Prime Minister did not have enough political power to make tough decisions and execute policies. After two election campaigns were held using this method, and having realized that the direct election reform had failed, the Knesset endorsed the new Basic Law: The Government in 2001, removing the direct election method. The era of direct elections will be remembered in Israel as the period in which the Prime Minister reigned supreme; candidates pursued personal ambition and parliamentary democracy continued to deteriorate.

175. Subsequently, the elections of 2003 marked the end of this unusual institutional concept. The parliamentary regime was restored, and the direct election method was abolished. Basic Law: The Government of 2001 re-established the principle that the government governs by virtue of retaining the confidence of the Knesset. At the same time, the legislature retained some of the arrangements that pertained to the relationship between the executive and the legislature, intending to bolster the standing of the Prime Minister and the government vis-à-vis the Knesset. For example, the constructive vote of no confidence was retained and further restrictions were imposed on moves to dissolve the Knesset, while the Prime Minister reserved his power to dissolve the Knesset by a Cabinet resolution. This idea of 'constructive non-confidence' has even been improved, making it much more difficult for the Knesset to bring down the government. From 2015, in order to revoke the government, the Knesset needs to pass a decision to form a new government, by a majority of sixty-one MKs. This means that not only must a member have a majority of sixty-one votes in order to become Prime Minister, but he/she also needs to present the Knesset with a full government, including all ministers and government guidelines. To conclude, debates regarding the appropriate regime for remain part of the Israeli political and public agenda.

IV. The Structure of Government Institutions

176. Israel is a parliamentary democracy in which three main branches operate:

- The legislative branch (the Knesset) consists of 120 Knesset members who are elected once every four years. The Knesset is mono-cameral. Its primary functions are the enactment of legislation and oversight of the government. The Knesset also has the power to pass laws possessing constitutional status.
- The executive branch, which includes the government. As is customary in parliamentary regimes, the government depends on the confidence of the Knesset.
- The judicial branch, which enjoys almost absolute independence and consequently is not dependent on any other governmental branch.

In addition to these classic branches of authority, Israel has a President, who is elected by the Knesset once every seven years. The presidency is primarily a ceremonial office with almost no legal powers.

§2. Political Parties, Lobbies and Interest Groups

I. Political Parties

177. In a democratic regime, a political party is a device for fulfilling the rights to freedom of association, to freedom of expression and the right to be elected to public office. The political party provides a framework for the political involvement of the wider public, and in this sense, it is a mediator between the citizen and parliament. In a representative democracy, the political party is today a necessary mediator and has an essential function in representing large groups of citizens.

178. In Israel, the political party is a constitutional unit and possesses constitutional status. The centrality of the party is reflected in the basic arrangement whereby only a party is entitled to submit a list of candidates for election to the Knesset. The central function of the party is also reflected on a practical, political level. The core of political power is found in the party and accordingly the parties largely determine the character of the regime, both on a personal and on an ideological level. The parties engage in political agreements which contain governance-related obligations, they form coalitions and chart the policy of the government.[128]

128. A. Rubinstein & B. Medina, *The Constitutional Law of the State of Israel* (6th ed. 2005, in Hebrew) at 777.

179. Israel decided to regulate the status and primary functions of its political parties by statute. The Parties Law, 1992 regulates various aspects of party organization, yet in practice, it accords political parties broad freedom of action in managing their internal affairs. Section 1 of the Parties Law provides that a 'party' is a group of persons who have associated in order to legally promote political or social goals and are represented in the Knesset by delegates. A party is founded by registering it in the party register (section 2), which is administered by the registrar of parties.

180. The law provides for restrictions concerning the founding and registration of a party. It is necessary for the association to be for the purpose of achieving political or social objectives by means of representation in the Knesset; the association must comprise at least 100 persons who are citizens and residents of the State; and the association must specify its purposes. The law also requires the party to submit its articles of association and set up the institutions listed in the law, such as a central institution, a body responsible for managing the affairs of the party and an auditing body. One of the main characteristics of the law is the absence of a demand for intra-party democratic structures. The law also establishes the institution of the 'registrar of parties'.

181. The registrar of parties is empowered to refuse the establishment of a party (by refusing to register it in the register of parties), and every adult citizen of Israel who is also a resident is entitled to oppose the registration of a party. Implementation of the power to refuse to register a party must be carried out with caution, after giving due weight to the members' freedom to associate as a party and to the fact that rejection of the application to register the party entails a denial of the right to be elected.

182. The most important section in the law is section 5, which provides that:

> a party shall not be registered if its purposes or acts, expressly or implicitly, contain one of the following: (1) negation of the State of Israel as a Jewish and democratic state; (2) incitement to racism; (2A) support for the armed struggle of a hostile state or a terrorist organization against the State of Israel; or (3) if there is 'reasonable ground to conclude that the party will provide a front for illegal activity'. The first three sections are identical to the provisions found in Section 7A of Basic Law: the Knesset, which prevents a list of candidates from standing for election to the Knesset.[129] This section also enables a party to be disqualified on the basis of the contents of its manifesto and clearly reflects the principles of a 'defensive democracy'.

183. A party is conducted in accordance with its articles of association. The Parties Law provides that 'the party shall establish regulations and it shall be managed in accordance with them'. The law also sets out provisions which must be incorporated in the regulations, including the conditions for admission of members to the

---

129. *See* in this Part, Ch. 3 on the disqualification of parties.

party, their suspension and expulsion; the rights and duties of members of the party; sections establishing the institutions of the party; and provisions for 'determining' the party's candidates for election to the Knesset. In essence, the regulations of the party form a contract between the party and its members.

184. The manner of conducting the internal affairs of the party is almost unrestricted, although the Supreme Court of Israel has indicated on occasion that the internal affairs of a party should be conducted in accordance with democratic principles. The Supreme Court has also held that 'considerable importance is to be attached to the existence of proper procedures and an orderly and fair system of decision-making in parties, which also maintains basic democratic principles within the party'.[130] At the same time, the Court has refrained from enforcing democratic rules in relation to a party, if such a democratic process is not required by the regulations of association. An attempt was made to introduce a provision into the Parties Law which would require the parties to follow democratic procedures internally; however, these attempts failed. This situation is unique, as in most countries in which a Parties Law operates, that law requires the internal structures to be democratic. In this context, it bears mention that religious and Orthodox parties operate in Israel. These parties consist of men only and candidates are selected by the religious spiritual authority. Likewise, the Party Law does not contain any provisions regarding the conditions for admitting, suspending or excluding members from a party, and these matters have been left for determination by the regulations. It would seem that a party is not limited in terms of the imposition of conditions for admission to its ranks.

II. Lobbies and Interest Groups

185. Lobbies in Israel, unlike in the United States, are not institutionalized, but they certainly exist, and they are active at the political level. NGOs and lobby activity are an integral part of the democratic political process, as they allow individuals or groups to express their opinions and to participate in policy-making. The activity of any particular lobby usually focuses around one specific issue rather than being concerned with a variety of topics. Some of the lobbies have close ties with political parties. The Histadrut, for example, is a vast, quasi-monopolist trade union, dominated by the Labour party.

186. In the Knesset, there are two types of lobbies:

(a) Lobbies of Interest Groups: These are lobbies consisting of public relations professionals who represent interest groups. The organization of their activity within the Knesset is anchored in the Knesset Plaza and Guard Law, 1968. The activists who enter the Knesset may do so only with the approval of the Knesset Speaker. A lobbyist is not allowed to coerce any MK to vote a certain way and is not allowed to mislead any MK regarding facts connected to any decisions or

130. CA 197/89 *Agudath Yisrael v. Shwartz*, 45(3) PD 320 at 326.

legislation. If any activist disregards these rules, the Knesset Speaker reserves the right to revoke their entrance permit. Today, approximately thirty lobbyists who work in advertising and public relations firms have fixed entrance permits into the Knesset. Currently, there is no periodic reporting or accounting of the activities of these lobbyists, and this issue has been turned over to the House Committee for processing and incorporation into the Knesset Rules of Procedure.

(b) *Knesset Members' Lobbies*
These lobbies consist of Knesset members who unite regarding a particular issue. The activities of these lobbies are anchored in the Knesset House Committee decision of 1 April 1997. That decision states that Knesset members are permitted to form lobbies without any explicit permission regarding issues that are currently being discussed in the Knesset committees.

187. Other NGOs are active in Israel, and have obtained remarkable success. One of them is the Israel Women's Network (IWN), Israel's foremost lobby group for women's rights. It is a non-partisan organization of women seeking to improve the status of women in Israel, and was established as a voluntary body in 1984 by a group of women professionals. IWN operates to provide free legal advice in relation to discrimination and sexual harassment in the workplace; and to run campaigns to raise public awareness about the fundamental need for equal rights for women. The lobby is very active in the Knesset, concerning laws affecting women, and provides legal representation in precedent-setting cases. Many cases concerning women's rights have been brought to Court by the IWN, for example, where the IWN represented Alice Miller in a landmark decision granting women the right to volunteer for pilot-training courses in the Israeli Air Force.[131] Some NGOs are particularly visible in their opposition to the government, such as the Association for Civil Rights in Israel (ACRI), B'tselem and Adalah. ACRI is Israel's oldest and largest human rights organization, and it mainly addresses human rights violations committed by Israeli authorities in Israel and the occupied territories. It has also been very successful in bringing landmark cases concerning areas such as freedom of expression, the right to privacy, freedom of and from religion, and lesbian, gay, bisexual, transgender and intersex (LGBTI) rights. Adalah concentrates on promoting and protecting the rights of Palestinians and Arab citizens of Israel as well as Palestinians living in the Occupied Territories. It frequently appeals to the HCJ and argues the cases of minorities whose human rights have allegedly been violated.

131. *See* Part IV, Ch. 2 on Fundamental rights and freedoms.

Chapter 2. Head of State: The President of the State

§1. The Organ of State

I. Historical Background

188. Upon the establishment of the State, the provisional council of State enacted the Law and Administration Ordinance which laid the foundations of government and its powers. The ordinance made no mention of the institution of the presidency. At the same time, at the first session of the provisional Council of State, its chairman, David Ben-Gurion, proposed the election of Dr Haim Weizman as President of that body. This proposal was accepted although it was clear to all that the position was essentially symbolic and did not carry any real legal powers.

189. The powers of the first President were undefined. The only reference to Presidential powers was that: 'The function of the President of the State will be the functions of a non-partisan head of State, who represents the whole State and people thereof abroad. All his official actions will be countersigned by the Prime Minister or a government minister empowered to act in that matter.'

190. The process of defining the functions of the President ended with the adoption of Basic Law: the President of the State in 1964. The very fact that the powers of the President are set out in a Basic Law shows that the position is 'constitutional'. Very few changes have been made to this basic law since it was adopted, and in practice, almost no changes have been made to the powers of the President of State. In the 1990s, following the change in the system of election to the office of Prime Minister (the Direct Elections Law), the President's function of choosing the person who would form the government was repealed, although after the redeployment of the old parliamentary system of election, this Presidential power was also returned.

191. This turn of events led to the establishment of the presidency as a representative or ceremonial institution, with very few powers. Apart from ceremonial functions, the President has three primary powers: granting pardons and reduction of sentences, appointing a member of the Knesset to form the next government, and consenting to the dissolution of the Knesset and early elections at the Prime Minister's request.

192. Israel has tried and imprisoned a former President. In July 2006, the attorney general ordered the police to commence a criminal investigation into President Moshe Katzav, who was suspected of committing sexual offences against and sexual harassment of several female employees of the Presidential residence and ministries where he had served before being appointed President. Upon conclusion of the investigation, it was decided to file charges of rape and other sexual offences against President Katzav, subject to the outcome of a pre-trial hearing. In May 2007, the attorney general conducted two pre-trial hearings before making a final decision on the indictment. These hearings produced a particularly lenient plea-bargain deal between the prosecution and the President. This deal omitted the rape charges and resulted in a guilty plea on the less serious offences. However, the President notified the Magistrate's Court of his decision to withdraw from the plea bargain and cancelled the deal.

Subsequently, the attorney general's office proceeded to re-examine the indictment and finally in March 2009, the attorney general notified the government of his decision to indict Katzav for rape and additional sexual offences relating to three different complainants. The trial was conducted *in camera* over the course of one year and, in December 2010, the judges of the Tel Aviv District Court unanimously found Katzav guilty as charged on all counts. The President was then handed a seven-year prison sentence and his subsequent appeal to the Supreme Court was dismissed.

For the State of Israel, the Katzav affair represented a momentous event. Clearly, the criminal conviction of an acting President is a source of great embarrassment, but at the same time, Israeli democracy demonstrated that equality before the law is not just a fundamental principle de jure, but that the state's legal system applies the same criteria and moral standards to the head of state as to its lowliest citizen.

II. The Election and Appointment of the President

193. In Israel, the President of the State is elected by the Knesset in a special secret ballot to hold office for a term of seven years. Every Israeli citizen is eligible to be a candidate for the office of President, and he may only hold office for one term. The President's term of office commences upon making a declaration of allegiance and upon the expiration of the tenure of the outgoing President.

§2. Legal Status

I. Presidential Immunity

194. As in most countries, in Israel the President enjoys substantive and procedural immunity. Members of Knesset also enjoy this dual immunity, as we shall *see below*. The substantive immunity prevents charges being brought against the President in respect of any matter connected to the fulfilment of his functions and the exercise of his powers. Procedural immunity prevents criminal charges from being brought against the President in respect of any offence committed while serving in office.

195. The President of the State has immunity against criminal charges during his period of office as President. Likewise, the basic law provides for immunity in relation to the performance of his functions, and this immunity continues to apply following the cessation of his term of office – 'The President of the State shall not be amenable to any Court or tribunal, and shall be immune from any legal act, in respect of anything connected with his functions or powers.'[132]

132. Section 13(a) of Basic Law: President of the State.

196. Within the framework of the discussion on the scope of this immunity, it is necessary to distinguish between two sets of issues. The first concerns personal immunity, i.e., immunity from 'any legal act' which applies to the President himself, and includes criminal indictments and civil suits. In this context, section 13(a) of the Basic Law confers the President with broad immunity which is similar in substance to that accorded to members of the Knesset. It would seem that the matters falling within the scope of this immunity, namely, 'anything connected with his functions or powers', will be broadly construed, in a manner similar to the broad construction commonly given to the substantive immunity accorded to MKs. This is because the purpose of the grant of personal immunity to the President and to Knesset members is essentially the same. Consequently, immunity will apply to those prohibited activities, which even though they are not part of the functions of the President, are closely connected to his functions and ensue from his special public position. The immunity provided by section 13(a) does not apply to prohibited actions which are unconnected to the functions of the President, such as the receipt of bribes. In such a case, only 'procedural' immunity will apply, as set out in section 14 of the Basic Law, and solely for the period that the President remains in office.[133]

197. Section 13 also accords the President immunity against judicial review of his decisions. This section precludes a judicial hearing on a petition directed at the President to revoke a decision. Consequently, a petition brought against the President himself, in which the Court is asked to examine the validity of his decision, will be struck out. At the same time, nothing prevents an examination of the validity of a Presidential decision on its merits; it is merely that such judicial review cannot take the form of a 'direct control' of the President or his actions but must be conducted as an 'indirect control' in relation to the act itself.[134] Put differently, the petition must be directed against the person intended to act on the basis of the presidential decision and not against the President personally. Thus, for example, a petition may be brought against the parole board with the aim of preventing the release of a prisoner, following a pardon by the President. Notwithstanding the above, the nature of the President's status leads to the scope of judicial review being very limited.

§3. Competence

198. Section 1 of Basic Law: President of the State provides that 'A President shall stand at the head of the State'. Notwithstanding this provision, it is clear from

133. Unlike the immunity of Knesset members, the procedural immunity of the President of the State cannot be removed. At the same time, nothing precludes inquiries from being conducted into allegations of improper behaviour on the part of the President – i.e., suspected offences and acts which are unconnected to his functions – and such inquiries may take place even against a serving President. In such a case, an indictment may be brought following the end of the President's tenure, as was the case with former President Moshe Katzav, convicted of sexual crimes and sentenced to seven years' imprisonment.
134. The types of judicial control will be further discussed in this Part, in Ch. 5 on judicial review.

the manner of formulation of the law that the President's functions are primarily ceremonial.

199. The functions of the President derive from the basic law and a number of other statutes, and principally entail granting formal validity to the governmental decisions of other bodies. Presidential functions include signing laws enacted by the Knesset, signing such conventions with foreign states as have been ratified by the Knesset and confirming the appointment of judges. These provisions are mandatory. In other words, the actions of the President in these cases are merely symbolic and it is likely that any refusal on his part to fulfil any of these functions would result in a judicial decision that the appointment or governmental acts were valid even without the signature of the President.[135]

200. Basic Law: The Government grants the President the power to appoint a member of the Knesset to form the government, receive the letter of resignation of the Prime Minister and accept the Prime Minister's decision to order the dissolution of the Knesset. The President is also empowered to receive from the government a report on its meetings. The President's powers of appointment are essentially symbolic. Decisions or recommendations are made elsewhere.[136] The President may also express his views on matters of public interest, even if the issues are controversial, and may act as an informal mediator between different societal groups.

I. Pardons

201. The President holds the important power to pardon by virtue of section 11(b) of Basic Law: President of the State. This section states that 'The President of the State shall have power to pardon offenders and to lighten penalties by the reduction or commutation thereof'. The power to pardon was initially established by section 16 of His Majesty's Order in Council, 1922, which empowered the high commissioner to pardon offenders, and later was transferred to the provisional government and subsequently to the President of the State. Accordingly, the government no longer possesses the power to pardon, and a governmental decision to release prisoners, within the framework of political agreements or in other circumstances, requires the consent of the President.

202. As noted, section 11(b) states that the President has the power 'to pardon offenders', in other words to grant a full pardon, which erases the punishment and the conviction. The power 'to pardon offenders' may be invoked by annulling the entire sentence, or by annulling the conviction by way of 'full pardon' before serving the sentence or during the course of the sentence imposed as punishment. The

135. A. Rubinstein & B. Medina, *The Constitutional Law of the State of Israel* (6th Ed. 2005, In Hebrew), at p. 1056.
136. Such as the President's power to appoint judges. The Committee for the Selection of Judges elects the judges. Following the election, the President of the State symbolically appoints them.

section does not provide any details regarding the power of pardon, a fact that provoked numerous legal questions over the years, for example, on what grounds it will be granted, the timing for the application of the Presidential power – e.g., only following conviction or also prior to trial, and whether judicial review may be exercised in relation to the power to pardon.

203. In Israel, it is generally accepted that the power to pardon is personal, and the President may set conditions for the grant of the pardon, or the lightening or commutation of a sentence. The pardon may be partial or full in terms of the punishment or it can take the form of rehabilitation of the offender by annulling the conviction as if it had never taken place.

204. The primary issue relating to pardons today is the scope of the discretion given to the President (and to the Minister of Justice who certifies the decision), and the scope of the judicial review which may be applied to the manner of executing that power. Initially, petitions for a pardon are considered by the Minister of Justice. If he recommends that a pardon be granted, the petition is placed before the President for his decision. Following a HCJ decision in 2010, the President has no exclusive power to grant a pardon, and he needs the approval of the Minster of Justice, who ratifies the President's decision. In a nine-panel ruling, the Court stated that although the Minister of Justice has no right to 'veto' on the president's pardon decisions, the purpose of the ratifying power of the Minister of Justice is to control and review pardon procedures and – in exceptional cases – even to prevent the granting of pardon.[137]

205. The case law has established a wide range of possibilities with respect to the grounds for granting a pardon, including absence of guilt, moral considerations, state reasons such as exchange of prisoners and, of course, considerations of justice.

206. A particularly interesting aspect of the President's power of pardon was considered in the well-known national security case of the 1980s termed the 'Bus 300 affair'.[138] This affair highlighted the legal question of whether the President was

137. HCJ (further hearing) 209/09 *Minister of Justice v. Nir Zohar (rendered on the 29th. Nov. 2010).*

138. In 1984, a bus (number 300) was hijacked by four terrorists who forced the driver to proceed towards the Gaza Strip. IDF forces halted the bus and rescued the passengers. During the course of the rescue, one passenger and two terrorists were killed. The following day it was published that all the terrorists had been killed during the assault. The inescapable conclusion was that two terrorists had remained alive following the action but were later killed by the security forces. This conclusion led to public outcry and the eventual formation of a committee of inquiry. The committee meetings revealed that members of the General Security Services (GSS) had been involved in the assault on the bus, and it was they who had intentionally beaten the two terrorists to death in accordance with instructions from the head of the GSS. On 15 Jul. 1986, about two years after this incident, and following the disclosure of all the details of the incident, the attorney general notified his decision to open a criminal investigation into those involved in the affair, including the head of the GSS, on suspicion that they had committed the offences of unlawfully killing the terrorists, perverting the course of justice and interfering with witnesses. In consequence of this decision by the attorney general, the President granted a pardon to all the GSS members in respect of 'all the

competent to grant a pardon to a person who had yet to be tried so as to prevent the actual criminal trial of that person. It should be recalled that the power to pardon is formulated as the power 'to pardon offenders'. The difficulty that ensued, therefore, was that a person who had not yet been tried and convicted could not fall within the definition of an 'offender'. The majority opinion in the *Barzilai* case[139] was that the President's power also applied to persons who had not been convicted. The majority judges explained their decision on the ground that it was necessary to assign a broad interpretation to a governmental power aimed at providing a benefit to an individual. Under this view, the term 'offender' could have one meaning in one circumstance, namely, under the penal law, where it refers to a person who has been convicted, and a different meaning in another circumstance, namely in relation to pardons, where it refers to a person who has not yet been convicted – depending on the purpose of the relevant legislation. Justice Barak, dissenting, held that the President had exceeded his powers and therefore the pardons were invalid.

207. Another question which has arisen in relation to the power to pardon – which was also considered in the Bus 300 affair – concerns the significance of a pardon. Does a pardon erase the criminal record of a person and turn him into a person eligible to assume any public position as if he had never been convicted? This question arose when one of the persons who received a pardon in the Bus 300 affair was appointed to the position of director general of a government ministry. The Supreme Court led by Justice Barak quashed the appointment and held that the Government – when appointing a director general – had to weigh the criminal record of the candidate. The result of this ruling is that a pardon does not erase a criminal past but leaves the record as a relevant circumstance when considering the appointment of the pardoned person to public office.[140] In the later *Yatom* case,[141] the Supreme Court again applied this principle and invalidated the appointment to public office of another senior participant in the Bus 300 affair. It follows from the case law that a Presidential pardon cannot erase the 'moral turpitude' attaching to a person who has committed a serious criminal offence.

208. The debate concerning the presidential power to pardon has also arisen in Israel in connection with Yigal Amir, who assassinated Prime Minister Yitzhak Rabin in November 1995. Amir was tried, convicted and sentenced to life imprisonment. Criminals convicted of murder in Israel are generally sentenced to a term of life imprisonment. Nonetheless, in Israel after a period of about seven years, it is customary for the President to 'fix' the sentence to a determinate number of years in accordance with the recommendation of the parole board. In December 2001, six years after the conviction of Yigal Amir, the Knesset amended the Parole Law as follows:

---

offences involved in the incident known as the Bus 300 affair following the events of the night between the 12th and 13th April 1984'.

139. HCJ 428/86 *Itzhak Barzilai v. Government of Israel and 52 others*, 40(3) PD 505, at 507–508.

140. HCJ 6163/92 *Yoel Eizenberg, et al. v. Minister of Construction and Housing*, 47(2) PD 229, at 269–270.

141. HCJ 4668/01 *MK Yossi Sarid, Chairman of the Opposition v. Prime Minister Ariel Sharon*, 56(2) PD265.

> Where a special parole board finds that a person imprisoned for life who was convicted of the murder of a Prime Minister acted for political or ideological motives, it will be deemed … that the board has recommended not to fix the sentence of the prisoner … and … that it has recommended not to exercise the power of the President in accordance with Section 11(b) of Basic Law: President of the State (Power to Pardon).

By enacting this amendment, the Knesset in effect prevented the parole board from recommending to the President that Yigal Amir's punishment be fixed at any time in the future. This is a personal law aimed at preventing Prime Minister Rabin's assassin from being released from prison. It does not directly infringe the President's power to grant pardons as the President may grant a pardon without a recommendation by the parole board, particularly since the amendment relates to an ordinary law which cannot affect the arrangements made in Basic Law: President of the State.

209. In summary, it is clear that notwithstanding that the President of the State of Israel is the Head of State, his functions are primarily ceremonial. The President symbolizes the State; he stands above the political parties and does not belong to any of the other governmental authorities of the State. He has few powers. His primary power, which entails a certain element of discretion, is the power to grant pardons. The functions and scope of the informal activities of the President depend largely on the personality of the office holder. Past Presidents of Israel were in the main elected following an eminent career in the public service and their selection reflected the confidence and respect in which they were held by the general public.

Chapter 3. The Legislature

§1. The Organ of State

210. The Knesset, both the Israeli legislative branch and the house of representatives, is mono-cameral. The Knesset is a unique body, holding not only legislative power but also constituent power so that it serves as a constituent assembly. According to Basic Law: The Knesset, the legislature comprises 120 members and is elected for a period of four years. In the absence of a full written constitution, there are prima facie no restrictions on the Knesset's legislative activities and powers, save for the entrenched sections found in the basic laws. Formally speaking, the lack of a constitution may mean that the legislative powers are unlimited. But the situation in Israel is much more complex.

I. Limited Power without a Written Constitution

211. Today there are two types of limitations on the power of the Knesset as the legislature. The first is embodied in the Supreme Court's recognition that the basic laws of 1992 possess supreme and constitutional normative status. In the *Mizrachi Bank* case, the Supreme Court held that the constituent authority may limit the legislature. This means that the legislative power of the Knesset is limited by the provisions of the basic laws on human rights. As in an ordinary constitutional state, a deviation by the legislature from a constitutional provision will result in judicial review of the statute.

212. The second limitation on the power of the Knesset as a legislative authority is, still, theoretical in nature. It concerns the possibility that the Israeli Supreme Court will repeal a statute which contravenes the fundamental principles of the legal system or even a basic law, within the theory of the 'unconstitutional constitutional amendment'. Israeli case law contains a long list of statements 'theoretically' recognizing the power to engage in judicial review of a law which seriously impairs a democratic value. This perception was acknowledged even before the constitutional revolution,[142] and further strengthened in the case of HC 4676/94 *Mitral v. Israel Knesset*,[143] where President Barak held:

142. EA 1/65 *Yardor v. Chairman of the Elections Committee*, 19(3) PD 385, principally in the opinion of Justice Sussman who speaks of the 'supreme' principle of a defensive democracy. *See also* HCJ 142/89 *'Laor' Movement v. Speaker of the Knesset*, 44(3) PD 529 at p. 554, where Justice Barak states: 'On a theoretical and fundamental level, it is possible that a court in a democratic society will declare the invalidity of a statute which contravenes fundamental principles of the system.' In CA 6821/93 *Mizrachi Bank v. Migdal Cooperative Farm*, 49(4) PD 221, Justice Heshin also thought – like Justice Barak in the *Laor Case* – that there are 'supreme' principles which limit the legislative power of the Knesset.

143. 50(5) PD 15 at p. 28.

> Even if we assume – without making any determination – that there are fundamental principles and purposes which a statute cannot violate, these are certainly fundamental principles and purposes upon which our entire constitutional structure, including the basic laws themselves, are based.

213. These are the 'framework rules' of the democratic system. To date, the Court has refrained from annulling a law which contravenes these rules, perhaps because of the lack of national consensus regarding the content of the fundamental principles underlying Israeli society. However, it is clear that the fundamental principles of the system provide a substantive limitation on the legislative power of the Knesset. Justice Heshin, for example, was ready to strike down a law because it violated the principle of equality, which in his view, is a basic principle of the State of Israel. In this case, the *Tal Law* case, petitioners argued that the law that exempts *yeshiva* students from military service violated the principle of equality. The HCJ determined that the right to dignity, as it appears in Basic Law: Human Dignity and Liberty, includes several aspects of the right to equality, and eventually decided to nullify the *Tal* Law because it disproportionately harmed the right to equality.[144] The fundamental assumption is that no representational democratic system is immune from exploitation, and the Court must have the ability to rectify 'flaws' in the governmental system, for example, when there is a danger of a dictatorship arising or serious violations of fundamental freedoms. Accordingly, over the years the Supreme Court has referred to this possibility in its case law, in the event that it ever becomes necessary to have resort to it. This 'non-conventional weapon' enabling the annulment of a law, and perhaps even a basic law, which seriously infringes democratic principles, is in the hands of the Supreme Court of Israel. In the *Bar-On* case of 2011,[145] the Supreme Court was asked to annul and judicially review a 'provisional' basic law that 'amends' Basic Law: The State's Economy, but does so only 'temporarily'. Each year, as in many other states, Israel regularly introduces an Annual State Budget Act, but in 2009, the Knesset decided to irregularly introduce a two-year budget, which it then decided to anchor in a provisional order of a basic law. A year after this provisional basic law was enacted, the government decided that the biennial budget was preferable and decided to extend the Act by another two years to cover 2011 and 2012. This amendment was unique because it was an extension of a provisional measure that was meant to be 'temporary' in nature.

Addressing a petition against this 'provisional constitutional amendment', the Supreme Court was faced with numerous constitutional issues. A seven-judge panel unanimously rejected a petition that challenged the constitutionality of amending a basic law. One of the arguments in this case refers to the boundaries of judicial review and the option of revoking a constitutional amendment. The petitioners argued that the amendment impairs a constitutional principle because, in Israel's parliamentary regime, the annual state budget is one of the tools that the Knesset uses to supervise government actions. In this respect, the Supreme Court addressed – for the first time in the history of Israel's constitutional adjudication – the unconstitutional constitutional amendment doctrine and its potential application to Israeli

144. HCJ 6298/07 *Ressler v. The Knesset* (published by Nevo on 21 Dec. 2012).

145. HCJ 4908/10 *Bar-On, MK v. The Knesset* (rendered on April 2011),

law. The Supreme Court established that the question of whether a basic law may be disqualified for conflicting with the fundamental principles of a regime is a rather complicated issue that addresses the very legitimacy of the constituent authority and the root of the Court's authority to judicially review laws. In this case, the judges held that the fact that the biennial state budget impaired the Knesset's ability to monitor government expenses was not so grave as to justify the annulment of a basic law.[146]

It seems that even though Israel's constitution is partial or 'invalid' in the words of the Supreme Court, the powers of the legislative authority no longer conform to the classic definition of the principle of parliamentary sovereignty.

214. Notwithstanding the existence of substantive limitations, in the absence of a constitution which provides for the manner of enacting or amending basic laws, the Knesset can currently enact or repeal basic laws by a simple majority, except in the case of three basic laws which require a majority of sixty-one Knesset members in order to amend or repeal them.[147]

II. The Electoral System

215. Undoubtedly, the most striking feature of the Israeli legislature is its electoral system, which is internationally unique. The general framework for the elections was laid down in section 4 of Basic Law: The Knesset, according to which the Knesset is to be elected in general, countrywide, direct, equal, secret and proportional elections. This section can only be amended by a vote of a majority of the Knesset members (sixty-one MKs). Israel is certainly not the only country practising the proportional system, but it is the only one not to have any constituencies. In other words, the entire country forms one single constituency, returning 120 representatives.[148]

A. *Principles of the Electoral System*

216. The principle of the generality of the elections ensures the active right of every Israeli citizen, who is at least 18 years old, to vote and the right of every Israeli citizen, who is at least 21 years old, to be elected. Even though Basic Law: The Knesset gives the legislature the power to deny the right to vote to anyone as it may see fit, the Knesset has never made use of this power. Those holding certain official positions, such as the President of the State, the State Comptroller, judges or

146. President Beinisch's opinion (*ibid.*, [34]) reads: 'Indeed, I too believe that there are fundamental principles supporting our existence as a state and society which, if harmed, might raise serious questions about authority, including doubts of whether we are looking at an amended constitution or the enactment of a new constitution. In such a case – which should never happen – the court will have to decide whether the Knesset violated its constituent authority and harmed the basic foundations of Israel as a Jewish and democratic state. This is not the case before us.'
147. Basic Law: Freedom of Occupation; Basic Law: The Government and Basic Law: Referendum.
148. The Dutch system is possibly the closest in terms of method to the Israeli electoral system.

dayanim (religious judges), career officers and senior civil servants, may not stand for election to the Knesset.

217. Israel is a single electoral district as far as the distribution of Knesset seats is concerned. Direct elections mean that the voter elects the Knesset directly. Equal elections mean equality of the votes cast and the Supreme Court has held that the principle of equality also relates to equality of opportunity for all the lists participating in the elections. The principle of secrecy ensures fairness in the elections and is meant to prevent the placing of effective pressure on voters, since no one has any way of knowing how they actually voted.

218. The principle of proportionality means that all the lists satisfying the qualification requirements are represented in the Knesset by a number of members that is proportional to their electoral strength. Israel has an electoral system based on nationwide proportional representation, and the number of seats that every list receives in the Knesset is proportional to the number of voters who cast ballots for it. Unlike most Western parliamentary democracies, the system in Israel is adhered to in a radical manner, and the only limitation imposed on a list which has participated in the elections is that it must pass the qualifying threshold, which is currently 3.25%. In other words, a party must receive at least 3.25% of the votes (nearly four seats in the Israeli Knesset) in order to be elected. The number of seats received by each list elected to the Knesset is determined on the basis of the number of valid votes that are received.

219. In the Israeli system, the voters cast ballots for a party list and not for a particular person on the list. Most parties select their candidates for the Knesset through internal proceedings and decisions, but one of the most striking features of this process, as mentioned earlier in the chapter dealing with the political parties, is that the internal proceedings for selecting the party candidates do not have to be democratic.

B. *Frequency of Elections*

220. Knesset elections are supposed to take place every four years but the Knesset can decide to hold early elections, and under certain circumstances can serve for more than four years. The Knesset can also decide, by a special majority, to prolong its term of office beyond four years. In one case – the elections of 1973 – the elections were postponed (through a special law) for three months; the elections were scheduled for October, the month in which the Yom Kippur War broke out, but they were finally held on 31 December 1973.

221. Israel's electoral system has experienced a certain degree of instability, and early elections are more and more frequent. Since 1990, the average term of every Knesset is 2.8 years. In the last eight Knessets, only one actually almost finished its four-year term.

222. Elections may also be held early by the enactment of a law for this purpose by the Knesset. Early elections also take place when the circumstances are such that 'the Knesset is deemed to have resolved to dissolve itself prior to the end of its tenure'. There are three sets of circumstances which meet this definition. First, circumstances where no Knesset member is able to form a Government which would obtain the confidence of the Knesset, following the election of a new Knesset or following a vote of no confidence in the government by the Knesset. A second set of circumstances arises where the budget law is not adopted within the first three months of the fiscal year. In such a case, the Knesset is regarded as having resolved to dissolve itself on the day following the end of the three-month period. Finally, early elections may be held by virtue of a decision by the Prime Minister, in accordance with the procedure set out in section 29 of Basic Law: The Government: 'Should the Prime Minister ascertain that a majority of the Knesset opposes the government, and that the effective functioning of the government is prevented as a result, he may, with the approval of the President of the State, dissolve the Knesset by way of an order to be published in Reshumot ... and the government will be deemed to have resigned on the day of the order's publication.' However, a majority of the Knesset members are entitled to prevent the dissolution of the Knesset and the holding of early elections by submitting a written request to the President of the State to charge one of its members who has so agreed in writing and who is not the Prime Minister, with the task of forming a government.

223. As for the actual method of voting, the casting ballot carries only the name of the party chosen by the voter. More specifically, the actual name of the party does not appear on the casting ballot; what does appear is a symbol, formed by a few letters, representing the specific party. In Israel, beyond the leaders of the different lists, the voter barely knows who the candidates are.

224. The seat is allocated in accordance with the following principles: Until 1988, the minimum threshold required to qualify for a Knesset seat was equivalent to 1% of all valid votes, after elimination of non-valid votes. Today, the threshold is fixed at 3.25%. The total votes in the lists that gained more than 3.25% are divided by 120; this electoral quotient then serves as the basis for the calculation of the seats to be allocated to the various lists. Lastly, an important technical issue, which arises in every proportional system, is the problem of non-allocated seats, since the votes gained by the various parties do not necessarily accord with the quotient or a multiple of the quotient. Of the two main methods used to resolve this problem – the 'largest remainder' rule and the 'highest average' rule or d'Hondt rule – Israel has in fact utilized both. In 1949, the d'Hondt rule was used, and from 1951 to 1973 the 'largest remainder' rule prevailed. In 1973, the d'Hondt rule was reintroduced. As is well known, the latter rule confers a certain advantage to the larger parties.

225. The Israeli electoral system does not require any form of by-election. Should a Knesset member resign, die or be expelled from the Knesset, the next non-elected candidate on the same list will replace him for that seat.

C. The Right to Vote

226. Section 5 of Basic Law: The Knesset provides that the right to vote is vested in 'every Israeli national of or over the age of eighteen' … 'unless a Court has deprived him of that right by virtue of any Law'. In practice, no statutory provisions have been enacted which deprive nationals of the right to vote. A national may only be deprived of the right to vote through the revocation of his Israeli nationality. The power to revoke Israeli nationality vests in the Minister of the Interior by virtue of section 11(b) of the Nationality Law, 1952, which allows him to do so where the national 'has committed an act of disloyalty towards the State of Israel'.

227. Apart from requirements of age and nationality, the Election Law sets forth additional preconditions for the implementation of the right to vote. Some of the preconditions derive from administrative requirements, for example, registration in the electoral register, registration in the population registry and use of an identity card to vote. Unlike other legal systems, the Election Law does not prescribe sanctions for persons failing to vote. Notwithstanding that the ballot of the individual voter is unlikely to have an impact on the overall result of the elections, the usual rate of voting for the Knesset is relatively high compared to other democracies and stands at about 70% of those eligible to vote.

228. In the Israeli system, the right to participate in elections does not include the right to abstain; in other words, the right to participate in the election, without expressing support for any particular list. Consequently, a blank voting slip will be disqualified.

D. Disqualification of Parties and Candidates

229. Israel, which is a relatively young democracy, did not restrict – upon its establishment – the participation in elections of citizens or lists.[149] Although the State was established in the aftermath of the Second World War, no statutory provision was enacted limiting the right of a person to present his candidacy, or limiting the right to be elected to the Knesset, and the right to be elected is granted to every Jew who has immigrated to Israel and has been registered as a new immigrant,[150] and Arabs who registered during the population census of 1948.[151]

149. It held, in its Declaration of Independence, that it would maintain the full equality of rights of all its citizens.
150. Today as well, the Law of Return, 1950 enables every Jew as of right to immigrate to Israel and receive Israeli nationality.
151. In practice, no independent Arab movement succeeded in sending representatives to the Knesset until the 1980s. Political associations in the Arab sector were established under the auspices of primarily 'Jewish' parties, such as the Israeli Communist Party. Parties of the Zionist Left admitted Arab citizens to their ranks and even enabled them to offer viable candidacies in elections.

230. It is possible to distinguish between three main periods in the Israeli law regarding the disqualification of parties. The first period ranged from the establishment of the State through to the 1980s, a period in which no legal arrangements existed for disqualifying a list or party by reason of its platform. The second period, 1985–1992, saw the first enactment in Israel of a law granting powers to disqualify a list by reason of the contents of its platform and its political views.[152] The third period began in 1992, with the enactment of the Parties Law, and saw the widening of the power of disqualification, a trend which reached its peak in 2002 with the enactment of amendments to the Election Law. The law now enables the disqualification of parties on new grounds including 'support or encouragement of terrorist activities or armed struggle against the State of Israel'.

231. The question whether it is possible to prevent a political party from participating in elections arose in 1965. The 'Socialist List' submitted its candidacy for the elections in 1965, to the Central Elections Committee (CEC). This list included a number of candidates who were members of the 'El Arad' movement, which was established in order to undermine the State of Israel.[153] The CEC, which conducts the elections, was at that time empowered to refuse the candidacy of a list of candidates only if it did not meet the formal requirements set out by the law.[154] The CEC refused to allow the list on the ground that the list of candidates was an unlawful association and its members denied the very existence and nature of the State of Israel.

232. The *El Arad (Yardor)* case clearly highlighted the problem known as the 'Weimar Syndrome'.[155] The CEC faced a serious legal problem, namely, the absence of power to disqualify a list on the ground of the contents of its platform or ideological motivation.[156] The law expressly stated that a list of candidates which was properly submitted '[would] be approved by the CEC'. As the CEC decided to disqualify the list, the candidate members of El Arad appealed to the Supreme Court. The Supreme Court approved by a majority the disqualification of the list and

---

152. Reference here is to Basic Law: The Knesset, s. 7A, which will be discussed below.
153. The '*El Arad*' movement was not allowed to operate as an association. On appeal against this decision to the High Court of Justice, the court dismissed the appeal and held that 'no free regime will allow and recognize a movement which seeks to undermine that very regime ... it is the elementary right of every State to safeguard its freedom and its existence against outside enemies and against other domestic foes'. HCJ 253/64 *G'eris v. Official in Charge of the Haifa District*, 18(4) PD 673, at pp. 679, 681. *See also* HCJ 241/60 *Kardush v. Registrar of Companies*, 15 PD 1511.
154. The Central Election Committee is a political body which is composed of representatives of the outgoing Knesset. Heading the Committee is a justice of the Supreme Court, who is supposed to explain the legal aspects of the elections; however, he only has one vote in the Committee. This procedure, which enables a political party to disqualify parties, is not free from criticism and raises difficult questions and problems, although it is possible to appeal its decisions to the Supreme Court. The final decision is ultimately made by a judicial body.
155. C. Klein, *The Defence of the State and the Democratic Regime in the Supreme Court*, 20 Israel Law Rev., 397 (1985).
156. The Knesset Election Law, 1959, which defines the powers of the Central Elections Committee, confines the disqualification power to technical grounds related to the manner of submission of the list, connected, *inter alia*, to the age of the candidates and their nationality and the number of signatures of supporters of the list.

dismissed the appeal. The decision of the Supreme Court in this case (known as the *Yardor* case)[157] is one of the most important in Israeli legal history. It is perceived to be an extraordinary decision and in many senses has become a 'symbol' of the notion of defensive democracy.

233. The issue of the disqualification of political lists arose again with the appearance of Rabbi Meir Kahane and the 'Kach' movement on the political scene in 1984. The CEC decided to disqualify the 'Kach' list led by Rabbi Kahane on the ground that its racial goals negated the fundamental principles of the democratic regime. At the same time, it disqualified the Progressive List for Peace (PRP) led by Mi'ari on the ground that central figures in the list identified in their activities with enemies of the State. The disqualification of the lists by the CEC took place this time, as in 1965, without any express statutory mandate, and in practice was *ultra vires*.

234. The Supreme Court in the *Neiman* case,[158] dealing with the appeals of the two lists, this time unanimously upheld the appeals, and contrary to the judgment in the *Yardor* case, allowed the participation of the two parties in the election. Most of the judges were of the opinion that the *Yardor* judgment in 1965, which disqualified the El Arad movement without any law actually allowing the disqualification, was correct in relation to its unusual circumstances, but that it could not be widened so as to disqualify parties which did not deny the existence of the State. The Supreme Court based its decision on the supremacy of the fundamental rights of the individual and in particular his political rights. Justice Barak actually proposed extending the principle laid out in *Yardor*. In his view, the CEC was entitled, even without express statutory mandate, to disqualify a list of candidates which rejected democratic principles, on condition that there was a 'reasonable possibility' that this list could execute its platform.[159]

235. In practice, the Court's decision forced the Knesset to deal with the issue of legislation regarding the disqualification of parties, particularly because the 'Kach' list, which had been approved to participate in the elections as a result of the judgment, formed part of the Knesset between the years 1984–1988. This period was particularly stormy in the Knesset, primarily because of MK Kahane's desire to realize his racist platform. MK Kahane attempted to table racist bills and spoke harshly against the Arabs in Israel. The Knesset took a number of steps in order to

---

157. EA 1/65 *Yardor v. Central Election Committee*, *ibid.*

158. EA 23/84 *Neiman et al. v. Central Election Committee*, 39(2) PD 225. For a detailed discussion of the judgment and the rationale of the judges, *see* Claude Klein, *The Defence of the State and the Democratic Regime in the Supreme Court*, 20 Israel Law Rev., 39 (1985).

159. The question that naturally arises is – if we have before us an anti-democratic list, at what stage can it be disqualified; that is, when is the test of 'reasonable possibility' met? If, for example, it has a reasonable chance of being elected or if it has a 'reasonable chance' of participating in Government. For further discussion of the problematic nature of the proposed test, *see* Claude Klein, *supra* note at p. 403. On the merits of the case, Justice Barak also concluded that the lists should not be disqualified, not because of a lack of statutory power – as was the view of his brethren – but because evidence had not been adduced to prove the existence of the element of probability required to disqualify the lists.

restrict Kahane's activities, and the latter was forced to petition the Supreme Court frequently against the decisions of the Knesset.

236. In 1985, a law was enacted for the first time in Israel enabling the disqualification of lists of candidates by reason of their objectives. This was not an easy decision for the Israeli legislature, and it should be viewed in the context of the *Neiman* case and the election of Meir Kahane to the Knesset.

Section 7A of Basic Law: The Knesset, as enacted in 1985,[160] states that:

> A list of candidates shall not participate in elections to the Knesset, if its acts or purposes, expressly or impliedly, contain one of the following:
> A. The negation of the State of Israel as the State of the Jewish people.
> B. The negation of the democratic nature of the State.
> C. Incitement to racism.[161]

237. The issue of the interpretation of section 7A arose in 1988, the first year in which elections to the Knesset were held following the section's enactment. Following the enactment of this law, the 'Kach' list was disqualified by the CEC and the matter again reached the Supreme Court. The Supreme Court unanimously dismissed MK Kahane's appeal and upheld his disqualification.[162] The Supreme Court was of the view that the interpretation of the provision should be strict, narrow and limited, and that in the light of this, the provisions of section 7A should only be applied in the most extreme circumstances. The Court held that this restrictive approach would be expressed in a list of 'conditions' or 'tests' which had to be met before the power to disqualify the list could be exercised. One of the conditions which had to be met was proof that the list indeed sought to carry out its purposes and that the improper acts and purposes of the list were vital to it and not marginal or unimportant. Another condition was the existence of clear, convincing and unequivocal evidence of the acts of the list prior to it being disqualified.

238. In 2002, section 7A of Basic Law: The Knesset was amended by the insertion of a new ground of disqualification and the introduction of the power to disqualify individual candidates. The possibility of disqualifying a candidate separately and independently of his list is an innovation in comparative law. A decision to disqualify a candidate requires the approval of the Supreme Court.

---

160. The section was amended in 2002 and 2008.
161. As noted, during that period Israel was not regarded as a constitutional state but rather as a state operating under the English principle of 'parliamentary sovereignty'. Notwithstanding the existence of many Basic Laws designed to form the framework for the future constitution, the Supreme Court refused to grant them constitutional status. Accordingly, it was possible to amend the Basic Laws relatively easily, with an ordinary majority of Members of Knesset. The amendment of the above section, enabling the disqualification of parties, passed with a special majority of more than half the members of the house.
162. EA 1/88 *Neiman v. Central Election Committee*, 42(4) PD 177. This was the first time that a list was disqualified in Israel by virtue of an express statutory power.

239. The new ground for disqualifying a list or candidate arises when their acts or purposes display support for armed struggle by a hostile state or a terrorist organization against the State of Israel. Concurrently with the amendment of the basic law, amendments were also made to the Parties Law, the Elections to Local Authorities Law (which prevents the candidacy of a party in local authority elections) and the Immunity of Knesset Members Law. The amendment was similar in each law and had a similar objective: to incorporate the ground for disqualification dealing with support for the armed struggle against the State of Israel, as a limitation on the freedom of speech in general and the right to vote and to be elected to the Knesset more specifically. It should also be recalled that these amendments were adopted at the end of the Knesset session and some months before the elections, which were held in January 2003. There were many who argued that these laws were *ad casum*, i.e., intended to deal with the problems of those Arab parties whose statements and support for terrorist activities against Israel – at least in the views of the initiators of the amendment – had attracted public outcry in Israel.

240. Before the elections to the Knesset in January 2003, the Central Election Committee (CEC) decided to disqualify the Arab party 'Balad' and the candidacy of MK Beshara, as well as the candidacy of MK Tibi, of the 'Ra'am' party. Concurrently, the CEC decided to authorize the candidacy of Marzel, one of the former leaders of 'Kach', who now sought to stand within the framework of another party and claimed that he had altered his views. The decisions of the CEC drew enormous public criticism, particularly because of their political character,[163] and the fact that some of the decisions were contrary to the position of the Chairman of the Committee who was not a politician but a justice of the Supreme Court. There were calls among the Israeli public, and in particular from the academic community, for the removal of the power to disqualify parties from the Knesset and for the transfer of this power directly to the Supreme Court.

241. The decisions reached the Supreme Court were deliberated upon by a bench of eleven justices. Ultimately, the Supreme Court upheld the appeal regarding the disqualification of MK Azmi Beshara and the 'Balad' party[164] by a majority of seven judges to four. Likewise, the final decision of the Supreme Court – to authorize the candidacy of Baruch Marzel, formerly a leader of 'Kach', within the framework of another party – was reached by a majority of seven judges.[165] In practice, the Supreme Court enabled all parties and all candidates to stand for elections.

242. The Supreme Court held in relation to the new ground of disqualification that the limitation on the right to be elected was justified in cases of persons supporting armed struggle against the State. Thus, for example, the Court referred to

163. The politicism was reflected in the disqualification of the Arab candidates and the approval of a right wing extremist candidate.
164. EA 11280/02 *Central Election Committee v. MK Tibi, MK Beshara and others* 57(4) PD 1.
165. Nonetheless, even though his candidacy was allowed, Baruch Marzel's party did not cross the electoral threshold.

the decision reached in December 1999 within the framework of the Venice Commission for Democracy through Law, one of the most important research bodies operating in the European Council, according to which:

> Prohibition or enforced dissolution of political parties may only be justified in the case of parties which advocate the use of violence or use violence as a political means to overthrow the democratic constitutional order, thereby undermining the rights and freedoms guaranteed by the constitution.

243. The Court held that section 7A was the 'peak' of defensive democracy. In this context, great importance was to be attached to the legitimate tools used by political parties. Support for armed struggle was not regarded as a legitimate measure. In the words of the Court: 'To aspire to change arrangements by means of support for armed struggle against the State … falls outside the democratic framework, and the democracy is entitled to defend itself against it.' The Court interpreted the law very narrowly by demanding that proof be given that the list of candidates had actually acted to implement its purposes and turn them from an idea into reality. According to the Court's ruling, a list could not be disqualified by virtue only of its objectives:

> A democracy does not take measures against a person who does not take action against it. This is the defensive democracy which does not prevent a list of candidates from participating in elections just because of the purposes of the list, but defends itself against acts directed against it.[166]

244. It would seem that the best evidence of the strict interpretation given by the Supreme Court actually lies in the outcome of the judgment. Notwithstanding that the law was enacted in order to sanction the exclusion of certain parties from the Knesset, the Supreme Court prevented this. Not one party was precluded from standing for elections to the Knesset. In practice, the right to participate in elections has been significantly strengthened. Since this last judgment, no party or single candidate have been disqualified. Although the CEC decided to ban an Arab MK (Hanin Zouhabi) in 2009, 2012 and 2015, the Supreme Court did not approve this ban.

The Israeli democracy is, indeed, a defensive democracy, but this concept is primarily true de jure rather than de facto.

§2. Legal Status

I. Representative Character of the Mandate

245. Basic Law: The Knesset lacks the principle commonly found in Western parliamentary constitutions whereby the mandate of the elected member is

166. *Ibid.*, in para. 6 of President Barak's judgment.

representative and free. Section 1 of the Parties Law provides for the principle of representation for parties. The purpose of uniting in a party is to allow its objectives or policies to be represented in the Knesset. According to the representative theory, the moment a party becomes a mediator between the public and the elected delegates, it in fact replaces the elected delegate and becomes the true 'representative' of the nation.

246. In my opinion, the case law in Israel expressly reflects the freedom of action accorded to parties. The case law dealing with parties' capacity to release themselves from political agreements teaches us – *a fortiori* – of their capacity to release themselves from their platforms, which are less binding and much less concrete documents. Thus, for example, it was held that a party platform does not create a contract between the party and the public. Further, in relation to political agreements, it was held that such an agreement is subject to judicial review, even though legally:

> A 'political agreement' is not a 'legal agreement' within the meaning of that term in civil law. It is not an agreement for the enforcement of which suit can be brought, or an agreement for breach of which an action can be brought for compensation.[167]

In the Israeli regime, the public grants the party a 'free mandate'. The party is not chained, legally, to its undertakings in its platform, *vis-à-vis* the public. It can 'release' itself and change its platform if the good of the State requires it do so.

247. With regard to the mandate received by a member of the Knesset, the question arises whether the MK receives a representative 'mandate' from the public, taking into account the fact that he is elected within the framework of a party, and that without his party he would not reach the Knesset at all. This question was considered by the Supreme Court of Israel in the *Velner* case. Justice Barak held that a Member of Knesset owes a duty of loyalty towards the public:

> A Member of the Knesset ... is not a 'representative' of the party. He is an organ of the State. He undertook to maintain allegiance to the State of Israel and to faithfully perform his duties in the Knesset (Section 14 of Basic Law: The Knesset). He does not undertake to maintain allegiance to his party and faithfully perform its duties in the Knesset. Every Member of the Knesset is a 'representative' of the entire nation.[168]

248. At the same time, interesting questions still arise regarding the relationship between the elected delegate and his party, and his subordination to party discipline. On this issue and this issue alone, controversy exists. Thus, for example, the question arises whether the approach accepted in other parliaments, whereby a

---

167. Justice Barak in HCJ 5364/94 *Velner v. Chairman of the Labour Party*, 49(1) PD 758.at 805. Justice Barak termed the political agreement an 'undertaking which is not an undertaking'.
168. *Ibid.*, at p. 807.

member of parliament is obliged to vote in accordance with his own conscience and not in accordance with instructions, even having consideration for the existence of party discipline, also applies in our system. This question has still not received an answer in Israeli law.

249. It is worth emphasizing in this context that in Israeli law, an MK may change his mind and even change his political party ('crossing the floor'), without any legal sanction being imposed on him. We can recall in this context the political crisis of 1990 when many MKs left their parties, many of them for private gain and without any ideological justification. The legislature found it necessary to restrict this 'migration' by statute (Amendment No. 12 to Basic Law: The Knesset). This amendment imposes restrictions on an MK who leaves his party and does not resign shortly after his departure.[169] It follows, therefore, that notwithstanding the absence of an express provision, the common view in Israel is that the mandate of the elected delegate is a free representative mandate.

II. Parliamentary Privileges and Immunities

250. The immunities enjoyed by Knesset members are relatively wide. Israeli Members of the Knesset enjoy a 'double immunity' as is the case in most European countries: immunity for acts performed within the scope of their functions (also known as 'inviolability'), and some procedural immunities, that may be lifted by the Knesset. Section 17 of Basic Law: The Knesset, determines that 'Knesset Members will have immunity: details will be stipulated in the Law'. These 'details' are laid down in the Immunity of Knesset Members, their Privileges and Obligations Law, 1951.

A. Inviolability for Acts Performed within the Scope of Their Functions

251. 'Professional immunity' or 'inviolability' refers to the protection accorded to a Knesset member for any vote, any written or spoken expression of a view, or any act performed within the framework of his function as a Knesset member. This immunity cannot be removed, and protects the Knesset member for life, even after his mandate ends and he is no longer in office.

169. Today s. 6(E) of Basic Law: The Government states that a 'Member of the Knesset who has left his party and has not resigned from office shortly after his departure, shall not become a minister during the tenure of the same Knesset; this provision shall not apply to the severance of a party on conditions set out by law'. In this regard, a person who has departed from his party is one who has voted against his party in a vote of confidence or no confidence in the government; however, a person who has not received any consideration whatsoever for such a vote shall not be regarded as one who has departed from his party. The law preserves the Knesset member's capacity to vote in accordance with his conscience; however, it prevents a vote for consideration, such as promises for the future, an appointment to a particular position or a promise for a place in the list of candidates.

252. Section 1 of the Immunity of Knesset Members Law states that:

1. A Knesset member will not be criminally or civilly liable, and will be immune from any legal action, by reason of voting, or by reason of an opinion expressed verbally or in writing, or by reason of an action which he performed – at the Knesset or elsewhere – if the voting, the opinion expressed or the act came within the framework of his function or for the fulfilment of his functions as a Knesset member.

(1A) For the avoidance of doubt, an act including an expression, which is not accidental, of a member of the Knesset which contains one of the following, will not be regarded, for the purpose of this section, as an expression or act performed in the framework of his function or fulfilment of his function as a member of the Knesset:
   1. Negating the democratic nature of the State;
   2. Incitement to racism;
   3. Support for the armed struggle of a hostile state or for acts of terrorism against the State of Israel or against Jews or Arabs by reason of their being Jews or Arabs, in Israel or abroad.[170]

253. Parliamentary immunity is not unique to Israeli law. It is recognized in every modern democratic state, and is highly controversial. No disagreement exists on the basic need for protection of a member of parliament in fulfilling his function. The issues which are controversial are the objects and aims of the immunity, the scope of the protection, the relationship between the immunity and other basic principles, such as the rule of law and the principle of equality and the limits appropriate for the parliamentary function of the Knesset member. In Israel, the activities included in the framework of immunity are threefold: voting, expressing an opinion and action.

254. In relation to expressions of opinion, the Israeli Immunity Law uses the terminology of some continental countries, giving protection not only to verbal expression but also to expressions of opinions through the submission of written questions and clarifications. The scope of the 'parliamentary expression' does not apply to some types of statements such as those negating the existence of the State, incitement to racism or support for armed struggle by a hostile state or a terrorist organization against the State of Israel.

---

170. This is an amendment to the law from 2002, and it was one of a list of amendments adopted by the Knesset during that period to laws regulating the right to vote and to be elected. The nature of the amendments was similar and their purpose identical: to include the disqualifying provision dealing with support for the armed struggle against the State of Israel, as a limitation on freedom of speech in general and the right to vote and to be elected to the Knesset more specifically. The amendment to the Immunity Law was born as an answer by the Knesset to a spate of controversial statements by Arab MKs, during a period of increasing terrorist attacks in Israel and when IDF forces were involved in numerous strikes in Judea and Samaria against suicide terrorists. These statements drew harsh responses from many MKs and brought about swift and comprehensive legislative measures designed to deal with this phenomenon.

255. The Supreme Court has considered the question of the appropriate interpretation of the words 'in the fulfilment of his function' in a number of recent cases. One of the first cases considered by the Supreme Court was the *Miari* case.[171] Miari's immunity was removed on the ground that he had participated in a terrorist's funeral and praised the deceased terrorist. Two judges dealt with the central question: whether Miari's action (i.e., support for a terrorist group) was protected by virtue of his professional immunity, or, put differently, whether Miari's action fell within the scope of his function as a member of the Knesset. The Court upheld the appeal by three judges to two. Justice Shamgar, one of the majority judges, viewed immunity in a broad way. He held that political speech outside the chamber walls of the Knesset came within the scope of the Knesset member's function, and therefore Miari's actions enjoyed immunity. Justice Shamgar proposed a standard to help determine whether an illegal action would attract immunity. He held that there was a direct connection between section 7A of Basic Law: The Knesset and section 1 of the Immunity Law, so that any written or spoken expression of a view, or performance of an act prohibited by section 7A would also not be protected by the professional immunity of a Knesset member.

256. In the *Pinhasi* affair,[172] the Supreme Court outlined different criteria for the interpretation of immunity. Justice Barak, for example, stated that a member of Knesset is obliged to act according to the law, but that sometimes the action 'glides' into the restricted area. Therefore, if the 'glide' falls within the range of 'natural risk' that a member of Knesset must accept in order to function in an effective matter, his action will be immune.

257. Some similarity exists between the tests laid down in Israeli law and the tests applied in continental law and even in American law. The basic assumption is that the Knesset member's function must be legal. This premise means that in the interpretation of the Immunity Law, the principle of the rule of law has priority. The judicial tests of interpretation are based upon the creation of a 'circle of exceptional activity'. All judges assume that the immunity applies to an activity which can be considered close, reasonable or normal in relation to the function of the Knesset member. It should be emphasized that the idea of 'normal and reasonable activity' is also the leitmotif in foreign doctrines. Both in the continental system and the American system, the use of the test of reasonability is conspicuous, meaning that only the normal and reasonable activities of members of parliament will be protected.

B. Procedural Immunities

258. The Immunity Law also grants MKs a 'procedural' immunity. This immunity may protect the MK from criminal proceedings for actions that are not

171. HCJ 620/85 *Miari v. Speaker of the Knesset*, 41(4) PD 169.
172. HCJ 1843/93 *M.K. Refael Pinhasi v. The Israeli Knesset*, 49(1) PD 661 (hereinafter: *the Pinhasi Affair*).

protected by functional immunity, i.e., actions which do not come within the scope of his function. As its name indicates, this privilege is procedural in nature.

259. Until recently, in cases involving a member of Knesset who has committed a criminal offence unrelated to the fulfilment of his function, the attorney general would ask the Knesset to remove his procedural immunity. This request would be submitted to the House Committee (a committee which deals with issues of immunity), and the committee would deliberate and decide whether or not to remove the Knesset member's immunity. If the committee decided to withdraw his immunity, the final decision on the matter would be left to the Knesset plenum. Following a number of cases in which the House Committee decided not to withdraw the immunity of Knesset members suspected of criminal activity, the legal position was changed. Public criticism of the Knesset was high primarily because it seemed that the Knesset was refusing, for political reasons, to withdraw the immunity of its members. In 2005, the Knesset enacted an amendment to the Immunity Law which essentially abrogated the need for the attorney general to appear before the House Committee and ask for the removal of immunity. Following the amendment, the rule is now that a Knesset member against whom an indictment has been filed will not enjoy procedural immunity. If he requests, on special grounds, to enjoy procedural immunity, he must do so expressly, and only then will a special hearing be held on his request. The Knesset member may, for example, seek immunity if he believes that the activity in respect of which he has been charged falls within the scope of his substantive immunity, i.e., the activity is in fact connected with an act performed as part of his functions. The amendment in essence reverses the burden of proof. In the past, the attorney general would have to ask for the removal of immunity; today, it is the Knesset member who must ask for the immunity to apply, and he can only do so on special grounds. This shift entails a certain constriction of procedural immunity.

260. A member of the Knesset also enjoys other privileges, such as freedom from arrest (unless there is *flagrante delicto*), exemption, in principle, from compulsory military service, and complete freedom of movement beyond that enjoyed by ordinary citizens.

III. Parliamentary Indemnity and Benefits

261. The normative framework for the salaries of Knesset members may be found in Basic Law: The Knesset. Section 39 of this law states that 'a member of the Knesset shall receive a salary as provided by law'. Until 2003, and the beginning of the tenure of the 16th Knesset, the salary arrangements of members of the Knesset were established by the Salary of Members of Knesset Law of 1949. This law was repealed, and a new chapter of the Knesset Law, 1994 has now been enacted. The new arrangement was intended 'to establish a public committee and empower it to determine the salary and other payments to Knesset members only, taking into account the special characteristics of their functions'. In practice, the

House Committee has the power not to accept the recommendations of the external committee.[173]

262. The Israeli model adopted by the Knesset Law leaves the determination of the salary of Knesset members in the hands of an external committee, which is an arrangement which exists in various countries, and also grants the Knesset the power to refuse to accept the recommendations of the committee. The participation of an external body prima facie reduces the suspicion of a conflict of interest which would otherwise exist if they were to set their own salaries.

IV. Termination of Tenure

263. The tenure of a member of the Knesset terminates with the termination of the Knesset's term, i.e., upon the convening of the next Knesset. The possibility of removing a Knesset member from office against his will is very limited. Unlike the arrangement established for the Prime Minister, who can no longer fulfil his function and the arrangements accepted in England and the United States, the termination of the tenure of a Knesset member is only possible in cases where he has been convicted of an offence which is tainted by moral turpitude. Accordingly, even where he is unable to fulfil his functions, for example, by reason of illness, he continues to hold his seat, and so long as he does not resign, he cannot be removed from office.

264. Section 42A of Basic Law: the Knesset provides that:

> If a Knesset member has been convicted of a felony by a final verdict, and the Court by its own initiative or at the request of the attorney general has determined that the offence bears moral turpitude, his membership in the Knesset shall end on the day the Court issued its final verdict, no matter if the offence was committed when he was a member of that same Knesset, a member of a previous Knesset, or before he was a member of Knesset.

The termination of the Knesset member's membership in such circumstances is automatic.

265. In addition to the possibility of transferring an MK from office, the law also allows for the suspension of an MK who has been convicted in a criminal case, where the decision is not yet final (due to an appeal process). According to section 42B(a), an MK is suspended from office temporarily as long as the criminal decision is not final, that is to say, during the period in which an appeal is pending

173. If the House Committee decides not to accept the recommendations of the public committee, the recommendations are returned to the public committee for fresh deliberations. The public committee will make new recommendations, and if the House Committee again decides not to accept the recommendations, the matter will revert once more to the public committee, and so on.

against the conviction or sentence. The suspension is not a punishment, but is a temporary measure designed to prevent an MK from sitting in the Knesset during the interim period between his conviction and a final verdict.

§3. Competence

266. As in other countries possessing a parliamentary regime, the Knesset is vested with various tasks and functions. First, the Knesset exercises legislative power.[174] Within the framework of the Israeli democratic system, in which there is a separation of powers between the legislature, the executive branch and the judiciary, the Knesset forms the legislative branch, with the exclusive authority to enact laws. The Knesset may pass laws on any subject, as long as a proposed law does not contradict an existing basic law, and as long as the legislative process is carried out as required by the law.

267. Second, the Knesset is also defined as the 'house of representatives of the State' (section 1 of Basic Law: The Knesset). This representative function is extremely important, especially in the case of a system with absolute proportional representation. Almost every sector of public opinion is represented through the elections.

268. Third, the Knesset supervises the executive branch. Section 3 of Basic Law: The Government states that: 'The Government holds office by virtue of the confidence of the Knesset.' The government resigns upon either the election of a new Knesset or a vote of constructive no-confidence by the Knesset.

269. Perhaps among all the traditional functions of the Knesset, as a legislative body and as a body supervising the government, it would seem that, in Israel, the most unique and striking Knesset function is that of being a constituent body holding constituent power.

I. The Constituent Power of the Knesset

270. The view accepted today in Israel is that the Knesset has a dual function – as a legislative authority and as a constituent body. The norms established by the Knesset as a constituent body ('basic laws') possess 'constitutional' status, that is to say, they stand at the apex of the pyramid of norms; whereas the norms established by the Knesset as a legislative authority ('ordinary' laws) are subordinate to the norms established by it as a constituent body. In other words, the Knesset's power, as a legislative authority, is restricted by virtue of norms which it itself has created, as a constituent authority. True, this is not an unusual phenomenon in a world in

174. It is interesting to note that the legislative power of the Knesset does not appear in Basic Law: The Knesset. Instead, it derives from the legislative power previously vested in the Provisional Council of State which the Knesset inherited when it replaced the latter institution.

which legislatures also possess constituent power (at least insofar as concerns the power to amend the constitution). The unique feature is that no special procedure is applied in exercising the power, and even more unusual is that the very existence of this Knesset power is not self-evident but requires the confirmation and recognition of the judiciary – as was held in the *Mizrachi Bank* case.

271. In the first twenty years following the establishment of the State, the traditional view was that the Knesset was parallel to the British parliament. The traditional approach gradually changed and was finally overturned in the judgment in the *Mizrachi Bank* case. According to President Barak, who won the support of the majority of the judges, the constituent power had indeed 'passed' from the constituent assembly (the First Knesset) to the 'Knesset', as a permanent institution. Justice Heshin, dissenting in this matter, held that the First Knesset had no intention whatsoever of transferring the constituent power to subsequent Knessets, and in any event, it was not entitled to do so.

272. It would seem that the public consensus is that the Knesset is indeed competent to enact 'constitutional' provisions as well as to amend or change them (and the practice of the Knesset itself is good evidence of this), but that this power is not unlimited. The societal consensus is that the Knesset is the body competent to determine the method of election to the Knesset, the nature of the regime and the restrictions on the right to vote and the right to be elected. The majority in the Knesset is competent to determine the 'rules of the game', but the accepted idea is that the 'entrenching' power is applicable exclusively to arrangements expressing the fundamental values of society.[175]

II. Legislative Power

273. The primary role of the Knesset is legislative. The legislative process consists of three readings of bills and includes debates on these bills. The division of the process into a number of stages is designed to enable the Knesset members to reconsider their position on the issues a number of times, to bring the bills to the attention of the public, and thereby to allow the public to express its opinions, and to ensure sufficient time for an examination of the various aspects of the matters at hand. The Supreme Court does not generally exercise judicial review over legislative processes. However, the *Poultry Growers* case,[176] which dealt with the fast track legislative procedures of a special law that accompanies the Budget Law, established four basic principles for the legislative process, violation of which would comprise 'a fundamental defect in the process' leading to the annulment of the law. The four principles are:

175. A. Rubinstein & B. Medina, *The Constitutional Law of the State of Israel* (6th Ed. 2005 In Hebrew), at 85.
176. HCJ 4885/03 *Poultry Growers Association of Israel Ltd. v. Government of Israel* PD 59(2), 14 (2005), paras 18–24 of the judgment of Justice Beinish.

- The principle of majority decision, whereby a bill only becomes a law if it has gained majority support;
- The principle of formal equality, according to which each MK has one vote;
- The principle of publicity, according to which the legislative process must be public; and
- The principle of participation, according to which every MK has the right to participate in the legislative process.

274. A central objective of the legislative process relates to the aspiration of ensuring that the Knesset's decisions are based on proper factual groundwork. Consequently, the Knesset committees have been accorded broad powers to summon experts and interested parties to express their views regarding bills under discussion in the committees. The bills may be initiated by the government, the committees and/or Knesset members. The government presents its bill to the Speaker of the Knesset, for tabling in the Knesset, and the bills, accompanied by explanatory notes, are published in a compilation known as 'bills'.

275. An MK who is not a minister or deputy minister may initiate a bill, and in such a case, it will be called a private member's bill. In recent years, there has been a considerable increase in private member's bills and therefore an attempt has been made to constrict private legislation, which entails increasing public expenditure. Section 3C of Basic Law: The State Economy provides that in the event that the Government does not support the bill, the support of at least 50 MKs is required during the first, second and third readings of a private member's bill. Regulations prescribe additional limitations in this regard and empower the House Committee to set a quota of private members bills which every faction is entitled to table during a Knesset session.

276. Bills which are initiated by the Government or by a Knesset committee are published as bills and are presented for first reading in the plenum.

277. A private member's bill must pass two preliminary stages before it can become a bill. The first is confirmation by the Speaker of the Knesset and his deputies that the bill is capable of being tabled in the Knesset and the second is a vote in the plenum approving the submission of the bill to a committee for preparation for a first reading. These two stages provide an initial filtering mechanism for private bills, from which Government and committee bills are exempt.

278. The debate of a bill is carried out in three stages. The first stage of the debate is known as a 'first reading'. This is a general debate only. The bill is presented to the plenum by the relevant minister or deputy minister or the Knesset member who initiated the bill. The first reading may result in either the bill being transferred to the most suitable committee or the bill being rejected. If the bill has achieved a majority in the first reading, it is transferred to the appropriate committee.

279. A bill which has passed the first reading is debated in a Knesset committee. There, the bill is worked on and the opinions of experts heard. Rubinstein and Medina have pointed out that experience has shown that the committee work is efficient, particularly because of the substantive discussions and weakening of party politics obstacles. Many bills have been completely rewritten in committee after taking into account the opinions of interested parties and experts which were not initially reflected in the government position.[177] Following completion of the discussions, the bill is tabled for a second reading in the Knesset plenum.

280. Each clause of the bill is considered separately during the second reading in the Knesset plenum. Each reservation is debated as are the various formulations of the clauses. If reservations are accepted, the Speaker is entitled to refer the bill back to the committee for the purpose of making the provisions of the bill compatible with those reservations. The third reading usually takes place immediately after the vote on each clause of the bill in the second reading, without further debate, unless reservations have been accepted during the second reading or votes have taken place on different versions of a particular clause, in which case the vote is deferred for a week. The legislative process ends with the approval of the bill in the third reading. Two further stages are then required. In the first stage, the President of the State must sign the law, and in the second, the law must be published in Reshumot.

III. The Knesset as Supervisor of the Activities of the Government

281. In Israel's parliamentary system, the Knesset is not only a legislature but also the institution which supervises the executive authority – the Government. The government holds office by virtue of the confidence of the Knesset, and the government is collectively responsible to the Knesset. Basic Law: The Government (a new amendment that came into force after the elections of 2015) states that a vote of no confidence in the government must be adopted by the majority of MKs, i.e., at least sixty-one members; and only by naming another MK as Prime Minister of a full government including government guideless. Accordingly, this is a 'constructive' non-confidence vote, and sixty-one members must agree not only upon someone else who shall form a new government, but they must also agree upon a new government, including its ministers and guidelines, and therefore this is a vote of confidence for a completely new government.

282. On a practical level, the fact that the government holds office by virtue of the confidence of the Knesset does not provide sufficient room for the Knesset to oversee its activities, as upon the establishment of a coalition, the government gains almost automatic support for its activities from the majority in the Knesset.

283. One of the central ways in which the Knesset can supervise the activities of the government is of course through legislation. By virtue of the principle of the

177. *Ibid.*, at p. 744.

separation of powers, the Knesset is charged with the task of making the decisions regarding essential social issues, and it is the Knesset which is exclusively empowered to determine the content of the legislation. Here, too, the possibility of engaging in supervision of the government by way of legislation is very limited by reason of coalition discipline. It is relatively rare for bills tabled by the Government to be rejected or for 'private' bills to be adopted contrary to the position of the government, so that in practice it is the government which controls the legislative process in the Knesset.

284. Additional supervisory measures derive from the statutory provisions dealing with the sources for financing the State budget and the use of the budget.

285. In the area of secondary legislation, one may find more efficient methods of supervising the work of the government – principally because the task of supervision is placed in the hands of the Knesset committees. Legislation establishes a variety of arrangements designed to ensure Knesset supervision over the content of secondary legislation. Thus, section 21A(a) of Basic Law: The Knesset states that 'Regulations that are promulgated by a Minister and that determine criminal punishment if they are violated shall not take effect unless they are approved, before being issued, by the Knesset committee responsible for the subject matter … .' and section 1(b) of Basic Law: The State Economy provides that:

> Where the amounts of any taxes, compulsory loans or other compulsory payments, or fees, payable to the Treasury are not prescribed in the Law itself, the amounts prescribed therefore by regulations shall require approval … by a decision of the Knesset or of a committee of the Knesset empowered on its behalf.

286. The supervisory powers of the Knesset are accompanied by a power to demand and receive information from the government regarding its activities. This information is routinely provided during Knesset debates in response to motions in the agenda, in government notices and statements by ministers in committee sessions.

IV. State Comptroller

287. An important supervisory power exercised by the Knesset takes the form of processes initiated by the State Comptroller who acts on behalf of the Knesset.[178] The State Comptroller is an independent entity, empowered to oversee not only government offices, local authorities and State institutions, but also bodies which are supported by the State and even workers' unions, with certain qualifications.

178. *See* further discussion in Ch. 6.

§4. WORKING

288. The work procedures of the Knesset are determined, to some degree, by legislation and the regulations of the Knesset, but they are largely based on customs which have been formulated over the years.

289. Section 19 of Basic Law: The Knesset states that:

> The Knesset shall determine its procedures; in so far as such procedures have not been prescribed by law, the Knesset shall prescribe it by rules; so long as the procedure has not been prescribed as aforesaid, the Knesset shall follow its accepted custom and practice.

Underlying this concept is the aspiration to accord the Knesset freedom of action in determining its own procedures, while placing considerable reliance on the traditions already generated in the Knesset in order to prevent harm to minorities and to increase the efficiency of its work. The rules are adopted by the Knesset, i.e., by vote in the plenum. Proposals for amending the rules are submitted to the Knesset plenum by the House Committee, and the Knesset is entitled to amend the rules by an ordinary majority.

290. The Supreme Court has the power to review the contents of the rules. Nonetheless, exercise of this power is limited to very rare cases:

> only in extreme circumstances, when a substantive defect which affects the basic principles of our constitutional regime and our democratic concepts is discovered in a provision of the rules adopted by the Knesset plenum, will judicial review be exercised over a provision of the rules.[179]

291. The interpretation of these rules lies in the hands of the chairman of the session, insofar as it is required during the session, and in the hands of the Interpretation Committee, which is competent to hear appeals against interpretations given to a rule by the chairman of the session. The rules provide that 'the decision of the Interpretation Committee will be final', i.e., the decision of the Interpretation Committee is a binding precedent from the point of view of the Knesset. At the same time, this does not negate the power of the Court to exercise judicial review in relation to a decision reached by the Interpretation Committee. Thus, it was held that 'the interpretation given by the House Committee [in relation to the significance of the provisions of the Knesset rules] does not bind the Court'.[180]

179. HCJ 669/85 *Kahane v. Speaker of the Knesset*, 40(4) PD 393, 399.

180. HCJ 73/85 *'Kach' Faction v. Speaker of the Knesset*, 39(3) PD 141, 152: 'In a democratic regime based on the separation of powers, the power to interpret all legislation … is a power held by the court . . . every statutory provision, as a natural and obvious element, vests the power of interpretation in the court.'

I. The Knesset Plenum

292. The principal body through which the Knesset acts is the plenum, i.e., the gathering of the entire body of Knesset members. The Knesset is entitled to debate and decide issues with any number of Knesset members present. This means that no quorum is necessary for Knesset proceedings to take place or even for legislative processes.[181] The resolutions of the plenum are made by 'majority decision of those participating in the vote … unless otherwise provided by the law'. Voting in the Knesset is generally open. In the past voting was carried out by a show of hands; today it is generally conducted by electronic means, which allows accurate reporting of the voting of each Knesset member. The Knesset holds secret ballots only when the vote relates to the election of an official to a statutory office, for example, the election of the President of the State or the State Ombudsman. The plenum debates are public. The rationale is that 'openness is the breath of life of parliamentary activity, as the central and direct expression of democracy in action; and without openness this activity has no justification and no significance'.[182]

II. The Speaker of the Knesset and His Deputies

293. The Knesset is organized according to the classic model of parliament. It is chaired by the Speaker, who is elected by a secret ballot for the period of the legislature. Despite the efforts of some Speakers, the position has certainly not achieved the status of the British Speaker of the House of Commons.

294. The Speaker of the Knesset possesses broad powers to manage the affairs of the Knesset. The Speaker of the Knesset, and in his absence, one of his Deputies, conducts the plenary sessions of the Knesset. The powers of the chairman of the session are wide: he conducts the debates, determines the order of voting on the various motions and decides the results of the votes; it is he who is entitled to grant the right to speak to Knesset members, make comments to speakers and call the Knesset members to order, and even order their removal from the chamber.

295. The Speaker of the Knesset is in charge of managing the affairs of the Knesset including preparing the annual budget of the Knesset, and has been granted numerous powers by multiple statutes. For example, when the President of the State is abroad, he/she stands in for him.

III. The Knesset Committees

296. Most of the Knesset's work is conducted in committees. The most significant debates concern the formulation of bills. Most of the work of overseeing the activities of the government also takes place in the committees. The composition of

181. Apart from basic laws or specific statutes which require a majority of Knesset members.
182. HCJ 5771/93 *Zitrin v. Minister of Justice*, 48(1) PD 661, 674.

the committees is determined by the Knesset according to the principle of proportionality, i.e., factional representation. For this purpose, when the Knesset convenes, it establishes an 'organizing committee', in which all the factions are represented according to their size, and it is this committee which makes proposals to the Knesset regarding the composition of the standing committees.

297. The committees hold sessions irrespective of the number of members present. The chairman of the committee is empowered to deal with all matters connected to the conduct of his committee. It is he who summons the committee members to hearings, and his presence is the sole precondition for convening a committee hearing. The chairman of the committee sets the agenda of the sessions, and he is empowered to take various significant measures against committee members. Unlike the Knesset plenum – where all sessions are public – committee hearings are open to the public only if the committee so decides. In recent years, there has been a tendency to open committee hearings to the public including to media coverage.

298. The powers of the Knesset committees are numerous. Many statutes grant Knesset committees power to create general or individual legal norms. The committees are empowered to debate and initiate bills, as well as to consider secondary legislation which requires the approval of or consultation with the committee.

IV. Judicial Review of Internal Proceedings in the Knesset

299. One of the unique aspects of Israeli law is the Supreme Court's power to intervene in the internal procedures of the Knesset. As early as in the 1980s, the Court held that it had the power to scrutinize the affairs of the Knesset, including its internal procedures. The Court's intervention in the affairs of the Knesset is dependent, therefore, on its desire and willingness to intervene, and is subject to the discretion of the Court. In contrast to traditional doctrines in other countries, in which there is no judicial power to intervene in the internal affairs of the parliament – by reason of the principle of *interna corporis* – in Israel the Supreme Court has emphasized that it does have such power. In practice, intervention in the internal procedures of the Knesset has always been restrained and controlled, and has been reserved for extraordinary and extreme cases only.

300. The accepted test for judicial intervention requires proof that fundamental constitutional principles have been violated. If so, the impact of this violation on the proper operation of the parliament will be examined. The rule which was established in the *Sarid* case was that:

> when the alleged harm caused by the internal parliamentary arrangements is light, and has no impact on the fundamental aspects of our parliamentary

> system, then the independence of the Knesset overrides the rule of law, and there is justification for the judicial authority to withdraw from hearing the matter.[183]

In the *Sarid* case, the Court refused to intervene in a decision by the Speaker of the Knesset to adjourn a debate on a motion of no confidence from the morning hours to the afternoon hours, an adjournment which was intended to enable Knesset members supporting the government to return to Israel from abroad and participate in the vote: 'even if the Speaker of the Knesset deviated from the provisions of the rules ... this was a minor deviation, which had to be resolved by the internal parliamentary procedures themselves'.[184] A similar approach was also employed in relation to an allegation of deviation from the rules regarding the manner of determining the agenda of the Knesset.

301. The Court has also refrained from intervening in relation to the reasonableness of a decision to appoint a Knesset member to the position of chairman of a committee, in view of the criminal record of that Knesset member. Only in a few cases so far has the Court intervened in decisions concerning the internal procedures of the Knesset, on the basis of the determination that there was an 'acute violation' of parliamentary life. Thus, for example, in the *Kahane* case, it was held that even though the Knesset presidency was vested with discretion to decide whether or not to approve for debate a bill tabled by a Knesset member, it could not disqualify a member's bill by reason of its content. In that case, the presidency (the Speaker and his deputies) disqualified a racist bill tabled by MK Kahane. The Court held that so long as the rules were not changed, the Knesset presidency was required to table MK Kahane's bill. It held that the decision not to table the bill was an 'acute violation of parliamentary life' which justified judicial intervention. It should be emphasized that the Court's decision was intended to protect a minority Knesset member from possible intimidation by the majority. Later the rules were changed in order to expressly provide that the Knesset presidency has the power to disqualify racist bills.

§5. MISCELLANEOUS

I. Delegation of Legislative Power

302. Basically, the entire approach to the question of delegated legislation is based upon the classic distinction between primary and secondary legislation. It is assumed that the Knesset will adopt the primary measures, whereas the executive, when enforcing the laws, will be empowered to adopt (enact) secondary measures. However, this distinction is not always respected. There is no independent source in Israeli public law for delegated, subordinate legislative power. In other words, the

183. HCJ 652/81 *Sarid v. Speaker of the Knesset*, 36(2) PD 197 at 202.
184. *Ibid.*, at p. 205.

administration can act only and exclusively when expressly empowered to do so.[185] The enabling provisions are generally part of the law; the last section will typically empower a minister to issue a regulation for the application of the law. Such power can be sub-delegated (*see* the following chapter).

303. With regard to certain important matters, the Knesset will retain oversight powers over the subordinate legislation; the most extreme case being that of prior approval, which is given by one of the standing committees of the Knesset.[186]

304. The principle of the separation of powers requires that in the delegation of powers, the Knesset will not be satisfied merely with a general decision regarding the existence of a governmental power in a particular area. The Knesset must delineate the principal arrangements by which the power will be exercised (primary arrangements or legislative guidelines). A sweeping grant of powers to a particular entity, without legislative guidelines, is equivalent to the transfer of legislative powers vested in the Knesset to another body. The principle of the separation of powers means that the Knesset is not entitled to discard its legislative powers.

305. In recent years, there has been an increasing tendency to widen the application of the rule regarding legislative guidelines, in such a manner as to restrict the powers of the executive authority. The Court has applied an interpretive presumption whereby the legislature is deemed not to have intended to empower the executive authority to determine primary arrangements.

306. Prima facie, in a parliamentary regime, in which the government holds office by virtue of the confidence of the Knesset, no practical importance attaches to the rule regarding legislative guidelines, as in any event, the majority in the Knesset supports the government, and accordingly, the government has the power to enact any legislation which it desires. Nonetheless, in practice, the principle of legality has great importance. Enforcement is intended to increase Knesset oversight of the exercise of governmental powers and allow public debate regarding the appropriate arrangements.

II. Legislation Having Retroactive Effect

307. One of the principal requirements ensuing from the principle of the rule of law is the prohibition on the retroactive application of norms. The prohibition on retroactive legislation is a fundamental principle of many constitutions around the world. Section 10(a) of the Law and Administration Ordinance and section 17 of

185. *See* A. Barak, 'Subordinate Legislation', in *Scripta Hierosolymitana*, Vol. XVI, 1966, at 219.

186. A good example is furnished by s. 5 of the Law of Return of 1950, as amended in 1970: 'The Minister of the Interior is charged with the implementation of this Law and may make regulations as to any matter relating to such implementation, and also as to the granting of immigration visas and certificates to minors up to the age of 18 years; regulations for the purpose of Sections 4A and 4B require the approval of the Constitution, Legislation and Judicial Committee of the Knesset.'

the Interpretation Ordinance establish a presumption against the retroactive application of general norms.

308. In Israel, retroactive legislation has not been made the subject of a constitutional prohibition, and accordingly, any prohibition derives from an interpretive presumption established by the Supreme Court. In the absence of a prohibition established by a Basic Law, however, the sovereignty of the Knesset means that the Knesset can prima facie also enact retroactive legislation. This question arose in Israel in relation to the capacity of the Knesset to enact a law in consequence of a judgment delivered by the Supreme Court, in order to effectively change the outcome of that judgment. It should be emphasized that the Knesset is entitled to respond to the judgments of the Court by way of amending legislation. Thus, for example, the Knesset is entitled to respond to a lenient punitive policy of the Courts regarding certain offences, by way of determining minimum mandatory sentences by law. The Court has held that 'there is no injury to the judicial authority when the legislative authority amends the law after the Court has given judgment, and the legislature has been dissatisfied with its interpretation'.[187]

309. The Knesset's power to amend the law in consequence of a Court judgment is subject to limitations regarding the date of commencement of the amendment and the scope of its application. The accepted approach is that the Knesset is entitled to give retroactive effect to an amendment which is a response to a judicial determination, provided, however, that this is expressly stated in the amendment itself. At the same time, the Knesset is subject to two primary restrictions in this context. First, the Knesset is apparently not entitled to retroactively repeal a verdict in a judicial proceeding with regard to the litigants to that proceeding. As President Barak stated, such a step would be 'grave and intolerable (and today apparently also unconstitutional)'.[188] Second, fundamental principles of the system restrict the power of the Knesset to retroactively apply an amendment to a statute by virtue of which a criminal sanction is imposed.

310. The guiding rule in this context is stated in the *Zandberg* case, where the Court was required to interpret a new law (the Tashrir law) which was intended to change a judgment. The law provided that 'the charges for holding a radio or television set determined for the years 1985 to 1992 are valid in every respect from the date of that determination'.[189] The Broadcasting Authority wished to impose fines for non-payment of the charges during those years, even though the Tashrir law was only enacted in 1992. The Court held that 'Ordering a holder of a television set to pay a fine for non-payment of the charge … which preceded the enactment of the Tashrir law, is unreasonable … and leads to an unjust result', and added that:

187. A. Witkon, *Law and Adjudication* (1988, In Hebrew) 136.
188. HCJ 5364/94 *Velner v. Chairman of the Israeli Labour Party*, *ibid.*, at 785.
189. Section 1 of the Broadcasting Authority (Authorizing the Validity of Radio and Television Charges) Law, 1992.

> the conclusion whereby the Tashrir law gives effect to the imposition of a retroactive fine would have created serious doubts regarding the constitutionality of this aspect of the Tashrir law. It would have been arguable (without us deciding this issue) that according to this interpretation the law violates the property rights of the holder of the television set beyond what is necessary.[190]

Accordingly, the Court held that the law should be interpreted so as not to impose a retroactive fine, by virtue of the principle that 'between two possible interpretations, one must choose the interpretation which is consistent with the constitution'.

190. HCJ 4562/92 *Zandberg v. The Broadcasting Authority*, 50(2) PD 793 at 810.

Chapter 4. The Executive

311. In Israel, the executive branch holds the State's governmental powers, and is charged with the 'execution' of decisions actually adopted by the Knesset. It has broad discretionary powers in relation to policy formulation and to the determination of the manner in which governmental powers are exercised. The executive branch actually comprises the entire complex of state bodies vested with governmental powers, which do not belong to the legislative or the judicial branches. Section 1 of Basic Law: The Government provides that 'The Government is the executive authority of the State'.

312. Over the last few years, varying opinions have been voiced regarding the optimal form of government for the State of Israel. Since the establishment of the State, and in fact even under the Mandatory government, the State has operated as a parliamentary system. Over the course of time, however, governments have experienced increasing difficulty in governing, primarily due to the numerical equality between the two main political parties, a factor that severely hampered the formation of stable coalitions. This process culminated in the adoption of a reform in 1992, whereby Israel was to become a country operating as a 'quasi-Presidential' system. The relevant legislation was scheduled to take effect in the 1996 elections. This system too proved defective, however, and consequently, in 2001 a new Basic Law: The Government was enacted, to take effect in the 2003 Knesset elections for the 16th Knesset. This legislation restored the original arrangement, and hence the government now serves on the basis of the confidence of the Knesset, similar to its operational mode since the establishment of the State, and until 1996. Nonetheless, Basic Law: the Government, 2001 introduced a number of changes affecting the Knesset's ability to express its lack of confidence in the government, while leaving the Prime Minister's power to dissolve the Knesset intact.

§1. The Organ of State

I. Composition and Organization

313. Basic Law: The Government regulates the government's composition. Section 5 of the Law provides that 'the Government is composed of the Prime Minister and other ministers'. Under the basic law, the Prime Minister must be a Knesset member, but this does not apply to his ministers. As a rule, however, most of the ministers are also Knesset members. The law regulates the service of ministers without portfolios as well as providing for the appointment of a minister who is a Knesset member to the position of acting Prime Minister. In 2005, Basic Law: The Government was amended, and a minister may now also serve as deputy Prime Minister.

314. The Prime Minister is charged with the formation of a government, and presents it for the Knesset's approval. With the Prime Minister's consent and governmental approval, the Minister may appoint a deputy minister for the ministry in his charge. This appointment does not require Knesset approval, and the minister need only give notification of the appointment. Appointment to the position of deputy minister is, however, limited to serving Knesset members. The Prime Minister has broad discretion in determining the composition of the government, given that a ministerial appointment is essentially a political, and not a professional, appointment based on professional qualifications.

315. Section 6 of Basic Law: The Government enumerates a number of conditions for eligibility to serve as ministers. First, the minister must be a citizen and resident of Israel. Furthermore:

> where a person holds a citizenship other than Israeli, and if the law of the country of which he is a citizen allows him to be released from such citizenship, he shall be appointed minister only after he has taken all measures necessary to be released from such citizenship.

316. An MK, who has seceded from his faction and did not resign from his position prior to his secession, is not eligible to serve as a minister during the incumbency of that Knesset. This provision is not applicable to the permitted secession from a faction under statutorily prescribed conditions. The provision was introduced to prevent the phenomenon of 'crossing the floor' ('*kalanterism*' in Israeli parlance) during the Knesset's incumbency in return for political benefits and/or in return for the appointment of a 'deserter' to a ministerial position.

317. In terms of eligibility, a ministerial appointment is prohibited for a person serving in a statutorily prescribed position, including, *inter alia*, the President of the State, the Chief Rabbis, holders of judicial positions, the State Comptroller and others. In addition to these restrictions, all ministers – including those who are not MKs – are bound by the restrictions prescribed in the Knesset Members (Immunity) Law, including the prohibition on serving as head of a local authority, or chairman of a governmental authority or institution, and being chosen to serve in a public body.

318. The Supreme Court has laid down additional restrictions on the service of a minister, pertaining both to his appointments and to his continued service as minister. These restrictions are essentially 'judicial', relating to cases of criminal indictment and judicial conviction. Regarding a conviction, two provisions have been enacted, namely:

(a) Section 6(a) of the Basic Law provides: 'If a person was convicted of an offence and sentenced to prison and if seven years have not yet passed since the day on which he finished serving his period of punishment, or since the handing down of his sentence – whichever was later – he shall not be appointed to be a minister, unless the Chairman of the CEC states that the circumstances of the offence do not carry moral turpitude;' and
(b) Section 23(b) of the Basic Law terminates the tenure of a minister convicted of an offence characterized by 'moral turpitude'. The cessation of the minister's tenure is immediate, beginning from the day of the verdict.

319. These are all statutory or constitutional provisions; their normative implications, details and interpretations have been addressed at length by the Israeli Supreme Court. For example, the Supreme Court has adjudicated the question of whether the Prime Minister is obligated to remove a minister from his post in the event of his being indicted for grave offences, notwithstanding that the basic law does not prescribe such an obligation.

Under section 22 of the basic law, 'The Prime Minister may [...] remove a minister from his post'. Prima facie, this power is discretionary, that is, it may be exercised at the Prime Minister's discretion in circumstances he deems appropriate. The Supreme Court ruled, however, that in certain circumstances, the exercise of this discretion is mandatory. In *The Movement for the Quality of Government* case,[191] Prime Minister Rabin was required to remove a minister from his post following the filing of an indictment against him, accusing him of 'the commission of grave acts which by their nature, essence, and circumstances, carry moral turpitude'. The Court relied on the doctrine of the Government serving as a public trustee, with a capacity mandating the establishment of, and compliance with, appropriate governmental norms. This enabled the Court to create an operative duty for the Prime Minister to dismiss a minister indicted in relation to acts involving moral turpitude, even if he has not yet been tried in Court.

320. Notably, the Supreme Court intentionally gave its ruling a narrow construction. In relation to the normative implications of this duty, the Court was not prepared to order the removal of a minister merely suspected of criminal offences, or against whom a decision was made not to file an indictment. Nor did the Court order the removal of a minister who relied on his 'right to remain silent' in a police interrogation and failed to proffer his own version of events when suspected of offences committed in the performance of his role. Apparently, the dismissal of a minister is mandatory only when the suspicions crystallize into an indictment detailing the accusations (which must be sufficiently grave) against him. The mere conduct of a criminal investigation against a minister does not compel his removal from office.

321. For example, the Supreme Court refrained from ordering the Prime Minister to remove the Minister of Justice due to the latter's involvement in the events leading up to a highly irregular appointment of the attorney general in 1997. In that case, it was decided that although the minister's involvement in the case constituted 'a deviation from appropriate norms of conduct', his acts were not of sufficient severity to warrant the filing of an indictment against him'.[192] The Court refused to interfere, and rejected the petition demanding that the Minister of Justice be removed.

322. The norms of Israeli political culture have created a situation in which resort to judicial review is perhaps the only means of compelling the Prime Minister to remove a minister. Nonetheless, it is emphasized that implementation of the aforementioned duty is replete with difficulties, due to the range of open questions

191. HCJ 3094/93 *The Movement for the Quality of Government v. Government of Israel*, 47(5) PD 404.
192. HCJ 2534/97 *Yahav v. State Attorney*, 51 PD (3) 39.

yet to be judicially or legislatively addressed. Thus, for example, the HCJ ruled that the city council had a duty to dismiss a mayor who had been accused of criminal offences, after the indictment was filed and before he was tried, despite the fact that, according to the law, a mayor must step down from his position only after having been convicted with a crime that carries moral turpitude.

II. Formation of the Government

323. The fundamental principles governing the formation of the government are that the government holds office by virtue of the confidence of the Knesset, meaning that the Knesset's support is the condition for the formation and existence of the Government, and that the government is collectively responsible to the Knesset.

324. The government is formed by the particular Knesset member chosen for that purpose by the President of the State. The Knesset member requested to form a government is given twenty-eight days to complete this task, and the President may extend this period for an additional period which cannot exceed fourteen days. Should the selected Knesset member be unable to form a government, the President is entitled to assign the task to another Knesset member, who also receives twenty-eight days to form a government, but with no possibility of an extension. Conversely, the President is entitled to refrain from imposing the task on another Knesset member and instead, to notify the Knesset Speaker, within three days, that he sees no possibility of forming a government. According to section 9 of Basic Law: The Government, if the process for the formation of the government fails, the government is regarded as having adopted a decision to dissolve the Knesset, and new elections are held within ninety days.

325. If the Knesset member selected by the President succeeds in forming a coalition, he must notify both the President and the Speaker accordingly. Within seven days of being notified, the Knesset Speaker must convene the Knesset, and the government in waiting will inform the Knesset of 'the basic lines of its policy, its composition and the distribution of functions among the ministers'. The government begins to serve from the moment that the Knesset gives its vote of confidence.

326. There are other instances in which the President is obligated to initiate proceedings for the formation of a new government, for example where a new Knesset is elected, or upon the resignation of the incumbent government. The government is deemed to have resigned in any one of the following cases:

(1) Prime Minister's resignation;
(2) Prime Minister's death or inability to fulfil his duties for a period in excess of 100 consecutive days. In such cases, a minister who was already a Knesset member and a member of the Prime Minister's faction is appointed by the government to serve as acting Prime Minister until the formation of a new government.

(3) Discontinuation of the service of the Prime Minister due to a conviction for an offence involving moral turpitude. If the Prime Minister is convicted of an offence in a final judgment, and the Court rules that the offence carries moral turpitude, the service of the Prime Minister is terminated and the Government shall be deemed to have resigned on the day the verdict becomes final.

(4) In the event of the Prime Minister ceasing to be a Knesset member. However, the Knesset does not have the authority to terminate the Prime Minister's membership in the Knesset.

III. Constructive No-confidence

327. Since the government holds office by virtue of the confidence of the Knesset, in that capacity, the Knesset can express no-confidence in the government. In this context, the Basic Law establishes a mechanism structured to enhance political stability, and turns the expression of no-confidence in the government into a formidable task. First, a majority of sixty-one Knesset members must support the no-confidence motion. Second, similar to the arrangement accepted in Germany, there is a requirement of 'constructive no-confidence'. The Knesset can only adopt a no-confidence motion where the majority of Knesset members support the establishment of an alternative government. As from 2015, as above mentioned, the no-confidence motion is carried out by a 'decision adopted by the majority of the Knesset members to vote confidence in an alternative government that has announced its guidelines and distribution of portfolios between the ministers. The new government will begin serving with the vote of confidence and the ministers will then step into their offices.'

328. The Prime Minister is also empowered to dissolve the Knesset. Section 29(a) of the Basic Law provides that, should the Prime Minister 'ascertain that a majority of the Knesset opposes the government, and that the effective functioning of the government is prevented as a result, he may, with the approval of the President of the State, dissolve the Knesset'.

IV. Transitional Government

329. The aforementioned scenarios (the resignation of the government or its dissolution pursuant to the passage of a no-confidence motion) place the government in the position of being a 'transitional' or 'caretaker' government. This is also the outgoing government's position following the election of a new Knesset. In these contexts, the cardinal question is: What is the constitutional status of the government after its resignation? What are its powers during the interim period, during the period of elections or until the formation of the new government? The question is perhaps endemic to most parliamentary regimes, though not always with the same degree of gravity. In fact, Israel has escaped the governmental instability that has plagued a number of parliamentary systems (despite its multi-party system). Nonetheless, the period between the resignation of a government and the establishment of a new government is sometimes quite long, and may extend for some months.

330. Section 30 of Basic Law: The Government established a unique arrangement to regulate this kind of situation. The outgoing government continues to function, without any curtailment of its powers. In other words, there is no application of the generally accepted position (in Europe) in which a transitional government has only limited powers (according to the concept of *expedition des affaires courantes* in France and in Belgium). Consequently, it has been suggested that a government in this position in Israel enjoys greater security than any 'established' government, first, because it is immune to the no-confidence weapon, and second, because its powers are unlimited.

331. A transitional government does not require Knesset approval to appoint a Knesset member as a Minister in place of a minister who has ceased serving, and the powers of the transitional government are unlimited, being ostensibly identical to those of a 'regular' government. The scope of the transitional government's powers was judicially reviewed following the government's decision at the end of 2000 to continue negotiations with the Palestinian Authority after the resignation of the Prime Minister, in an attempt to conclude an agreement even before the national elections. In HCJ 5167/00 *Weiss v. Prime Minister*,[193] President of the Supreme Court Barak stated that 'Israeli constitutional law does not recognize any special doctrine whereby upon the Prime Minister's resignation … the powers of the outgoing government become restricted to ongoing acts ('maintenance functions'). At the same time, in exercising its powers, the transitional government must be aware that it does not enjoy the Knesset's confidence and should refrain from pursuing policies that are a source of public controversy, and which may lead to an irreversible change, unless an urgent public interest compels such action'. The Court ruled that the resigning Prime Minister and the ministers of his government should 'conduct themselves with a degree of restraint that is commensurate with the status of an outgoing government'.

§2. Legal Status

I. Immunities

332. Members of the government enjoy the same immunity as the Knesset members. Section 15 of the Knesset Members (Immunity, Rights and Duties) Law (1951) provides expressly that: 'For the purpose of this Law, a minister who is not a member of the Knesset shall be deemed to be a minister who is a member of the Knesset.'

333. In terms of scope, the Immunity law subjects all ministers, including non-Knesset members, to the restrictions applicable to all Knesset members, such as the prohibition on additional occupations. Furthermore, the State Comptroller is

193. 55 PD (2) 455, 468.

charged with the enforcement of the rules prohibiting ministers from having conflicts of interests. A number of statutory prohibitions, however, apply exclusively to members of government. Section 14(c) of the Immunity law prohibits a member of government from being a member of the board of directors of a company or other association for a period of three years after the termination of his tenure, if that corporation or association received a concession from the State during his tenure. Section 14(d) extends this prohibition to deputy ministers with respect to rights received from the State as a result of the office in which they served.

334. The prohibition on conflicts of interests applies equally to ministers.[194] In exercising ministerial or governmental functions, a minister is enjoined from handling matters in which he has a personal interest. In their book, Rubinstein and Medina propose an arrangement whereby a member of government would be disqualified from participating in government meetings (or ministerial committees) dealing with matters in which the minister's personal interest is liable to influence his position. Implementation of this criterion should depend on the generality of the issue under discussion. For example, where the matter concerns taxation policy, the mere fact that a minister is also a tax payer would not suffice to justify a prohibition against his participation in the decision-making process. Similarly, there is no justification for excluding all those with interests in the agricultural sector from participating in governmental deliberations on policy pertaining to that sector. The appropriate balance between the relevant interests dictates that the prohibition be limited to situations in which the minister has a personal stake in the adoption of a decision which in essence is a private one. In other words, the prohibition is of limited application.

II. The Principle of Collective Responsibility

335. A fundamental principle governing the activities of the government is the doctrine of collective responsibility. Section 4 of Basic Law: The Government provides: 'The Government is collectively responsible to the Knesset.' This principle makes every member of the government a full partner to all government decisions, irrespective of whether he supported or opposed the passage of any particular decision.

336. The principle of collective responsibility relates to government members' public and parliamentary responsibility for government decisions and policy. This principle is part of the political culture, meaning that its enforcement by legal or formal means is, naturally, restricted.

194. Section 3 of the Rules for the Prevention of Conflicts of Interests of Ministers and Deputy Ministers, provides that a minister shall fulfil his role without bias, in fairness to all, and without having any personal stake, even if only a semblance thereof, in any of his decisions, and actions.

337. The doctrine of collective responsibility restricts the activities of members of the government with respect to their criticism of the government, the initiation of legislation and voting in the Knesset against the government's position on a particular issue. Divergence from these limitations exposes the member of government to public and parliamentary criticism, and may culminate in his being removed from his post by the Prime Minister. A minister must support the position of the government in all Knesset sessions and committees. Each member of government may express his view at the time of deliberations, attempting to persuade his fellow members that his is the correct position. However, having adopted a decision on a matter, the government's decision binds all its members, including those who opposed it. A minister can only be released from the yolk of collective responsibility by resigning from the government. Enforcement of collective responsibility is essentially a political task, and the Prime Minister is empowered to remove a minister from his post if he acts against or undermines the government's position.

338. During Israel's early years, the Prime Minister was not empowered to dismiss ministers, and the violation of collective responsibility occasionally precipitated the resignation of the entire government in order to remove a dissident minister, after which the government was constituted anew, without him. This procedure was unsatisfactory, and as early as 1962, a provision was enacted authorizing the Prime Minister to dismiss a minister from his post. This arrangement enabled the Prime Minister to dismiss a minister from office when he violated the principle of collective responsibility.

339. The Israeli unilateral withdrawal (disengagement) from the Gaza strip provides an interesting example of the exercise of Prime Ministerial discretion to remove ministers from their posts. Before presenting the Disengagement Plan for Knesset ratification, Prime Minister Ariel Sharon required governmental approval for the plan. Two ministers of Sharon's government, members of the right wing 'National Union' party, were expected to vote against the plan in an attempt to foil Sharon's attempt to muster the majority required to give the plan the force of a government decision. Consequently, Sharon decided to remove them from office, utilizing his statutory prerogative under section 22(b) of Basic Law: The Government.[195] The ministers concerned petitioned the legality of the Prime Minister's decision in the HCJ,[196] thereby confronting the Court with a highly sensitive question. They argued that their political views indeed contradicted the policy that the Prime Minister was attempting to promote – but this, they argued, did not entitle him to remove them from office. The Prime Minister's decision to dismiss them was therefore illegal, especially since the policy in dispute, which the Prime Minister was attempting to realize, actually deviated from the government's basic guidelines in which the Knesset had expressed its confidence.

---

195. The section provides: The Prime Minister may, after notifying the government of his intention to do so, remove a minister from his post.
196. HCJ 5261/04 *Adv. Yossi Fux v. The Prime Minister of Israel*, 59 PD (2) 446.

340. The petitions were unanimously rejected, providing the Prime Minister with a legal 'life jacket' for his decision to fire the dissident ministers ahead of the vote in the government. But the Court both criticized the Prime Minister's exercise of his statutory power to fire a minister, and demarcated the parameters for the exercise of his discretion.

341. According to President of the HCJ Barak:

> The Prime Minister is empowered to remove a minister from office only where he is convinced that it will promote the government's ability to function properly […] the government and its ministers are not ancillary to the Prime Minister […] the government – and not the Prime Minister – is the executive authority of the State.

President Barak further ruled that the fundamental principles of constitutional law compel the conclusion that the Prime Minister does not have absolute discretion in this context. The Prime Minister operates within certain parameters of reasonableness, and as long as his decisions fall within those parameters, the Court will avoid interfering with his decision. Nonetheless, President Barak maintained that a decision to remove a minister from office must rely on a substantiated factual foundation and on a relevant reason pertaining to the promotion of the government's ability to function properly. But this, as stated, does not preclude recourse to political considerations. 'Political considerations are therefore a legitimate component of the Prime Minister's decision to remove a minister from office. They should be assessed within the entirety of the circumstances.'[197]

342. The principle of collective responsibility requires both the government and the Prime Minister to involve all members of the government in the decision-making process. All government members must be afforded the opportunity of examining the protocols of deliberations in various ministerial committees, and every minister must be allowed to challenge decisions adopted in the committees, in the broader forum of the government plenum. The principle of collective responsibility expresses the concept that governmental decisions are adopted after deliberation – and subsequent compromise – between and amongst the ministers. In reality, however, these requirements are not always complied with.

§3. Competence

I. Powers and Ministerial Responsibility

343. After receiving the Knesset's initial vote of confidence, the government may exercise its full executive powers, in accordance with section 1 of Basic Law: The Government, which defines the government as 'the executive authority of the State'. The government's executive powers are exercised, *inter alia*, by each of the

197. *Ibid.*, at para. 26 of Barak's decision.

ministers in the domain of their own respective ministries. In fulfilment of their ministerial duties, Ministers are entitled to delegate powers, but, as noted above, and in conformity with the English law still predominating in this country, any delegated power must be delegated explicitly, *expressis verbis* by law.

344. The ministers have a wide array of governmental powers. By virtue of his responsibility for a government ministry, a minister has powers delegated to him by the government. Each minister also has the powers conferred upon him by the specific laws pertaining to the activities of his ministry. The extensive range of ministerial powers occasionally compels ministers to delegate their powers to other bodies.[198] Nonetheless, a minister is not permitted to delegate the power to enact regulations. Inasmuch as regulations generally establish a general and binding law, it is more appropriate that the minister himself exercises this regulatory power. Delegation of his powers does not divest the minister of the powers delegated, both with respect to responsibility for the manner of its exercise and with respect to his ability to actually exercise the power delegated and in doing so to nullify the delegation.

345. The principle of 'ministerial responsibility' renders each minister responsible for all activities performed by the portfolio within his control. The actual scope of ministerial responsibility is broader than the statutory expression thereof in section 4 of Basic Law: The Government, which provides that: 'each minister is responsible to the Prime Minister for the field of responsibility with which the minister has been charged'. The minister must report to the Knesset and to the public at large regarding all acts, omissions and failures of the ministry within his charge, as well as of the entire complex of bodies connected to his ministry. He bears public responsibility for all such acts and omissions. Ministerial responsibility finds expression both in 'procedural responsibility' – in prescribing criteria for the exercise of powers by various administrative bodies choosing position holders, determining work procedures that ensure appropriate inspection and review,[199] – and in responsibility for determining general policy in the areas within his portfolio. In order for the minister to bear the full weight of responsibilities, he must be empowered to determine how the powers exercised by bodies within his control are actually exercised. His ministerial responsibility does not extend to responsibility for actions of those not subordinate to him in terms of their appointment.

346. In addition to the determination of general policy, the Minister is also entitled to directly intervene and to exercise governmental powers that are statutorily assigned to other bodies, by way of assigning these powers to himself.[200]

---

198. Section 33 of the Basic Law provides that a minister is entitled to delegate to a 'civil servant' any power that is granted by law to a minister, or a power that was granted to that minister, or which was transferred to him pursuant to a government decision.

199. A. Rubinstein & B. Medina, *ibid.*, at pp. 866–867.

200. Section 34 of Basic Law: The Government states: 'A minister charged the implementation of the law may assume any power, with the exception of powers of a judicial nature, granted by law to a civil servant, provided that no other intention is evidenced by the law; the minister may do the above for a particular matter or for a specific period.'

347. Members of the government are in charge of mapping out the policy of the executive branch. When functioning as government members, their service bears a distinctively political character. Consequently, their actions in that capacity are not bound by many of the administrative laws binding upon other public bodies, including the obligation to base all decisions on an appropriate factual basis, the obligation to hear all bodies liable to be harmed by a decision, the obligation to give reasoned decisions, the obligation to publish decisions and others. At the same time, when a minister discharges his duties, he must strictly comply with appropriate administrative procedures; he must act as a 'public trustee', which means acting fairly and reasonably, on the basis of equality and without prejudice. These are the normative pronouncements of Israeli case law regarding a minister's actions.

§4. Working Procedures

348. The law affords the government considerable discretion in the determination of its working procedures. Section 31(f) of Basic Law: The Government provides only that: 'The government will set working and debate procedures, and decision-making processes in the Government, whether permanent or for a specific matter.' No statutory provision determines the number of members required to constitute a quorum in government meetings.

349. Section 31 of the Basic Law provides that:

> the government may, with the approval of the Knesset, change the division of roles among the ministers … unite or divide government ministries … abolish or establish new ministries … and transfer areas of actions from one ministry to another.

350. Section 35 of the Basic Law relates to the publication of contents of debates and decisions. According to these provisions, the debates and decisions of the government and those of the ministerial committees regarding 'State security' and 'foreign relations of the State' are confidential, and 'their disclosure and publication is prohibited'. Similarly forbidden are the disclosure and publication of additional matters declared by the government in an order, if the Government deems their secrecy to be 'essential to the State'. The Government is also entitled to keep certain matters confidential.

351. In order to prevent leaks, the government increasingly tends to convene regular meetings concerning any ordinary political matter, and to then declare itself a Ministerial Committee for Matters of National Security. In that capacity, the rules enjoining publication come into effect. Nonetheless, this course of action has not prevented leaks from government sessions. Leaks have become a permanent feature of the Israeli political scene, and the Israeli public is accustomed to regarding such leaks as a natural feature of the workings of the political system. Hence, the number of decisions adopted in narrower, more discrete fora has increased, notwithstanding the absence of formal statutory status.

§5. MISCELLANEOUS

I. Role of the Administration

352. For many years, the administrative service was dominated by a system according to which each party could appoint civil servants from its members. This applied to the lowest ranks of the administration as well as to the higher ranks. The system was gradually eliminated after 1959, with the adoption of a civil servant code. Today, government employees are recruited through a merit-based system, with appointment, promotion, transfer, termination, discipline and conditions of employment regulated by law. They are prohibited, especially in the upper spheres, from engaging in partisan politics by the Civil Service (Restriction of Party Activities and Fund-Raising) Law of 1959.

353. The civil service in Israel is managed by the Civil Service Commission, which is headed by the commissioner appointed by the government. The commission is appointed to implement the government's policies in the fields of management and human resources. Within the framework of its task, the commission is responsible for approval of the organizational structure and division of responsibilities between governmental units; approval of permanent positions in government ministries; appointment of employees (excluding positions that are positions of 'trust', i.e., fiduciary nominations); and qualifying and training employees etc.

354. The commission's jurisdictions have been determined by various laws relating to employees in the Civil Service, as well as in the Civil Service Regulations – the 'Takshir'. The commissioner has broad responsibility for the examination, recruitment, appointment and discipline of civil service personnel.

Chapter 5. The Judiciary

§1. Introduction

355. The Israeli judiciary is one of the main achievements of the Israeli legal system. Its structure was influenced by the legacy of the British Mandate, introduced in Israel after 1917. The judiciary enjoys tremendous prestige; it is independent, and enjoys extensive public trust. This is true primarily of the Supreme Court, but applies equally to other Courts. The Court plays a central role in the determination of legal norms, and the Supreme Court plays a decisive role in Israel's public life.

356. In principle, the Israeli judiciary is divided into three central sectors: criminal, civil and public. Matters falling within the first two categories are generally adjudicated by the general Courts, namely the Magistrate's, District, and Supreme Courts, in accordance with the jurisdictional allocation outlined below. At the apex of this framework, the Supreme Court hears appeals from judgments given by the lower Courts, namely the District and Magistrate's Courts. Adjudication of public matters, however, pertaining to disputes between citizens and the sovereign authorities, comes under an entirely different judicial rubric. Citizens' claims against the governing authorities are submitted directly to the highest judicial authority in the state, that is, the HCJ, which is in fact the Supreme Court sitting in its capacity as the HCJ. In such cases, the High Court is the first, last and sole judicial body with jurisdiction. This arrangement is an exceptional one, apparently without parallel in other states.

The following chapter presents a detailed outline of the division of jurisdiction in Israel,[201] with special attention given to the HCJ.

§2. Judicial Organization

357. The Israeli judiciary consists of the general Courts and *batei din*, which are special Courts dealing with specific issues, *inter alia*, religious Courts, labour Courts and administrative Courts. The civil Courts have general jurisdiction in relation to criminal, civil and administrative matters. Religious Courts have special jurisdiction over specific matters and specific persons, for example, in matters relating to personal status, and primarily in matters of marriage and divorce. The labour Courts have jurisdiction in relation to matters flowing from labour relations. The military Courts have jurisdiction over persons in the military service, for the duration of their service. In Israel, the need to establish special tribunals and Courts with jurisdiction over specific areas stemmed from a variety of reasons, some of them

201. Most of the material is summarized in the comprehensive book by Professor Shimon Shetreet, 'On Judging' (2004, In Hebrew). For elaboration in English, *see*: S. Shetreet, *Judicial Independence and Accountability in Israel*, Int'l & Com. Law Quarterly, 979 (1984).

historical, and others prompted by the need to apply a special law, such as the religious law in matters of marriage and divorce. Hence, just a few years ago, a number of other special Courts were established. The Court for Administrative Affairs was established to alleviate the burden on the Supreme Court, and the Family Courts were established in recognition of the need to concentrate all matters pertaining to the family in a single Court, to be adjudicated by judges specializing in family law.

I. Ordinary Law Courts

358. Basic Law: Judicature and the Courts Law [Consolidated Version], 1984 provides the statutory basis for the Israeli judiciary. Section 1 of Basic Law: Judicature provides:

(1) Judicial power is vested in the following Courts:
- (a) The Supreme Court;
- (b) The District Court;
- (c) The Magistrate's Court; and
- (d) Another Court designated by Law as a Court.

The Israeli judiciary therefore consists of three bodies: the Magistrate's Court, the District Court and the Supreme Court. Each Court has defined and distinct powers, stipulated in the Courts Law [Consolidated Version] 1984 (hereinafter: 'the Courts law'), but their powers occasionally overlap.

A. *Magistrate's Court*[202]

359. The distribution of jurisdiction among the different Courts is based primarily on the division of jurisdiction between the Magistrate's Court and the District Court. The Magistrate's Court's jurisdiction in criminal matters extends to most of the offences punishable by a fine only, and offences for which the statutory punishment does not exceed seven years of imprisonment. In civil matters, the Magistrate's Court has jurisdiction over all civil claims except for claims relating to immovable property, provided that the sum of the claim or the value of the subject matter does not exceed NIS 2,500,000.[203] In claims involving immovable property, the Magistrate's Court hears actions concerning the possession (i.e., claims for possessory rights) or use of immovable property, irrespective of the sum of the claim. The Magistrate's Court usually sits as a panel of one judge, but the President of the Magistrate's Court may order that a particular matter be heard by a panel of three judges. Judgments of the Magistrate's Court may be appealed to the District Court.[204]

202. Magistrate's Courts operate in all the Israeli cities.
203. Section 51(a)(2) of the Courts Law. When this text was written, the sum stood at around EUR 600,000.
204. Section 52 of the Courts Law.

B. District Court[205]

360. Section 40 of the Courts Law defines the powers of the District Court, which essentially fulfils two functions: it acts as a trial Court for any matter not falling within the jurisdiction of the Magistrate's Court, and, naturally, it acts as an appellate Court for judgments delivered by the Magistrate's Court. As a trial Court, the jurisdiction of the District Court is 'residual' (i.e., all matters not within the jurisdiction of the Magistrate's Court). Thus, it deals with all civil claims valued at over NIS 2,500,000 and all criminal offences punishable by more than seven years' imprisonment. The District Court usually hears cases as a panel of one, but in relation to a long list of subjects, the District Court is statutorily required to sit as a panel of three judges. Those subjects requiring a panel of three judges include offences punishable by ten or more years of imprisonment, appeals against judgments of other Courts and *batei din*, and any other matter ordered to be heard by a panel of three by the President of the District Court.

C. The Supreme Court

361. The Supreme Court is the highest judicial authority in the State of Israel, and it too serves two functions: as a final appellate Court for judgments of the District Court, that is, it is a Court of criminal and civil appeal, and as the HCJ. There is only one Supreme Court, comprising fifteen justices. The Supreme Court usually sits in a panel of three justices, but the President of the Supreme Court can decide and order that a case be heard by an expanded panel. Over the last few years, numerous cases have been adjudicated by expanded panels, primarily in the context of petitions to the High Court, which raise constitutional questions. Constitutional cases are often heard by panels of up to nine, and sometimes eleven justices.

362. The judiciary operates in accordance with a number of guiding principles. All judgments of a trial Court may be appealed. Thus, a District Court judgment regarding a felony punishable by seven or more years of imprisonment may be appealed – as a matter of right – to the Supreme Court. However, there is no automatic right of appeal against judgments given on appeals by an appellate Court, and a second appeal can only be heard if an appeal was granted by either the Court giving the judgment or the Court of the (second) appeal itself. Hence, a decision of a District Court sitting on appeal against a Magistrate's Court judgment can be appealed in the Supreme Court.

363. Decisions of the Supreme Court cannot be appealed, even when the Supreme Court sits as a First Instance Court (e.g., when sitting as the HCJ, in which,

205. Israel is divided into six districts in accordance with an order issued by the Minister of Justice, and there are six District courts: Jerusalem, Tel-Aviv, Central district, Haifa, Bear Sheva, and Nazareth.

as stated, it sits both as a first and final tribunal). However, when sitting as a panel of three justices, after giving judgment, the Supreme Court may decide to conduct a 'further hearing', presided over by five justices or more. The law prescribes specific grounds justifying the conduct of a further hearing, including where a Supreme Court ruling contradicts a previous ruling of the Supreme Court, or where the importance, difficulty or novelty of a decision warrants an additional hearing. The institution of a further hearing is an exception to the rule of the 'finality of proceedings', but is justified when the decision is of exceptional importance, or amounts to the establishment of a new law. In such a case, an examination of the law before an expanded panel is justified in order to ensure the stability of the system.

D. The High Court of Justice

364. The HCJ is the product of a particular constellation of historical circumstances. The bizarre position described above, whereby certain categories of claims (administrative claims of a person aggrieved by actions of a sovereign authority) are submitted directly to the Supreme Court, was not the result of prior planning.

365. During the British Mandate period, judges in the lower Courts (Magistrate's and District Courts) were generally locals (Jews and Arabs) whereas Supreme Court justices were British. The policy of the Mandate Government was that in regular civil and criminal matters, local judges would be entitled to adjudicate in regular Courts. However, if the dispute involved the Mandate Authorities themselves, they preferred that it be heard from beginning to end by judges belonging to the British establishment.[206] The result was that all administrative disputes were under the direct jurisdiction of the Supreme Court. The practical justification for this structure disappeared with the establishment of the State, but the legal situation was never amended accordingly.

366. With the establishment of the State, it was decided in principle that the existing legal and administrative structures of the Mandate would remain intact, and the HCJ therefore continued to operate in the same format, except that its judges were now Jewish. Within a short period, the Supreme Court had assumed a central position in the development of the law, and almost immediately after the State's establishment, it proceeded to lay down the constitutive principles for a democratic state governed by the rule of law. A well-known case bearing mention in this context, from the early days of the State, was the case of *AlCarbutli v. Minister of Defence et al.*[207] An Arab citizen was arrested pursuant to the Emergency Regulations, which had been enacted by the High Commissioner in 1945. He was placed

206. R. Gavison, M. Kremnitzer & Y. Dotan, *Judicial Activism, For and Against* (2000, In Hebrew) pp. 5–7.
207. HCJ 7/48 *Al-Carbutli v. Minister of Defence*, 2 PD 5.

under administrative detention, without trial, and for an unlimited period. Pursuant to the Regulations, an advisory committee ought to have been established, charged with the examination of the detention, and if necessary to instruct the military commander to revoke the order. The detainee was denied the possibility of applying to the committee, which in fact had not even been established.

The HCJ ruled that the Regulation was illegal, because it effectively denied the detainee his right to appeal his detention before the advisory committee. The HCJ ruled that 'the sovereign authorities are subject to the law like all other citizens of the State, and the rule of law is one of the sturdy foundations of the State'. The echoes of this decision reverberated, throughout the State, leaving a distinct impression on both the Jewish and Arab sectors of the public.

367. Over the years of its existence, the HCJ has consistently demonstrated its ability to confront the government authorities, even in security-related matters. In the absence of a constitution, it was the High Court that created, by virtue of judicial interpretation, the 'judicial bill of rights'.

368. The procedure in the HCJ differs from that of the other Courts. Witnesses are not cross-examined, nor is oral testimony accepted. The deliberation of the matter is structured to enable a prompt, immediate remedy. The HCJ is accessible to the private citizen, its procedures are simple and the speedy procedures combine with the relative facility of filing a petition to convert the HCJ into a magnet for citizens' grievances occasioned by Government actions. As a result, the HCJ has established itself as an institution of far-reaching repute, importance and power.

369. Basic Law: The Judiciary outlines the powers conferred upon the HCJ. Section 15(c) of the law provides that 'the Supreme Court shall also sit as an HCJ. When so sitting, it shall hear matters in which it deems it necessary to grant relief for the sake of justice and which are not within the jurisdiction of another Court'.

370. Besides the general provision of subsection (c), the HCJ has explicit authority to adjudicate the matters enumerated in section 15(d) of the Basic Law:

(1) To issue orders for the release of persons unlawfully detained or imprisoned i.e., Habeas Corpus; and
(2) To order State and local authorities, and the officials and bodies thereof, and other persons fulfilling public functions under law, to do or refrain from doing any act in the lawful exercise of their functions or, if they were improperly elected or appointed, to refrain from so acting;
This is the section that gives the High Court the formal power to interfere in any decision made by a person carrying out a public function under law. The definition is particularly broad, encompassing all holders of public positions in the State, right from the President and the Prime Minister, via the Knesset Speaker, to the ministers and members of Knesset, down to the lowliest of clerks. All of these people are persons carrying out public functions under law.
(3) to order Courts [general Courts and *batei din*] and bodies and persons having judicial or quasi-judicial powers under law, other than Courts dealt with by this

law and other than religious Courts, to hear, refrain from hearing, or continue hearing a particular matter or to void a proceeding improperly taken or a decision improperly given.
This section enables the HCJ to supervise the activities of Israel's judicial system. For example, the HCJ can invalidate a decision of the military on the grounds of its unreasonableness or disproportionality or for exceeding its powers, or it may intervene in the decisions of the labour or other Courts.

(4) To order religious Courts to hear a particular matter within their jurisdiction or to refrain from hearing or continue hearing a particular matter not within their jurisdiction.

This is a special section that deals with the HCJ's power of review over the rabbinical Courts, which is the product of a political compromise. On the one hand, the religious establishment opposed any form of supervision by the HCJ over the religious Courts system that operated under the religious law, inasmuch as the HCJ operated in accordance with the state law, as distinct from religious law. On the other hand, it was not feasible for any kind of judicial network to be immune to any form of supervision or review. The result was the enactment of this section, which prima facie limits the HCJ powers of intervention exclusively to cases of exceeding the limits of powers. In fact, the HCJ interferes in the decisions of the Rabbinical Courts in accordance with the same criteria utilized for reviewing the activities of all other Courts and judicial tribunals, namely procedural and even substantive compliance with principles of natural justice, absence of bias, the equality-based nature of the proceedings etc.

371. As a rule, the law prescribes precise rules to demarcate the Courts' powers, and the Courts are careful not to exceed the borders established by the constitution or by law. But here, too, the status of the HCJ differs from that of the other Courts. Its authority is broadly and flexibly formulated, for example, the wording that enables it 'to hear matters in which it deems it necessary to grant relief for the sake of justice'. High Court justices use this section extensively to extend the scope of their intervention to encompass all of the State authorities. An examination of HCJ rulings over the past few years leads to the conclusion that, at least from the justices' perspective, the 'power' at the disposal of the HCJ is practically unlimited. This explains the absence of cases in which the HCJ has refused to rule due lack of power to adjudicate on the issue before it. Hence, the HCJ generally invokes its discretionary power to explain its rejection of petitions or their referral to other judicial fora. The HCJ's rhetoric is replete with pronunciations whereby petitions have been rejected notwithstanding the HCJ's competence to hear them, due to considerations of judicial restraint. Ostensibly, the HCJ has almost unlimited control over the demarcation of its powers; an approach which has enabled the extension of its supervision to sectors previously deemed 'out of bounds'. For example, the HCJ extended its review powers to the internal working procedures of the Knesset, and broadened the applicable range of the rules of public law (such as the principle of equality) to all bodies, even those not subordinate to governmental authorities, such as governmental companies and even certain private bodies.

II. Administrative Courts, Special Courts and Religious Courts (*Batei Din*)

A. *Courts for Administrative Affairs*

372. Until the year 2000, decisions in relation to administrative matters fell within the substantive jurisdiction of the Supreme Court, sitting as the HCJ. In 2000, the Administrative Affairs Courts Law, 2000 was enacted. This law empowers the District Court, sitting as the Administrative Affairs Court, to adjudicate matters that were previously within the jurisdiction of the High Court. The law purported to reduce the burden on the High Court, which, as mentioned, also functions as an appellate Court for civil and criminal appeals.

373. The power conferred upon the Administrative Affairs Court related to the adjudication of matters not involving violations of basic individual rights by the authorities, which matters were, and have remained, the exclusive province of the HCJ. The matters in relation to which jurisdiction was transferred to the Administrative Affairs Court concerned municipal taxes, education, religious councils, tenders, non-profit organizations, the licensing of businesses, tourism, planning and construction, weapons, population administration, public housing, transport, renovation and maintenance of houses, parties, credit supply services, registration of currency supply services and animals.

374. The judges in the Administrative Affairs Court are District Court judges who have been specially trained in administrative law, serving in that capacity for four years. Hearings are usually conducted before a sole judge. The establishment of the specialized Administrative Affairs Court does not preclude the jurisdiction of the HCJ, and as stated, its aim was to reduce the caseload burden of the Supreme Court. The law thus provides that, where the Administrative Affairs Court finds that an administrative petition raises a matter of exceptional importance, sensitivity or urgency, it may order that its adjudication be transferred to the Supreme Court, sitting as the HCJ.[208]

B. *Family Courts*

375. Until the middle of the 1990s, all matters pertaining to the family and personal status were adjudicated by the District Court. In wake of recommendations by a public committee, it was decided to establish a Court to deal exclusively with family affairs. In 1995, the Family Courts Law, 1995 was passed. This law was intended to consolidate in the Family Court all of the judicial powers pertaining to family affairs and disputes, apart from matters of marriages and divorces conducted in

208. It should be stressed that the first condition, that the 'matters … are not within the jurisdiction of another court or bet din' is not always satisfied, for there have been cases in which the High Court of Justice has heard petitions relating to matters within the jurisdiction of another court or *batei din*, when it was deemed that the alternative remedy was inefficient.

accordance with the personal religious law of the individual, which fall within the exclusive jurisdiction of the religious Courts.

376. Subjects connected to the family include maintenance, guardianship, maternity and paternity, return of abducted minors and actions based on specific legislation, such as marriage age, legal competency and guardianship, determination of age, property relations between spouses, adoption of children and prevention of domestic violence. The Family Court is in essence a Magistrate's Court sitting as a Family Court, albeit with certain unique characteristics. For example, each family has its own judge; hence, the same judge will adjudicate any matter reaching the Court and concerning that particular family. The rationale underpinning this arrangement is the desirability of having one judge who is familiar with the entire family and its individual components and circumstances. The judge's comprehensive understanding of the family in all its aspects equips him with a deeper understanding of the essence of the dispute. In practice, this idea is not realized in full, because the religious Courts have retained sole jurisdiction over certain cardinal issues pertaining to the family, namely marriage and divorce.

377. The Family Court operates under the basic assumption that the dispute between the parties is not a regular civil dispute, and that a family dispute cannot be adjudicated in the same manner as a regular dispute between parties who are strangers to one another. The Family Court thus attempts to exhaust all possible avenues of dispute resolution without harming the integrity and unity of the family unit. In most cases, this preference is manifested in the Court attempting to mediate between the parties. For example, even in the preliminary stages of proceedings, the Court examines the possibility of transferring the case to a mediation context. The Court has at its disposal a network of social workers and psychologists who assist the Court in reaching professional decisions. The Court accepts professional opinions from its auxiliary units consisting of psychologists and social workers. Similarly, the Family Court is not bound by the laws of civil procedure and evidence that bind the general Courts. It may operate in any way deemed necessary for achieving justice. Deliberations are conducted in camera to preserve the privacy of all the parties involved in the hearing.

C. The Rabbinical Courts System

378. The establishment of the Rabbinical Courts system has its roots in the pre-State period. As early as in the Mandate period, and even during the Ottoman Regime, the accepted approach was that matters of personal status were governed by the religious law of the community to which the affected person belonged. Accordingly, the various communities were granted legal and adjudicative autonomy in matters of personal status. With the establishment of State, it was resolved to preserve this arrangement. For Jews, the basic principle was that divorces and marriages of Jews would be conducted exclusively in accordance with *Din Torah* (Jewish religious law).[209]

379. To apply the religious law of each community, a separate system of religious Courts (*batei din*) was established, each of which conferred jurisdiction on the members of the specific communities then existing in Israel. As a result, Israel has Shara'ite Courts, Druze Courts and Rabbinical Courts. Each network of religious Courts is based on a number of regional Courts and one central, appellate Court. The jurisdiction of the Rabbinical Courts is anchored in the Rabbinical Courts Jurisdiction (Marriage and Divorce) Law, 1953. The law provides that the jurisdiction of the Rabbinical Courts is limited to matters of marriage and divorce of Jews in Israel, who are citizens or residents of the State. This jurisdiction was only conferred upon the rabbinical Courts, and so, as stated, marriages and divorces are conducted exclusively in accordance with Jewish religious law. Nevertheless, the HCJ supervises the activities of the religious Courts, and quite often intervenes in their decisions, as shall be observed below.

380. The Shara'ite Courts of the Muslim community enjoy more extensive autonomy than the rabbinical Courts, insofar as they enjoy exclusive, general jurisdiction over all matter of personal status, and not just matters of marriage and divorce, as is the case with the rabbinical Courts.

D. *Labour Courts*

381. The labour Courts were established with the intention of providing a specialized judicial forum for labour disputes, and to ensure that appropriate weight was given to the unique interests of workers and their employers. The regional branch of the labour Courts is the lowest authority in the framework, while the National Labour Court functions as an appellate Court. Labour Courts deal with worker-employer relations and disputes. They also have jurisdiction over certain criminal matters by virtue of specific legislation such as the Minimum Wage Law, the Equal Opportunities for Labour Law, the Prevention of Sexual Harassment Law and others. A particularly interesting feature of the labour Courts is the composition of their judicial panels. Together with the professional judges, the panel also comprises public representatives, i.e., a workers' representative and an employers' representative. The inclusion of representatives from workers' and employers' organizations ensures that consideration is also given during deliberations to non-legal factors.

---

209. The application of the religious law leads to a plethora of problems, and causes severe discrimination against women. This matter is referred to in Part IV in the Chapter on fundamental rights and freedoms.

E. Administrative Courts

382. Israel's judiciary does not have any equivalent to the European continental system of administrative Courts. Nevertheless, there are numerous administrative tribunals, dealing with specific matters. Parallel to the general Courts and special Courts, including the religious Courts, a broad network of judicial and quasi-judicial fora has developed under the auspices of the administrative authorities. These Courts resolve disputes between the citizen and the authorities with greater efficiency, saving both time and expenses. The system consists of tribunals or special Courts, before which the citizen can appeal administrative decisions that concern him, for example matters of national insurance, local authorities' decisions etc. Over the years, about one hundred of these judicial or quasi-judicial tribunals have been established pursuant to the provisions of various administrative laws.

III. Legal Status of Judges

A. Appointment of Judges

383. Judges in Israel are, theoretically, appointed by the President of the State. However, as the President has a formal role only, the election is actually made by the Judges Election Committee. The Judges Election Committee is a unique Israeli creation consisting of nine members: two ministers (one of whom is the Minister of Justice who also serves as the Chairperson of the Committee), two members of the Knesset (elected by the Knesset), three Supreme Court justices (including the President of the Supreme Court) and two advocates, who are representatives of the Israel Bar Association. The Committee's composition ensures representation for the legislative, executive and judicial branches. Numerically, members of the legal profession constitute the majority (two representatives of the Bar Association and three judges), thereby preventing the judiciary's politicization. Over the years, the committee has proven its worth, generating worldwide interest in the Israeli system of judicial appointments. Its decisions are substantive, reasoned and relatively free of extraneous or political considerations, thereby ensuring the appointment of judges of a high professional level, who are not dependent on political bodies. The committee's decisions are final and cannot be appealed. Judges are elected to the three judicial bodies, but for our purposes, the election of the Supreme Court judges warrants special consideration.

384. The interesting, perennial question surrounding the committee's appointments of judges in general, and particularly Supreme Court justices, is whether judges as a group should be 'representative' of the mosaic of sectors, views and backgrounds of the population over whom they preside, and who they ideally presume to serve. Ultimately, a judicial decision is largely the product, or at least is reflective, of the judge's personal outlook, his background, his education and even his religious beliefs. Consequently, it is claimed that the composition of the judiciary should give expression to the multicultural character of Israeli society. The counter-argument is that the representative character of the judiciary must not be attained at the expense of its high professional level, and that the judiciary discharges its 'representation onus' by ensuring that its judgments and decisions 'reflect' the heterogeneous nature of Israeli society. Moreover, in fact, the Supreme Court partially embodies Israel's cultural variety of Israel, as its panels traditionally include female judges, religious judges and an Arab judge.

385. A judicial appointment is 'for life', which, in practice, is until age 70. The permanence of his position and the difficulty of removing him from his position naturally affect the criteria applied to a judge's appointment, which may change according to the nature and level of the judicial appointment. Magistrate's Court judges must be qualified lawyers, members of the Israel Bar Association,[210] who have practised or taught law for five or more years (two of them in Israel). To qualify for the position of a District Court judge, a candidate must have served as a Magistrate's Court judge for a period of four years, practised law or been engaged in a judicial position or taught law continuously for six or more years.

386. The qualifying criteria for appointment to the Supreme Court are five years' service as a District Court judge or alternatively, having worked as an attorney, or having served in a judicial capacity or having taught law for a period of ten years or more. A person not satisfying these criteria, but regarded as an 'eminent jurist', may also fill the position of Supreme Court justice. This exception applies exclusively to the appointment of a justice to the Supreme Court.

387. Once appointed, the judge's position is permanent, and can only be terminated in accordance with certain statutory conditions: namely, resignation, reaching the age of 70, election or appointment to a position the holders of which are barred from being candidates for the Knesset, or removal from his position. Section 7 of Basic Law: Judiciary enables the dismissal of a judge from office prior to retirement age, pursuant to a decision of the Judges' Election Committee or a decision of the Judges' Disciplinary Court, both of which are very rare.

388. An ombudsman's office for public complaints against judges was recently established, headed by a Commissioner elected by the Judges Election Committee (Ombudsman for Public Complaints against Judges Law, 2002). The purpose of this law is to investigate complaints 'against any judge in a matter relating to his conduct in the framework of the fulfilment of his duties as a judge including his manner of conducting a trial'. The ombudsman is empowered to recommend that disciplinary proceedings be instigated against a judge, and even recommend to the Judges Election Committee that the judge's tenure be terminated. The Ombudsman submits an annual report surveying the overall functioning of Israel's judges. This arrangement ensures a commensurate degree of supervision over the judges without impinging on the independence of the judicial system.

---

210. In Israel, membership of the Bar Association is a necessary precondition for working in the profession.

In the event of a criminal act, section 12 of the Basic Law: The Judiciary provides that a criminal investigation cannot be opened against a judge without the consent of the attorney general (AG), and that an indictment against a judge can only be filed by the AG General. Subsection (b) provides that criminal charges against a judge may only be heard by a District Court consisting of three judges.

B. Basic Principles

1. The Independence of the Judicial Branch

389. Israeli law is structured to ensure the judiciary's absolute independence, and to do so, the judges are guaranteed substantive, personal and institutional independence.

390. Substantive Independence: Basic Law: Judiciary states that a judge shall not be subject to any authority other than that of the law. This provision guarantees the fundamental principle of judicial independence; hence, a judge does not receive orders from any other person. To preserve the substantive independence of the judges, the law provides that a person vested with judicial power shall not be criminally liable for any act performed in the discharge of his judicial functions, even in excess of the boundaries of such power. The term 'person vested with judicial power' has been interpreted as applying to persons fulfilling judicial roles in the regular legal system as well as in the religious Courts and other special Courts. The immunity applies both to actions and to omissions, i.e., a failure to perform an action that should have been performed. Judicial immunity against tort actions is stipulated in section 8 of the Torts Ordinance, which confers broad protection against any action grounded in a tort. The section protects both the civil Courts and *batei din*, and any individual fulfilling a judicial function, including arbitrators. It should be stressed that judicial immunity applies to negligent breaches of judicial duties, although it is unclear whether it also applies to cases where there was a lack of good faith.

391. Personal Independence: The personal independence of the judges means that the conditions of their tenure are not subject to the supervision of the executive branch, which might manifest itself in their removal from their post, suspension, transfer to another Court, or from one position to another, or a salary cutback, or ordering their retirement for pension by force of a regular administrative decision. The judge's personal independence further manifests itself in the fact that the legislature has guaranteed the judges' tenure by permanent appointment to their judicial posts until they reach the statutory retirement age of 70. A judge can only be removed from his office in exceptional cases or pursuant to a decision of the Judges Election Committee, by a majority of seven of the nine members.

392. Furthermore, Basic Law: The Judiciary stipulates that judges' salaries and other payments are prescribed by the Knesset or one of its committees. The Knesset

Finance Committee determines the amount of judges' salaries, by force of the principle of separation of powers that mandates the independence of the judiciary and the limitations on its contact with the executive branch. Judges' salaries are linked to the consumer price index, and increases in judges' salaries are determined by the Knesset Finance Committee. The judges' personal independence is also expressed in the enjoinment of collective or individual reductions of judges' salaries. Basic Law: The Judiciary provides that reductions of judicial salaries must be linked to parallel reductions in the salaries of another sector.

393. Institutional Independence: In Israel, the judicial system does not constitute an administratively autonomous unit, and administratively, it is actually a unit of the Ministry of Justice. As such, the formal status of the judiciary is not entirely clear. This linkage between the judiciary and the Ministry of Justice means that compliance with the principle of separation of the branches of powers in this respect is not absolute, and as such, the judiciary has only partial, qualified discretion in the supervision of its staff, the Courts' budget and the maintenance of Court buildings. The law grants the Minister of Justice extensive powers in all matters pertaining to the administration of the Courts and the procedures practised therein. Section 82 of the Courts Law provides that the Minister of Justice is responsible for the administration of the Courts and to that end, with the consent of the President of the Supreme Court, he may appoint a judge to serve in the position of administrator of Courts. Supplementing his powers under section 82, the administrator is also charged with the implementation of the Minister's decisions to establish District and Magistrate's Courts, as well as determining their location and areas of jurisdiction. The Minister of Justice has additional powers in his capacity as the chairman of the Judges Election Committee, and in his sole authority to instigate disciplinary proceedings against judges. These supplementary powers also include the temporary appointment of judges to higher or lower Courts, the appointment of presidents for the District or Magistrate's Court, and the transfer of judges from one Court to another under certain circumstances.

394. In a formal sense, this situation is problematic because prima facie, the judicial branch is dependent on the executive branch, and ideally, the Court system should be entirely disconnected from, and independent of, the Ministry of Justice. Currently, the Minister of Justice has extensive standing and clout in a range of matters directly concerning the judiciary, thus contravening the meaning of section 2 of Basic Law: The Judiciary that states: 'a person vested with judicial power shall not, in judicial matters, be subject to any authority but that of the Law'. On the face of it, the procedure governing the conduct of judicial proceedings properly belongs to the category of matters in which the judge enjoys independence. In reality, however, many of these matters are determined by the Minister of Justice. All the same, the tradition that has developed over the generations, and which has been endorsed by successive Ministers of Justice, has been to refrain from interference in the administration of the Courts.

2. The Principle of the Publicity of Judicial Proceedings

395. Maintaining the stature of the judiciary as an independent authority, and the aspiration to ensure public confidence, is also expressed in the restrictions currently imposed on the freedom of expression, which are intended for the protection of 'the integrity of the judicial process'. The principle of the publicity of judicial proceedings is set forth in section 68 of the Courts Law, which provides that, subject to statutorily specified exceptions, the Court's proceedings take place in public.

396. Concurrently, the law imposes some restrictions on the ability to express an opinion in response to 'the activities of judges in the fulfilment of their duty'. An example of this is the sub-judice rule, intended to prevent the exertion of influence on a proceeding pending in Court. Section 71(a) of the Courts Law prohibits the publication of 'anything concerning a matter pending in any Court if the publication is calculated to influence the course or the outcome of the trial'.[211] Pursuant to this provision, it suffices that there is a reasonable possibility of influencing the result of a proceeding for the prohibition to apply. The influence on the outcome of the trial need only be a reasonable possibility and not 'probable' or 'imminent'.[212] It bears mentioning that the historical origin of the sub-judice provision was the British legal system, which is based on the jury system, in which jurors, who are not professional judges, were far more likely to be influenced by external publications and influences. Its retention in the Israeli system, in which professional judges hear all cases, has thus been the subject of scathing criticism. As a result, the prosecuting authorities almost never file indictments for violation of this particular prohibition, in deference to the other, supremely important principle of freedom of expression.

IV. Judicial Proceedings

A. Judicial Proceeding in the General Courts

397. Civil [and criminal] trials in Israel are conducted within the framework of the adversarial system, generally adopted in common law countries. This system relies on the skill of the rival advocates who present their parties' positions, and not on a neutral party, usually the judge, who endeavours to ascertain the truth of the case. In theory, the onus of conducting the trial, the evidence submitted, and the questions asked, are the exclusive province of the parties themselves, or of their attorneys. Nonetheless, it would be misleading to speak of trials being conducted in accordance with a 'pure adversarial model', for the judge too plays an active role in

211. Following the amendment adopted in 2002, the prohibition was restricted to publications concerning criminal matters. Section 71(c) establishes an exception to the rule, whereby 'The prohibition of publication shall not apply to the *bona fide* publication of anything that has been said or has occurred in an open session of the court'.

212. Cr. A *Disenchik v. Attorney General*, 17 PD 169; Cr. A 696/81 *Azulai v. State of Israel*, 37(2) PD 565.

Court proceedings, bearing a large measure of responsibility for the conduct of the trial in all its aspects, and for ensuring compliance with procedural and substantive justice. In this context, judges interfere with the proceedings, shorten the time designated for pleadings and for cross examination, and ask clarifying questions. The judge decides on the permissibility of questions and admissibility or inadmissibility of evidence. In certain cases, he even requests the submission of certain evidence or asks certain questions that the parties themselves (for strategic or tactical reasons pertaining to the success of their case) may have deliberately refrained from submitting, or asking. The judge is likely to adopt this path when it is necessary for ascertaining the factual truth of a matter. To the extent that the issues at stake are more sensitive, pertaining to matters of life and death, the Court has greater discretion and flexibility in its conduct of the trial, for example, where the Court regards itself as responsible for the interests of minors. In this context, the special Courts are empowered to deviate from the laws of evidence and procedure, and in the family Courts, for example, the judge is at liberty to conduct the proceeding in any way he deems appropriate in the circumstances.

398. The trend over the last few years has been towards increasing judge-based interference in the conduct of the trial, motivated by the aspiration to do justice in Court, an aspiration that often takes priority over rigid procedural requirements.

B. Judicial Proceedings in the High Court of Justice

399. Deliberations in the HCJ differ substantively from those of the general Courts. Its procedures are simplified, and the deliberation as a whole is characterized by speed, efficiency and the absence of cumbersome procedural formalism.

400. An HCJ hearing commences with the filing of a petition, supported by an affidavit. The petition is initially heard before a single (Supreme Court) justice, who is empowered to issue a temporary injunction in the petitioner's favour, based exclusively on his affidavit, without conducting a hearing in the parties' presence on the question of whether or not to issue an injunction. Where an injunction is thus granted, the judge then sets a date for submission of a response to the petition. The judge may also conduct an initial session exclusively in the petitioner's presence, or decide to transfer the petition to a panel of three judges. A single justice cannot dismiss a petition, and if he considers that a petition ought to be summarily dismissed, it must first be transferred to a panel of three judges, which is empowered to dismiss the petition. In relation to the petition itself, after the respondent submits his response (in an affidavit), the HCJ does not sit as a regular judicial forum, and only rarely is the petitioner permitted to submit additional evidence and examine witnesses and the authors of any affidavits. In the Court session itself, the respondent begins by presenting his pleadings, after which the petitioner has the right of reply. The respondent can also apply for leave to give a counter-response to the petitioner's response to his petition.

High Court proceedings are terminated with the Court's decision to either cancel the injunction (if issued) in the petitioner's favour, or to make it final. The uniqueness of the HCJ lies in its power to grant prerogative orders.

401. In the words of the President Barak to the justices of the HCJ, 'The HCJ has neither a sword nor a wallet – all it has is the confidence reposed in it by the public at large'. As stated above, the High Court enjoys tremendous prestige, and since the State's establishment has gained repute and power. Its orders are therefore complied with by all of the State authorities.

C. Standing and Justiciability in the HCJ

402. A salient characteristic that distinguishes the HCJ from the general Courts is the justices' broad discretion to decide whether to even hear the petition filed before them. The HCJ justices have formulated a series of preconditions to be fulfilled by petitioners to the HCJ. The purpose of preconditions such as 'standing', coming to Court with 'clean hands' (purity of motive and actions), and justiciability, is to sieve out those petitions that do not pose matters warranting HCJ intervention. The Court's exercise of its discretion to refuse to hear certain matters serves primarily to alleviate its intense workload, created as a result of the Supreme Court's dual role – serving as the highest and final appellate Court in the State as well as being a First Instance Court for administrative matters. In exercising its discretion not to hear certain cases, the HCJ may refuse to intervene as a matter of judicial policy, or decide to transfer the case to another Court.

403. The principal threshold conditions historically required for a petition to be heard by the HCJ are 'right of standing', and the barrier of justiciability.

404. The requirement of 'standing' means that a petitioner must show that he is personally, significantly, and directly, affected by the matter dealt with in the petition, i.e., that he has a personal interest in the petition. The petitioner cannot discharge the 'standing' requirement just by indicating a defect in the authority's actions. He must first show why he, and no other, is entitled to a remedy from the High Court. In the past, the Court regarded the requirement to demonstrate standing as a precondition for its intervention. This approach was based on the principle that:

> there can be no judicial proceedings unless there is a '*lis*' (dispute) … the more the subject of the complaint is of a public nature … the more it is necessary to strictly enforce the requirement that the complainant suffer substantive harm in his private domain, in order for him to acquire a right of standing before the judicial authority.[213]

405. The implementation of the requirement to show a 'right of standing' has enabled the Court to avoid hearing matters it considered to be better suited for other

213. HCJ 40/70 *Becker v. Minister of Defence*, 24(1) PD 238, 246–247.

avenues of review. Over the years, however, the 'right of standing' doctrine has received an increasingly liberal and broad construction, and exceptions have been recognized to the requirement of proving standing. The new approach is that in important, high profile cases, the Court would exercise its discretion to intervene even if the petitioner had no personal interest in the matter. In fact, since the 1980s, the HCJ has intervened in almost every petition presented to it, paying scant or no attention to the question of whether or not there is a defined 'dispute', or the nature of the petitioner's personal interests.

406. According to the doctrine of justiciability, certain petitions are inappropriate for consideration by a judicial forum because they raise political questions, issues that are the focus of public controversies and which ought to be resolved within the framework of the political branches of government. Similarly to the requirements of the right of standing, the justiciability doctrine has enabled the HCJ to avoid having to decide sensitive public questions. In the past, the Court would generally reject attempts to bring about judicial intervention in matters concerning political parties, in areas of foreign relations, and in cases involving the review of branches of governmental authority such as the military authorities. The 1980s evidenced a growing tendency to limit the justiciability threshold, thus enabling the filing of petitions relating to sensitive questions. Some of the justices have even expressed the view that the justiciability doctrine ought to be rejected outright. The cases dealing with the exemption from military service for *Yeshiva* students may serve as a good example for the change in the Court's approach towards standing and justiciability.

407. The question of exemption from military service on grounds of religion has been the subject of ongoing social, political and judicial debate, since the establishment of the state of Israel in 1948. Israeli Law establishes compulsory military service. The 1986 Defence Service Law (Consolidated Version) compels every Israeli citizen, both men and women, to serve in the military. Yet, according to an administrative practice dating from the first days of the State, the Minister of Defence has the discretion to exempt certain persons from the obligation of compulsory military service. Since the early years of the State, the Minister of Defence had the discretion to exempt male ultra-Orthodox Jews who upon reaching recruitment age are full-time students at a religious institution (a *Yeshiva*). The first Prime Minister of Israel, David Ben-Gurion compromised on this issue with the ultra-Orthodox Jews, agreeing to exempt Yeshiva students from serving in the Army.[214] The result of this agreement is that the ultra-religious portion of the population is, in effect (*post facto* at least), exempt from any military duty.

408. This exemption has been the source of a continuous and acrimonious struggle between secular and orthodox Jews for over fifty years. The first exemptions for Yeshiva students were of a small scale, and it was not until 1970 that the

214. It is of note that the word 'exemption' is not used, and formally, the enlistment of *Yeshiva* students is 'postponed' as long as they keep studying in the *Yeshiva*.

issue was brought before the HCJ. The first petition to the HCJ was rejected,[215] without even discussing the issue. In a short decision, the Court stated that the appellant had no 'right of standing', meaning that he had no direct interest in the subject matter of the case. The classical doctrine of standing applied by the justices did not acknowledge *actio popularis* petitions. In anything related to a public petition – one that sought to fight a public battle rather than that of the individual petitioner – the Court refused to recognize the right of standing of the public petitioner. Justice Witkon argued that the appellant's complaint was 'collective and public', and it is settled law that the Court will not grant an injunction in relation to such cases. Justice Witkon drew a connection between the 'standing' doctrine and the political aspect of the exemption's case:

> the Court is careful not to be dragged into the general public debate, which is better left to the political branches ... the issue in this case is of a purely political nature and that is the reason for a strict reading of the standing principle.

409. Ten years later, in the early 1980s, a renewed attempt was made to persuade the Court to rule on the legality of the exemptions.[216] Again, the Court refused to judicially review the Minister of Defence's discretion, averring that the petitioner – Mr Ressler – did not have 'standing'. But in an interesting obiter dictum, Justice Kahn remarked that even if the 'standing' obstacle were overcome (or waived), the Court would still not interfere with the exemption policy. The Court based its decision on a new restriction: the 'justiciability' doctrine, according to which there are questions which do not permit, or are unsuitable for, judicial consideration. The question of whether to enlist *Yeshiva* students – said Judge Kahan – is primarily a 'public' question and the Court has no legal criteria upon which to base a decision. In 1986, Ressler attempted to raise the exemption issue again.[217] By that time, the Supreme Court had relaxed the 'standing' requirement[218] and had recognized the possibility of an *actio popularis*. This petition represented the 'turning point' in the Court's attitude: the abandonment of the traditional barrier of lack of standing. The Court introduced the new rule of standing as being an 'exception' to the old 'legitimate interest doctrine'. When the topic is of grave importance to the community – stated Justice Barak – a 'public' petitioner may lodge a petition. In principle, there is no reason why the public Court should not open its doors to the 'public petitioner'. Issues of public interest, of constitutional concern or serious

---

215. HCJ 40/70 *Becker v. Minister of Defence*, 24(1) PD (1970) 238.
216. HCJ 448/81 *Ressler v. Minister of Defence*, 35 PD (1981) 81.
217. HCJ 910/86 *Ressler v. Minister of Defence*, 42(2) PD (1988) 441. Note that the decision and reasoning were published in 1988. For translated extracts of the case *see*: Zamir and Zysblat, *Public Law in Israel, supra* n. 2 at 275. For further discussion *see*, by author: S. Navot, *Exemption from Military Service Granted to Orthodox Students in Israel – a Case Study on Justiciability, Equality and Judicial Review*, 6 European Public Law (2000) 12.
218. This change was especially due to two important decisions rendered in 1986, *Barzilai v. Government of Israel*, 40(3) PD 505, and *Aloni v. Minister of Justice*, 41(2) PD 441. In both cases, it was decided that if the issue brought before the court was of constitutional and public nature and the principle of the rule of law is threatened, the court would review it even if no interest of the petitioners had been harmed.

wrongdoing by an authority, all generate legitimate standing before the HCJ, even if the appellant has no specific, personal interest in them.

410. Once the standing barrier was overcome, the Court had to deal with one more preliminary obstacle: the military exemption issue is of political nature, and is therefore, prima facie, unjusticiable. In a long and detailed judgment, Justice Barak formulated a new theory of 'justiciability'. The major innovation of the Court was its distinction between cases of 'normative non-justiciability' and those of 'institutional non-justiciability'. Normative justiciability is concerned with whether there are legal means of dealing with the dispute. A dispute is justiciable in the normative sense if legal standards exist for its resolution. Where there is a legal norm – states Justice Barak – there are legal standards to judge it and therefore, it is justiciable. Institutional justiciability deals with the question of whether it is appropriate for the Court to rule in the dispute, or whether it is best left for the decision of other branches of government. Institutional justiciability deals, therefore, with the question of whether the law and the Courts are the appropriate framework for resolving the specific dispute. The political aspect of any action does not preclude its legal aspect – argued Justice Barak – and the Court's mandate is to preserve the rule of law by ensuring that all branches of Government act within the law. Justice Barak refused to place political questions outside the scope of judicial review, and his ruling in Ressler soon became known by the simple motto: 'everything is justiciable'.

411. The Court agreed that the legality of military exemptions was a 'legal' question, and therefore suitable for judicial review. Finally, having overcome the obstacles of 'standing' and 'justiciability', the Court was ready to examine the statutory discretion granted to the Minister of Defence.[219] The *Ressler* case of 1988 was dismissed, and ultimately the Court decided not to intervene. However, unlike the cases described above, the decision this time was on the merits of the case.[220]

412. The issue of the exemption of Yeshiva students exemplifies the metamorphosis in the High Court's perception of its role over the last few years. The traditional approach that recognized, and accepted, the classic threshold requirements of standing and justiciability, conformed with the concept of the HCJ being first and foremost a Court, whose duty was to resolve concrete disputes. The Court did not view itself as the 'gate keeper' of the rule of law, monitoring its enforcement in society. In practice, the HCJ's willingness to grant legitimacy to the phenomenon of public petitioners who were not personally aggrieved but who came to the Court in the name of the rule of law attested to the fact that the Court had arrogated itself the role of supervising the rule of law. Its task was to intervene and prevent governmental unlawfulness, even if the act did not concern a concrete legal dispute, and

219. The formal legal framework for judicial review of governmental and administrative decisions was already well rooted in Supreme Court judgments. From the beginning of the 1980s, a general doctrine of 'reasonableness' had been developed as a standard for examining governmental decisions. The Minister of Defence's discretion is limited – remarked Judge Barak – but his decision to grant an exemption to Yeshiva students – for the moment – is not unreasonable.

220. Further developments in relation to this topic have caused the Knesset to pass a law allowing for this exception, a law that was declared unconstitutional in 2012.

even if no one was directly and personally harmed by the decision. Where the rule of law was violated, the HCJ was prepared to intervene. This tendency also manifested itself in increased flexibility in the application of the other preliminary requirements for High Court intervention. For example, in the past, unjustified delay in filing a petition was liable, as such, to dictate its dismissal in time. Today, however, the accepted approach is to assess the consequences that actually resulted from the delay in the application of judicial review.

413. Similarly, the Court generally avoids summarily dismissing a petition by reason of the petitioner's 'lack of clean hands', in other words, for reasons connected to his conduct external to, and/or in the course of, the judicial proceeding. A petitioner's conduct may influence the results of the proceeding to the extent that they personally affect him, but it is not taken into account when assessing the legality of the sovereign's act.

414. The 1980s saw a gradual change in the attitude towards preconditions for High Court intervention, but it should be stressed that this change was an integral part of a broader, and more deeply rooted, transition, which culminated in the application of judicial review to legislation, as we will observe in the next section.

§3. Judicial Review

I. Introduction

415. Judicial review of Knesset legislation is a highly controversial, 'loaded' topic. On a number of occasions, it has ignited stormy parliamentary altercations – peaking in a proposal for a basic law to establish a constitutional Court in which Supreme Court justices would be the minority – and precipitating outbursts of public indignation and demonstrations. The central bone of contention is the absence of broad national consensus on fundamental basic questions pertaining to Israeli society, such as the status of religion in the state, the Jewish nature and character of the state, and the scope and status of human rights. Furthermore, many contend that resolution of these matters must be the product of a broadly based consensual and representative procedure, i.e., a political-parliamentary process, and not by way of a judicial resolution.

416. In this context, and conceivably playing a factor in the intensity of the public debate, judicial review of Israeli legislation is not constitutionally based. As such, it differs from the norm accepted in most Western democracies in which the power to judicially review legislation is constitutionally based, along with the grounds for review and the remedies offered. In Israel, judicial review is the product of the case law of the Supreme Court.

417. The subject of the status of the basic laws has been discussed extensively in Israeli academic circles over the years. It is noted, as mentioned above, that the

Harari Decision, which introduced the concept of basic laws, was silent on the question of their legal status.

418. One of the hallmarks of a constitution is naturally the fact of it being a stable document with a special procedure for its amendment. The search for these features in the Israeli basic laws discloses an interesting phenomenon; the vast majority of the basic laws were passed without any 'entrenchment' provision i.e., a provision that can only be amended by a special majority of members of the Knesset. Hence, most basic laws in Israel can be either revoked or amended with the same ease required for the revocation or amendment of a regular Knesset law, that is, by way of a regular majority of those present in three readings.

419. It is conceded that the Basic Law: the Knesset of 1958 established three entrenched provisions (in other words, provisions requiring a special majority for their amendment, that is, a majority of 61 of 120 members of the Knesset). But even here, the entrenched provisions comprise three sections only, out of the forty-six sections included in the original Basic Law: The Knesset.

420. The connected questions regarding the status of the basic laws in Israel and the authority for judicial review of legislation arose in Israel for the first time in 1969 in the *Bergman* case. The judicial deliberation in *Bergman* focused on an entrenched section in the Basic Law: The Knesset, which dealt with the electoral system. Yet, despite the *Bergman* ruling, which relates to the status of an entrenched decision in a basic law, the Supreme Court still refused to recognize the normative superiority of basic laws. Nor did the Court even refer to the question of its authority to judicially review Knesset legislation.

421. Intuitively, it would seem that an entrenched section should be bestowed with supra-statutory status. In reality, however, the Knesset could have made relatively light work of overcoming the requirement of a special majority mandated by section 4 of the Basic Law: the Knesset, and passed a law which violated the principle of equality in the elections by mustering a majority of sixty-one. Needless to say, in such a case, the Supreme Court would have been unable to subject the law to judicial review.

422. Until the enactment of the basic laws on human rights in 1992, the Supreme Court continued to recognize the superiority of the formal entrenchment provision in a basic law. Nonetheless, it avoided conferring particular normative significance to the basic laws themselves. In other words, absent any formal entrenchment provision, a new law could amend, and even violate an arrangement prescribed by a basic law. This approach underwent a far-reaching metamorphosis with the enactment of the basic laws concerning human rights.

423. The enactment of the basic laws on human rights in 1992, Basic Law: Freedom of Occupation, and Basic Law: Human Dignity and Liberty, was accompanied by a significant change in the meaning of constitutional entrenchment. Both of the basic laws dealing with human rights included sections that came to be known as 'substantive entrenchment' sections. Accordingly, a law which substantively speaking is inconsistent with a particular provision of the basic law is invalid. This invalidity, however, is conditional upon the law's failure to satisfy the conditions enumerated in the 'limitation' clause. Hence, the Basic Law: Human Dignity and Liberty includes a clause which provides:

> There shall be no violation of rights under this Basic Law except by a law befitting the values of the State of Israel, enacted for a proper purpose, and to an extent no greater than is required, or by regulation enacted by virtue of express authorization in such law.

424. In relation to the power of judicial review, the turning point in Israeli constitutional law arrived in 1995. In the *Mizrachi Bank* judgment[221] – the Supreme Court ruled that the limitation clause was intended to circumscribe the Knesset's legislative authority. In a pioneering, broadly based decision, eight out of the nine Supreme Court justices recognized the possibility of invalidating any law adopted by the Knesset, if it infringed human rights stipulated in a basic law, and did not satisfy the conditions of the limitation clause. In this context, no importance attaches to the size of the majority passing the law. Thus, the Supreme Court finally accepted the concept of judicial review of laws, not only in the formal-technical sense of examining the required majority, but also in the substantive sense. In other words, the Supreme Court recognized the possibility of invalidating a law that contradicted or was inconsistent with substantive conditions established by a basic law.

425. In a manner similar to the American ruling in *Marbury v. Madison*, it was the constitutional status of Israel's basic laws that provided the basis for the Court's power to judicially review laws that contradicted basic laws. As stated, in the *Mizrachi Bank* ruling, the Court ruled that it had the power to exercise judicial review. Its claim was that our 'legal tradition', in the spirit of the tradition characterizing most of the world's democracies, necessitates the existence of a body that is external to the Knesset, which is empowered to conduct judicial review – namely, the Court. In that capacity, the Court can rule on questions of whether limitations applicable to the Knesset by virtue of the basic law have been complied with. The empirical-evaluative basis of this conception is that the Court is the body best qualified to determine whether a particular legislative provision deviates from the provisions of the basic laws. This process, namely, the enactment of the basic laws on human rights in 1992, and the *Mizrachi Bank* ruling in 1995, in which the Court officially recognized the normative supremacy of basic laws in the Israeli legislature, is referred to in Israel as the 'constitutional revolution'.[222]

---

221. HCJ 6821/93 *Mizrachi Bank Ltd. v. Migdal Cooperative Village*, 49(4) PD 221. (For an English translation of certain paragraphs, *see Mizrachi Bank v. Migdal* (Gal Amendment) – translated extracts with commentary in 31 *Israel Law Review* (1997), p. 754.

222. For further discussion on this matter, see Part I, Ch. 2 on the Constitution, and *see* (in English): C. Klein, *Public Law in Israel: A General Background*, European Public Law 1(171) (1995); C. Klein, *Basic Laws, Constituent Power and Judicial review of Statutes in Israel, The Bank Hamizrachi case*, 2 European Public Law, 233; Zamir & Zysblat, *Public Law In Israel* (Oxford University Press 1996), p. 140 et seq.

426. The *Mizrachi Bank* ruling established the constitutional principles governing the supremacy of a basic law, judicial review of legislation and the principle of a restricted Knesset. As a result of this judgment, Israel ceased being a state structured on the English model of parliamentary supremacy and became a constitutional state.

427. Since 1995, the Supreme Court has continued to judicially review Knesset legislation that infringed rights protected by the basic laws and which was not consistent with the limitation clause. Nonetheless, the Court has generally been extremely cautious in exercising its power of review. To date, only a dozen statutes have actually been declared invalid.[223]

428. Given that judicial review in Israel is the product of case law, the procedural rules governing judicial review lack statutory regulation. The central problem is that these rules lack both stability and clarity. Because of its case law basis, it could be argued that judicial review of Israeli legislation is ultimately dependent upon the Court's willingness to engage in such review. The basic laws of the State of Israel contain no provisions governing applications for the exercise of judicial review of legislation. Nor do they enlighten us as to the specific grounds for such an application, or the constitutional remedies to which a person is entitled by reason of an infringement of his basic human rights, which are constitutionally protected by the basic laws. Absent legislative guidance, I will attempt to clarify the basic procedural principles governing judicial review of legislation, as elucidated by the Supreme Court.

223. Some examples as to the cases in which the HCJ struck down specific laws or sections of a certain law include the case of the Investment Managers Chamber, where a transitional provision was invalidated in the Regulation of Occupation (Investment Consultancy and Management of Investment Portfolio) Law, 1995. According to the transition provision, any person who had been engaged in the profession for less than seven years would be obliged to pass an examination. The Court ruled that this provision unlawfully violated the freedom of occupation of those dealers who have extensive and substantive experience, albeit for a period of less than seven years; the *Tzemach* case (53(5) PD 24), in which the Court declared the invalidity of ss 234 and 237 of the Military Justice Law, 1955, which allowed the detention of a solider for up to seventy-two hours before bringing him before a judge; HCJ 1030/99 *Oron v. Israeli Government*, 56(3) PD 640, in which case the Court declared the invalidity of the arrangement prescribed in s. 3(7) of the Telecommunications Law, 1982. The provision granted broadcasting licenses to radio stations that had operated without licenses for at least five years, without a tender. It was invalidated in view of its violation of the freedom of occupation of potential competitors; the landmark decision to declare unconstitutional the privatization of prisons; the case dealing with a security measure that enabled courts to conduct detention hearings involving suspects charged with security offences *in absentia*. This provision was a temporary law amending the Criminal Procedure Law, which permitted the court to extend detention periods – hearings conducted in the absence of the detainee – in order to allow effective interrogations of terror suspects. The Court decided to strike down the law, and by a majority of eight judges, held that the article was unconstitutional; recently, a decision of the HCJ to invalidate an amendment to the Anti-Infiltration Law that allows the incarceration of asylum seekers from Africa for up to three years. In this dramatic decision, an expanded panel of nine judges ruled that the law was unconstitutional and disproportionately impinged on a person's right to liberty, as well as being in conflict with Israel's Basic Law on human freedom and dignity. Moreover, a new amendment to this law was declared unconstitutional as well.

II. The Power of Judicial Review

429. The accepted view today is that the power of judicial review vests exclusively in the Supreme Court, even though the particular question of the identity of the body exercising judicial review was actually left pending in the *Mizrachi Bank* ruling, and still awaits a definitive ruling. This is, however, only the 'accepted' view. In fact, despite this view, prima facie at least, any Court – even the Magistrate's Court – is empowered to invalidate Knesset legislation. This is the consequence of the lacuna left by the *Mizrachi Bank* judgment, and is the unfortunate by-product of the absence of statutory procedural guidelines for the exercise of judicial review and its predication on 'case law', as stated above. This situation is undesirable. On only one occasion since 1995, a Magistrate's Court judge in Tel Aviv invalidated a provision in the Income Tax Ordinance, in view of its disproportionate violation of the freedom of occupation.[224] Understandably, the Knesset was infuriated by the judgment, regarding it as a patently illegitimate use of judicial power.

430. The question of the source of the power to exercise judicial review is another issue awaiting a definitive legislative answer. The draft bill of the Basic Law: Legislation proposed that the power of judicial review should be bestowed exclusively on the Supreme Court. However, this basic law still awaits adoption by the Knesset.

III. The Procedure for Challenging Legislation[225]

431. In Israel today, judicial review of the constitutionality of laws takes two basic forms.

A. *Direct Judicial Review: In the HCJ ('Direct Attack')*

431.1. The first form of judicial review arises by way of private or public petition, which is essentially a 'concrete' petition. Any person alleging a violation of his protected rights in one of the basic laws dealing with human rights can apply to the Supreme Court, in its capacity as the HCJ, in the form of a 'direct' petition. Such a petition challenges the constitutionality of the violation in question. In this context, the petitioner must claim that:

---

224. CC 4696/01 Tel-Aviv Magistrate's Court, per Judge David Rosen. Indeed, the judge made it clear that 'when examining the preliminary claim, I was guided by my conception of judicial care and caution that are dictated by the nature of the subject. The judge must take an extremely measured and restrained approach when deciding on whether to declare the invalidity of a statute or even a small part thereof'. Ultimately, however, the judge ruled that the statutory provision did not satisfy the conditions formulated by case law, and as such was invalid.

225. In this section, I rely predominantly on a previous article. *See* S. Navot, 'Procedural Principles of Judicial Review: An analysis of Israel's New Model'; D. Oltzen & S. Schwartz (eds.) *The Seventh Joint Annual Exchange and Conference: Judicial Review in Comparative German Israeli Perspective* (Baden-Baden, Germany 2004).

(1) A law was enacted (already published) that violates one of the rights protected in the basic laws.
(2) In other words, the infringement of a human right is 'unlawful'; that is, in contravention of the conditions stipulated in the 'limitation clause' (a clause closely resembling the parallel clause in the Canadian Charter). This means that the violation is not proportional, and that it does not befit the character of Israel as a Jewish and Democratic State, and was not enacted for a proper purpose.
(3) At all events, the petitioner must prove that that his rights were unlawfully violated, in view of the interpretative canon that any legislative act in Israel is presumed to be valid, and is presumed to be constitutional.

432. In Israel, there is no procedure for 'filtering' such petitions in order to assess their prospects of success.

433. In a private petition, the petitioner complains of the infringement of a personal right. His petition will be considered 'private' even if the petitioner belongs to a group of citizens aggrieved by the particular decision, for example, failure to grant licenses to the entire public of investment managers, as a result of new legislation. A public petition however, concerns 'public harm', affecting an entire sector of society. In a public petition, the petitioner becomes the representative of a sector of the society, whose interests have been violated. Despite his standing as a representative of the interests of a particular sector, the petitioner does not require an act of official authorization – either by the public, or by the sector being represented.

434. The classical doctrine of standing traditionally applied by the judges did not acknowledge *actio popularis* petitions. However, as mentioned above, in the early 1980s, attempts were made to persuade the Court to adjudicate 'public' questions, and the Supreme Court has tended to broaden the boundaries of justiciability, and by extension, to broaden the scope of judicial review. This process culminated in the recognition of the possibility of an *actio popularis*. Since then, the public petition has been an accepted phenomenon in Israeli law.

B. Indirect Judicial Review (Collateral Attack): In all Courts

435. In Israel, absent any provision to the contrary, the power to examine the constitutionality of a law theoretically resides with the particular judge presiding, within the framework of the proceeding in question. Consider the case of a criminal proceeding in which the accused claims that his indictment is based on a law that violates the provisions of a basic law. In such a case, the judge presiding over the criminal matter can also adjudicate the constitutionality of the law. These were the circumstances in the case referred to above, in which a Magistrate's Court judge invalidated a section in the Income Tax Ordinance. Admittedly, this case is the sole (and an extreme) instance of indirect judicial review by a Magistrate's Court, but to the best of my knowledge the case was not appealed, and as such, the precedent stands. As mentioned above, universal judicial review, exercised by all Courts, as opposed to being limited to the Supreme Court, is highly problematic, and may *inter alia* lead to conflicting judgments regarding various laws, thus generating uncertainty and instability. De facto, as above mentioned all 'judicial review' cases are dealt by the HCJ.

IV. The Absence of Abstract Judicial Review

436. At this time, Israeli law does not have a procedure for abstract judicial review. The absence of the possibility for abstract judicial review is the source of numerous difficulties, and generates protracted and superfluous adjudication of constitutional questions. For example, a constitutional question arose in 2005 concerning the date of the Israeli elections. This question arose as a result of a lacunae in the law, and it transpired that there were two alternative ways of interpreting the relevant basic law, that is, Basic Law: The Knesset. Assuming that there was a process of abstract judicial review in Israel, the Knesset or one of its committees could have initiated an application to the Supreme Court, requesting its ruling on the correct interpretation of the law. In fact, the matter arrived at the doorstep of the Supreme Court in a roundabout, circuitous fashion. The decision regarding the interpretation of the law was referred to the chairman of the CEC (a Supreme Court Justice), and a petition against her decision on the interpretation of the law was subsequently filed in the Supreme Court. In the wake of Knesset deliberations over this particular issue, a proposal was made to establish a new procedure, enabling the presentation of an abstract question to the Court. In my view, there ought to be a formal procedure, enabling those with standing (as statutorily defined) to refer questions of law to the Supreme Court. As mentioned, to date the Knesset has not enacted any formal arrangement for such a procedure.

V. The Grounds for Judicial Review

437. Before discussing the grounds for judicial review presented by the basic laws on human rights, it should be mentioned that the Basic Law: Human Dignity and Liberty does not have retroactive application. The section dealing with preservation of laws provides that the Basic Law: Human Dignity and Liberty will not affect the existing legislation at the time of its enactment in 1992. As such, the option of judicial review of legislation affecting human rights is limited to laws enacted after the passage of the basic law. This limitation does not appear in the Basic Law: Freedom of Occupation.

438. Judicial review in Israel has many possible grounds.

A. *Invalidity of Legislation Due to Procedural Flaws*

*438.1.*This question arises when laws are enacted pursuant to a procedure that deviates from the fixed procedure for enactment of laws, prescribed by the Knesset

Rules. This situation might arise, for example, when a law was not tabled for the required number of readings, or where the required majority was lacking in one of the readings. The conception expressed in case law, to date in obiter dictum only, is that 'once the Knesset prescribed its own legislative procedures … it must comply with its own procedures'. Accordingly, even if legally adopted, until its official publication, a law is invalid. Theoretically, at least, the conclusion is that a law adopted in contravention of, or in a manner deviating from, those procedures may be invalidated. The Supreme Court was prepared to examine the propriety of legislative procedures in the Knesset in the *Poultry Growers* case,[226] which dealt with the fast track legislative procedures of a special law that accompanies the Budget Law. In this case, the Court established basic principles for the legislative process, violation of which would comprise 'a fundamental defect in the process' leading to the annulment of the law. However, this case was dismissed, meaning that to date all petitions that have attempted to invalidate legislation by reason of flaws in the legislative procedure have been rejected.

B. Invalidity of a Law Which Fundamentally Violates Protected Human Rights

439. The power of judicial review of legislation is particularly broad in circumstances in which the limitation of the power of the legislature is not just 'formalistic' but also substantive. Substantive restriction means the establishment of conditions, which all legislation must satisfy. Its enforcement entails the exercise of broader judicial discretion. Consequently, the Court was prepared to enforce the formalistic restrictions prescribed in section 4 of Basic Law: the Knesset without even examining the question of its authority to do so, as the *Bergman* judgment did not deal with the Court's authority for judicial review of legislation. However, enforcement of substantive limitations of the kind prescribed in Basic Law Human Dignity and Liberty and Basic Law: Freedom of Occupation is a far more complex matter.

440. In the *Mizrachi Bank* judgment, the Court ruled that it was authorized to exercise judicial review and to enforce 'substantive' limitations on the legislative power of the Knesset. In this process, the substance of the basic principles is not self-evident, thus exposing it to scathing criticism levelled against the Court's arrogation of power to conduct judicial review of legislation.[227] Notably, the judicial review of legislation is conducted with considerable judicial constraint. Since 1995, when the Court explicitly declared its power to subject legislation to judicial review, the Court has used its power in a few cases only. The Court's power to overturn laws is analogous to non-conventional weapons:

> everyone knows how destructive such weapons can be, even though not all are aware of the entire scope of the destruction they may wreak. Those responsible for such weapons must exercise the highest degree of restraint … . The

226. HCJ 4885/03 *Poultry Growers Association of Israel Ltd. v. Government of Israel*, 59(2) PD 14.
227. *See* e.g., M. Mandel, *Democracy and the New Constitutionalism in Israel*, 33 Israel Law Rev. 259 (1999).

> Court is not supposed to exercise is power to invalidate a law except in an outstanding case of fundamental infringement of basic rights or of basic values.[228]

441. In Israel today, a violation of protected human rights is the central ground for challenging the constitutionality of a law. The relevant claim would therefore be that the law unlawfully and disproportionately infringes rights that are protected within the framework of the basic baw. The Supreme Court recognized the 'supra-statutory' constitutional status of the basic laws in the *Mizrachi Bank* ruling, and thus established the substantive framework for the conduct of the Knesset's legislative function in its adoption of regular laws. The Court is prepared to assess whether the provision of a 'regular' law contradicts the provisions of the basic law. In accordance with its recognition of the strength of this power, and the derivative imperative of judicial restraint, as mentioned above, since the *Mizrachi Bank* case, the Court has only invalidated some twelve statutes de facto. Furthermore, in many of these cases, the Court did not invalidate the entire law. Rather, it restricted its declaration of invalidity to specific provisions. This is indicative of the tremendous judicial restraint that characterizes the functioning of the Supreme Court in this context.

C. Invalidity of a Law that Violates the Basic Principles of the State

442. This is perhaps the most interesting ground for invalidation of a law, and it relates to a theoretical possibility, not yet applied in case law. The argument is that a law may be invalidated if it violates the basic principles of the State, even if these principles lack positive and explicit expression in its basic laws. Normative status is thus bestowed upon the concept of the innate natural law that 'hovers' over the Kelsian pyramid of norms. This claim was first referred to in Israeli case law in the *El Arad* judgment delivered in 1965, when the Israeli Supreme Court dealt with the case of a political party whose electoral platform sought to negate the existence of the State of Israel.[229] In the words of the Supreme Court:

> Conceivably, it is no accident that the Supreme Court of the Federal Republic of Germany … was the first Court to endorse the principle that the judge must also decide in accordance with rules that are not written in the codex of statutes; for not only are these rules above the regular laws, enjoying superior normative status – they are also above the constitution itself, and constitutional provisions which contradict these rules will be rejected.

This concept surfaces in case law every few years, and may be regarded as a legal foundation for the invalidation of a law which conflicts with basic democratic values. It would seem that the Supreme Court is preparing a 'non-conventional weapon' should it be called upon to declare the invalidity of a law conflicting with basic principles that are not currently expressed in the basic laws. However, to date

228. HCJ 7111/95 *Centre for Local Government v. Knesset*, 50(2) PD 485, 496.
229. For discussion of this case, *see* Part II, Ch. 3 on the disqualification of political parties.

at least, the Court has avoided exercising judicial review in reliance upon unwritten basic principles. The rule is that a declaration of the invalidity of legislation is restricted to cases in which there is a fundamental divergence from the basic principles of the Israeli legal system.

D. *Invalidity of a Basic Law: The Unconstitutional Constitutional Amendment doctrine*

443. One of the new questions posed to the HCJ is whether the Court has the power to judicially review an unconstitutional amendment. The *Bar-On* case in 2011[230] dealt with an amendment which was passed to the Basic Law: the Economy, according to which the state budget will be passed once every two years. The amendment was passed by a temporary provision for a period of two years, and then extended again, by another temporary provision. The constitutionality of these amendments was brought before the Supreme Court, which dismissed the appeal and ruled, unanimously (by seven judges), that the temporary amendments were constitutional. The Court allowed the use of this procedure – to amend a basic law by a temporary provision – but explicitly ordered that it should be used only in extraordinary circumstances. In this case, the petitioners argued that a temporary amendment to a basic law was invalid, as basic laws are of an 'eternal' nature as part of the constitution, and should not be amended by temporary provisions. They also claimed that approval of the budget on an annual basis is one of the basic principles of a parliamentary regime, as the budget is one of Parliament's main tools in order to oversee the work of the government. The temporary basic law limits the use of this tool and the power of the Knesset, and alters the relationship between the government and the Knesset. Therefore, the petitioners concluded, this amendment should be considered to be an unconstitutional constitutional amendment.

The doctrine of constitutional amendment has been extensively discussed in foreign legal systems, and in this case, it was discussed for the first time in Israeli case law. The approach of the Israeli Supreme Court is that, in the broadest sense, this doctrine of comparative law has no place in Israel. But still, the constituent power of the Knesset is limited. The Knesset must act within the framework of the fundamental principles and fundamental values of Israel's constitutional structure. According to this view, the character of Israel as a Jewish and democratic state is 'eternal', meaning that there are principles in the very bases of Israel's existence as a society and a state, which may raise the question of the unconstitutional constitutional amendment.

The budget case brought before the Court was not such a case. The relationship between the government and the Knesset is an important relationship. The power of the Knesset to oversee the government is an essential part of the doctrine of the separation of powers. But does the requirement that the Knesset's approval will be received once every two years, instead of once a year, for example, constitute a denial of the Jewish or democratic character of the state? The answer, according to

230. HCJ 4908/10 *Bar-On, MK v. The Knesset* (4 Jul. 2011).

the Supreme Court, is negative. Quoting Professor Barak's article on the topic, the Court concluded:

> When the project of enacting basic laws is completed and ratified *by* the people, that will be the time to make a decision regarding amendments that are not constitutional. It may be that eternity clauses will be determined in the constitution, that will assist in solving the question; it may be that the constitutional text will be silent on this issue, and the Supreme Court will have to make a decision whether to adopt the doctrine of the basic structure of the constitution, or a similar doctrine, or to reject such doctrines; it may be that the amendment process will be so difficult and complicated that the question will never be raised for discussion.

VI. Constitutional Remedies: Relative Invalidity, Temporary Suspension and the 'Ripeness Doctrine'

444. Judicial review in Israel is still in its formative stages. During these stages of its development, it is receptive to, and influenced by, the rules of judicial review accepted across the Western world. These influences are expressed *inter alia* in the Supreme Court's resort to the doctrines of 'relative invalidity' and 'temporary suspension', which enable flexibility regarding the question of the remedy offered when a law is found to be unconstitutional. The 'ripeness doctrine', for example, takes Israeli constitutional law closer to the American law and may actually change the principles of judicial review that have dominated the last two decades of Israeli constitutional law. According to the ripeness doctrine, which is now supported by some of the justices in the Supreme Court, and which was primarily applied by its former President Justice Grunis, the Court would refrain from judicial review if the law in question had still not been implemented. For example, in 2014 an expanded panel of nine Supreme Court justices discussed a constitutional petition against an amendment to the Cooperative Societies Ordinance, passed in 2011, and also known as the Admissions Committees Law.[231]

The Admissions Committees Law allows small communities to require new residents to receive approval by an admissions committee before joining the community. The law specifies a list of reasons for which the committee is entitled to refuse to accept a candidate into the community, including that the candidate is not suitable for the social life of the community, or that the candidate does not fit into the social-cultural fabric of the community. The petitioners (the NGO Adalah) argued that this law is discriminatory. President of the Court, Justice A. Grunis, stated that the petitions should be rejected because they are not 'ripe' for decision.

This doctrine may justify, in appropriate cases, the rejection of a petition when no administrative decision has yet been made, based on the relevant law that is under judicial review, and when there are no clear petitioners, and when it is not yet clear how the law will actually be implemented in practice. The importance of this ground lies in the fact that the Court, in view of its limited resources, will not engage in adjudicating hypothetical or theoretical arguments. Lately, the Court has

231. HCJ 2311/11, 2504/11 *Sabah v. The Knesset* (2014).

been referring to this doctrine also in other cases and refusing to judicially review laws that have not yet been implemented.

445. The doctrine of relative voidability makes a basic distinction between the relevant defect and the remedy. This distinction facilitates the exercise of judicial discretion with respect to the outcome of a legislative act that has been invalidated, allowing consideration to be had to the circumstances of the particular case. The model of relative invalidity accommodates judicial sensitivity as to the nature of the illegality, taking into account questions such as, *inter alia*, the extent of the 'illegality', that is, whether it was grave or minor; whether there has been any reliance on the legislative act; whether it create expectations; and what are the expected consequences of the invalidation of the law.

446. Referring to this model, the Court stated:

> The model of relative invalidity (referred to by Field as 'The Case to Case Theory', SN) is an interim model between the two models referred to above.[232] According to this model, the essence of the illegality and the surrounding circumstances must be considered. Occasionally the illegality is so basic and fundamental that it can be safely said that the law is 'nothing more than a piece of paper' and therefore invalid and void even in the absence of any formal judicial declaration. In other cases, the voidability of a statute may be disputed (which is the more frequent scenario). In these cases, a formal act of invalidation is required in order to terminate the normative effect of the statute. Invalidation can be retrospective, active or prospective. The decision will be adopted having consideration for, and with regard to, the particular piece of unconstitutional legislation and the scope and intensity of reasonable expectations generated thereby. According to this approach, the invalidity of a law might be restricted to a particular set of circumstances or a particular factual framework, leaving it intact and valid in respect of other circumstances or factual frameworks. As such, the model enables the adaptation of the result dictated by the particular determination to the nature of the illegality and circumstances, and in doing so may provide an optimal solution to the potentially harsh consequences flowing from the declaration that a particular legislative act was illegal.[233]

447. In relation to temporary suspension, the question as to whether the Court is entitled to postpone the effective date of invalidity in circumstances in which a law is declared invalid has not yet arisen in Israel.

1. However, this issue did arise in connection with a question of constitutional significance, namely, the exemption granted by the Minister of Defence to

232. In this context, Field refers to two models of invalidity: absolute invalidity – void *ab initio*, and potential invalidity – presumption of validity. *See* O. Field: *The Effect of an Unconstitutional Statute* (1935) 2–8.

233. HCJ 86652/96 *Citizens Rights Association v. Minister of Interior*, PD (3) 117.

students studying in Yeshivot. In 1997 the Court ruled that this arrangement was illegal but deferred the practical effects of the judgments, stating: 'The judgment in the petitions (dated 9 December 1998) was that the current arrangement, under which the Minister of Defence defers the military service of Yeshiva students who are full time students, is illegal. We also ruled that the authority to establish an arrangement on this matter resides with the Knesset. Even so, we ordered that the results of our decision would not become immediately effective. We established a suspension period of 12 months from the date of judgment. The postponement was intended 'to allow the Minister of Defence or the Knesset to conduct substantial and organized discussions of the matter and all its ramifications.' Conceivably, the underlying rationale for the postponement of effect would also apply to a case in which a law was declared invalid.

VII. Conclusion

448. As stated above, the procedural rules for the exercise of judicial review of legislation are the products of case law, and are not statutorily based. While the Court has already engaged in judicial review of legislation for almost a decade, its existence, its legitimacy and the manner of its implementation are still the subject of lively and often acrimonious political and public dispute. These features gave rise to a unique situation in which judicial review in Israel is particularly restrained. This tendency is manifested in a number of contexts.

449. While the claim of a violation of basic principles has frequently been made, the Court has generally chosen to interpret legislation in a manner rendering the law under challenge consistent with the basic principles, instead of overturning it. In doing so, it has been guided by the interpretative canon that an interpretation that leaves the law intact is preferable. In other words, it is preferable [and a conscious effort is made to that effect] to give the law an interpretation that leaves it intact, i.e., an interpretation that renders it consistent with the constitution. Furthermore, even in cases where the Court has actually been willing in principle to judicially review legislation, the legislation still enjoys the initial 'presumption of constitutionality'. As a result, the person claiming that a piece of legislation is constitutionally invalid bears the onus of proving that the illegality infringes basic principles entrenched in the basic law, and that the illegality does not satisfy the conditions prescribed in the limitation clause.

450. Furthermore, the Court has tended to avoid declaring the invalidity of statutory provisions of limited duration, even if they substantively infringed fundamental constitutional principles.

451. Our discussion would be incomplete without mentioning the fact that, in recent years, there has been public discussion of the question of the nomination of Judges to the Supreme Court, and sometimes even the establishment of a constitutional Court. This proposal was advanced by the opponents of the Courts' activist decisions and mostly by orthodox religious Knesset members. Its objective is to veto the exercise of judicial review by the Supreme Court in its current format, and to transfer that power to a special constitutional Court, comprising representatives of the different sectors of Israeli society (national religious, ultra-orthodox, oriental, Western-secular etc.). Such a Court would deal exclusively with petitions regarding the constitutionality of laws. The proposal is not free from political considerations, and has been raised primarily by the circles that regard the Supreme Court and its liberal rulings as a 'threat' to the character of the State. Lately, new ideas have been presented, such as the enactment of an 'override clause' to the Basic Law on Human Dignity and Liberty, so as to allow the Knesset to re-enact a law that has been declared unconstitutional by the HCJ.

Chapter 6. Independent Non-political Bodies with an Advisory or Supervisory Task

§1. Advisory Bodies

I. The Attorney General[234]

452. Advisory bodies, in the generally accepted sense, do not abound in Israel, apart from the bodies of 'consultative' administration. These bodies are part of the sovereign-governmental system and are more developed. In the context of consultative administration, the most important advisory body is the attorney general (AG), which is one of the most important and influential public offices in the State of Israel. A full and informed understanding of Israeli public life is impossible without reference to this unique institution. The AG is responsible for four principal areas. He heads general State prosecutions. He represents governmental authorities in judicial fora. He is the legal consultant of the government and other sovereign authorities, in which capacity he is empowered to determine the binding legal policy for the government and its respective branches on a broad range of issues. Finally, he is responsible for protecting the public interest and for promoting the rule of law. On several occasions over the years, proposals have been made – and rejected – to divide up the AG's functions. The proposals have been rejected, primarily in cognizance of the fact that such a move would undermine the stature of the AG, and 'would deprive the public of an effective source of supervision over the rule of law'.[235]

453. Despite the AG's broad array of powers, his powers are not anchored in any law or basic baw, nor is there any statutory definition of the essence of his role, the manner of his appointment, his dismissal, and the overall status of the AG *vis-à-vis* the other governmental authorities.

454. A tradition has developed, originating during the Mandate period,[236] whereby the AG is a civil servant, and in contrast with the practice in other states, he has no political standing. In the early years of the State, those who filled the position were politically affiliated, but since the middle of the sixties, a tradition has

234. This chapter is primarily based on the book of A. Rubinstein & B. Medina, *The Constitutional Law of the State of Israel* (6th ed. 2005, In Hebrew) pp. 996–1024.

235. Report of the Public Committee for Examination of the Methods of Appointing the Attorney General and other Matters Connected to his Office (Shamgar Commission) 53 in pp. 48, 52–56, and 90–93; R. Gavison, 'The Attorney General: A Critical Review of New Trends' *Plilim* (In Hebrew), 5 (1997) 27.

236. During the Mandate period, there was an office of the AG. In contrast to the holder of the equivalent office in the United States and England, where the office was a political one, the holder of which was a member of the government, the AG during the Mandate period was a civil servant whose position was not a political one. Prior to the establishment of the State, the People's Council, which was to become the Provisional Government, decided that the position of AG would be assumed by the Minister of Justice, who was generally responsible for the rule of law. The AG would be a senior clerk whose role was to provide legal opinions to the Government and the drafting of its bills. Ultimately, this was not the model adopted.

developed wherein appointees to the role have been apolitical persons, coming primarily from the judiciary or academia. The convention that has developed is that the replacement of the government do not lead to the replacement of the AG.

455. There is no statutory format for the appointment of the AG. Pursuant to a government decision, a public committee examines candidates' qualifications and credentials and gives its recommendation for a number of qualified candidates suited for the position, after which the Minister of Justice gives the government notice of his chosen candidate. The candidate must be formally qualified to serve as a Supreme Court justice.

456. The AG's period of office is not fixed. The Shamgar Commission recommended a period of tenure of six years, not admitting of extension. The goal is to ensure the independence of the attorney general, and this arrangement was actually applied as from 2004.

A. The Attorney General as Head of the State Prosecution

457. The AG's powers in the field of prosecution consist essentially of decisions to file indictments in specific matters, to stay proceedings or close a police investigation file, and the filing of appeals against decisions in criminal matters. The power to prosecute is a quasi-judicial power with far-reaching ramifications, and this necessitates a significant degree of independence on the AG's part, and his eschewal of any consideration of the political aspects or implications of his decisions.

458. As early as 1962, with the publication of the Report of the Lawyers Commission on the Powers of the AG ('Agranat Commission'), it was determined that the AG would be conferred exclusive discretion to determine whether or not to pursue criminal proceedings, both in terms of the examination and evaluation of the evidence, and in terms of assessing the public interest. The Report stated that in exercising his power, the AG must exercise independent discretion, and is not subordinate or otherwise bound by the orders of the Justice Minister or of the Government itself. The governmental responsibility is expressed in its duty to appoint a suitable person to the position of AG, but this does not include the power to interfere in the manner in which the AG exercises his powers.

459. Accordingly, and in line with Israeli practice, the Minister of Justice, like the government itself, does not intervene in the manner in which the AG exercises his powers. The result is that the Government bears a limited degree of public responsibility for the AG's acts. Likewise, Knesset supervision of the AG's acts and omissions is restricted. In this context, the Agranat Commission stated that 'this is the small price that must be exacted for [the need to] confer responsibility to an apolitical institution that embodies important judicial-legal qualities which independently maintain and promote the public interest in the criminal domain'. The Knesset cannot amend the decisions or the policy of the AG other than by way of legislation, and it cannot order the government to fire him. The upshot is that judicial supervision is the only form of supervision and review regarding the scope of the AG's discretion in his decisions on indictments.

460. Section 62 of the Criminal Procedure [Consolidated Version] Law states that:

> Where it appears to a prosecutor to whom the investigation material has been transmitted, that there is sufficient evidence to charge a particular person, he shall prosecute him, unless he is of the opinion that there is no public interest in the prosecution.

This section establishes the normative parameters that should guide the AG in the exercise of his powers to prosecute or to refrain from prosecuting, and it became the focus of questions pertaining to judicial review of his considerations. In this context, it must be remembered that the AG is empowered to refrain from conducting a criminal proceeding, even where the evidence suffices for a conviction, if he does not see a public interest in the conduct of the criminal proceedings.

461. All the same, it would seem that the AG is not empowered to categorically refuse to enforce particular offences. The HCJ has stated, 'For the Court to intervene in the enforcement level of any particular law it must conclude that the empowered authorities intend to abandon their duty to enforce the law … or unreasonably avoid the fulfilment of their duty'.[237] It is similarly clear that the AG is not permitted to enforce the law selectively on the basis of extraneous considerations.

462. It was specifically the concluding phrase of section 62, granting discretion to refrain from filing an indictment, which prompted a plethora of decisions. In the past, and until the present, the grounds for interference in the discretion of the AG were restricted to extreme cases only, and all of the petitions challenging the manner in which the AG exercised his discretion to prosecute have been rejected.

463. Gradually, however, the Court has broadened the scope for judicial intervention in circumstances in which the AG has decided not to prosecute because of the public interest. The leading judgment in this context was the *Ganor* decision.[238] This case dealt with the involvement of the heads of the Israeli banking establishment in the regulation of bank shares, which precipitated the collapse of the Israeli stock market in 1983. In the wake of this crisis – 'the Bank-Shares Crisis' – a public commission of enquiry was established, which ultimately found fault in the conduct of the bank heads. Nonetheless, the AG did not deem it necessary to prosecute them, claiming *inter alia* that in the circumstances, there was no public interest in doing so. A petition was filed in the HCJ, which subsequently intervened and cancelled the AG's decision. The HCJ's decision provided guidelines for the exercise

237. HCJ 6579/99 *Filber v. Israeli Government* (unpublished), cited in Rubinstein & Medina, *supra* n. 1 in p. 1014.
238. HCJ 953/89 *Ganor v. Attorney General*, 44(2) PD 485.

of discretion regarding State prosecutions, stating that the term 'public interest' represents a value judgment as to the benefit gained by society by prosecuting and the benefit gained by refraining from doing so. A public interest in avoiding prosecution exists only in cases where the prosecutor deems that the potential damage to the interests and values that the society desires to protect outweigh the interests and values that the criminal code seeks to promote by the prosecution.

Still, all attempts to judicially review the AG's decision to prosecute or not, have failed. The case of the former President of the State, Moshe Katzav, may serve as an example. In 2007, after the decision to prosecute Katzav for sexual crimes, the AG conducted two pre-trial hearings before making a final decision on the indictment. These hearings produced a particularly lenient plea-bargain deal between the prosecution and the President. This deal omitted the rape charges and resulted in a guilty plea on the less serious offences. Immediately after the deal was signed, petitions challenging the reasonableness of its terms were filed with the HCJ. Petitions seeking the annulment of the plea bargain were heard, but the majority of the expanded five-judge panel, headed by President of the Supreme Court Dorit Beinisch (who was in the minority), rejected them. Nevertheless, the media and leading legal pundits openly opposed the deal. Moreover, hostile public opinion was demonstrated through the staging of several stormy protests. However, the final decision of the Court was not to interfere with AG's discretion.

B. The Attorney General as the Guardian of the Rule of Law

464. One of the AG's central duties is to ensure that the government and the sovereign authorities conduct themselves in accordance with the law. For example, the AG examines secondary legislation before its publication. He also plays an important role in the informal supervision of the contents of coalition agreements, and is empowered to appear as a party in any proceeding – including civil, administrative and private complaints – in which there is an important public interest.[239]

465. The AG has a number of means of ensuring that governmental authorities respect and uphold the rule of law. He can order the indictment of violators of the law, and where necessary, he can apply to the Court to compel the authority to comply with the law. The rule is that:

> when representing an authority before the Court, the AG makes those claims that, in accordance with his legal understanding, justify the actions of the authority in accordance with the law. As such, if the AG deems that the

239. *See* s. 1 of the Procedure (Appearance of the Attorney General) Ordinance: 'If it appears to the Attorney-General that any right of the State of Israel or any public right or interest is or may be affected or involved by, or in any proceeding in any court … he may, at his discretion, appear in such proceeding and be heard therein.'

governmental authority is acting in violation of the law, he is entitled to notify the Court that he is unable to defend that act in Court.[240]

466. The AG is also the authorized interpreter of the law for the purposes of the government. The rule is that the AG is empowered to interpret the law, and his interpretation binds the government in all of its internal workings. The Court ruled that it is incumbent upon the AG to interpret the law and to ascertain the legality of sovereign decisions in accordance therewith, and that he is not permitted to let the sovereign make its own decision regarding the legality of its actions. A violation of the AG's guidelines, may, per se, constitute grounds for High Court intervention. Over the years, High Court rulings have conferred binding authority to the guidelines of the AG *vis-à-vis* the government, and have emphasized the Government's obligation to conduct itself accordingly.

467. Another question arising in this context as to the content of the law when the government believes that, from a legal perspective the AG's position is mistaken. Can the government ignore the AG's position and be represented by a private attorney who pleads on its behalf against the position represented by the AG? To date, these questions yet have to receive an unequivocal answer. Assuming that a judicial proceeding is underway, the AG's role is to present the Court with what he considers to be the path of action mandated by the law, even if this position does not reflect the position of the government. Accordingly, the AG may refuse to represent the government in relation to a particular issue if he deems that the government's actions will not stand up in Court, and instead he can present his own position regarding the illegality of the government's actions. Concurrently, the AG may also present government's position to the Court.[241] In exceptional cases, the AG may permit the government to be represented by its own 'private' attorney.

C. Conclusion

468. The AG commands extensive powers, and fills a singularly important public role. Proposals to distribute the powers of the AG among different bodies are occasionally raised, the aim being to prevent the concentration of such extensive powers in the hands of one authority, rendering it effectively a one-man show. Those supporting the division of his position according to his different roles claim that there ought to be an administrative-professional division between the AG's consulting functions and prosecuting functions. The function of providing legal consultation to the government requires an ongoing connection with sovereign position

240. HCJ 4267/93 *Amitai-Citizens for Proper Government and Integrity v. Prime Minister*, 47(5) PD 441.

241. This has occurred once, in the petitions requesting that the Prime Minister be instructed to dismiss a minister and Deputy Minister from their positions, following the submission of indictments against them. In these cases, the attorney general supported the petitioners' positions, in opposition to the Prime Minister's position. *See* HCJ 3094/93 *The Movement for the Quality of Government v. Israeli Government*, 47(5) PD 404.

holders, and as such, the AG should not be the one to decide on prosecution, occasionally of the very same position holders. Nor is it desirable that there be even a semblance of an impression that the AG's decision, in his capacity as the head of the law enforcement branches, is influenced by the fact that he also serves as the AG. The two roles are substantively different, and may even be conflictual. The issue is still prominent on the public agenda, and is the source of a public controversy, which has led to further proposals to split the AG's powers. It would appear that the nature of the role should be regulated and defined in a special law for the AG. Such a law would provide substantive solutions to the various problems attendant to the multiplicity of the powers conferred upon him.

§2. Organs of State Control

I. The State Comptroller

469. A State Comptroller (SC) operates in Israel, whose office and powers are outlined in the Basic Law: State Comptroller, and in the State Comptroller Law, 1958. State audit, or inspection, is an important tool in the hands of the Knesset for overseeing the Government's activities, and this function is carried out by the SC on the Knesset's behalf. 'In carrying out his function, the Comptroller shall be responsible only to the Knesset and shall not be dependent upon the Government'. The Knesset appoints the SC pursuant to sections 7–8 of Basic Law: State Comptroller, and receives the SC's audit reports.

470. The SC is an independent body, uninvolved in political life, and both he and his staff are bound by rigid restrictions regarding their work, both during their service and thereafter. Section 9 of Basic Law: State Comptroller enumerates the bodies audited by the SC, including Government ministries and offices, local authorities and other state institutions and state-supported bodies.

471. The scope of the SC's audit is particularly broad: It extends to accounting, inspection of administrative propriety, compliance with the law, responses to public complaints, working efficiency of the audited bodies, learning, internalization and implementation of the findings of previous audit reports, and examination of the integrity in the ongoing work of the audited bodies.

472. For the purposes of discharging his functions, the SC is vested with a relatively broad range of powers. Audited bodies are obligated to submit annual financial reports to the SC, together with a report detailing their activities, and any other information requested by the SC. His investigative powers resemble those bestowed upon state commissions of enquiry, including the power to summons any person to testify before him and to submit information to him. The Knesset Committee for State Audit Affairs discusses the Comptroller's reports, after which it submits its conclusions to the Knesset. The Committee is similarly entitled to order the establishment of a state commission of enquiry to examine a particular issue dealt with in the SC's report. In the event of the audit report raising suspicions of the commission of criminal acts, the SC must bring the matter to the attention of the attorney general, who is then required to report to the Comptroller regarding his handling of the matter.

473. The prevailing approach to date has been that the HCJ almost totally avoids judicial review with respect to the validity of the SC's findings, preferring to leave the task of clarification in the hands of the Knesset. In the *Turner* case, the HCJ ruled that, generally, there was no justification for judicially reviewing the findings of the State Comptroller. 'Objections and appeals should be discussed within the framework of the right of response given to the inspected authorities ... and in the course of reporting to the State Audit Committee, which conducts a detailed discussion of the findings of the report'.[242] Judicial review is limited to the procedural aspects of the audit, and primarily considers the right to be heard of any person liable to be affected by the findings of the audit. The Court refused to order the SC to give details regarding his audit findings. Nevertheless, recently there has been a growing readiness on the SC's part to deviate from its long accepted policy of anonymity, by mentioning the names of the people under inspection. According to its current policy, in cases concerning exploitation of office, or suspicion of dishonesty, the SC no longer avoids publication of the names of those involved. The accepted policy today is that the publication of the inspection findings is one of the central tools of enforcement at the disposal of the SC. The Court noted that 'a public stigma attaches to officeholders as a result of his integrity being impugned by an authority such as the State Comptroller and the high public profile of his findings and determinations'.

474. By law, audit findings have no binding normative status. The SC has no power to enforce the reports, so his power derives primarily from media coverage of his findings and recommendations, and the force of his personality. The practice over the last few years has been to divide the reports into different sections, and to periodically submit the various sections over the course of the year, as well as initiating special reports on subjects currently on the public agenda. Recent years have seen a tendency towards buttressing the status of the audit findings. Until now, case law has refrained from compelling audited bodies to implement the SC's recommendations for rectifying flaws, although it did determine that audited bodies are obliged to take the SC's recommendations into account, and to furnish reasonable explanation for its failure to do so in any particular case. For example, the Court noted that 'proper administration requires that the SC's substantive criticism of the inspected body not remain a dead letter'.[243]

475. In 2001, a number of amendments were introduced to the State Comptroller Law. Under the new provisions, an audited body is obligated to appoint a team,

242. HCJ 4914/94 *Terner v. State Comptroller*, 49(3) PD 771.
243. HCJ 766/87 *Zuker v. Tel-Aviv Jaffa Mayor*, 42(2) PD 610–619.

headed by the inspected body's general manager, and charged with the rectification of defects noted in the SC's inspection. The head of the audited body is instructed to report to the SC (and to the government) regarding the actions taken to rectify those defects. The law allows the inspected body 'to postpone the rectification of a particular flaw' but obligates it to report such decisions to the SC, stating the reasons for such postponement.

A. *The State Comptroller as the Ombudsman for Public Complaints*

476. In addition to his function of State audit, the SC also functions as the Commissioner for Public Complaints. Any person is entitled to complain about 'an act directly injurious to, or directly withholding a benefit from the complainant'. However, if the complainant is a Knesset member, he can also file a complaint regarding an act that is 'directly injurious to, or directly withholding a benefit from another person, and which [in both cases] is contrary to the law or done without lawful authority or contrary to good administration or involving a law too inflexible or flagrant injustice'.

477. Similarly, the Ombudsman may also adjudicate legal claims, and nothing prevents him from hearing matters that may ultimately be subject to judicial review. The Ombudsman is also conferred far-reaching powers which protect a civil servant who complains about an 'act of corruption committed in the body in which he works'. In respect of such an employee, the Ombudsman may 'give any order he deems appropriate, including a temporary injunction, to protect the worker's rights'. The intention is to forestall situations in which an employee who complains about acts of corruption committed by his superiors ends up being punished or even dismissed. Accordingly, the Ombudsman is entitled to order the retraction of the dismissal, or to award special indemnification for the worker, in cash or in rights, or to order that he be transferred to another position in his employer's service.

478. In respect of the Ombudsman, section 45(b) of the State Comptroller Law provides that 'No Court shall entertain an application for relief against decisions of findings of the Ombudsman in the matter of a complainant'. Similarly, section 38(5) states that the Ombudsman is not permitted to investigate a complaint as to 'a matter pending in a Court or tribunal or in which a Court or tribunal has given a decision with regard to the substance thereof'.

II. Commissions of Enquiry

479. Israeli law provides for the establishment of three central forms of commissions of inquiry: Public Commissions of Enquiry, State Commissions of Enquiry and Parliamentary Commissions of Enquiry.

A. Public Commission of Enquiry

480. Public Commissions of Enquiry are investigative or examining committees comprising employees of the administrative authority as well as other position holders e.g., public figures and experts. In the public administration, this form of enquiry is an accepted tool for gleaning relevant information by way of fact finding, investigations and hearings of the opinions of interested and/or relevant bodies, all aimed towards the crystallization of recommendations. The establishment of this kind of commission does not require statutory authorization. Essentially, these committees operate 'internally' and function as auxiliary tools within the authority itself, as part of its system of exercising sovereign discretion.

B. State Commission of Enquiry

481. These are commissions of enquiry established pursuant to the Commissions of Enquiry Law, 1968 for the purpose of factual clarification and recommendations regarding matters deemed by the government to be of vital public importance. Since the Agranat Commission (which examined the events surrounding the Yom Kippur War in 1973), the State Commissions of Enquiry have attained broad public standing, so that their actions are today perceived as being primarily for 'external' purposes. They are established by a government decision and serve as an important means for examining the actions of government authorities, and even of position holders within the public service. Their recommendations concerning personal liability and structural changes have decisive influence. In fact, a State Commission of Enquiry is strikingly similar to a judicial forum.

482. The composition of the commission is determined by the President of the Supreme Court in a manner that occasionally reflects the aspiration of ensuring representation in the commission of various sectors relevant to the matter under investigation. The commission is headed by a judge (usually a justice of the Supreme Court), but its panels may also include non-legal position holders. The commission is not bound by procedural or evidentiary law. Nevertheless, though not a judicial forum, the commission's findings have legal consequences, especially in relation to the personal responsibility of persons serving in public positions.

483. Over the last decade, no commissions of enquiry have been established. The turning point was the Second Lebanon war, in 2006.[244] The war evoked a sharp sense of failure among the Israeli public and the feeling that, overall, the war had been grossly mismanaged. Consequently, immediately after the ceasefire, a public campaign began, calling upon the Government to establish a state commission of

244. On 12 Jul. 2006, Hezbollah forces opened fire on Israel with a barrage of missiles targeted at Israeli northern settlements and kidnapped two IDF soldiers from Israeli territory to Lebanon. The Israeli government immediately convened an emergency meeting in which it decided on an Israeli military response. The fighting that ensued in the wake of these events (the Second Lebanon War) lasted thirty-four days.

enquiry to investigate the failures of the war, and demanding the resignations of the national leadership, namely, the Prime Minister, the Minister of Defence and the Chief of Staff. After much hesitation, the government decided against the establishment of a state commission of enquiry, deciding instead to set up a 'governmental commission of inquiry' to examine the conduct of the political and military authorities at all stages of the war. The circumstances surrounding the Commission's establishment generated expectations for the Government's resignation in its wake, and accordingly, for over a year, the Israeli public waited impatiently for its conclusions. As mentioned, the public sentiment was that the war had been a dismal failure, the likes of which compelled the politicians involved to acknowledge their personal responsibility and resign. Accordingly, it came as a great surprise when the final report lacked personal conclusions relating to specific individuals and omitted, intentionally, personal recommendations regarding the continued service of the senior office holders involved and responsible for the failures of the war. Since then, no State commission of enquiry has ever been established.

484. The Government is the body empowered to establish a state commission of enquiry. According to section 1 of the Commissions of Enquiry Law: 'When it appears to the Government that a matter exists which is of vital public importance and requires clarification, it may decide to set up a commission of inquiry which will inquire into the matter and shall make a report to it.' At the same time, an amendment adopted in 1995 determined that, following the submission of the State Comptroller's report, the Knesset Committee for State Audit Affairs was empowered to set up a commission of inquiry which would be subject to the Commissions of Inquiry Law. On the basis of this provision, the Beisky Commission was set up to investigate the bank shares crisis.

485. The commission's powers are demarcated in its letter of appointment, but in fact it has relatively broad discretion regarding the areas of its investigation. Naturally, the letter of appointment requires interpretation, which is the role of the commission. The commission may decide to investigate and deliberate on the background to the particular factual occurrence under investigation, and the scope of such an investigation. The accepted view is that investigative proceedings within the framework of a commission of enquiry are not a substitute for criminal proceedings. In most of the commissions of enquiry established by force of the law, the commissions have faced the question of the personal liability of office holders, and on a number of occasions, these proceedings have led to the imposition of criminal culpability, in a separate proceeding. This view is based on the recognition that the commission's mandate is not limited to 'legal' responsibility, but also extends to 'public responsibility'. In fact, the Commissions of Enquiry Law explicitly refers to the possibility that the commission's findings may raise 'a suspicion that a particular person committed an offence'.

486. Testimony given before the Commission of Enquiry, and the report itself, will not serve as evidence in a legal proceeding. The Commission of Enquiry is intended primarily for the imposition of personal responsibility in the public sense and not as a substitute for judicial proceedings. This point was noted by the Court in the *Elon* case, stating: 'A commission of enquiry should not be established if its purpose is to fulfil the function of the Court, i.e., to determine the guilt or innocence of a person suspected of having committed a criminal offence.'[245] For example, the second Shamgar Commission, established to examine the circumstances surrounding the assassination of Prime Minister Rabin, refrained from deliberating on the guilt of the assassin. The Or Commission, set up to investigate the events of October 2000, decided to avoid deliberations over the guilt of the security forces who opened fire on the demonstrators, sufficing with a recommendation to open a criminal investigation into the matter.

487. A State Commission of Enquiry has broad investigative powers. It may summon any person to appear before the commission to give testimony and produce documents in his possession, and it may enforce compliance with that summons, in a manner resembling the powers of the Court in a civil proceeding, and may even fine a person who does not obey with the summons.

488. Under section 18 of the Commission of Enquiry Law, the deliberations of the commission are conducted in public. Its report is published for the entire public, unless the commission has decided against publication, whether in full or in part. The report of the commission of enquiry includes a detailed presentation of its factual findings, and as a rule, also includes recommendations regarding future courses of action. The Government is obliged to accept the commission's factual findings, this being one of the goals of its establishment. However, the Government is not obliged to accept all of the commission's recommendations, which are for the government's consideration and decision only, by reason of the government's exclusive mandate to formulate policy. However, beyond the question of whether the recommendations are accepted by the government, the commission's recommendations are of singular importance with respect to public figures involved in the matter under investigation. The custom is for the Government to accept the commission's recommendations concerning personal conduct and liability.

C. Parliamentary Commission of Enquiry

489. In addition to the State Commission of Enquiry, in recent years, use has increasingly been made of the parliamentary commission of enquiry. As mentioned above, the Knesset Committee for State Audit Affairs is empowered to establish a commission of enquiry regarding matters raised in the State Comptroller's report. In relation to other matters, the Knesset is empowered to set up 'Parliamentary Commissions of Enquiry'. According to section 2 of Basic Law: The Knesset, 'The Knesset may appoint commissions of enquiry – either by empowering one of the permanent committees in that respect or by electing a commission from among its members – to investigate matters designated by the Knesset; the powers and functions of a commission of enquiry shall be prescribed by the Knesset'. The members

245. HCJ 152/82 *Elon v. Israeli Government*, 36(4) PD 449.

of these commissions are Knesset members. In most cases, the commission's deliberations concern substantive or professional matters, as distinct from political or party matters.

490. The Knesset Regulations regulate the manner of setting up a Parliamentary Commission of Enquiry. In the past, this institution was almost never used. However, since the 11th Knesset, a whole series of Parliamentary Commissions of Enquiry have been established. To date, the reports of these commissions have not succeeded in commanding the esteem and public stature which are bestowed upon the reports of the State Commissions of Enquiry.

Part III. The State and Its Subdivisions

Chapter 1. State Form

491. Geographically, and demographically, the State of Israel is a relatively small country and not highly decentralized. It lacks any of the regular hallmarks of a federal system, and only the area of local government is decentralized.

492. The Israeli system of government is likewise a particularly centralized system. Legally and formally, political power is concentrated in the hands of the central government, vested with most of the substantive powers, both on a national and local level. Centrality of government is not just the by-product of the state's small geophysical dimensions, but also of the circumstances of its establishment – being part of the British legacy that preceded its establishment, and particularly as a result of the military and social challenges that confronted the state immediately upon its establishment, all of which necessitated coordination between all the governmental, sovereign bodies, leading to the strengthening of the central government.

Chapter 2. Decentralized Authorities

493. The structure of local government in Israel is an extension of the framework that crystallized under British rule in Mandate Palestine. This framework was based on a number of local governing units that were consolidated into legal structures, finding their expression in the Municipalities Ordinance of 1934, and thereafter in the Local Councils Ordinance of 1940. The Jewish Yishuv in Palestine ascribed tremendous importance to the development of the mechanisms for local Jewish government, which constituted the first steps of Jewish autonomy, albeit on a local level, and which enabled independent management of public life. With the establishment of the State, the legislature ensured the legislative and administrative continuity of the local government structure, and determined that the local councils and other local authorities would continue to operate within the same jurisdictions, and in the framework of the same powers that found expression in the aforementioned ordinances.

494. In terms of the general structure of the local government, almost the entire area of the state is 'covered' by a network of local authorities, comprising about 60 municipalities, about 140 local councils and about 50 regional councils. In other words, all told, in Israel there are over 260 local authorities, ranging from the large cities whose populations exceed 200,000, to small settlements numbering less than 2,000 people. There are two categories of local authorities: the municipal authorities and the village authorities. The municipal authorities are further classified into two separate legal categories, namely, cities and local councils.

495. The municipal authorities are governed by two bodies: the Head of the Authority (Mayor) and the council, both of which are elected by the residents. The council functions as the municipal legislature, whereas the Mayor constitutes the executive branch. The Local Authorities Law of 1975 was intended to lead to the direct election of the Head of the local authority by the residents, thereby ensuring that the Mayor would not be dependent upon incidental, chance coalitions, but in fact it revolutionized the area of municipal government in Israel. Until its enactment, residents of the local authority would choose a group of people who subsequently comprised the council of the local authority, and the elected council of the authority would choose the Head of the Authority: the Mayor, or the Head of the Local Council. However, just as it chose the Mayor, the council was also empowered to dismiss him. This state of affairs gave rise to a glut of defections between and among the parties that constituted the city council, and to the phenomenon of 'crossing the floor'. Such defections led to the dismissal of the Mayor and his replacement by another. The legislature therefore decided to separate the function of Mayor from the composition of the council, thereby releasing him from dependence on the benevolence of the council in order to perform his executive functions.

496. The central difference between cities and local councils is in the number of residents. In the past, there was an unofficial rule stating that a settlement with a population of over 2,000 merited the status of a 'local council', whereas a population exceeding 20,000 residents usually entitled it to the status of a 'city'.[246] The Municipalities Ordinance and the Local Councils Ordinance were recently amended, and today the minimum number of residents required for the status of a city and for a local council is 10,000, with an exceptions provision empowering a minister, in special cases, to grant a particular area the status of a city or a local council if the number of residents exceeds 5,000.[247]

497. The regional councils consist of a number of settlements (all of which were originally cooperative agricultural settlements). In terms of governmental hierarchy, the regional council is at the highest level, having control of the entire area and responsibility for provision of services to all the residents located within its jurisdiction. The local committees are at the lowest level. These are bodies that represent the specific settlements within the territorial expanse of the regional council. Israel has over 970 local committees, which are associated within the framework of 53 regional councils, and which rule over 80% of the territory of the state, despite the fact that their population constitutes less than 10% of the total state citizenry.[248]

498. The Centre for Local Government in Israel is a body which consolidates and unifies all of the local authorities in the State of Israel. The Centre was constituted in 1938 and since then has dealt with the representation of the local authorities and their leaders in their relationships with the state bodies such as the Knesset, the Government and its ministries.

§1. The Local Authorities' Historical Background

499. The structure of government in the local authorities originated in the first decade of the State, and was based on the concept of local autonomy and a cooperative-agrarian world view, parallel to the centralistic British municipal model that reigned in Israel prior to the establishment of the state. The first local authorities to be created during the Mandate period were intended to provide the Jewish settlements with the broadest possible autonomy, and were regarded as an essential tool for the achievement of the national goals of the Zionist movement. With the establishment of the state, the need arose to confront formidable difficulties, both domestically and externally, and simultaneously to continue providing municipal services to the entire state population, which had grown dramatically in the wake of mass immigration. Israel's leaders therefore decided to preserve the structure of local government in the same format as it had existed under the British Mandate.

246. D. Newman, 'Creating Homogenous Space: The Evolution of Israel's Regional Councils', in *Israel: The First Decade of Independence*, 495–496 (S.I. Troen and N. Lucas eds., 1995).

247. For elaboration on this subject *see*: I. Rozen-Zvi, *Taking Space Seriously: Law Space and Society*, Contemporary Israel (2004), pp. 23–27. *See also* in: I. Rozen-Zvi, *The Place of Justice: The Law of Local Government and Social Injustice*, 28(2) Y'unei Mishpat (In Hebrew) 2004, 417.

248. For a discussion of the structure of Regional Councils, *see* D. Newman & L. Applebaum, *Conflicting Objectives for Rural Local Governments: Service Position to Exurban Communities in Israel*, 13 Environment & Planning C (1995) 253.

The fact that the population of Mandate Palestine had comprised a variety of ethnic groups, religions and nationalities intensified the urgency of preserving these structures. Furthermore, the various villages, cooperative settlements and Kibbutzim also reflected a broad spectrum of political-ideological positions, thus constituting self-contained homogenous political units. In fact, the local authorities were the natural extension of the political communities that preceded the establishment of the State.

500. With the establishment of Israel, the local government was regarded as the executive arm of the central government, which required local branches for the efficient provision of services to the residents of the state. In the words of Issachar Rozen-Zvi, the local authority was no more than a 'branch' or an 'extension' of the central government, intended exclusively for administrative convenience and efficiency, and as such it was not an autonomous sovereign in its domain, being powerless to perform any action apart from the matters specifically and explicitly delegated to it by the central government.[249]

§2. The Law of Local Government

501. The formal standing conferred upon a local authority under local government law is that of a 'contractor', or an 'agent', of the central government, which is absolutely subordinate to the authority of the Ministry of the Interior. The Ministry of the Interior has the exclusive power to establish or abolish a local authority, or to unify a number of local authorities into one authority, to annex territories of the local authorities, and to demarcate its borders anew.

502. The central government is vested with powers of supervision over the local government, and the Ministry of the Interior is empowered to cancel any decision of the local authority, and in certain cases, even to arrogate its powers to itself, and act in its place. Any act of local government is conditional upon the approval of one of the Government ministries, usually the Ministry of the Interior. For example, the Ministry of the Interior approves the authority's budget and any loan it takes. The local authority has particularly limited discretion in determining the rates of municipal taxes (*arnona*) and the levels of deductions and exemptions, and any deviation requires the approval of the Minister of the Interior. The Education Ministry is required to approve the opening of new schools located within the borders of the authority, and the authorities are subject to the various government ministries (such as Interior, Health, Internal Security, Labour, and Environment), in all matters related to their activities as licensing authorities under the Licensing of Businesses Law.

503. By force of the principle of legality, a local authority can only operate within the framework of powers explicitly conferred on it by law, and any action performed by an authority without having been explicitly authorized is null and void

249. In his article 'The Place of Justice: The Law of Local Government and Social Injustice'.

due to the doctrine of *ultra vires*. The *ultra vires* doctrine was applied for the first time in 1951 in the case of *Chet v. Haifa*:

> The municipality is a body created by law, having no existence other than by force of law. The scope of its powers is defined by law and any matter diverging from its legal boundaries is null and void (*ultra vires*). In considering whether a particular matter is in excess of the council's power or not, the criteria is not whether it is enjoined by the Municipalities Ordinance or not, but rather whether it is permitted thereunder. In other words, it is not sufficient that the matter is not forbidden; it must actually be permitted in order to be valid in the eyes of the law. The law does not leave an empty vacuum to be filled at will.[250]

504. Since the establishment of the State, in a series of judgments, the Court has annulled decisions of local authorities that were adopted without explicit legislative empowerment. An example of this is the judgment in the matter of *Sh.Z.M v. Jerusalem Municipality*.[251] In that case, the Jerusalem municipality refused to grant the applicants a license for a shop that sold sexual aids and pornographic literature, basing its refusal to grant the license on democratic grounds, that is, the wishes of the local residents. The Municipality claimed that Jerusalem is a unique city, comprising a variety of populations, characterized by a high degree of cultural tension. The sensitivity involved precludes the establishment of a business of this nature in Jerusalem without harming this delicate balance. The Municipality argued that a business of this kind would gravely offend the lifestyles of the religious Muslim population, the Christian population and the religious Jewish population; an offence which they were incapable of sustaining without severe harm to their own well being and the public peace in general. The Court ruled that the Municipality's decision was unauthorized because there was no explicit provision in the laws regarding registration of businesses empowering it to withhold a license on those grounds. The Court's judgment emphasized that 'with all my sympathy for the commendable and desirable motives of the Jerusalem Municipal Council … neither the Municipality nor any other local authority are the institution charged by the Legislature as the custodian of public feelings'.

505. Another example in this context is the *Solodkin* case. The adjudication in this case concerned the local authority's power to prohibit the sale of pork in their jurisdiction, which meant forbidding the opening of shops that would sell un-kosher meat. In its judgment, the Court ruled that a balance must be struck between the desire to protect the religious and national feelings from the offence caused to them by the sale of pork, and the protection of freedom of conscience and the freedom of occupation of individuals wishing to purchase and to sell pork. The Court ruled that in the decision of any local authority on such a matter, two principal considerations are required: the protection of the feelings of the offended residents, which was dependent upon the proximity of their residential areas to the place where pork was

250. HCJ 36/51 *Chet v. Haifa Municipality*, 5 PD 1553 at p. 1557.
251. HCJ 230/73 *Sh.Z.M v. Jerusalem Municipality*, 28(2) PD 113.

sold, and the percentage they constituted of the entire population; and on the other hand, the need to ensure the possibility of purchasing pork at a near and accessible location:

> The local authority must examine the nature of the territorial unit; it must assess the degree of social consensus in that unit, and its degree of mutual tolerance. The different alternatives must be considered, and in particular, there must be an examination of the availability in the immediate vicinity of shops that sell pork and pork products.[252]

506. The Court was aware that, in principle, the local authority was empowered to forbid the sale of pork in a particular area. The local authority has discretion in this area, and it 'must consider the composition of the population of each particular place, its habits, lifestyles, and the general character of the area'.

507. Notwithstanding these guidelines, the Courts have tended to avoid interfering in all matters relating to the determination of municipal borders. By law, the Minister of the Interior has exclusive authority to constitute and to abolish local authorities, to unify them, and to delineate their borders. In this regard, the Court has ruled that only rarely would it interfere with the Minister of the Interior's power to establish or to alter the borders of the local authorities. The Court emphasized the breadth of the discretion granted to the Minister of the Interior, and clarified that it would only interfere in exceptional cases in which the Minister had exceeded the scope of his powers, and his considerations attested to arbitrariness or some other defect.[253] In the *Rishon Le-Tzion Municipality* case, the Court stated that:

> The only question which we can ask ourselves is whether the Minister of the Interior was aware of what he was doing, whether he was acting intentionally, and whether he was not motivated by extraneous motives. If the answer to these is affirmative, this terminates our examination.[254]

508. Despite the broad supervisory powers of the central government over the local government, in fact, the overall degree of government supervision over the local authorities has been negligible. Paradoxically, it is precisely the formal legal structure, conferring the central power with numerous supervisory powers, which is nonetheless one of the factors responsible for the absence of actual supervision. A large number of government ministries have power in this realm, and the lack of coordination between them frequently enables the local government to exceed the formal boundaries of its powers, preventing the central government from exercising effective supervision over the local authorities.[255] The view has thus been expressed that, at least in certain areas, Israel has been witness to a steadily increasing degree

252. HCJ 953/01 *Solodkin v. The Municipality of Be'it Shemesh* (in English at Israel Law Reports [2004] IsrLR 232).
253. *See* HCJ 51/68 *Azur Local Municipality v. Minister of the Interior*, 22(2) PD 226; HCJ 94/74 *Rishon Le-Tzion Municipality* v. *Minister of the Interior*, 28(2) PD 711.
254. *Ibid.*, p. 716.
255. I. Rozen-Zvi, *ibid.*

of 'de facto decentralization' of powers since the 1980s. This decentralization finds expression in the broad powers conferred to the local planning and construction authorities, in the transition to independent financing of the local authorities, and in substantially less governmental participation in the activities of the local authorities.

509. Since the 1980s, there has also been a revolution in the budgetary structure of the local authorities. As a result of various legal changes and innovations, the relative proportion of independent income in the authorities' budgets has risen considerably, and there has been a dramatic, parallel decrease in government participation. These changes have increased the independence of a number of the authorities, which have simultaneously become less dependent upon government participation in their budgets.

Part IV. Citizenship and the Administration of Justice

Chapter 1. Rules Concerning Citizenship and the Relevance of Citizenship

§1. General

510. The State of Israel is a Jewish state (variously referred to the State of the Jews or the State of the Jewish people) in the sense that it is the political framework in which the Jewish people's right to self-determination is realized. As a Jewish state, one of its constitutive characteristics is the right of every Jew to immigrate to the State of Israel, as a state in which the Jewish people will constitute a majority, in which Hebrew is the primary and official language of the state, and in which the principal festivals and symbols are Jewish. The State of Israel is therefore a 'nation state' i.e., a state in which the Jewish people exercises its right to national independence.

511. The issue of Israeli citizenship is particular and fundamental. It is, in many ways, the essence and the history of the State of Israel. Even in the Declaration of the Independence, it was determined that the State of Israel would be open to Jewish immigration (*aliyah*) and the gathering of those in exile. There were hundreds of thousands of Jewish refugees, both from Europe and from Arab states in North Africa, for whom the nascent Jewish state was the only path to security and life from post-Holocaust Europe and from the Arab states in which they could no longer reside from the moment the state was established. It was thus imperative to enact legislation that would allow the immediate granting of citizenship to any Jew desiring to be absorbed into Israel. The principal legislation in this context dealt with the right of 'return' or repatriation, and the ability of Jews 'returning' to Israel to receive almost automatic Israeli citizenship.

512. The question of the conditions to be satisfied for receiving citizenship involves national and personal aspects. From the national perspective, the conditions prescribed for obtaining citizenship are determinative for the character of the state, and important also from a demographic perspective. The preservation of a Jewish majority among Israeli citizens is largely dependent upon a policy of granting citizenship that expresses clear preference for Jews as opposed to Arabs. Likewise, the policy for granting citizenship decisively affects the nature of the State's

'Jewish' character, which gives rise to disputes over the definition of a 'Jew' which would gain preferential treatment in acquiring citizenship. These questions are complemented by the personal circumstances of each applicant interested in attaching his fate to that of the state, for, like other welfare states, the State of Israel is also required to deal with the desires of foreigners to join it, whether temporarily or on a permanent basis.

513. In general terms, immigration and citizenship procedures in Israel are characterized by the ease with which citizenship is granted to Jews. The accepted understanding is that an essential condition for the preservation of Israel as a Jewish state, in which the Jewish people realize its right to self-determination, is the existence of a decisive Jewish majority. This concept receives expression in the recognition of the right of every Jew to receive citizenship immediately upon treading on Israeli soil ('Citizenship by Virtue of Return') after having expressed his desire to settle in Israel.[256] Automatic citizenship is thus granted, not qualified by fulfilment of any other obligations, or even by the requirement of residence in the state for a certain minimum period. In fact, as will be observed below, the Court has recognized that every Jew has a basic, innate right to receive Israeli citizenship, and denial of that right is only possible in exceptional circumstances. Hence, the right to citizenship under the principle of return is also given to 'a child and grandchild of a Jew, the spouse of a Jew, the spouse of the child of a Jew and the spouse of the grandchild of a Jew, even if the Jew in respect of whom the right is claimed has not even immigrated to Israel'.

514. However, the potential for non-Jews (or those who are not the relatives of Jews) to receive citizenship is highly restricted, and characterized by the granting of broad discretion to the Minister of the Interior. The strictest restrictions, even including the total negation of the possibility of attaining citizenship (or even permanent residence status) are imposed on Palestinians, in view of the desire to ensure the preservation of a Jewish majority among the Israeli citizenry and in view of Israeli security considerations.

§2. The Law of Return

515. By virtue of the Law of Return, the State recognizes the right of every Jew to receive immediate citizenship upon arriving in Israel, after having expressed his desire to settle there permanently. Section 4B of the Law of Return defines a Jew as 'a person who was born of a Jewish mother, or has become converted to Judaism and who is not a member of another religion'. In relation to the family members of a Jew, section 4A(a) stipulates that the law does not apply to a person 'who has been a Jew and has voluntarily changed his religion'. Furthermore, section 4B of the Law provides that 'For the purposes of this Law, 'Jew' means a person who was born of

256. Section 3 of the Law of Return, 1950 and s. 2 of the Citizenship Law, 1952.

a Jewish mother, or has become converted to Judaism and who is not a member of another religion'.

516. The aforementioned definition of 'Jew' did not, however, appear in the original version of the law, which did not actually define what the term 'Jew' meant. This definition was added by an amendment to the law in 1970, in the wake of two controversial Supreme Court rulings, the first being the *Rufeisen* case in 1962, and the second being the *Shalit* case in 1970. In the first case, the Court refused to grant a right of return to a Jew who had become a Catholic, and whose claim to being Jewish was based on the fact that under Jewish religious law, having been born to a Jewish mother, he was Jewish. In the absence of a positive statutory definition of the term 'Jew', the majority ruled that the 'cultural-national' definition of the term should be applied, i.e., the definition of 'Jew' should be consistent with the accepted view among Zionist thinkers and the Israeli public, which was that a Jew who had converted to another religion had thereby severed his connection with the Jewish people,[257] and could therefore no longer be considered Jewish.

517. The second case concerned Benjamin Shalit, an officer in the Israeli Army, who, while studying abroad, married a non-Jewish, Scottish woman. After coming with his non-Jewish wife to Israel, and following the birth of their two children, Shalit attempted to register his children in accordance with the Registry Law, both in the system designated for religion, as having no religion, and in the system of national affiliation, as Jews. The registration clerk rejected his request that his children be registered as Jewish in the national affiliation system, as a result of which Shalit petitioned the Supreme Court.[258] Shalit argued that a distinction ought to be made between questions of religion and of nationality, contending that a person could belong to the Jewish nation without necessarily being a member of the Jewish religion. In his view, the proper criterion for assessing whether or not a person belongs to the Jewish nation was the criterion of identification with the Israeli-Jewish culture and values, and in his view, his children satisfied that criterion. In an unprecedented (at the time) panel of nine justices, the Supreme Court called upon the Government to delete the national affiliation rubric from the Population Registry, thus obviating the need to decide a question (of the children's 'Jewishness') which, as stated by then President Agranat, was 'essentially ideological and not legal, and is the source of deep dispute among different groups in Israeli society'. The Government refrained from assenting to the request. Accordingly, the Court had no choice but to rule on the matter, and by a majority of five against four it decided to grant the petition and instructed that the children be registered as belonging to the Jewish nation, thus accepting the proposition that national affiliation was a question of a subjective definition (clearly in contradiction to the Halakhic position). The judgment was erroneously understood as reflecting a substantive decision on the status of a Jew for the purposes of the Law of Return, and provoked a public storm and political crisis.

257. HCJ 72/62 *Rufeisen v. Minister of the Interior*, 16(4) PD 2428.
258. HCJ 58/68 *Shalit v. Minister of the Interion*, 23(2) PD 477.

518. In response to the rulings in *Rufeisen* and *Shalit*, in 1970 the Knesset adopted an amendment to the Law of Return (and to the Population Registry Law). This amendment gave rise to the enactment of section 4B, which stated that 'For the purposes of this Law, "Jew" means a person who was born of a Jewish mother, or has become converted to Judaism and who is not a member of another religion'. The result was that the first part of the law adopted the position of Jewish religious law with respect to the requirement of maternal lineage (i.e., a Jew must be born to a Jewish mother), whereas the concluding part adopted the cultural-national definition (i.e., a Jew is not a member of another religion). A similar provision was also adopted in the Population Registry Law, but in order to prevent the abridgement of the rights of a child born to a non-Jewish mother, section 4A(a) was added to the Law of Return, which as mentioned above, conferred the right of return upon a child and grandchild of a Jew, the spouse of a Jew, the spouse of the child of a Jew and the spouse of the grandchild of a Jew. As mentioned above, in the concluding part of the law, the right of return was denied to a person who had been a Jew and who had voluntarily converted to another religion.

519. The Supreme Court has yet to rule on the interpretation of the term 'converted' in the definition of 'Jew' in section 4A of the law. In section 4B the Knesset intentionally refrained from determining that a Jew was one who 'had converted in accordance with the Halakhah', thus leaving open the question of the validity of the conversion performed by non-orthodox communities. In series of judgments, the Court has ruled that, for purposes of population registration, the validity of a non-orthodox conversion should be validated.[259]

520. Israeli immigration policy thus reflects an absolute preference for Jews (and the family members of a Jew), due to the automatic citizenship conferred upon every Jew arriving in Israel, who expresses a desire to settle there, together with the almost impregnable barrier preventing those who are not Jewish from receiving Israeli citizenship.

521. During the early years of the Israeli State, in addition to providing immediate citizenship for homeless Jewish refugees from persecution, who had no other place to go, the Law of Return was a crucial demographic tool in the creation of a decisive Jewish majority among Israeli citizens. Today, too, the Law of Return continues to fulfil its role in the preservation of that majority. In maintaining a Jewish majority the state does not only suffice with the automatic conferral of citizenship upon Jews coming to Israel, but also allocates large portions of the public coffers to the encouragement and promotion of Jewish immigration to Israel (*aliyah*), which also includes sending emissaries abroad from Israel and granting financial benefits to new (Jewish) immigrants.

---

259. HCJ 239/86 *Shoshana Miller v. Minister of the Interior*, 40(4) PD 436; H.C. 264/87 *United Religious Sepharadic Jews-Shas v. Director of the Population Authority in Min. of Interior*, 43(2) PD 728; H.C. 1031/93 *Pessaro (Goldstein) v. Minister of the Interior*, 49(4) PD 66.

522. It should be remembered that the preference of national ethnic groups is accepted practice in many democracies around the world (albeit not with the same intensity as the practice in Israel), falling within the legal rubric of legitimate repatriation laws. There are three categories of justifications for the existing immigration policy, despite its possible criticism on the grounds of discrimination. First, it may derive from the right of the Jews of the world to immigrate and become citizens in the state in which they realize the Jewish people's national right to self-determination. Second, it is based on recognition of the collective right of the Jewish nation to absorb and grant citizenship of the country designated for its self-determination, to the specific members of the public needed in order to realize that right. Finally, there is recognition of the collective right of the Jewish people to prefer, for immigration and citizenship purposes, those belonging to their own national community.

523. In other words, one of the justifications of the Law of Return is the recognition of every person's right to immigrate to the state in which the right to self-determination of the nation of which he is a part is realized. The second justification for the current immigration preferences is the recognition of the Jewish people's collective right to absorb and grant citizenship to the public it requires in order to realize its right to self-determination. An essential precondition for Israel's maintenance of a Jewish state, i.e., one in which the Jewish people realizes its right to self-determination, is the existence and preservation of a decisive Jewish majority among the state citizenry. So long as there is fear of the disappearance of the Jewish majority, or fear of other grave harm to the interests of the Jewish majority in the event of the loss of a Jewish majority, the continued application of the Law of Return can be justified.

§3. Acquiring Citizenship by Return

524. Israeli citizenship is acquired exclusively in accordance with the provisions of the Citizenship Law, which enumerates the different methods of acquiring citizenship, the first of them being by virtue of return. A distinction must be made between the right of return and the right to citizenship. The Law of Return grants every Jew the right to come to the country as an *oleh* (Jewish immigrant) and the right to an *oleh's* visa or an *oleh's* certificate.

525. Citizenship is granted automatically from the day of receiving an *oleh*'s certificate. An *oleh* not wishing to receive citizenship must give a declaration to that effect within three months of his aliyah (date of immigration under the Law of Return) and must be a citizen of another state. Having failed to do so, Israeli citizenship is conferred upon him automatically, and should he wish to waive citizenship he must submit a special application, which is subject to the discretion of the Minister of the Interior.

526. The Law of Return confers citizenship subject to the cumulative fulfilment of all the following conditions: the applicant is Jewish[260] or a family member of a Jew; he arrived in Israel and expressed his desire to settle there; the Minister of the Interior was not persuaded that he 'is engaged in an activity directed against the Jewish people or is likely to endanger public health or the security of the State, or that he had a criminal past and is likely to endanger the public peace'.

527. The possibilities open to non-Jews for attaining citizenship (if they are not family members of Jews) are extremely limited. Israeli citizenship is not conferred by virtue of residence in Israel.[261] Furthermore, birth in Israel also does not confer citizenship, except to persons whose father or mother were Israeli citizens at the time of birth. The Citizenship Law prescribes a number of conditions that must be satisfied for a person to receive Israeli citizenship, including a requirement of three years of residence in Israel during the five years preceding the application, and a requirement that the applicant be entitled to reside in Israel permanently. The Law grants the Minister of the Interior broad discretion in this context. Accepted policy since the establishment of the State has been to severely limit the authority to grant citizenship under this provision. Furthermore, in 2003 the Citizenship Law (Temporary Provision) was enacted, which annulled the Minister of the Interior's authority to grant citizenship (or even a permit for permanent residence in Israel) to Palestinians residents of the Territories, even in cases of marriage to an Israeli citizen. This 2003 amendment to the Citizenship Law, which bans family reunions between Israeli Arabs and Palestinians who reside in the Palestinian Authority (PA) territories, was introduced as a temporary provision, but its validity was extended on numerous occasions. In early 2012, the HCJ rejected a petition against this law by a majority of six of the eleven judges. Most of the judges maintained that even though it impairs the Israeli Arabs' basic right to maintain family life, it is 'proportional' due to matters of security and the fact that the 'reunion' in question relates to residents of a hostile entity. This is in addition to the blanket denial of the rights of Palestinians and their families, who left the State, to return within the borders of the State of Israel.

§4. Acquiring Citizenship by Marriage to an Israeli and 'Family Reunion'

528. A particularly complex issue is the question of the right of the spouse of an Israeli citizen to acquire citizenship. The citizen's right to select a spouse and to establish a family in Israel requires the recognition of the right of the Israeli citizen's spouse to acquire citizenship. All the same, in practice, the realization of this right is subject to significant restrictions.

---

260. For discussion of this subject, *see*: B. Akzin, *Who is a Jew, a Hard Case*, 5 Israel Law Rev. 259 (1970).

261. HCJ 7052/03 *Adalah v. Interior Minister*, (2006) ver 51(2)202. See the English version of the verdict at: http://elyon1.Court.gov.il/files_eng/03/520/070/a47/03070520.a47.htm.

529. The spouse of an Israeli citizen, whether or not he is Jewish, can only attain citizenship by the process of 'naturalization'. Section 5 of the Law regulates the receipt of citizenship, and section 5(b) provides that the obtaining of citizenship is not only subject to the satisfaction of the conditions enumerated in section 5(a), but also to the discretion of the Minister of the Interior, who can grant citizenship 'if he deems it appropriate'.

530. The policy adopted by the Minister of the Interior in the past was that the non-Israeli spouse was only able to initiate naturalization proceedings if he had previously been entitled to permanent residence in Israel. A permit for permanent residence could only be granted following a protracted process, which included a trial period of more than five years' duration, and which was intended to assess whether the marital contract had remained intact, and whether there were any other impediments to granting citizenship.

531. In the year 2000, the Minister of the Interior issued new guidelines which established a graded process of naturalization for the non-Israeli spouse. A temporary resident was obliged to live in Israel for at least four years before his application for citizenship would be considered. At the second stage, the spouse must prove that his life has been centred in Israel for at least three of the past four years. Having done so, he becomes entitled to citizenship presuming that there are no criminal or security impediments. Supplementary guidelines published in 2004 provided that this procedure would also apply to the non-married spouse of an Israeli citizen, including same-sex couples.

532. In exercising his powers under section 5(b) of the Citizenship Law, the Minister of the Interior is also empowered to have consideration to security issues. In this context, it may be reasonable to deny citizenship to an applicant for reasons of a perceived danger to public security, on the basis of information concerning the applicant himself. The question is to what extent the Minister of the Interior – or the Knesset itself – can make a blanket ruling in this context, based on the national identity of the applicant. This question arose in a series of cases in which the Court was requested to review the policy adopted by the Minister of the Interior, based on a Government decision, not to grant citizenship, or even a license for permanent residence in Israel, to Palestinians who had married Israeli citizens.[262] This policy is statutorily anchored in the provisions of the Citizenship and Entry into Israel Law (Temporary Provision), 2003. This law stipulates that:

262. According to the Government decision dated 12 May 2002, 'In view of the security situation and due to the implications of migration and settling processes in Israel of foreigners of Palestinian origin, including by way of unification of families, the Ministry of the Interior, in coordination with the other relevant Government offices, will crystallize a new policy for handling applications for unification of families. Until such a policy is crystallized, new applications of residents of the Palestinian Authority to receive the status of permanent residence or any other status will not be accepted. An application already filed will not be approved, and the foreign spouse will be required to remain outside Israel until another decision is adopted.'

> During the effective period of this law, notwithstanding any other legal provision, including Article 7 of the Citizenship Law, the Minister of the Interior shall not grant the inhabitant of an area citizenship on the basis of the Citizenship Law, and shall not give him a license to reside in Israel on the basis of the Entry into Israel Law, and the Area Commander shall not grant a said inhabitant a permit to stay in Israel, on the basis of the security legislation in the area.

The legality of this law was contested before the Supreme Court.

533. In a decision delivered in May 2006, by an expanded panel of eleven judges, the Court decided by a majority vote of six to five against the petition to strike down the temporary provision of the Citizenship Law.[263] The government argued that the legislation is based on security concerns, because many Palestinians given licenses for family reunions were involved in terrorist attacks against Israeli citizens. However, the restrictions also touched upon a sensitive demographic issue, namely, the fear that Israel's Jewish majority could be threatened if too many Palestinians were granted citizenship. In this monumental decision of 262 pages, the majority, headed by Justice Heshin (who retired from the Supreme Court and this was his last decision), granted special importance to the fact that Israel is at war with the Palestinians. 'We deal with life' – wrote Justice Heshin – 'with life and death, with the right of Israeli citizens to live'. The right of marriage and the right to live as a family in Israel must be balanced against another 'very powerful' right – the right of Israeli residents to life and security. He concluded that, in times of war, there is no right to bring into Israel a member of a family who resides in a hostile state, which is actually at war with Israel. Therefore, the majority of the Court found that the temporary provision should not be declared void.

534. The minority vote, headed by President Barak, was ready to strike down the law, even though 'this is a hard decision'. President Barak stated that Israel does not have two separate law systems, one for times of peace and one for times of war. Human rights are always present. Barak wrote that the constitutional right of Israeli citizens to live in Israel as a family is violated by the temporary provision. Even though the purpose of this law is proper due to security reasons, the means chosen to promote the purpose are not proportionate, and therefore, are inconsistent with the provisions of the 'limitation clause' in Basic Law: Human Dignity and Liberty. Despite the fact that the minority was of the view that the law is unconstitutional, President Barak wrote that, because it is a temporary provision of the law, soon to be due for reconsideration, it should not be declared void. Rather, the Knesset should be given time to amend it.

535. Even though it leaves the temporary provision of the Citizenship Law intact, this decision held that the policy included in the law will not be allowed to continue. The majority of the judges expressed strong criticisms of the law, which negates the possibility of family reunion on a general basis, and not on individual

263. HCJ 7052/03 *Adalah v. Minister of Interior ibid.*

grounds. The decision reveals that, despite the fact that the petition was rejected, the law is inconsistent with the provisions of Basic Law: Human Dignity and Liberty. The judges called upon the Knesset to review the law, and base the restriction for Palestinians to live in Israel with their families on an individual consideration, based on security grounds. The law is still being prolonged in its current form, without any major changes to its provisions, so we may see another round of this issue before the Supreme Court in due course.

§5. Obtaining Citizenship by Residence in Israel, Birth and Adoption

536. As a rule, the Citizenship Law does not recognize the principle of *Jus soli* (Latin for 'right of the territory'), or birthright citizenship, i.e., a right by which nationality or citizenship can be conferred upon any individual born in the territory of the relevant state. Though accepted in other migrant states, this principle was not compatible with the predominant policy of the Israeli legislature, which was to promote the connection between the nation and its land.

537. Until 1980, Israel's citizenship policy was based on the principle of *Jus sanguinis* (Latin for 'right of blood') i.e., a right by which nationality or citizenship can be conferred on any individual born to a parent who is a national or citizen of that state. Accordingly, any child born to Israeli mother and father, irrespective of his birthplace, would be considered as an Israeli. However, the law has been changed, and under the current practice, citizenship by force of birth is granted to a person born in Israel, provided that his mother or father are Israeli citizens, and to a person born outside Israel only if at the time of birth his father or mother were Israeli citizens by virtue of return, residence in Israel, naturalization, birth in Israel or adoption.[264] The result of this policy is that citizenship does not devolve to the children of Israeli citizens who were born outside Israel and continue to live there without having migrated to Israel. In adopting this policy, the Israeli legislature went from one extremity to another: from continued citizenship based on the *jus sanguinis* right of blood, bestowed on all progeny for posterity, to the forced severance of citizenship for members of the third generation.

538. Another means of obtaining citizenship is via adoption. Under section 4B of the Citizenship Law:

> A minor will become an Israeli citizen by way of adoption, effective from the date of his adoption, provided that the following conditions are satisfied: the minor was adopted under the provisions of the Adoption of Children Law, 1981, when his adoptive father or mother were Israeli citizens; or if the minor was adopted outside of Israel, when his adoptive father or mother were Israeli citizens but were not residents of Israel on the date of adoption.

264. Under s. 4(b) of this Law, 'For purposes of this section, where a person was born after the death of one of his parents, it is sufficient that that parent was an Israeli citizen at the time of his death.'

§6. Naturalization

539. A person who does not satisfy the conditions for obtaining citizenship by return, residence in Israel or birth, can nevertheless receive citizenship by way of naturalization. Section 5 of the law enumerates six conditions which an adult must satisfy in order to merit citizenship: residence in Israel; residence in Israel for three out of the five years preceding the date of submission of his application; entitlement to permanent residence in Israel; having settled, or intending to settle in Israel, and having some knowledge of the Hebrew language, and having renounced his prior nationality, or having proven that he will cease to be a foreign national upon becoming an Israeli resident.

540. The Minister of the Interior is empowered to set additional conditions for the granting of citizenship by naturalization, and may exempt a person from fulfilment of one of the conditions. For example, in the case of regular service in the IDF for a period of at least eighteen months, a person's naturalization also confers citizenship on his minor child, if resident in Israel on the day of naturalization.

541. Prior to receiving citizenship, the applicant must make the following declaration: 'I declare that I will be a loyal citizen of the State of Israel', and the citizenship becomes effective from the date of the declaration. This declaration is not required in any of the other instances of obtaining citizenship, and expresses the candidate's desire to accept the duty of loyalty to his country. The discretion of the Minister of the Interior is relatively broad, based not only in section 5(b) of the Law, but also on the power vested in him to grant a license for permanent residence in Israel, by virtue of the Entry Into Israel Law. To date, the Court has not demonstrated willingness to intervene in his discretion on this matter.

542. The fundamental problem in the laws of citizenship is the legislature's failure to define the conditions for entitlement to permanent residence in Israel, leaving the matter for the discretion of the Minister of the Interior. The result is that there is an overly broad margin left for the influence of the particular world view of the Minister in charge of formulating immigration policy.

§7. Loss of Citizenship

543. By force of the Citizenship Law, Israeli citizenship can be lost, whether at the citizen's behest or by force of law. The statutory arrangements are based on the concept that a person cannot be permitted to waive his citizenship unless he has ceased, or intends to cease, being a resident of Israel, or upon the fulfilment of other conditions as stipulated below. In all of these cases, the waiver of citizenship requires the consent of the Minister of the Interior.

544. An adult Israeli citizen may request to waive his citizenship if he is not an Israeli resident, or having given notice of his desire to cease being an Israeli citizen. In addition to his authority to determine the validity of the waiver, the Minister of the Interior is likewise empowered to determine the date on which citizenship is revoked. The notion guiding the exercise of the Minister's discretion is that a person should not be allowed to waiver citizenship as a means of evading the obligations it imposes. The most important ramification of this concept pertains to the duty of serving in the IDF, imposed on every Israeli citizen or permanent resident. The Minister of Defence has generally used his discretion to exempt from the duty of military service Israelis regarding whom the circumstances indicate that they have severed their connection with Israel. However, the Court has ruled that 'It is legitimate for the Minister of the Interior to consider whether the petitioner has fulfilled a duty imposed on him by the state law precisely by virtue of his being a citizen ... and which to date he has failed to fulfil, thereby being in breach of the law'. This includes the duty of military service.[265]

545. In the case of an Israeli citizen who is also an Israeli resident, the possibilities for waiving citizenship are significantly restricted. The citizen must be an adult, whose citizenship was obtained by force of return, after having immigrated to Israel, and for whom the waiver is intended for the purpose of retaining his other citizenship. The waiver requires the consent of the Minister of the Interior, who may accede to it only in 'special circumstances'.

546. By virtue of the Citizenship Law, an Israeli citizen loses his citizenship if he unlawfully exited Israel to one of the states enumerated in the Prevention of Infiltration (Offences and Jurisdiction) Law, 1954, such as Lebanon, Syria, Saudi Arabia or Iraq, or became a citizen of one of those states. The loss of citizenship is conditional upon the exit from Israel being 'unlawful' and does not apply to departure to states with which Israel has signed a peace agreement. The Minister of the Interior is also authorized to revoke citizenship in cases of disloyalty to the state or where citizenship was obtained on the basis of submission of false particulars.

§8. Conclusion

547. Two factors have contributed to make Israel's citizenship laws particularly interesting and worthy of discussion. The first question concerns the definition of the term 'Jew' and its implications for the question of conversion. The Supreme Court rulings on this question in sixties and seventies of the twentieth century, popularly referred to as the 'Who is a Jew' jurisprudence, led to a significant change in the legislation. The definition was simultaneously limited in accordance with religious-halakhic criteria and broadened with respect to the right of family members of Jews to immigrate to Israel and obtain Israeli citizenship. The amendment solved the issue with respect to Jews who had voluntarily converted, but nonetheless precipitated a new crisis, which continues until today. It opened the gates of immigration under the Law of Return to tens of thousands of people who are not Jewish in the eyes of the Halakhah, but who by virtue of the law have become Israelis and identify with the Jewish people. The result is that the question mark

265. HCJ 296/80 *Bokovza v. State of Israel*, 35(1) PD 492.

regarding the definition of the term 'Jew', which the amendment may have purported to solve, still awaits an authoritative answer.

548. The second factor relates to the Zionist ideology underpinning the laws of citizenship. This ideology purports to give a home to every Jew, and to guarantee a Jewish majority in the State of Israel, thus enabling it to remain a Jewish state. The question of justifying this policy in light of accepted international norms proscribing all forms of discrimination has been addressed extensively in academic literature. As a rule, however, repatriation laws, such as the Law of Return, conferring ethnically based privileges in the areas of citizenship and immigration, also exist in other states and do not violate the provisions of the International Convention on the Elimination of All Forms of Racial Discrimination. The central problem of Israeli citizenship laws is rooted in their prevention of the grant of citizenship to non-Jews and the leaving of their fate in the hands of the Minister of the Interior.

Chapter 2. Fundamental Rights and Liberties

§1. General

I. Introduction

549. At the time of its establishment in 1948, the State of Israel did not adopt a constitution. Israel has been involved in a struggle for survival since its Declaration of Independence, and consequently has been subject to a continuous state of emergency. The early efforts of the Knesset to adopt a complete constitution, including a bill of human rights, failed. The First Knesset, which acted as the Constituent Assembly, decided that the constitution would consist of a series of chapters entitled 'basic laws'. The basic laws dealing with the institutional structure of Israel were enacted long ago.[266] However, all efforts to formulate a 'bill of human rights' within the framework of one Basic Law have proved futile. In these circumstances, where the country cannot rely on a written constitution and lives in the shadow of a state of emergency, the Israeli defence of human rights and adherence to basic democratic principles is impressive. In the absence of a written constitution, it was the Israeli Supreme Court which took on the task of protecting rights and creating what became to be known as the 'judicial bill of rights' in Israel. The Supreme Court did so by developing special rules of interpretation and by relying on the Declaration of Independence, which comprises the fundamental legal source for Israel's commitment to the protection of human rights.

550. This chapter discusses the attempts made to enact a bill of human rights in Israel and the process which led to the adoption of two basic laws relating to human rights in 1992 – Basic Law: Human Dignity and Liberty and Basic Law: Freedom of Occupation. The Chapter will focus on the most important rights and those aspects unique to Israeli law, as well as the status of the basic rights which were not incorporated into the basic laws of 1992, for example, the right to equality and the right to freedom of expression. I shall also consider the protection of minorities in Israel and the protection afforded to human rights by the Supreme Court in times of emergency.

II. General Review

551. Immediately following the establishment of the State, elections were held for the constituent assembly, which devoted considerable time to discussing the

---

266. For discussion, *see* Part I, Ch. 2 on the Constitution. To date, 12 Basic Laws have been enacted, Basic Law: The Knesset (1958); Basic Law: Israel Lands (1960); Basic Law: The Government (first enacted in 1964, and since then replaced twice: in 1992 and in 2001); Basic Law: President of the State (1964); Basic Law: State Economy (1975); Basic Law: The Army (1976); Basic Law: Jerusalem Capital of Israel (1980); Basic Law: The Judiciary (1984); Basic Law: The State Comptroller (1988); and the two Basic Laws enacted in 1992, which we shall discuss below: Basic Law: Freedom of Occupation and Basic Law: Human Dignity and Liberty and Basic Law: Referendum (2014).

constitution. During these discussions in the Knesset, no decisions were reached, for various reasons I have discussed in previous chapters. At the end of the debate, the First Knesset reached the 'Harari Decision', whereby Israel's constitution would be constructed as a series of chapters comprising 'Basic Laws', which would be adopted from time to time and eventually make up the State's constitution.

552. In almost every Knesset since 1958 – the year in which the first basic law was enacted, Basic Law: The Knesset – multiple efforts have been made to bring about the ratification of a Basic Law: Bill of Human Rights. The debates on the various proposals have been accompanied by acute controversy and all efforts have failed.

553. The 12th Knesset (1988–1992) saw another proposal tabled for Basic Law: Human Rights and, as was the case with all previous proposals, this time the Orthodox and religious parties frustrated the progress of the law. Seeking to save the law, MK Amnon Rubinstein[267] divided the proposed Basic Law: Human Rights into separate bills, each of which was intended to secure individual fundamental rights. The Bill of Human Rights was disassembled following precisely the same format as the Harari Decision, whereby the constitution would be constructed in stages – by means of basic laws. The rationale for this move was that several separate basic laws dealing with an individual right or class of rights would be adopted, and finally would become an entire bill of rights. In pursuit of this approach, the Knesset adopted Basic Law: Human Dignity and Liberty and Basic Law: Freedom of Occupation in March 1992 thereby bringing about what legal scholars term the 'constitutional revolution'.

III. The Status of Human Rights Prior to 1992

554. The Declaration of Independence established two fundamental principles on which the Israeli legal system would be based, namely, that the State would be 'Jewish' and that it would be 'democratic'. At the same time, because of the absence of a constitution, the Israeli legal system was based in practice on the English principle of the supremacy of Parliament. Prima facie, the Supreme Court's capacity to create human rights in a situation where there is a state of emergency, in which rights cannot be entrenched in a constitution or basic law, and in which the principle of parliamentary sovereignty prevails, is limited. Attempts to give effect to the Declaration of Independence, the text of which mentions a series of basic rights – such as complete social and political equality for every inhabitant of the State without distinction as to religion, gender or nationality, and freedom of religion and

267. Professor Rubinstein is one of the most outstanding jurists in the field of Constitutional Law in Israel. He is the author of several books on constitutional law. At the time he was an MK, and served as Chairman of the Constitution, Law and Justice Committee, responsible for presenting the bills regarding basic laws.

conscience – were unsuccessful. From the earliest days of the State, the Supreme Court held that the Declaration of Independence was only intended to establish the fact of the foundation of the State for the purpose of recognition by international law. It expressed the vision of the people and their 'raison d'être', but it was neither a constitution nor did it have the force of law.

555. Nonetheless, over the years, the Supreme Court began to refer to the Declaration of Independence as a legal source for the interpretation of laws promulgated by the Mandatory authorities or the Knesset. Thus, for example, in *Kol Ha'am v. Minister of the Interior*,[268] Justice Agranat held that although the Declaration of Independence did not have binding legal force, statutes had to be interpreted in accordance with the principles entrenched in it. In this judgment, Justice Agranat laid the basis for legal recognition of civil rights. He held that Israel is a democratic state, and that the democratic regime cannot survive if the legal system does not recognize freedom of expression. Even though it is not possible to strike down a law which contravenes freedom of expression, because of the absence of a constitution, the Court will prefer an interpretation of the law which is consistent with freedom of expression. The judge also adopted the idea of a 'balancing test' between civil rights and other social interests, and held that only the prevention of an 'almost certain'[269] severe violation of the public peace could justify the infringement of freedom of expression.

556. The Supreme Court's recognition of the importance of human rights became a legal norm in the Israeli legal system, due to the principle of 'binding precedent'. Infringement of the duty to respect human rights gave rise, and today continues to give rise, to a cause of action which allows every person to apply to the HCJ.

557. The judgments which recognized new rights entrenched those rights in what has become known as the 'judicial bill of rights' – a collection of human and civil rights which have been recognized by the HCJ; rights which are not written in the statute books but in the judgments of the Court. Long before the enactment of Basic Law: Human Dignity and Liberty, the rights set out in the basic law were recognized by the Supreme Court, without them having any normative basis.

558. Thus, for example, the Supreme Court recognized the right of every citizen to the privacy of his person. In the *Katlan* case,[270] the question turned on whether the prison authorities were entitled to perform an enema on a detainee, without his consent, in a search for swallowed drugs, after it had become clear that drugs were being smuggled into the prison in this manner. The Supreme Court held that every

268. HCJ 73/53 *Kol Ha'am v. Minister of Interior* (1953) 7(2) PD 871.
269. This balancing test, also known as the 'imminent certainty' or 'close possibility' test, is similar to the American 'clear and present danger' test.
270. HCJ 355/79 *Katlan v. Prison Services*, 34(3) PD 294, 298.

person in Israel, including detainees and prisoners, enjoys the basic right to the integrity of his person and respect for his human dignity. Performing an enema on a detainee, without his consent and for non-medical reasons, violated the integrity of the detainee's person, infringed his privacy and violated his human dignity. Justice Barak added that human dignity originates, *inter alia*, from the Declaration of Independence and therefore from that moment it was recognized as a 'superior' right in the Israeli legal system. Accordingly, an administrative authority was not entitled to violate it in the absence of express statutory authorization:

> Every person in Israel enjoys a basic right to the integrity of his person and respect for his human dignity. These rights are contained in the 'judicial bill of rights' which was recognized by this Court. The walls of the prison do not separate prisoners from their human dignity ... freedom is denied to the prisoner; his human dignity is not taken away from him.

559. Following this approach, the Supreme Court recognized almost all the basic human rights, such as equality and freedom of expression, as well as political rights, such as the right to vote and to be elected, economic and social rights. However, it should be recalled that this recognition was limited. In the absence of a constitution and in the absence of judicial review, the Court could not invalidate statutes which expressly violated human rights. Thus, for example, in the case of *Rogozinksy v. State of Israel*,[271] the Supreme Court held that:

> a statute which placed issues of marriage and divorce of Jews in Israel within the jurisdiction of the Rabbinical Courts, and provided that such marriages and divorces would be carried out in accordance with the law of Torah, had preference over the principle of freedom of conscience.

560. To summarize, prior to the enactment of the basic laws on human rights, the Court recognized them using presumptive and interpretative tools: the presumption that the legislature did not intend to violate human rights; the principle that a statute open to two interpretations should be interpreted in such a way as to best protect human rights; the principle that a statute violating human rights should be construed restrictively; and the rule directed at all administrative authorities according to which the violation of human rights is prohibited unless specifically authorized by statute. This approach created a 'judicial bill of rights' in Israel, setting out the rights created by the Court. The bill took the place of the constitution insofar as human rights were concerned. This may be one of the most impressive and important contributions of the Supreme Court to Israel's democracy. But, these 'judicial rights' are weaker than the rights listed in a formal constitution or in the basic laws on human rights, as they are unwritten and fall outside the normative hierarchy. Consequently, if a statute expressly violates these rights, the statute will override them, and the Court will not be competent to invalidate it.

271. CA 450/70 *Rogozinksy v. State of Israel*, 26(1) PD 129.

IV. The Status of Human Rights After 1992

561. The 'constitutional revolution' took place in Israel in March 1992 with the enactment of the two basic laws on human rights. These basic laws imposed restrictions on the legislature, thereby giving rise to the Supreme Court's power for judicial review.[272] Basic Law: Human Dignity and Liberty and Basic Law: Freedom of Occupation changed the legal status of the rights contained therein and also altered the Court's perception of the entire body of human rights. The basic laws not only recognized rights but also provided that these rights could be violated in certain circumstances. The Supreme Court took on the task of determining whether the infringement of rights is 'constitutional'. The two basic laws open with a statement capable of affecting the status of the Declaration of Independence itself. Thus, the first section of each basic law states:

> Basic human rights in Israel are based on the recognition of the value of the human being, and the sanctity of his life and his freedom, and these will be respected in the spirit of the principles of the Declaration of Independence of the State of Israel.

562. Referring to this section, the Supreme Court held that:

> with its enactment a substantive change took place … regarding the source of validity of these basic rights. Until the enactment of this purposes provision, their validity was derived from the Declaration of Independence "which expresses the vision and *raison d'être* of the people" … however, the absence of legal effect of the Declaration of Independence meant that these were "basic rights which were unwritten" and instead derived directly from the nature of our country as a democratic state aspiring to freedom … . With the coming into force of Basic Law: Human Dignity and Liberty, and particularly its purposes clause, these basic rights became written rights, and the purpose of their enactment too has been recorded in the statute books … elevating the status of these basic rights.[273]

563. The adoption of these two basic laws transformed Israel into a constitutional state. They expressly altered the status of the written rights in the basic laws, including the rights to life, freedom and dignity, the rights to privacy and property, the right to move freely across state boundaries and the freedom of occupation. The basic laws refrain from referring to certain rights such as the right to equality, the right to freedom of expression, the right to freedom of religion and conscience, and social rights. However, it must be noted that the basic laws of 1992 and the constitutional institutional revolution which followed, i.e., the judicial review of legislation, almost stopped the constitutional process in Israel. Since 1992, only one

---

272. For a discussion of the constitutional revolution, *see* Part 1, Ch. 2. *See also* the monumentally important decision in *Mizrachi Bank v. Migdal*, by a panel of eleven judges in 1995 and the discussion of this judgment in Part 1, Ch. 2.

273. CA 294/91 *Hevre Kadisha (Burial Society) v. Kastenbaum*, 46(2) PD 464.

basic law has been enacted (Basic Law: Referendum) and the continued entrenchment of human rights in basic laws has come to an abrupt stop.

564. Nonetheless, an interesting development has taken place in the case law of the Supreme Court. Since the enactment of Basic Law: Human Dignity and Liberty, judgments have yielded expanding constitutional interpretations of the phrase 'human dignity', acknowledging the constitutional status of rights that were not explicitly mentioned in this basic law, even if this acknowledgement is somewhat partial in the sense that only matters directly and practically associated with human dignity were accorded constitutional status in the context of that right. The rights in question here include freedom of expression, freedom of faith and worship, various rights in criminal proceedings and certain aspects of the right to equality. Granting constitutional status to those rights substantially changed Israeli constitutional law because it meant that the Knesset was restricted in its power to infringe them with laws that do not meet the terms of the limitation clause. Furthermore, acknowledging the constitutional status of rights that were not included in basic laws means that it is the HCJ's prerogative to judicially review laws enacted by the Knesset that allegedly violate those rights.

Today it is evident that the true constitutional revolution did not take place within the arena of human rights, but actually within the area of institutional constitutional law. The constitutional revolution is important because of the shift in the status of the basic laws, and the possibility of judicial review of the law. The status of the rights themselves has not changed significantly in consequence of the basic laws. They already existed in the case law of the HCJ. Some are now entrenched in the Basic Laws. The substantive change does not lie in the existence or absence of the rights themselves, but in the ability of the Supreme Court to invalidate a law which violates protected rights; an action which it could not carry out previously. The two basic laws of 1992 will be discussed in detail below.

§2. Civil and Political Rights

I. Basic Law: Human Dignity and Liberty and Basic Law: Freedom of Occupation

A. The Principles and Purposes Clauses

565. The first two sections of the basic laws, the principles clause and the purposes clause, were drafted in order to provide an introduction common to each of the basic laws in relation to human rights to be enacted in the future. These are general clauses which provide a general standard for all human rights.

566. Basic Law: Human Dignity and Liberty and Basic Law: Freedom of Occupation open with a first section devoted to a statement of the basic principles underlying human rights in Israel. These are 'the value of the human being, the sanctity of his life and his freedom'. One of the interesting questions now open in Israeli law is whether the basic principles clause should only be accorded interpretive value or whether it should be ascribed a 'stronger' status, as a source of human rights in addition to those set out in the basic laws. This question has not yet received a clear answer; however, the case law of the HCJ has hinted at the possibility of recognizing this clause as one which is 'independent', i.e., an independent source of human rights.

567. The second section, known as the 'purposes clause', states that: 'The purpose of this Basic Law is to protect human dignity and liberty, in order to anchor in a Basic Law the values of the State of Israel as a Jewish and democratic state.' This clause sets out the general purpose of the law as well as the presumption that the State of Israel possesses values as a Jewish and democratic state; values which we shall discuss in depth further on.

B. The Limitation Clause

568. Like all human rights, the human rights listed in the basic law are always relative. The violation of human rights is permitted if that violation occurs for proper purposes in accordance with the rules set out in the basic law itself. The Israeli legislature chose to establish a statutory test which is similar in nature to that established by the Canadian legislature,[274] and did so within the framework of the 'limitation clause'. The limitation clause refers to the question whether an ordinary law, which infringes a basic law, can be valid in Israeli law. The Israeli legislature answered this question in the affirmative, but conditionally. An ordinary law which 'infringes' a human right set out in the Basic Law will be valid, but only if it complies with the conditions set out in the limitation clause, which states:

> There shall be no violation of rights under this Basic Law except by a Law fitting the values of the State of Israel, designed for a proper purpose, and to an extent no greater than required or by such a law enacted with explicit authorization therein.

569. As its name implies, the limitation clause establishes limits. The limitation clause defines the circumstances in which it will be possible to violate the right to human dignity and liberty and the right to freedom of occupation. The clause has a dual function: it limits the power of a law to violate human rights on one hand, while limiting the protection given to the rights on the other.

570. The limitation clause provides constitutional protection to human rights by establishing the constitutional standards which enable the violation of human rights. It expresses the notion that the rights are relative and exist within a social framework which is committed to implementing national goals.

---

274. *See* the limitation clause in s. 1 and the Canadian Charter of Rights and Freedoms. The wording of s. 29(2) of the Universal Declaration of Human Right influenced the formulation of the Israeli limitation clause. *See also* the limitation clause appearing in Section 5 of the New Zealand Bill of Rights Act 1990.

571. Accordingly, when the HCJ hears an argument that a right has been violated by the legislature, it must first examine whether the violating law is compatible with the values of the State of Israel. It must also examine whether the law was intended for a proper purpose, i.e., the Court must consider the purpose of the law from the point of view of the subjective intention of the legislature at the time of enacting the law, as well as the objective purpose. In this regard, a purpose is proper if it serves an important social goal which is sensitive to human rights. The purpose must violate human rights to only a minimal extent.

572. An additional component of the limitation clause examines the principle of proportionality. The requirement for a violation which 'does not exceed what is necessary' establishes the component of the 'measure'. The fact that the purpose of a violating law is proper is insufficient by itself to meet the constitutional test. It is a precondition for validity that the measure adopted by the law which violates human rights is an appropriate measure. Over the years, the HCJ has developed subsidiary tests for examining the principle of proportionality.[275]

573. If at the end of the process of examination, the law violating human rights meets the requirements of the limitation clause, the law will be valid. If the Court is convinced that the law does not meet the requirements of the limitation clause, the Court will declare it invalid.[276] Prima facie, a substantive change has taken place in relation to the ability of the Court to conduct judicial review of Knesset legislation which is alleged to violate protected human rights. However, the legislature has taken steps to prevent judicial review of legislation which was enacted prior to Basic Law: Human Dignity and Liberty coming into effect. Section 10 of the Basic Law states that '(t)his Basic Law shall not affect the validity of any law in force prior to the commencement of the Basic Law'. The significance of this provision is that all laws which were in force in March 1992 will continue to be valid despite the fact that their contravention of the provisions of Basic Law: Human Dignity and Liberty might otherwise have led to their invalidation. The old law is shielded against constitutional judicial review. This outcome was the result of political compromise and creates, in the words of Aharon Barak, a 'constitutional anomaly'.[277] At the same time, the interpretation of the old law is influenced by the enactment of the Basic Law and will be conducted in the 'spirit' of the provisions of the Basic Law.

---

275. These tests include consideration of the following questions: Is the means compatible with the purpose? Is there a rational connection between the means and the purpose? Is there another law or other means which can achieve the purpose, i.e., an alternative way of achieving the purpose which is less injurious? Thus, for example, a situation may exist in which a lesser result is achieved but the injury is also substantially less, and accordingly it will be preferred. See Aharon Barak, *Proportionality: Constitutional Rights and their Limitations* (Cambridge Studies in Constitutional Law) 2012.

276. Since 1995, the Supreme Court has engaged in judicial review of Knesset legislation which violates rights protected by the Basic Laws dealing with human rights and is incompatible with the limitation clause; however, this judicial review is very measured. To date, a dozen statutory provisions have been invalidated.

277. A. Barak, *Constitutional Interpretation* (1993, In Hebrew) at 561.

C. The Entrenchment Clause in Basic Law: Freedom of Occupation

574. Similarly to other constitutions around the world, Basic Law: Freedom of Occupation contains an express clause setting out the process by which the law may be amended. This 'entrenchment clause' provides that '(t)his Basic Law shall not be varied except by a Basic Law passed by a majority of the members of the Knesset'. The purpose of this clause is to provide the Basic Law with formal rigidity. The two preconditions which must be met before the Basic Law may be amended – (1) amendment by a Basic Law, and (2) adoption by a majority of Knesset members (namely, a majority of 61 of the 120 Knesset members) – are formal in nature. A similar provision in Basic Law: Human Dignity and Liberty was voted down at the last moment. The entrenchment clause has not had a restrictive effect on the Israeli legislature, and when the need arose to amend Basic Law: Freedom of Occupation it proved easy to enlist a majority of sixty-one Knesset members to approve the desired amendment.[278]

D. The Override Clause in Basic Law: Freedom of Occupation

575. A law which violates freedom of occupation and does not satisfy the requirements of the limitation clause may remain valid in view of the special provisions contained in the Basic Law:

> A provision of a law that violates freedom of occupation shall be of effect, even though not in accordance with Section 4 [the limitation clause S.N.], if it has been included in a law passed by a majority of the members of the Knesset, which expressly states that it shall be of effect, notwithstanding the provisions of this Basic Law; such law shall expire four years from its commencement unless a shorter duration has been stated therein.

576. This clause was introduced in 1994 and does not appear in Basic Law: Human Dignity and Liberty. It ensued from the need to enact a specific statute which it was feared would violate the freedom of occupation and also fail to satisfy the conditions of the limitation clause. The Knesset feared that the proposed statute would be invalidated by the Supreme Court.[279] A section found in the Canadian

278. This problem arose in 1994, when it became necessary to enact a statutory provision which would restrict the importation of *non-kosher* meat to Israel in accordance with the demands of the Orthodox parties then forming part of the coalition. Doubt was expressed as to whether this provision would satisfy the conditions of the original limitation clause, whereby 'this right shall not be restricted save by law, for a proper purpose and for the public benefit'. The Supreme Court stated *obiter* that if the law were enacted, any legislation making the importation of meat contingent upon it being *kosher* would be legislation which restricted freedom of occupation, and would be inconsistent with the limitation clause. Accordingly, such legislation required an amendment to the Basic Law. Basic Law: Freedom of Occupation was amended, the limitation clause set out therein was amended, and the override clause was inserted.

279. *See id.*, the *Meat Legislation* case (Mitral), making the importation of meat dependent on it being *kosher*.

Charter[280] provided the model for the Israeli legislature. So far, the override clause has only been applied once, in order to enact a statute which makes the import of frozen meat contingent upon it being kosher.[281]

II. The Rights Expressly Listed in the Basic Laws

A. *Freedom of Occupation*

577. Freedom of occupation has been recognized as a human right from the earliest days of the State.[282] The principle embodied in the freedom of occupation is that every man has an inherent right to engage in the work or trade that he chooses, provided that this work or trade is not prohibited by law. Concomitant with the right of a person to work in a profession or trade is the obligation of the State to refrain from interfering with his exercise of his profession. At the same time, in many cases, matters such as the need to regulate the economic activity of the State, and the need to protect consumers against unskilled professionals, justify restricting the right to freedom of occupation. Such restrictions extend from the setting of preliminary conditions for performing work, such as the grant of a license or permit, to the imposition of restrictions on the right of a person to engage in a particular occupation, and even extend to the imposition of prohibitions on engaging in an occupation in which a group or body has a monopoly.

B. *Sanctity of Life, Body and Dignity*

578. According to section 2, 'All persons are entitled to protection of their life, body, and dignity'. It follows that every person has the right not to be subjected to physical force, a death sentence, torture as a means of punishment, or degrading conditions of detention or imprisonment. Thus, for example, Justice Heshin has held that 'the right to life and to everything that life depends on – the right to breathe, the right to drink, and the right to eat – is the mother of all rights, it is the man'.[283] Justice Strasberg-Cohen has held that 'there are basic rights, such as the right to life and dignity, which cannot be violated or negated even when held by a person who is not a citizen or resident of the State'.[284]

280. Section 33 of the Charter, known as the override clause.
281. In March 1994, the Knesset enacted the Importation of Frozen Meat Law, 1994 which stated that 'notwithstanding the provisions of any law, a person shall not import meat unless he has received a certificate of *Kashrut* in relation to it; this law shall be valid notwithstanding the provisions of Basic Law: Freedom of Occupation' The Meat Law passed by a majority of sixty Knesset Members.
282. HCJ 1/49 *Bezerano v. Minister of Police*, 2 PD 80.
283. HCJ 606/93 *Kidum Yazamuth Ve'Molot (1981) Ltd. v. Broadcasting Authority*, 48(2) PD 1, 25.
284. EA 3969/97 *State of Israel v. Abu Rabiya Haled*, 41(5) PD 470.

579. Embodied in this right is every person's right to minimum living conditions. Recent developments show that the right to 'human dignity' gives rise to additional rights, beyond those set out in the basic law. The tendency of the Court is to include in the right to 'human dignity' several aspects of the right to equality, the right to due process, and freedom of speech, as we shall see further on. However, here too we may assume that, should the Supreme Court wish to further develop social rights, the only path open to it would be to include them within the right to dignity.

C. Personal Freedom

580. The basic law does not expressly refer to the right of a person to freedom. At the same time, section 5 of the Basic Law provides that '(t)here shall be no deprivation or restriction of the liberty of a person by imprisonment, arrest, extradition or by any other manner'. Naturally, this provision does not negate the constitutionality of all the penalties imposed for the breach of criminal prohibitions which involve the deprivation of personal liberty, or the possibility of arresting a person before he is convicted. It follows from the provision that a person may not be subjected to degrading or harsh conditions of detention or imprisonment; a sentence of life imprisonment may not be imposed where there is no possibility of early release; and it is prohibited to impose a punishment which is not proportionate to the offence committed. Severe violation of personal freedom was also the reason for a landmark decision of the HCJ dealing with the privatization of prisons in 2009.[285] A panel of nine judges headed by President Dorit Beinish declared that the amendment to the Prisons Ordinance, passed by the Knesset in 2004, which permitted the establishment of private prisons in Israel, seriously violates protected human rights. The Court stated that the transfer of authority for managing prisons from the state to a private contractor whose aim is monetary profit would severely violate the prisoners' basic human rights to dignity and freedom. The Court was well aware that, so far, no American or British Court has had to rule on whether privatizing prisons is unconstitutional. From the opinions of several experts, wrote Beinish, we learn that if this question were to arise in Europe, it would be rejected by the different Courts. Therefore, this case appears to be the first case in comparative constitutional law, in which a Supreme Court declared a prison privatization to be unconstitutional.

D. The Right to Property

581. Section 3 of the Basic Law gives constitutional expression to the right to protection of property: '(t)here shall be no violation of the property of a person'. This right was recognized by the case law as a basic right even before it was

285. HCJ 2605/05 *Academic Centre of Law and Business v. Minister of Finance* (19 November 2009).

entrenched in the basic law, and when it was raised to the rank of a constitutional right, the right to property attracted even greater protection.

582. In the *Mizrachi Bank* case, the Supreme Court held by a majority that the Basic Law had a superior normative status, and therefore a statute infringing a basic right protected by the Basic Law – in this case, the right to property – otherwise than in accordance with the conditions of the limitation clause – was invalid. All the judges agreed that the constitutional protection accorded to property is broad in the sense that it is not limited to tangible rights, but also applies to contractual rights. It is also clear that the requisitioning of an asset violates the right to property.[286]

E. The Right to Leave and Enter Israel

583. Section 6 of the Basic Law recognizes the constitutional status of a person's right to leave Israel, and the right of a citizen to enter the country: '(a) All persons are free to leave Israel. (b) Every Israeli national has the right of entry into Israel from abroad.' This right too is relative, and its implementation is subject to balancing against competing interests. It should be emphasized that freedom of movement, i.e., the right to move freely within the boundaries of the State of Israel, was not expressly written into the law. The reason for this was the desire to placate the religious community, which feared that an express right to this effect might undermine the status quo concerning travel on the Sabbath in certain areas.

584. The Court has the power to issue an injunction, valid for a limited period of time, prohibiting persons – such as criminal suspects – from leaving the country, in order to ensure their availability for interrogation by the police; or prohibiting the departure of debtors or defendants who might otherwise not appear for trial, in order to ensure payment of their debts or execution of judgment against them. The law also empowers the Minister of the Interior to prohibit a person from leaving Israel if it is suspected that his departure would harm national security.

585. In view of the determination that the right to leave the country possesses constitutional status within the Basic Law, the HCJ has restricted the ability of the Courts to prohibit the foreign travel of litigants. The Court has held in a series of cases that in view of the provisions of the basic law, greater weight must be given to freedom of movement. Similar rulings have been delivered regarding restraining orders against leaving the country issued by the Rabbinical Courts,[287] by the Execution Office[288] and by Courts dealing with defendants in criminal trials.

---

286. HCJ 5091/91 *Nusseiba v. Minister of Finance*, Tak-El 94(3), 1765.
287. HCJ 3914/92 *Lev v. Regional Rabbinical Court in Tel Aviv-Jaffa*, 48(2) PD 491; HCJ 4358/93 *Zuk v. Great Rabbinical Court in Jerusalem*, 48(4) PD 563.
288. CLA 7208/93 *Weissglass v. Weissglass*, 48(4) PD 529.

F. Privacy

586. Section 7 of the basic law guarantees protection of the human right to privacy. The law provides general protection for privacy but does not define the right to privacy except in terms of prohibitions, for example, 'There shall be no entry into the private premises of a person who has not consented thereto'; 'No search shall be conducted on the private premises or body of a person, nor in the body or belongings of a person'; 'There shall be no violation of the secrecy of the spoken utterances, writings or records of a person'. The constitutional protection given to a person against searches of his premises has ramifications for the scope of the searches conducted by the police on the bodies of suspects. The rules established in this regard even prior to the adoption of the basic law prohibited searches of a person's body, without his consent, in view of the ensuing violation of his dignity.

587. Following the attribution of constitutional status to this right, the protection was expanded. The Court has consequently stated:

> Even when we are speaking of an external search of the body of a person, there is still room to determine and demand that the conditions and circumstances in which such a search is conducted – particularly when we are dealing with stripping a person and searching intimate parts of his body – will be such as not to violate his dignity and privacy, save to a minimal extent, in so far as possible in the circumstances of each and every case.[289]

588. The right to privacy is also established in legislation, for example, the Protection of Privacy Law, 1981, and the Secret Monitoring Law, 1979. The entrenchment of the right to privacy in the Basic Law accords constitutional status to this right – which has already been recognized by the case law as a basic right. At the same time, it is accepted that this entrenchment does not vest the right to privacy with superior normative status *vis-à-vis* other basic rights which have not been entrenched.

III. Basic Rights which Are Not Expressly Referred to in the Basic Law

A. The Right to Equality

589. The principle of equality is at the heart of every democratic regime. This right – which ought to have been the primary right, entrenched in the Israeli charter of human rights – was not included in the Basic Law: Human Dignity and Liberty bill. The omission was designed to enable broad consensus in favour of the bill. The principle of equality is problematic in Israel and creates deep divisions and disagreements. Some of the issues presenting these problems include equality between

289. Cr. A 2145/92 *State of Israel v. Guetta*, 46(5) PD 704, 713.

Jews and non-Jews; equality in a State in which there is no separation between religion and state, and numerous rights are determined by religious law which does not give equal treatment to women; and equality regarding civil obligations such as the duty to perform military service.

590. The principle of equality in Israel shall be elaborated below. From an historical point of view, it was not possible to achieve consensus regarding the incorporation of the principle of equality as a basic right. It is likely that such consensus still does not exist. At the same time, the HCJ has ruled that the principle of equality derives from the need to protect the dignity of a person. After 1992, it was held that it is possible to entrench and protect several aspects of the principle of equality within Basic Law: Human Dignity and Liberty.

591. It is commonly accepted that the principle of equality has now achieved constitutional status, so that the primary legislature must comply with it, subject to the provisions of the limitation clause. In 2012 for the first time, a law was invalidated because it contravened the principle of equality.[290]

B. *Freedom of Expression and Freedom of Association*

592. Freedom of expression too has not achieved formal entrenchment in the basic law. This is an important right in Israeli law, and it too will be discussed in further detail below. Based on the provisions of the purposes clause, the basic principles clause and the interpretation given to the expression 'human dignity and liberty', it is commonly accepted today that the normative status of freedom of expression changed with the adoption of the basic law, and the legislative authority is no longer permitted to infringe the right to freedom of expression, where such infringement does not meet the conditions of the limitation clause.

C. *The Right to due Process*

593. The Basic Law on Human Dignity does not contain express provisions relating to the rights of defendants, although there is a general provision stating that 'There shall be no deprivation or restriction of the liberty of a person by imprisonment, arrest, extradition or by any other manner' (section 5 of the Basic Law) and prohibiting searches in the private premises of a person. Much like the right to equality and freedom of expression, the rights arising in the context of the criminal process may also be anchored in provisions of Basic Law: Human Dignity and Liberty. Thus, for example, the right of a defendant to representation by defence counsel was recognized as a constitutional right, derived from the basic law. Similarly, the right to silence – the right of a suspect or defendant to refrain from giving his version of events and his right to refrain from making incriminating statements or

290. HCJ6298/07 *Ressler v. the Knesset* (February 2012), dealing with the law that exempted Yeshiva students from military service.

giving incriminating testimony – may be supported on the basis of the right to dignity. The right to dignity may also be interpreted to mean that the use of interrogational measures which violate a person's dignity, such as exerting physical or mental pressure, is unconstitutional.

In 2009, the HCJ decided to strike down a law because it violated the right to due process. The provision in question was a temporary law amending the Criminal Procedure Law, which permitted a Court to extend detention periods in order to allow effective interrogations of terror suspects. The extensions would be granted on the basis of hearings conducted in the absence of the detainee. The appellant argued that the provision in question was unconstitutional on the basis that it interfered with a detainee's right to be present at hearings concerning his detention, his right to due process, and his rights to dignity and to freedom. The Court decided to strike down the law, and held the article unconstitutional. Justice Rivlin (the Deputy President) writing for the Court, stated that preventing the appellant from being present violates his due process right, which was part of the constitutional right to freedom, established in the Basic Law.[291]

D. Personal Autonomy and Freedom of Contract

594. It is commonly accepted that the right to personal autonomy and the rights derived from it – freedom of testacy, the freedom to enter into contractual arrangements and the principle of freedom of contracts – form part of the basic right to human dignity. The case law has held that 'freedom to enter into contractual arrangements is a basic constitutional right, albeit, like all other rights, it is not an absolute right but one which is relative and one which must be balanced against other interests worthy of protection'.[292]

E. Freedom of Religion

595. Freedom of conscience and freedom of religion have been recognized as basic rights of the individual in Israel. The Declaration of Independence states that Israel is a Jewish state, which guarantees freedom of religion and conscience to all its inhabitants. By intertwining freedom of religion and freedom of conscience, the Declaration of Independence proclaims equality between religious inhabitants (whether Jewish, Muslim, Christian or other) and secular inhabitants. The former enjoy freedom to adhere to their religion or beliefs and pursue their rituals of worship without interference, while the latter enjoy the freedom to act in accordance with their conscience, without being coerced into complying with religious rules in which they do not believe.

596. The enactment of Basic Law: Freedom of Occupation and Basic Law: Human Dignity and Liberty led to the transformation of the basic rights appearing

291. Crim. App. 8823/07 *Anonymous v. The State of Israel*, 11 Feb. 2010.
292. CLA 2512/90 *Supergas Israel Gas Distribution Company Ltd. v. Tofine Sa'ar*, 45(4) PD 405.

in the Declaration of Independence from unwritten rights to rights now binding the legislature itself. As noted, notwithstanding the fact that neither of the two basic laws expressly mentions the rights to freedom of religion and conscience, there is a tendency to interpret 'human dignity and liberty' as including a body of unwritten rights, and among them, the right to freedom of belief and religion.

597. Notwithstanding the recognition given to the principle of freedom of religion and conscience and the protection accorded thereto, it cannot be said that freedom of religion, in the broad sense of that term, exists in Israel. There is freedom to hold particular beliefs, to belong to a religious community and to worship without interference, but in certain areas the laws of the State oblige citizens to subject themselves to religious law, whether they are Orthodox or not. This is, of course, a problematic right in a State in which one of the fundamental principles is that the State is 'Jewish' and where there is no separation between religion and state. One particularly problematic area is that of marriage and divorce in Israel.[293] Thus, for example, every person in Israel is required to marry and divorce in accordance with the religious law applicable to him – a provision which, of course, violates the right to freedom from religion. The Jewish non-Orthodox communities have no right to marry their members in a religious ceremony, as the Orthodox community holds the 'monopoly' on issues of Jewish religion.

598. The status of the right to freedom of religion has arisen in Israel in a variety of contexts, for example, with regard to the right of Jews to realize their right to freedom to worship and pray in places holy to them, such as the Temple Mount. Most of the applications to hold such prayers are rejected by the Chief of Police in Jerusalem, on grounds of danger to public safety, and the fear of possible rioting. Most of the petitions submitted by worshippers against the Chief of Police are also rejected. The approach usually taken in the case law is that freedom of religion and freedom of worship will retreat where there is a real possibility of danger to public safety. The difficulties in this area will be illustrated by way of two specific examples, relating to burials and the issue of kosher food.

1. Burials

599. Since its establishment, the State has declined to operate civil cemeteries. All the cemeteries (except those operating in Kibbutzim, that is, collective agricultural villages) are managed by the religious institutions of the various religious communities. The citizens of the State are buried, therefore, in accordance with their religious affiliation. If the deceased did not belong to a religious community which operates a cemetery, or belonged to a known religious community but did not wish to be buried in accordance with his religion, special solutions had to be found.

---

293. For further discussion, *see* S. Shetreet, *State and Religion: Funding of Religious Institutions – The Case of Israel in Comparative Perspective*, 13 ND J. L. Ethics & Public Policy 421 (1999); E.R. Clinton, *Chains of Marriage: Israeli Women's Fight for Freedom*, 3 J. Gender Race & Justice 283 (1999).

600. The Jewish cemeteries are managed by various Burial Societies, which only allow deceased persons who are Jews according to Orthodox law and in a ceremony which is conducted in accordance with Orthodox ritual.

601. In 1988, the 'Menucha Nechona' ['Rest in Peace'] Association – the goal of which is to bury deceased Jews in a liberal Jewish burial ceremony or in a secular ceremony – submitted a petition to the HCJ demanding a license to operate as a burial society and an allocation of land for use as a cemetery. In a judgment given in May 1992, the Court ordered the Minister of Religious Affairs to issue the requested license to the association, and also ordered the Israel Land Administration to allocate land for a cemetery, all within a reasonable period of time.[294] In 1994, the 'Menucha Nechona' Association submitted a new petition to the HCJ, complaining that two years down the line it had still not received the license or the land allocation. At this time, waves of immigrants were arriving in Israel from the former Soviet Union, and many of these new immigrants lacked religious affiliation.

602. The crisis of these immigrants – who did not have a burial place – spurred the government to decide in December 1993 to create alternative burial sites, and after many delays, the first cornerstone of an alternative cemetery was laid in April 1996 in Be-er Sheba. Nowadays many alternative cemeteries can be found in several Israeli cities.

2. Kosher Food

603. The issue of ritually clean (Kosher) food exemplifies the problematic nature of the relations between religion and state in Israel, and of the tension prevailing between the character of the State as Jewish on one hand and a State which guarantees individual freedoms on the other. In this regard, a distinction has been created between the public and private domains. Whereas it has been decided – either by statute or as part of public policy – that Kashrut will be maintained in the public domain, on the face of it, the State does not intervene in the private domain.

604. Seeking to preserve the Jewish character of the State of Israel, to refrain from violating the sensitivities of the religious community, and to enable both religious and secular people to eat together, Israel has followed a policy of maintaining Kashrut in public kitchens (food served in public institutions, army camps, hospitals and the like), and in public places (as a result of which there are prohibitions on selling pork, and a prohibition on showing leavened products on Passover).

605. The Kashrut (Prohibition of Deceit) Law, 1983, provides that a person who sells food is prohibited from representing it as Kosher unless he has been given a certificate of Kashrut, and if the food premises have been given such a certificate, no commodities may be served or sold which are not Kosher according to religious

294. HCJ 397/88 *'Menucha Nechona' Association v. Minister of Religious Affairs*, Tak-El 92(2) 1175.

law. Similar limitations apply to the manufacturers of commodities, sellers of commodities, importers and butchers. The law is intended to ensure that a person who is interested in consuming Kosher food may rely on the representation of the food as Kosher, but it empowers only the Council of the Chief Rabbinate of Israel, or a rabbi who the Council has authorized, to grant a certificate of Kashrut for the purpose of the statute.

606. These provisions hurt those groups which do not recognize the competence or exclusiveness of the Council of the Chief Rabbinate. These groups include, on the one hand, Orthodox groups – whose Kashrut requirements are much more stringent than those of the Chief Rabbinate, and on the other hand, traditional groups, which take care to eat Kosher food, but do not object, for example, to a restaurant opening on the Sabbath. The exclusive jurisdiction of the Chief Rabbinate to grant certificates of Kashrut accords the Council great power, and this power is not always used for the purpose originally designed.

607. Thus, for example, in 1989, the belly dancer Ilana Raskin petitioned the HCJ against the policy of the religious council in Jerusalem to make it a condition of the grant of a certificate of Kashrut that no 'immodest' shows (including belly dances) were put on in the hall in which food and drink was served. The Court held that in granting the power to issue a certificate of Kashrut, the legislature did not intend to empower the rabbi to force that business to behave in a particular manner, even if that behaviour was prohibited by religious law. The Court even added that the certificate could not be made conditional on a prohibition against the applicant conducting Christmas or New Year's celebrations in the hall or hotel in which the food being served was given a certificate of Kashrut.[295]

608. By contrast, in a judgment given in December 1995, the HCJ held that a rabbi could not be compelled to conduct a wedding ceremony in a place in which non-Kosher food was being served, recognizing that 'compelling rabbis to conduct a ceremony in a place which did not maintain Kashrut harmed them and was equivalent to forcing them to do something which their conscience forbade and might bring disgrace upon them'.[296]

609. The clash between individual freedoms and religious principles has become more acute in recent years, including in relation to the issue of meat imported to Israel, referred to above. Since its establishment, the government has maintained control of meat imports to Israel, and has only imported Kosher meat. In 1992, the government decided, on the basis of recommendations of a professional committee, to privatize the importation of meat, and to enable unlimited imports without need for licenses.

---

295. HCJ 465/89 *Raskin v. Jerusalem Religious Council*, 44(2) PD 673.
296. HCJ 6111/94 *Committee for Traditionalists v. Council of the Chief Rabbinate of Israel*, 49(5) PD 94.

610. This decision was not implemented prior to the elections to the 13th Knesset, and it was not long before Basic Law: Freedom of Occupation was adopted. The new government decided to regulate the privatization of meat imports in primary legislation, in such a manner as to ensure the preservation of the status quo. In view of the comments of the HCJ that a statute which restricts meat imports to Kosher meat might unlawfully contravene the provisions of Basic Law: Freedom of Occupation, the Basic Law was amended by the insertion of the override clause. Concurrently, a law prohibiting the import of meat into Israel was enacted,[297] except where that meat was issued a certificate of Kashrut by the Council of the Chief Rabbinate. The law was enacted within the framework of the override clause and in accordance with the conditions set out therein.

611. These are merely a few examples of how the freedoms of religion and conscience are implemented in Israel. Most arrangements today seek to maintain the status quo in the relations between the religious and secular communities. It should be recalled that until the last Knesset, the Orthodox and religious parties always formed part of the political coalitions in Israel, thereby precluding any possibility of change.

F. Freedom of Movement

612. Freedom of movement is a basic right, which ensues from the definition of a person as a free man, and is an essential precondition for the realization of many other freedoms and rights. The State is entitled to limit this right when its implementation conflicts with other important public interests, such as national security or public order. Freedom of movement is anchored in international documents, which deal with human rights;[298] however, apart from the right to leave and enter the State, this right has not been entrenched in a Basic Law. The Basic Law: Human Rights bill (elements of which were adopted in Basic Law: Human Dignity and Liberty), included a section dealing with freedom of movement and established, *inter alia*, the right of every person, lawfully present in Israel, to move freely within Israel and the right of every inhabitant of Israel to choose a place of residence in Israel. This section was not included in Basic Law: Human Dignity and Liberty in deference to the religious parties which feared a violation of the principle of no travel during the Sabbath in religious neighbourhoods.

IV. The Status of Human Rights Not Included in the Basic Laws

613. Following the enactment of the basic laws on human rights, a key question on the Israeli political agenda during the following years concerned the status of

297. Import of Frozen Meat Law, 1994.
298. Section 13 of the Universal Declaration of Human Rights (1948); s. 12 of the International Covenant on Civil and Political Rights (1966); and Section 5 of the Convention on the Elimination of All Forms of Racial Discrimination (1966).

rights which were not expressly mentioned. Do the rights expressly referred to in the basic law form a 'closed list', which reflects the protected rights ensuing from the principle of 'human dignity and liberty'? Over the years, while the legislature failed to complete the basic laws on human rights, attempts have been made to convince the Court to broadly interpret 'human dignity' in order to include human rights that have not been constitutionally anchored. When it started addressing petitions that sought the inclusion in the right to dignity of rights such as the equality principle, freedom of speech, right to a family life, right to due process and so on, the Court assumed that if the original basic law did not include these rights, it did not negate them either. In many cases, the HCJ chose to interpret broadly the right to dignity. For example, as we have seen, the Court determined that a defendant's right to be present at his own trial is part of the right to due process, which is a constitutional right protected by Basic Law: Human Dignity and Liberty.

614. In recent years, the prevailing approach has been one that defines the rights protected by the basic law as not only those expressly mentioned in it, or those which ensue naturally and directly from the right to 'dignity', but also additional rights, which are derived from the essence of the right to 'human dignity and liberty'.

615. This process by which the Supreme Court completes the constitution – cautiously, with restraint, but steadily – is interesting. While the basic assumption is that certain rights (the right to equality or the freedom of expression) are implied by the human right to dignity, a complete bill of rights cannot be recognized under this limited right. Therefore, the Supreme Court reserves the right to consider whether a certain aspect of equality, for example, should be acknowledged and constitutionally protected because it is closely associated with the right to dignity. Similarly, the Court may refuse to include another aspect of equality in the right to dignity and refuse to judicially review a law that impairs equality. One of the most far-reaching developments refers to the right to equality, as we shall see further on. When the legislature kept silent, the Court granted parts of the equality principle – not entirely; only certain aspects thereof – the constitutional status that allows judicial review of laws that disproportionately limit them.

616. I assume that this approach, which aspires to expand the application of Basic Law: Human Dignity and Liberty, will continue to play a central role in Israeli case law concerning human rights in the coming years.

V. The Right to Equality

A. General Remarks

617. Israel is one of the few states in the West which has not entrenched a person's right to equality in all areas of his life in a constitution, perhaps because this is the most problematic right in Israeli constitutional law.

618. The principle of equality has a place of honour in the historical heritage of Judaism. 'One law and one manner shall be for you and for the stranger that sojourneth with you' (Numbers, 15:16). 'Ye shall have one manner of law, as well for the stranger, as for one of your own country' (Leviticus: 24:22). During the British Mandate over Eretz Yisrael, the British undertook to prevent discrimination on the grounds of race, religion and language. The British government articulated this undertaking in important legislation in 1922 which established the legislative powers of the High Commissioner in Eretz Yisrael.

619. Upon the establishment of the State, the Jewish heritage and the importance of the principle of equality found expression in the Declaration of Independence: 'The State of Israel will ensure complete equality of social and political rights to all its inhabitants irrespective of religion, race or sex.' Over the years, some aspects of the right attracted concrete statutory consideration, either by way of a statute expressly referring to the principle of equality or by way of legislation intended to guarantee the principle, albeit tacitly.

620. Thus, for example, the Knesset passed the Women's Equal Rights Law, 1951 in relation to gender equality, and entrenched the principle of equality in section 42(a) of the Employment Services Law, 1959 and in the Equal Opportunities in Work Law, 1988, in relation to the prohibition on discrimination in the labour market on account of age, sex, sexual preference, race, religion, ethnic group, country of origin, views or party affiliation.

621. These and similar statutes have not been accorded superior normative status, and the Knesset is entitled to deviate from their provisions in subsequent legislation.

622. In the absence of a general sweeping statement regarding the supremacy of the principle of equality, the Supreme Court has acted as the source of the duty of the governmental authorities to act equally towards citizens of the State. A line of cases has established the principle whereby it is presumed that the purpose of a piece of legislation is to further equality and preserve it. Accordingly, express language is needed in order to contravene this presumption.[299]

623. Justice Landau referred to this in the following way: 'it is right that in borderline cases, when a provision of primary legislation is open to two interpretations, we shall prefer the interpretation which preserves equality for all before the law'.[300] Even when it is clear that the legislature deviated from the principle of equality, the Court will attempt to limit – by way of interpretation – the scope of the deviation.

624. Following the enactment of Basic Law: Human Dignity and Liberty, the accepted view of the HCJ is that, notwithstanding that the principle of equality is not expressly mentioned in the basic law, it still has constitutional normative status.

---

299. HCJ 104/87 *Nevo v. National Labour Tribunal*, 44(4) PD 749, 764.
300. HCJ 98/69 *Bergman v. Minister of Finance*, 23(1) PD 693.

Thus, for example, Professor Barak writes in his book: 'From now on, equality is a supra-legal principle ... it has become a central constitutional principle.' This approach is based on a broad interpretation of the right to 'human dignity and liberty', and a reference to the principles of the Declaration of Independence. This approach lead to the requirement that legislation, which impairs a man's right to equality, will meet the conditions of the 'limitation clause', set out in section 8 of the basic law. At the same time, in any event, the legislation, which was in force prior to the enactment of the basic law, will not lose its validity because, as mentioned, the basic law has no retroactive effect.

625. In a decision handed down in May 2006, by an expanded panel of eleven judges, the Court decided by a majority vote of six to five, against a petition to strike down a temporary provision of the Citizenship Law. This provision, which is highly controversial, severely restricts the rights of Palestinians in Judea and Samaria from living with their spouses and children who are Arab citizens of Israel.[301] The law, passed in 2002 at the height of Israeli Palestinian fighting, was argued to violate the principle of equality. The government argued that the legislation was based on security concerns, because many Palestinians granted licenses for family reunions were involved in terrorist attacks against Israeli citizens. The majority ruled that the temporary provision should not be declared void.

626. However, the importance of this case reaches far further than issues of citizenship, or the final decision on the merits. It was in this decision, along with another decision delivered only three days before it,[302] that the Supreme Court judges agreed to include the principle of equality within the framework of Basic Law: Human Dignity and Liberty. These cases provoked in Israel a new 'constitutional revolution' concerning human rights. The recognition of some aspects of the right to equality as a constitutional and protected right in Israel may lead to the further inclusion of all remaining rights into the basic laws.

627. In both cases, the expanded panel of Judges agreed upon the idea that several aspects of the principle of equality are now protected in the basic law. Those aspects of equality that are 'closely related' to the principle of human dignity are constitutionally protected. This is a new approach in Israeli jurisprudence. Until now, some obiter dictum about the principle of equality being constitutional could be found in different cases, but not a joint statement of almost all the judges in the Supreme Court. It means that from now on, any new law violating the principle of equality can be judicially reviewed by the Supreme Court. It should be remarked that this basic right has been deliberately left out of the basic law by the Knesset.

301. HCJ 7052/03 *Adalah v. Minister of Interior* (not yet published, delivered on the 14 May 2006). *See* Ch. 1 on this Part, on nationality.

302. HCJ 6427/02 *The Movement for quality government v. the Knesset* (delivered on 11 May 2006). This case dealt with a petition for judicial review of the law granting an exemption for Yeshiva students from the army. The Court decided, eight judges against one dissenting, that the law is constitutional.

628. The fact that in both of these 2006 cases the law was not declared void should not mislead as to the importance of the decisions' reasoning. Both laws were temporary laws, and the Court decided to give the Knesset reasonable time to deal with these two controversial issues: namely, the exemption of yeshiva students from army service, and the temporary provision on the Citizenship Law restricting Palestinians from living in Israel with their families. The importance of the cases lies in the recognition of the principle of equality, as part of Basic Law: Human Dignity and Liberty. New petitions filed with the HCJ asked the Court to invalidate the law that exempts *yeshiva* students from military service once the temporary law was extended again. This time, in 2012, the HCJ determined that the right to dignity, as it appears in Basic Law: Human Dignity and Liberty, includes several aspects of the right to equality, and eventually decided to nullify the Tal Law because it disproportionately harmed the right to equality.[303]

629. In recent years, there has been a growing tendency to apply the duty to act equally on the basis of gender, religion, nationality and the like, to private bodies as well. This tendency is reflected both in legislation and in case law, which requires private bodies which provide services to the public to act equally and fairly.

630. Within the principle of equality, we shall focus on two specific examples. The first is the approach taken by Israeli law towards minorities. The second is equality between the sexes and between persons of different sexual orientations.

B. *Minorities in Israel and the Problem of Discrimination on the Basis of Religion and Nationality*

631. Insofar as concerns the status of Israeli Arabs, it should be made clear that we are not considering the classic issue of civil rights and minority rights, but rather a special situation. This situation is characterized by the absence of peace with the Arab-Muslim world, a persistent security crisis and the natural identification by the majority of Israeli Arabs with their national and cultural heritage.

632. The Declaration of Independence of the State of Israel guarantees complete equality of civil and political rights to all inhabitants, without discrimination on the basis of race, religion and gender, and calls upon the Arab citizens of Israel to take part in the building of the state, and to be represented in its institutions. Nonetheless, concurrently with the guarantee of equality, Israel was defined as a 'Jewish State in Eretz Yisrael', a definition which hints at a distinction between the status of the Jews and non-Jews. In practice, it is difficult to speak of equality in a situation in which on one hand Israeli Arabs are not subject to a duty to perform military service and national service, while on the other hand, they do not enjoy, in practice, those civil rights mandated by the full rules of equality.[304]

---

303. HCJ 6298/07 *Ressler v. The Knesset* (published by Nevo on 21 Dec. 2012).
304. S. Samooha, *Minority Status in Ethnic Democracy: The Status of the Arab Minority in Israel*, 13 *Ethnic & Racial Studies* 349 (1990).

633. The tension between the definition of Israel as a Jewish State and its declared commitment to democracy and equality between Jews and Arabs has characterized Israel's attitude towards the Arabs from its establishment, and has been reflected in express statutory provisions as well as in rulings of the Supreme Court.

1. Equality and the Jewish State

634. The Law of Return, 1950 provides the clearest definition of the State of Israel as a Jewish State, and it enshrines in statutory form the essence of the Zionist concept, namely, the bond between Jews in the Diaspora and the State of Israel. The Law of Return recognizes the right of every Jew in the world to immigrate to Israel, and to become a citizen of the State. It follows that all the Jews in the world are potential citizens of Israel. The preferred legal status given to Jews and their family members is expressed in the right to immigrate and the grant of automatic citizenship. Every immigrant who settles in the country otherwise than in accordance with the Law of Return must be naturalized and meet the conditions set out in the Nationality Law.

635. Prima facie, the preference accorded to Jews is inconsistent with the principle of equality. Nonetheless, this special status does not undermine the rule of law. The grant of the right of return and the right to citizenship is not subject to the principle of equality for the simple reason that in this area, the State has a recognized right to decide the composition of its population and its character. This right was expressly recognized by the International Covenant for the Elimination of All Forms of Racial Discrimination adopted by the UN on 21 December 1965, a covenant which was signed and ratified by Israel on 3 January 1979.

636. Additional statutes accord special recognition to the character of Israel as a Jewish State, including the World Zionist Organization – Jewish Agency (Status) Law, 1953. This law refers to the historical functions fulfilled by the World Zionist Organization and the Jewish Agency, and declares that these institutions will act as in the past to gather the exiles, supervise the absorption of immigrants and develop settlement. Other statutes in Israel regulate the observation of the Sabbath and other Jewish holidays as rest days, as well as Holocaust Day, the Flag and Emblem Law, 1949, which define the flag and national emblem as possessing Jewish character, and other statutes which create cultural and remembrance institutions possessing Jewish content.[305] All of them emphasize the Jewish character of the State of Israel.

---

305. For additional statutes which confer special status upon Judaism, *see* for example, the Foundation of Law, 1980. This law enables a Court faced with a legal question to which there is no answer in statute or case law or by analogy, to decide it 'in the light of the principles of freedom, justice, equity and peace of Israel's heritage'. While the interpretation of this section is subject to dispute, this law clearly gives statutory recognition to the definition of the State of Israel as a Jewish State. Likewise, the Chief Rabbinate of Israel Law, 1980 defines the structure of the Chief Rabbinate of Israel and its functions. It should be emphasized that there is no parallel law regulating the establishment of religious institutions for other faiths.

637. The Declaration of Independence, which expressly defines the State of Israel as a 'Jewish State', does not have formal constitutional status which enables the invalidation of contravening statutes. However, as noted, it has important constitutional ramifications. These ramifications are most patent in the context of elections to the Knesset, where the question has arisen whether an Arab list, which rejects the characterization of the State as Jewish, can be disqualified from participating in the elections. A particularly interesting example of this issue concerned 'Al Arad' party members, who stood for election to the Knesset in 1965. The CEC held that the Al Arad list could not act as a society or association, as it was a movement seeking to undermine the existence of the State. According to the law, the CEC, which conducts the elections, is empowered to disqualify a list of candidates if the list does not meet the formal conditions established by statute.[306] The Elections Committee refused to approve the list because of the fact that its members negated the integrity and very existence of Israel.

638. The Elections Committee disqualified the list without having the statutory power to do so. It was an *ultra vires* decision which was appealed to the Supreme Court. The Supreme Court upheld the disqualification of the list by a majority, and dismissed the appeal. The Supreme Court's decision in this case (known as the *Yardor* case)[307] is one of the most important in Israeli legal history and perceived as an exceptional and unusual decision. In many senses, it has become a 'symbol' of the notion of defensive democracy.

639. The then President of the Supreme Court, Justice Agranat, held in the majority opinion, that the existence of the State of Israel as a Jewish State is a 'basic constitutional fact' which cannot be appealed, and a party which rejects this basic fact is not entitled to stand for elections to the Knesset. He concluded from this that the Elections Committee was entitled to disqualify the list which had as its goal the complete negation of the existence of Israel. Since 1985, Basic Law: The Knesset has permitted the disqualification of a list which negates the existence of the State of Israel as a Jewish and democratic State.

2. The Duty to Perform Military Service

640. The Defence Service (Consolidated Version) Law, 1986 imposes a duty to perform military service upon all citizens of Israel who have reached the age of 18. The basic period of regular service is three years for men and two years for women. Following discharge, citizens are subject to annual military reserve duty which may take sixty days. While the law does not distinguish between citizens on the basis of religion or nationality, the enlistment officers are entitled to exercise discretion at the time of enlistment. Since the establishment of the State, defence policy has been to refrain from enlisting Arabs, apart from Druze men who have been enlisted since the end of the 1950s.

306. For the disqualification of parties *see* also Part II, Ch. 1, and below in this chapter.
307. EA 1/65 *Yardor v. Central Elections Committee*, 19(3) PD 365.

641. The formal reason given to Israeli Arabs for their exemption from military service is the desire not to face them with the problem of making them use weapons against their own people. The reason for the exemption is less important than the fact that the vast majority of Jews are enlisted and the vast majority of Arabs are not enlisted. Consequently, if military service is a criterion for the grant of rights, its significance will be that the majority of Jews will enjoy them whereas the majority of Arabs will not.

642. The non-enlistment of Arabs does not fundamentally detract from their national and other rights. Service in the IDF vests a series of rights which ensue from the service itself, such as priority in returning to a place of work following service and exemptions from charges in particular circumstances.

643. In the past, patent discrimination existed which caused great resentment among Israeli Arabs in relation to 'ex-military servicemen's benefits'. This benefit, which was introduced in the beginning of the 1970s by virtue of the Discharged Soldiers Law, was paid by the Institute of National Insurance together with the ordinary children's benefit, and granted significant additional financial funds to families of soldiers with three or more children. The law defined a 'soldier' as one who served in the armed forces, and a 'family member' as a spouse, child or parent. In practice, most Jews who had three or more children received the benefit, whereas most Arabs did not receive it. The discharged soldier's benefit provided a practical means of improving the lot of one group in the population and not of another, without connection to the financial situation of any of them.

644. This state of affairs changed following the elections to the 13th Knesset, when the government decided, shortly after being formed, to create a uniform set of rules relating to children's benefits. According to prevailing law, all are entitled to the same social rights, the same academic university fees, the same housing and the same child benefits. The compensation given to IDF servicemen for losing years in which they might otherwise have studied or worked is established by the Absorption of Discharged Soldiers Law, 1994. It is specific and connected to the service performed, such as a particular payment of money for the service, and grants and loans for housing and higher academic studies.

3. Equality in the Allocation of Resources to the Arab Population

645. The basic undertaking in the Declaration of Independence to grant full equality of rights to Israeli Arabs was not fully realized in practice. Arab citizens suffered, and continue to suffer from, discrimination and oppression in numerous areas of life. While it cannot be denied that with respect to civil and political rights the Arab citizens enjoy basic rights, in other areas, primarily those relating to participation in public institutions and resource allocation, *inter alia* – housing, education, settlement policy, welfare, budgets of local authorities and employment, discrepancies between Arabs and Jews remain substantial. In a number of public sectors as well, the respective levels of resource allocation and Government services to the Jewish and Arab populations are disproportionate. A number of factors have contributed to this phenomenon, among them the political and social environment, the priority that all governments have given to the promotion of the Jewish economy and settlement, the fact that the Arab population is exempt from service in the IDF and naturally, Israeli legislation.

646. By contrast to the accepted norm in other states, Knesset legislation does not generally prescribe binding standards for a basic level of public services – educational, health, sewage, etc., – to which every citizen is entitled. These matters are generally left to the discretion of the ministry in charge, which determines its priorities in accordance with budgetary constraints. This is the source of preferences, disparities and even discrimination in resource allocation that favour stronger populations in terms of their influence in government, and their political identification with the State and the government. Furthermore, even government allocations are not all regulated by a substantive law determining allocation criteria. The cumulative result is gross discrepancies in resource allocation between different sectors of the population.

647. Here too, the absence of a fundamental and basic principle of equality governing resource allocation has compelled the Supreme Court to enter the fray. In a series of decisions over the past few years, the Supreme Court has conducted in-depth examinations of discrimination in resource allocation, and where necessary, has intervened in government decisions regarding budgetary allocation. Hence in the HCJ in *Adalah v. Minister of Labour and Welfare*,[308] the petitioners claimed that the Ministry of Labour and Welfare was pursuing a discriminatory policy when designating Ministry funds to the indigent in anticipation of the Passover festival but failing to ensure parallel allocation of funds to the Arab indigent, prior to their festivals. The Ministry of Labour and Welfare conceded that it was obliged to act on the basis of equality in allocation of funds to the poor of different religions. Accordingly, it agreed to amend its criteria for the support of needy families in anticipation of the upcoming Passover Festival, in a manner that would ensure equal allocation to members of other religions too.

648. In HCJ *Adalah v. Minister of Religious Affairs*,[309] the petitioners claimed that the Ministry of Religious Affairs had been derelict in fulfilling its duty to ensure equal allocation of resources for the cemeteries of the Arab minority. The petition was accepted, and the Supreme Court ordered the Ministry of Religious Affairs to allocate the Ministry's budgetary funds for cemeteries on an equal basis for the different religions. In that judgment, Justice Zamir wrote as follows:

308. HCJ 2422/98 *Adalah – The Legal Centre for Arab Minority Rights in Israel v. Minister of Labour and Welfare*, Tak-El 98(2) 531.
309. HCJ 1113/99 *Adalah – The Legal Centre for Arab Minority Rights in Israel, Minister of Religious Affairs*, 54(2) PD 164.

> Discrimination in the allocation of state resources based on religion or nationality is prohibited even if done indirectly. It is certainly forbidden, *a fortiori*, when done directly. A striking example of this is discrimination in the allocation of funds from the State budget by a government ministry ... Indeed, the norm is that budgetary funds do not suffice to cover all needs and all the needy, giving rise to the need for criteria-priority based funds allocation and leading to sectorial and personal distinctions. Nonetheless, the priorities and the discrepancies must be based on relevant considerations, which are consonant with the principle of equality, and not on extrinsic considerations, such as religion or nationality.

649. Today the preservation of the principle of equality in budgetary allocation is mandated both by case law and by legislation.[310] In practice, however, things are different. Arab organizations are frequently compelled to turn to the HCJ, petitioning the latter to order equality-based allocation. Moreover, when the Court grants injunctive relief pertaining to the principle of equality, it does so prospectively, with a view to coming budgetary year. This remedy is problematic since it does not function adequately as a deterrent against ongoing discrimination, and tends to perpetuate existing disparities. At the same time, it is stressed that since the 1990s, there has been a marked improvement in the implementation of principles of equality between Jews and Arabs in the area of the allocation of state resources.

4. Allocation of Lands

650. A similar situation prevails with respect to allocation of State lands to the Arab population. In principle, pursuant to section 1 of the Israeli Lands Law, it is forbidden to sell state lands or transfer ownership therein, and their administration is under the aegis of the Israeli Lands Authority.

651. Since the establishment of the state, hundreds of new settlements have been established for Jews, whereas apart from the creation of Bedouin villages in the Negev, and the recognition granted to a few previously unrecognized villages, not a single Arab settlement has been established.

652. A groundbreaking judgment on the settlement policy of the Zionist movement is *Kaadan v. Israel Land Authority*,[311] which dealt with the legality of the Israel Lands Authority's allocation of lands designated exclusively for Jewish settlement. The petitioner was an Arab requesting to purchase a house or plot of land for his family in the precincts of a Jewish settlement – the Katzir settlement. The settlement was built on State lands allocated to the Jewish Agency and in effect the

310. Section 3A Budgetary Principles Law, 1985.

311. HCJ 6698/95 *Kaadan v. Israel Lands Administration*, 54(1) PD 258 (hereinafter – *Kaadan*). The decision was given in the year 2000.

settlement only accepted Jewish residents. Having received a negative response, the petitioner filed a petition to the HCJ.

653. The Court allowed the petition, ruling that the State was duty bound to premise all of its actions on the basis of equality, and that this duty was constitutionally based. The ruling was given by President Barak, who ruled that different treatment based on religion or nationality is 'suspect' and is, prima facie, discriminatory treatment. Justice Barak conceded that circumstances may arise in which different treatment deriving from considerations of religion or state is justified, such as in a case of rectificatory discrimination or affirmative action in accordance with the law. However, in the instant case, the Court found no legal basis for state-sponsored discrimination, and therefore decided to allow the petition, declaring that 'the State was not permitted by Law to allocate state Land to the Jewish Agency for the purpose of establishing the communal settlement of Katzir based on discrimination between Jews and non-Jews'. This was the first time that a Court had ruled that when the Government allocates state lands, it is enjoined from discriminating between those benefiting from the allocation, directly or indirectly, based on their religious or national affiliation.

654. The Court based its decision on two considerations, a practical one and one of principle. On a practical level, the State did not allocate areas for exclusively Arab communal settlements, and hence, in the absence of any policy for allocating lands for Arab settlements, the Arabs should be allocated land in Jewish settlements.[312]

655. The second issue, of principle, was based on the Court's refusal to regard the case as falling into the category of 'equal, but separate'. Relying on the rationale of the famous American decision in *Brown v. Board of Education*,[313] the Court ruled in Kadaan that a policy of 'equal, but separate' was inherently unequal when it was the majority that desired to separate. Separation of this kind 'is insulting to the minority group being removed from the general public, stressing the difference between it and the others, and perpetuating feelings of social inferiority'.[314] The Court instructed the State to consider the petitioner's request to purchase a piece of land for them in the Katzir settlement, for the purpose of building their house, based on the principle of equality.

312. R. Gavison, *Does Equality Require Integration: A Case Study*, 3 Democratic Culture 36, 77–78 (2000).
313. *Brown v. Board of Education*, 347 US 438, 74 S.Ct. 686 (1954).
314. *Kaadan, ibid.*, at p. 279. The concept of 'separate but equal' was adopted in one case in Israeli case law, in HCJ 528/88 *Avitan v. Israel Lands Administration.* In that case, the petitioner was a Jew who requested to lease a plot in a settlement earmarked for Bedouins. The Court rejected the petition, ruling that there is a public interest in assisting Bedouins to live permanently in urban areas, for reasons pertaining to the provision of proper public services, such as education, health, sanitation and others. These interests, when combined with the long felt need to change the customs and lifestyle of the Bedouin sector, justify granting priority to the Bedouins in the allocation of plots under subsidized conditions, in a settlement designated for their permanent residence.

656. The Ka'adan couple was not granted a direct injunction allowing them to purchase land in Katzir. Instead, the justices held that the State of Israel was not permitted to allocate state land on the basis of discrimination between Jews and non-Jews.

657. Legally speaking, this case deals with the abolition of a discriminatory phenomenon. However, the decision must also be read politically, disclosing a disturbing reality. Since the establishment of the State of Israel, land allocation has been almost exclusively for Jews. The Zionist ethos is based on establishing a Jewish country in the Land of Israel, which implies building and developing settlements for Jews. As such, the Arab population has not enjoyed allocation of land for its own expansion. This import of the case is not that from now on, Arabs will be admitted into new Jewish settlements. The majority of the Arab population does not actually want this. In Israel there are almost no 'mixed settlements',[315] mostly because of the will of each population to preserve its own identity and way of life. For the Arabs in Israel, this case may mean the possibility of the state allocation of land for their own development. This possible reading of the decision, or its evolution in this direction, may lead to new appeals. Therefore, the application of *Ka'adan*'s *ratio decidendi* in the future remains to be seen.

658. In 2012, the Knesset introduced the *Admittance Committees Law*, which created a way for communal and rural Jewish settlements in the Negev and the Galilee to refuse settlement candidates because, among other things, 'they do not match the social-cultural fabric'. Clearly introduced to counter the *Ka'adan* verdict, this law practically legalized the screening processes which have been practised in those settlements primarily to refuse the entry of Israeli Arabs. In September 2014, in a five to four decision, an expanded panel of the Israeli Supreme Court decided to dismiss a petition brought by Adalah three years ago against this law. The majority at the HCJ stated that it cannot determine at this stage whether the law violates constitutional rights. Therefore, the petition was rejected on the basis of the ripeness doctrine.

C. Gender-Based Discrimination

659. With respect to the status of women, similar to the previous examination of Israel's Arab minority, one of its striking aspects is the need for affirmative action. In both cases, there was a clear need for a policy that is not based on equality, but on 'discrimination' that favoured the members of one group, which was intended to increase the equality between that group and others.

315. According to the Israeli Statistical Yearbook, there are eight 'mixed' settlements, with a decisive Jewish majority, but a significant Arab or other minority: Tel-Aviv-Jaffa, Haifa, Ramle, Acre, Lod, Ma'alot-Tarshiha, Upper Nazareth and Neve-Shalom.

660. Naturally, there is a dispute as to whether affirmative action constitutes an exception to the principle of equality, inasmuch as it is not blind to gender, religious, or national affiliation, or even disability, and effectively causes discrimination against others. However, it may be subsumed within the equality principle as one of the means of achieving substantive equality.

661. In the case of *Israeli Women's Network v. Government of Israel,*[316] Justice Matza referred to this point, stating that 'In my view, it [the principle of affirmative action S.N.] should be recognized as a corollary of equality. Its status should be that of a necessary derivative and central guarantee of equality and not just a permitted exception to the principle of equality'. Nonetheless, it is clear that affirmative action can only be implemented in appropriate cases.

662. The principle of gender equality was not recognized by the Mandate charter or in the King's Order in Council 1922, apparently due to the fears of the Mandate government that such recognition would be construed as an attempt to interfere with the customs of the various communities, a factor that was primarily relevant with respect to the Muslim communities. However, the principle of gender equality was included in the Partition Plan and in the third section of the Declaration of Independence.

663. Even though the franchise was granted equally to men and woman with the establishment of the State, and there was a recognized prohibition on gender-based discrimination, in reality, equality was not achieved. Inequality was expressed in various statutory provisions, and primarily in the area of personal status,[317] in which the woman's position was inferior to that of her spouse, and in the election and appointment of woman to senior positions in the public service and in the private sector. The result was growing demand for active intervention; in other words, for affirmative action to rectify the position of women.[318]

664. The predominant statutory expression of the recognition of equality between the sexes was already established in the early days of the State, in the Women's Equal Rights Law, which includes a general provision that anchors the overarching principle of women's equality (section 1 of the law): 'A man and a woman shall have equal status with regard to any legal proceeding; any provision of law which discriminates with regard to any legal proceeding, against women as women, shall be of no effect.'

665. In the amendment of the law in 2000, a number of significant new rules and principles were added. Under section 1B, entitled 'Permitted Distinction and Affirmative Action', the following situations will not be regarded as infringing equality

316. HCJ 453/94 *Israeli Women's Network v. Government of Israel*, 48(5) PD 529.

317. Gila Stopler, *Article Countenancing the Oppression of Women: How Liberals tolerate Religious and Cultural Practices That Discriminate Against Women* 2 Colum. J. Gender & Law 154, 171 (2003).

318. For further discussion *see* F. Raday, *Culture, Religion, and Gender*, 1 Int. J Constitutional Law 663–715 (2003).

or constituting prohibited discrimination: (1) distinction between a man and a woman where the distinction is dictated by substantive differences between them, or the nature of the matter; (2) a directive or act intended to rectify prior or existing discrimination, or a directive or act intended to promote women's equality […]. Section 6C, entitled 'Appropriate Representation', provides that all tenders and appointments in public bodies must give expression to the appropriate representation of woman. Section 6D, entitled 'Equality in the Security Forces', states that all women who are candidates for, or currently serving in, the security forces, shall have a right equal to that of a man, to serve in any position … [.] The main purpose of this legislation was to ensure statutory anchorage of equality between men and women with regard to various legal rights.

666. This basic provision gives binding expression to absolute equality of rights for women. Formally, the law is a normal one, and did not merit the title 'basic law' and entrenchment against amendment by the provisions of a later law. All the same, the Court regarded it as having established a general provision regarding the rights of woman to equality in all areas of law. In the legislative context, it bears mentioning that the principle of equality established in the Woman's Equal Rights Law quite frequently conflicts with the provisions of the woman's personal law, namely her religious law. Thus, with respect to the laws of marriage and divorce, which fall within the jurisdiction of the personal law as determined by Rabbinical Courts, and precisely in the areas in which women are currently subject to discrimination, section 5 of the same law provides that: 'This law shall not affect any legal prohibition, or permission relating to marriage or divorce.'

667. The Rabbinical Courts have exclusive jurisdiction in all matters concerning the marriages and divorces of Jews who are citizens or residents of Israel. The religious Courts, including the Rabbinical Courts, rule in accordance with the religious law, and not secular law. One of the questions which arose related to whether the provisions of the Women's Equal Rights Law superseded the discriminatory substantive provisions of the religious law. The Supreme Court distinguished between the ritual aspects of marriage and divorce, which supersede the provisions of the Women's Equal Rights Law, and the monetary or property related aspects.[319] In the landmark decision of *Bavli v. Rabbinical Court of Appeals*,[320] the Supreme Court ruled that matters of division of property cannot properly be considered to be

319. R. Halperin-Kaddari, *Symposium Issue Colonizing Women: The Ethical and Legal Issues Surrounding Systematic Gender and Race Discrimination: Women, Religion, and Multiculturalism in Israel*, 5 UCLA J Intl & Foreign Affairs 339, 348 (2001). A few examples of inequality are as follows. In the marital ceremony, the husband 'buys' the wife, and the husband's consent is an absolute condition for the divorce. Indeed the methods for compelling a recalcitrant husband to grant a divorce writ (*get*) to the wife have been toughened up of late, but according to Jewish Law, a woman cannot be given permission to marry without the husband's consent – as opposed to the permit that may be given to a husband where the wife does not and/or is unable to give her consent to the divorce. Furthermore, the substantive provisions of personal status are determined by institutions from which women have always been excluded, and they are not determined in accordance with democratic principles.

320. HCJ 1000/92 *Bavli v. Rabbinical Court of Appeals*, 48(2) PD 221.

matters of ritual religious law, in which the Women's Equal Rights Law does not apply.

668. The Women's Equal Rights Law further provides that the law does not derogate from any provision of law protecting women as women. The priority given to her in any law by virtue of her being a woman is not affected by the law. This matter has found expression in a number of laws, *inter alia*, in the special provisions relating to woman's labour,[321] pregnancy-related rights and shortening the period of military service for women.

669. A question arises regarding the distinction between protection of women and discrimination against them. Does the establishment of a lower retirement age for women protect them or discriminate against them? In the past, the rule was that different retirement ages applied for men and for woman. The Supreme Court expressed its opinion that the distinction regarding the age of retirement constituted discrimination against women. Today there is a single statutory age of retirement for men and women employees, while a woman's right to early retirement is also retained.

670. In relation to the issue of equality for women and affirmative action, the Supreme Court made a special, decisive contribution to Israeli law. In order to promote the values of equality, the Supreme Court was prepared to intervene in areas which were customarily regarded as unjusticiable, such as army training. For example, the famous judgment in *Miller*[322] was a landmark case for women's equal rights. This case dealt with a petitioner who challenged the rules of the army which prevented women from participating in the IDF pilot's course.

671. In this case, the Supreme Court ruled that even if the training of women for the pilot's course was more expensive due to the shorter period of women's service in their roles, the army authorities should have to bear that cost.

672. Justice Matza stressed that the relative weight of budgetary considerations, which were at the basis of the Army's decision not to accept women for the pilot's course:

> is measured and determined by being balanced against other considerations […]. In any event, when the issue is one of a claim for the realization of a basic right – which indeed is the right being dealt with before us [i.e., the right to equality – S.N.] – the relative weight of budgetary considerations cannot be great.

---

321. Employment of Women Law, 1954 prohibits the employment of women in any work or production process or workplace which may be especially prejudicial to their health, and night work, subject to exemptions and permits that may be granted. The law also guarantees a working woman's right to a leave of absence for the purposes of childbirth, and to be absent from work during periods of pregnancy and breastfeeding.

322. HCJ 4541/94 *Miller v. Minister of Defence*, 49(4) PD 94 (hereinafter '*Miller*').

Absent any definitive proof substantiating the claim that the cost of accepting female pilots in aviation jobs is unreasonable, the IDF cannot exclude women from the pilot's course.

673. Justice Strassberg-Cohen, too, in her judgment, referred to the financial burden of accepting women into the pilot's course, but stressed that resources should be allocated in a manner that accommodates the same starting point for both genders. Her approach is based on her basic conviction regarding the equal weight to be ascribed to equality and to state security, as a function of military needs. Accordingly, the 'value of (military and security needs) prevails over the lower value (equality) only if there is near certainty of real harm being caused to state security', and 'in all these cases, there must be an examination of whether there are alternate measures which could prevent the close possibility of a serious danger'. Since the military authorities did not prove that such damage could be expected at the required level of certainty, she ruled that their position violated the principle of equality. The judgment had far-reaching ramifications for the army, and since the ruling, a whole range of military courses have been opened to women, which in the past were regarded as too 'manly' for women.

674. The Supreme Court trail-blazed a similar revolution in the direction of equalizing women's rights to serve in public positions connected to provision of religious services, i.e., membership of the body that appoints the local rabbi, and membership on religious councils. The landmark case here was *Shakdiel.*[323] In this case, the Supreme Court ruled that the principle of equality between the sexes prevails, and rejected the claims that the appointment of women to serve in these positions should be prevented, due to the disruption caused to the functioning of theses bodies. In doing so, the Court did its best to ensure that religious law was not used as a tool for discriminating against women, and in his leading judgment, Justice Elon cited and relied upon an array of leading contemporary religious-halakhic authorities according to which women were indeed permitted to serve in public positions, and according to which this did not in any way contradict religious law.

675. It would thus appear that, whereas in the financial areas, progress has been made towards realization of equality between the sexes, in the area of marriages and divorces, such progress would require the establishment of an alternative to the religious framework, which would enable couples to create an equality-based relationship that is not based on the patriarchal system.

D. Discrimination Based on Sexual Orientation

676. The right to equality includes the right not to be discriminated against by reason of sexual orientation. The protection is against an affront to a person's dignity and rights by reason of his sexual orientation, and the freedom to form emotional and sexual relations and to form a family without discrimination based on his

323. HC 87/153 *Leah Shakdiel v. Minister of Religious Affairs et al.*, PD 42(2) 221.

spouse's gender, while receiving the same protection and social support that heterosexual families receive.

677. Israel has never known or practised persecution of homosexuals of the type that was once rife in other Western states, despite the religious, biblically based prohibition of homosexual sexual relations, and despite an old criminal prohibition against the conduct of 'unnatural sexual relations'. Israel has always been tolerant in this area. At the same time, recent years attest to a number of dramatic changes in the community's attitude towards homosexuals and lesbians.

678. Until the last few decades, alternative sexual leanings were regarded as deviant, and the very existence of homosexuals and lesbians as a significant societal group was denied. Today, lesbians and homosexuals enjoy a considerable degree of social equality and dignity, which may be seen in an increased societal openness to alternate forms of family and spousal relationships. For example, even though the criminal prohibition was never actually enforced and criminal indictments were never filed against offenders, the retention of the offence in the Penal Code prevented the realization of the right to equality and the prevention of discrimination based on sexual preference. In 1988, the Knesset amended the Penal Code, and repealed the offence of carnal knowledge between males. With the repeal of this prohibition, the road was paved to recognition of this right. An additional step in that direction was expressed by the removal of all limitations on the service of homosexual soldiers in the IDF.[324]

679. The principle of equality in terms of sexual tendency also received expression with respect to labour relations and social rights. In 1992, the Equality of Opportunities in Labour Law was amended, and a provision was added under which employers are forbidden to discriminate against employees, or those seeking employment, in their employment and in their conditions of work, on the basis of 'sex, sexual orientation, and personal status'. The blanket approach taken in labour relations reflects the tremendous importance attaching to ensuring the equality of employment opportunities and of the ability to make a living with dignity.

680. In 1994, the High Court ruled on the petition of an air steward, Yonatan Danilowitz,[325] who argued that the prohibition on discrimination based on sexual orientation in the Equality of Opportunities in Labour Law also prohibits employers from discriminating against same-sex couples, as opposed to heterosexual couples, when they give their spousal benefits, even when the spouses are not legally married (i.e., where they are 'common law partners'). Incidental to its discussion of the right of the El-Al steward to receive an annual free ticket for 'his spouse', the HCJ ruled in a majority opinion that conferring a benefit to heterosexual common law spouses and denying it to same-sex couples constitutes unlawful discrimination.

---

324. Tzili Mor, *Law As a Tool For a Sexual Revolution: Israel's Prevention of Sexual Harassment Law, 1998*, 7 Mich. J. Gender & L 291, 314 (2001).
325. HCJ 721/94 *El-Al Airlines v. Danilowitz*, 58(5) PD 749.

681. In another case filed after three years of litigation and negotiations, Adir Shteiner, who was the spouse of a deceased senior officer, was conferred the financial benefits that had previously only been granted to spouses of the opposite sex.[326] Furthermore, he received the rights of commemoration of his deceased spouse, such as the right to be invited to official commemoration ceremonies of the Ministry of Defence.

682. Another key ruling, setting an important precedent, was handed down in the *Yarus-Hakak* case,[327] in which the Supreme Court allowed a lesbian couple to adopt each other's biological children. Later, the attorney general issued detailed instructions concerning same-sex adoptions that were even more advanced and flexible. Nevertheless, the public and legal struggle of same-sex couples is not over. No Court verdict has ever explicitly stated that same-sex couples are equal to heterosexual couples in every respect. Verdicts on such issues are rarely handed down. In its judgments in cases that have addressed the rights of same-sex couples, the Supreme Court has repeatedly insisted that the Court's decision does not acknowledge the validity of same-sex marriages. The Court has left the issue of the legality of same-sex marriage unaddressed and unresolved, believing it to be a matter for the legislature. Although an HCJ decision ruled in favour of five same-sex Israeli couples who married in Canada and requested that their marriages be registered in Israel, same-sex marriages are not generally acknowledged. Nonetheless, the gay and lesbian community has politically, legally and culturally moved from the margins of Israeli society to increased visibility and growing acceptance.

VI. The Right to Vote and Be Elected and the Disqualification of Parties

683. Since the establishment of the State of Israel, security considerations have been deemed relevant for the purposes of restriction of freedom of association, where the association is regarded as having the intention of harming state security, and if the members of the association identify with enemies of the state. The central legislation restricting freedom of association was enacted in 1948, and remained substantively unchanged until the beginning of the 1980s. Notably, these laws have no 'direct application' to the right to vote and be elected to the Israeli Parliament: The Knesset, given the omission of any substantive or ideological limitation of the right to vote and to be elected.[328]

---

326. HCJ 5398/96 *Steiner v. Minister of Defence* Tak-El, 197(1) 244. For a detailed analysis of this case, *see* A.M. Gross, *Challenges to Compulsory Heterosexuality: Recognition and Non-Recognition of Same-Sex Couples in Israeli Law*, in *Legal Recognition of Same Sex Partnerships: A Study of National, European and International Law*, 391–414 (R. Wintemute and M. Andenas, eds., Oxford 2001).

327. CA 10280/01 *Tal Yarus-Hakak v. the Attorney General*, 59(5) PD 59(5), 64 (2005).

328. Basic Law: the Knesset provides a broad definition of the right to vote and to be elected. The sole limitation relates to conviction for an offence carrying moral turpitude, for which the punishment is imprisonment, prior to the passage of seven years from the date on which he completed serving his sentence. There are also restrictions concerning ideology, on which we will focus below.

684. The issue of invalidating a political party and therefore restricting its freedom of association and the right to vote and be elected, was first adjudicated in Israel in 1965 in the case of *El-Arad*,[329] and again when Rabbi Meir Kahane and his 'Kach' movement appeared on the political scene in 1984, running for election on a racist platform directed against Arabs. In the famous *Neiman* judgment,[330] the Supreme Court ruled that, in the absence of any legislative basis for disqualifying a list on ideological grounds, there was no choice but to confirm Kahane's list and to permit his party to participate in the Knesset Elections. In the wake of this judgment, a statutory amendment was passed, permitting the disqualification of lists of candidates on the basis of their objectives. Section 7A of the Basic Law, as passed in 1985 (and amended in 2002 and 2008), provides that:

> 7A (a) 'A candidate's list shall not participate in elections to the Knesset, and a person shall not be a candidate in elections to the Knesset, if the objects or actions of the list or the actions of the person, as the case may be, expressly or by implication, include one of the following:
> 1. The negation of the State of Israel as a Jewish and democratic state.
> 2. Incitement to racism.
> 3. Support for an armed struggle by a hostile state or a terrorist organization against the State of Israel.
>
> (b) A decision of the Central Elections Committee to disqualify a candidate from participating in the elections requires the confirmation of the Supreme Court.

685. Despite the constitutional limitation of the political right of being elected, this law has only been used sparingly. Since its adoption, only Kahane's list and those sharing similar characteristics have actually been disqualified. The law has not been utilized to disqualify Arab lists, and until the printing date of this book, it had not even been used to disqualify a party that supported the armed struggle of terrorist organizations against Israel, notwithstanding efforts to have the party in question disqualified, based on the provisions of section 7A. The Supreme Court emphasized that it would not allow the majority to abridge the freedom of a political minority.

Apparently, the damage caused by the stifling of a political opinion and excluding a party from the political process outweighs the benefit gained thereby. The essence of democracy lies in the license given to the minority opinion to endeavour to mould the character of the State, even if the majority is convinced of the absolute, incontestable truth of its own ideology.

---

329. EA 1/65 *Yardor v. Central Elections Committee*, 19(3) PD 365. This topic is discussed in detail in Part II, Ch. 3.
330. EA 23/84 *Neiman et al. v. Chairman Central Elections Committee*, 39(2) PD 225. For a detailed elaboration of the judgment and of the argumentations of the justices, *see* Claude Klein: *The Defence of the State and the Democratic Regime in the Supreme Court*, 20 Israel Law Review, 397.

VII. Freedom of Expression

686. In Israel, the right to freedom of expression is considered to be one of the foundations of the democratic system, and already in early rulings of the Supreme Court, it was termed 'a fundamental right', from which other rights are derived. Courts have given a broad interpretation of the manifold expressions included within the protection of freedom of expression, including all manner of books, films, plays, words, actions, theatre performances and sculptures. It comprises political, literary and commercial expression. Hence, '[F]reedom of expression is not just the freedom to express or to hear words that are accepted by all. Freedom of expression is also the freedom to express views which are odious, infuriating, and perverse, which provoke the revulsion and loathing of the entire public'.[331] Even expressions which are nothing but a 'sordid concoction of erotica, politics and all manner of perversity'[332] are included. So too are expressions which offend a person's feelings or his good name, which are racist or even obscene.

687. Naturally, freedom of expression is not absolute and unlimited, and where it conflicts with other interests or human rights, a balance must be struck to decide which interest has priority in the circumstances. Israeli law distinguishes between freedom of expression per se, which extends to all utterances and expressions and all the various fora in which they are presented, and the scope of the protection given, which is partial and measured, and is the product of the balance struck with competing, conflicting values.

688. Due to its omission from the list of basic rights enumerated in Basic Law: Human Dignity and Liberty, the formal constitutional status of freedom of expression as a basic right is disputed. Nonetheless, violations of freedom of expression are treated by the Court as a violation of a formal constitutional right, and the criterion for evaluating an abridgment or violation of the freedom is expressed in the 'limitation clause'.

689. In recent years, the Supreme Court justices have invoked the limitation clause to assess the legality and constitutionality of violations of the freedom of expression, originating in the actions of the sovereign authorities. However, the limitation clause did not replace the various balancing formulae adopted in case law, such as the test of 'close possibility'. The Court's practice has been to integrate the criteria of 'imminent certainty' or 'close possibility', which is a probability-based criterion, with the value-based criteria of the limitation clause that primarily assesses proportionality. In applying the proportionality criteria of the limitation clause, the Supreme Court continues to resort to the balancing formulae that developed in case law prior to the adoption of the Basic Law.

331. HCJ 399/85 *Kahane v. Managing Committee of the Broadcasting Authority*, 41(3) PD 255.
332. HCJ 14/86 *Laor v. Council for Film Censorship*, 41(1) PD 433.

690. According to the balancing formula established in the *Kol Ha-am* case, which is the most widely accepted formula, where a conflict arises between freedom of expression and the public peace and security, the restriction of freedom of expression will only be permitted if two cumulative conditions are satisfied: (1) that the damage caused by the expression to the public peace and security is grave, harsh and serious. The damage must exceed the 'tolerance level' generally prevalent in a democratic society and shake its very foundations. (2) The likelihood of the damage to the public peace and security must be one of 'imminent certainty' or 'close possibility'. However, the Court ruled that the diversity of possible situations compels a diversity of balancing points, and held that it is impossible to establish a single test for assessing the multifarious possible situations.

691. As stated above, despite the tremendous importance of freedom of expression as a supreme basic right, this right is not legislatively anchored. The attempt to explicitly entrench the freedom of expression in the Basic Law was unsuccessful. Already in 1992, a draft proposal for Basic Law: Freedom of Expression was tabled, yet the legislative procedures have been stopped. Nonetheless, in a number of its decisions, the Court has ruled that the freedom of expression and the freedom of political expression are tightly and practically associated with the right to human dignity.[333]

A. *Freedom of the Press*

692. Freedom of the press, too, as such, is neither protected, nor even anchored in any Israeli legislation, and it was likewise omitted from the democratic rights enumerated in the Declaration of Independence. Until this very day, the print media is governed by a colonial law – the Press Ordinance of 1933, the declared goal of which was to curtail the activities of the press in Mandate Palestine, which, in the views of the British Mandate Authorities, enjoyed exaggerated freedom. Despite the fact that freedom of the press is without explicit statutory anchorage, it is indisputably one of the basic rights in Israeli law. The High Court conferred it with this elevated status in its famous ruling in *Kol Ha-am* in 1953.

693. The print media is supervised by the executive branch, by force of Mandate Provisions such as the Press Ordinance, and the Defence Regulations (Time of Emergency) 1945. These provisions remained in force even after the establishment of the State, but the Supreme Court has given an exceedingly restrictive construction to their provisions, commensurate with the elevated status of the freedom of expression.

---

333. CA. 105/92 *Re-em Engineers Contractors Ltd. v. Upper Nazareth Municiplity*, 47(5) PD 189; LCA *Geva v. Walt Disney Company*, 48(1) PD 251; HCJ 2481/93 *Dayan v. Jerusalem District Commander*, 48(2) PD 456, 468. HCJ 10203/03 *The National Census Ltd. v. Attorney General*, para. 26 of Justice Naor's verdict (published in Nevo, 20 Aug. 2008).

694. The broadest restriction on the freedom of the press in Israel is the result of the obligation of licensing, prescribed in the Press Ordinance. To the best of my knowledge, Israel is the only democracy in the world in which a newspaper's publication is contingent upon a governmental license. The difficulty created by the regulation derives from the fact that the power to approve a license also constitutes the power to refuse to grant a license. Notably, in recent years, there have been no instances of refusals.

695. In addition to the District Commissioner, the Minister of the Interior is empowered to close down a newspaper, on the basis of security considerations. Section 19(2) of the Press Ordinance empowers the Minister of the Interior to suspend publication of a newspaper. This power was discussed at length in the *Kol Ha-am* case cited above, as well as in the case of *Omer International Inc. New York v. Minister of the Interior.*[334] In this case, the petitioners requested the cancellation of an order to suspend publication of the Al Pag'r newspaper published in East Jerusalem, for a period of a month. The order was given after the Minister of the Interior was satisfied that its publication contained 'praise of acts of murder and terror and encouragement of their continuation, and acts that were likely to endanger the public peace'. In its decision, the High Court relied on the ruling established in *Kol Ha-am*, under which the Minister of the Interior is empowered to use his power of suspension if the publication poses a 'close possibility' of endangering the public peace. The balance test was used by the Court to reach a conclusion opposite to that reached in the *Kol-Ha-am* case. The Court ruled that the publication of the paper posed just such imminent danger, and therefore rejected the petition, and determined that the Minister of the Interior had made lawful use of his power to suspend publication of the newspaper.

696. Another restriction on the freedom of the press in Israel can be imposed by the Military Censor. Pursuant to the Defence (Emergency) Regulations 1945, a military officer, namely, the Chief Military Censor, is authorized to request and to submit his criticism of any material intended for publication in the press and to prohibit its publication if he deems that it 'would be, or be likely to be or become, prejudicial to the defence of the country or to the public safety or to public order'. The regulations further confer the Censor with the authority to prohibit by order the publication of any matter that 'may or is liable to endanger the defence of Israel, and public safety'.

697. The Chief Military Censor's authority was discussed at length in *Schnitzer v. Chief Military Censor,*[335] in 1988. In that case, the Court deliberated over the Military Censor's disqualification of certain paragraphs of an article published in a newspaper. The article criticized the head of the Mossad's [Agency for Intelligence and Special Duties] effectiveness as well as the impending change in leadership of the Mossad. The Censor felt that a publication of this nature could focus attention

---

334. HCJ 644/81 *Omer International Inc. New York v. Minister of the Interior*, 36(1) PD 227, 234.
335. HCJ 680/88 *Schnitzer v. Chief Military Censor*, 42(4) PD 617.

on the head of the Mossad and endanger his safety, and thus adversely affecting the Mossad's ability to function in general and in the field of security policy.

698. The Court allowed the petition and permitted publication of the article in the above respects, holding (per Justice Aharon Barak – as he was then known) that although the Defence Regulations were promulgated by the Mandatory regime, they are now part of Israeli legislation and should be interpreted in harmony with Israeli democratic values, among them the prominent values of freedom of expression and freedom of the press. The instant case concerned a conflict between the value of state security and the values of freedom of expression and the public's right to information. A balance must be struck between these interests. Justice Barak concluded that the Censor had disqualified the newspaper publication without being convinced that the publication created the requisite 'imminent certainty' or 'close possibility' of danger, and the exercise of his power was therefore flawed. This judgment significantly curtailed the Censor's powers, and was of tremendous significance with respect to the status of the Supreme Court and its activist ruling. The judgment is an example of the High Court's willingness to intervene even in matters bearing a military nature, which until that time were considered unjusticiable.

B. *Expressions Offending Public Feelings*

699. Conflicts between freedom of expression and the offending of public feelings and morality have often been the subject of discussion and deliberation in Israeli constitutional law. These deliberations have their source in the Mandate period, in the Cinematograph Films Ordinance 1937, under which the screening of a film in public in Israel requires prior approval for screening by a Board established under the Ordinance. Under the provisions of the Ordinance, the Board is empowered to ban a film in its entirety or in part, to disqualify certain sections therein, to impose limitations on the permitted viewing age, or to approve it, at its own discretion. Despite its broad license to abridge freedom of expression, the Ordinance did not establish criteria for the Board's exercise of its censorship capacity.[336]

700. The development of case law in this respect has been particularly interesting, giving expression to the metamorphosis in the Supreme Court's conception of freedom of expression and its appropriate degree of protection.

701. For example, in 1973 the Supreme Court handed down the *Avidan* decision,[337] ruling that:

336. Originally, and for a number of decades, the Board also operated as a censorship board in relation to the presentation of theatre performances, in accordance with the Public Performances (Censorship) Ordinance, but later on, the authority for preliminary censorship of plays was repealed.
337. HCJ 383/73 *Avidan v. Gary*, 28(2) PD 766, 769.

> the law does not provide guidelines for the exercise of the Board's discretion, and it has absolute freedom in its decisions. In this case, where the public authority has unlimited authority, the Court will not intervene in a topic that may be the subject of a public controversy ... I am almost unable to conceive of a case in which we would regard ourselves as authorized to cancel its decision. After all, the Board was chosen to represent the public interest in this case, and for as long as it exists, its opinion must be decisive.

On the face of it, this was a minimalist judicial approach, whereby the Court would not interfere with the Board's decision, in view of the broad discretion granted to the Board.

702. A few years later, the Court adopted a substantially different approach to the very same issue, in its ruling in the *Universal* case.[338] That case concerned the Board's decision to ban the 'Last Temptation of Christ' from screening in Israel, given that its presentation would give grave offence to religious sensibilities and the beliefs of the Christian public. The Supreme Court accepted the petition, and annulled the Board's decision. The justices made it clear that despite the broad formulation of the Board's discretion, only an extreme, vulgar and deep affront to public feelings could justify restricting the freedom of expression. The degree of probability required for such damage to justify restriction of freedom of speech must be that of 'close possibility'. The Court concluded its ruling with the determination that 'There is no evidentiary foundation for deciding that what the Christians of Rome and Paris are permitted to see should be forbidden in Jerusalem', and thus approved the film for screening in its entirety.

703. Since the ruling in the *Universal* case, the Court has displayed a consistent trend of limiting the powers of the Film Censorship Board to a minimum. One of the Supreme Court justices even averred that the Court's decisions regarding this issue amounted to a 'requiem' of the Film Censorship Board.

704. This trend received its starkest expression in the Supreme Court's decision in *Bakri v. Film Censorship Board*,[339] (more commonly known as the *Jenin Jenin* case), which is one of most problematic cases to have come before the Supreme Court over the last few years on the issue of freedom of speech. According to its producers, the film in question purported to present the Palestinian narrative of the battle in the Jenin refugee camp in April 2002, during 'Operation Defence Wall', and as noted by Justice Dorner herself: 'the petitioner declared that he did not attempt to present the Israeli position, or even to present a balanced version of events. His goal was to present the Palestinian story regarding the events surrounding the IDF's entry into the Jenin refugee camp'.[340]

---

338. HCJ 806/88 *Universal City Studios Inc. v. Film & Theatre Censorship Board and Others*, 43(2) PD 22.
339. HCJ 316/03 *Bakri v. Israel Film Council*, (not published) (hereinafter '*Jenin Jenin*').
340. On 29 Mar. 2002 following a terrorist attack two days previously on the Park Hotel, the IDF began the 'Military Shield' operation. On 30 Apr. 2002, IDF forces entered the Jenin refugee camp. A

705. Upon the termination of the IDF military operation in the Jenin refugee camp, film producer Muhamd Bakri entered the camp and videoed the responses of the Palestinian residents to the IDF operation. All of these responses were combined and presented in film form in the 'Jenin Jenin' movie, which was a deliberate attempt to present the Palestinian perspective of the IDF operation and the ensuing battles. The film's central claim was that the IDF had purportedly perpetrated a massacre in Jenin, a claim which had already been proved groundless by the Supreme Court, and by international bodies.

706. The film was submitted for the approval of the Film Censorship Council, prior to being commercially screened. The Board decided by a majority of eight out of eleven members to disqualify the film, based on a number of considerations: first of all, the film presented a distorted picture of the battle under the guise of documentary truth, with the intention of misleading the public; second, the manner in which the film presented events amounted to incitement that included de-legitimation of the very existence of the State of Israel; and third, the film severely offended public sensibilities and the feelings of the soldiers' families, whose sons had fallen in the course of the operation. The film producer, Bakri, petitioned against the Board's decision to ban the film before the HCJ.

707. The main judgment was written by Justice Dorner, who focused on the Board's first reason. She ruled that the falsity and distortion of expression as such may still be protected by freedom of speech. In her words, 'The mere fact that an expression is false does not constitute a cause for the removal of protection'. Similarly, Justice Proccacia added resolutely that 'issues of truth in expression, including artistic productions, cannot usually constitute a cause for the restriction of freedom of expression'. Justice Dorner assessed the violation of the freedom of speech through the limitation clause and stated that the disqualification of the film does not satisfy the requirements of the clause. She wrote that:

> an absolute prohibition against the screening of a film is the most drastic action which the Council is authorized to take. It must be a measure of last resort and its adoption must be restricted to those cases in which there is no other way of achieving the same goal.

708. Justice Procaccia concurred with Justice Dorner's conclusion, but contended that the main dilemma in the case concerned the third reason given by the Council, which related to the offence to the feelings of the public. Her approach was that, in view of the tremendous importance of freedom of expression, 'only in exceptional and extreme cases, where the offence exceeds the level of tolerance which should be borne in a democracy, and where the offence will substantially

---

harsh battle ensued, in the course of which IDF forces were engaged in house-to-house fighting and at the end of which twenty-three soldiers had been killed, and thirty injured. According to IDF statistics, fifty-two Palestinians were killed, about half of them citizens, while houses and property were damages.

harm public safety and public order, will it be justified to limit freedom of expression'. On the merits of the issue, the justice ruled that in this case even though the offence was grave, genuine and harsh, the offence did not shake the foundations of human tolerance to the extreme and exceptional extent required to justify restricting the freedom of expression.

709. The Supreme Court decided to permit the screening of the film, and rejected an application for a further hearing in an expanded judicial forum. In fact, the judgment divests the authority of any real substantive power to disqualify films and plays, which still exists (in theory). The conclusion emerging from the *Bakri* decision is that only in a rare and exceptional case is it possible to exercise the power to ban films, and cases of this nature do not appear likely at all.

C. *Freedom of Expression and the Prohibition on Incitement to Racism*

710. In the first thirty years of the State's existence, the phenomenon of incitement to racism was rare, and while the legislation included provisions enabling prosecution and punishment of inciters, the emphasis was primarily on seditious publications under the Penal Law, the definition of which included the prohibition on promoting feelings of ill-will and enmity between different sections of the population. There were also criminal prohibitions regarding slandering the public, which afforded a theoretical framework for filing an indictment for incitement to racism.

711. In the 1980s, however, this situation changed with the ascent of Kahane, and the phenomenon of incitement to racism became a concrete reality. The advent of the Kach movement, which promoted the creation of a State, based on Orthodox Jewish law, free of all non-Jews, galvanized public awareness of the pressing need to discuss and confront racist ideologies. Concurrently with the legal system's response to the phenomenon of racism, i.e., the prevention of participation of racist lists in the Knesset, there was also a need to deal with its criminal aspect.[341] Accordingly, along with the legislation of section 7A of Basic Law: The Knesset preventing the participation of lists that incite to racism, the Penal Law was also amended.

712. Section 144A of the Penal Law, 1977 defines racism as 'persecution, humiliation, degradation, the display of enmity, hostility or violence, or the causing of riots against a public or parts of the population, all because of their colour, racial affiliation, or national, ethnic origin'. Section 144B prohibited the publication of racist incitement.

713. The Supreme Court justices are divided over whether freedom of speech even extends to racist expression. Justice Barak, for example, expressed the view that the internal grain of freedom of expression even extends to expression with racist overtone or content.[342] Other views were, however, expressed by his colleagues

---

341. D. Kretzmer, *Freedom of Speech and Racism*, 8 *Cardozo L. Rev* (1987) 445.
342. HCJ 399/85 *Kahane v. Managing Committee of Broadcasting Authority*, 41(3) PD 281–282.

on the bench. The election of Kahane to the Knesset triggered a series of decisions dealing with his activities in the Knesset.[343] One of these decisions examined the freedom of racist expression in Israel. The *Kahane* case[344] judicially reviewed the Broadcasting Authority's refusal to broadcast planned interviews with MK Kahane, to ensure that he would not exploit governmental broadcasting tools for incitement to racism,[345] and its decision to only survey those activities in which Kahane participated which 'were intrinsically newsworthy'. Kahane petitioned against the Authority's decision to effectively 'ban' him to the HCJ. Justice Barak ruled that in a democratic society it was incumbent upon the Broadcasting Authority not only to provide ongoing objective news coverage, but also to give expression to the opinions and views of the various streams of society.

714. According to Justice Barak, this case concerned a candidate who was permitted to participate in the Knesset elections, which begs the question of how a person can be permitted to participate in the Knesset elections and thereafter have his views banned for presentation to the public. The Court allowed the petition against this decision, overturning the decision of the Broadcasting Authority, and ruling that the Broadcasting Authority was not entitled to categorically refuse to broadcast the views of MK Kahane, even if his views give rise to substantial and acute revulsion. The criterion for freedom of expression, including political expression, is the test of 'close possibility'.

715. The Supreme Court was also required to address the criminal aspect of incitement to racism in the *Elba* case,[346] which discussed the expressions of Rav Elba, who published an article entitled 'Clarification of the Laws concerning the Killing of a Non-Jew', in which the author argued that it was both permitted and justified to kill Arabs. The Supreme Court ruled that the prohibition on the publication of incitement to racism abridges freedom of expression, but that the infringement is for an appropriate purpose, namely, the prevention of racism, the preservation of human dignity and equality of those offended by racism. It is further intended to preserve the public peace. Nonetheless, the appropriate interpretation of the criminal prohibition must ensure that the ambit of the prohibition would be limited to what is critical for the realization of that appropriate purpose, and that the violation of freedom of expression would not exceed what is necessary.

716. Summing up, Israeli law provides broad protection to freedom of expression, even in times of emergency and war. This protection is even broader than the protection provided by other Western democracies, even despite the absence of explicit constitutional entrenchment of the freedom of expression. The Supreme

343. The MKs attempted to curtail his activities, and thus prevented him from tabling draft proposals, and disqualified bills that he submitted to the Knesset presidium. In all of these cases, the High Court found itself in the unenviable position of having to protect Kahane, who was a parliamentary minority, against the 'dictatorship' of the majority.
344. *Ibid.*, p. 235.
345. It bears mentioning that the Broadcasting Authority is a public authority in Israel, and during that period, there were neither competing broadcasting authorities, nor any cable television.
346. Cr. A 2831/95 *Elba v. State of Israel*, 50(5) PD 221, p. 221.

Court's point of departure was that freedom of expression is the 'crown jewel' of a democracy, and as such, merits maximum protection. A frequent criticism is that the protection afforded to freedom of expression in Israel is excessively broad, and is provided at the expense of other important interests that are not sufficiently stressed in the Supreme Court's decisions. Particularly harsh criticism was directed against the *Jenin Jenin* decision, which was one of the grandest monuments to freedom of speech in recent Israeli case law. Presumably, even in the event of the enactment of a Basic Law: Freedom of Expression, the scope and protection of the right in Israel would not differ substantively from the guidelines established in the Supreme Court rulings discussed above, which is already, particularly (even to the point of being overly) broad. In my estimation, were such a law to be enacted, the only addition would be the broadening of the possibility of judicial review of laws abridging the freedom of expression.

§3. Human Rights in the Occupied Territories

717. Since its establishment, the State of Israel has found itself in an exceptionally grave and perilous security situation. In the geopolitical environment of the Middle East, Israel has been engaged in an ongoing confrontation, at various levels, with states and organizations that have yet to reconcile themselves with the fact of its existence, and which are liable to initiate military actions against it. Since its establishment in 1948, Israel has fought a number of battles with Arab states, and these exceptional security circumstances have compelled the state to adopt emergency measures which can provide an appropriate response to these dangers.

718. Furthermore, over the last few decades, Israel has confronted times of threats to its citizens' security, stemming from heinous terrorist attacks which originated in the territories of the Palestinian Authority, that have been under Israeli occupation since 1967. Since October 2000, for a few years, the Israeli Palestinian conflict, that many thought was coming to an end, entered a new phase. Suicide bombers in Israeli cities and curfews in the West Bank cities became a part of everyday routine. The renewed Intifada of the 2000s and the Israeli military operations in Palestinian cities at that time posed a number of serious questions regarding the balance between defence of human rights and meeting the security needs of the state during a time of war. Is the collective punishment of a city's population legitimate? Is it permissible to destroy the homes where suicide terrorists lived? What legal instruments, if any, should the Court use in reviewing the actions of the security forces? Should the legal powers of the IDF and of other bodies dealing with terrorism be increased? What should be the scope of judicial intervention when dealing with counter-terrorism measures?

719. Terrorism defies democracy. It poses difficult challenges to a democratic state. Not every means available to fight terrorism is also a legal and justifiable one. Fighting terrorism may require decisions that are inconsistent with democratic values. In this fight, the ends may be confused with the means. It may require difficult and delicate assessments, and balancing between the claims of national security and the principles of human rights. Standard legal tools, that are suited to periods of normalcy, may prove inadequate when the cannons are booming. For example, the accepted, protracted legislative procedures do not provide an appropriate response to the needs for urgent legislation necessitated by an emergency situation.

I. The HCJ and the War against Terror

720. The last Intifada brought the Supreme Court into 'the eye of the storm', the middle of the battlefield. Numerous appeals were brought to Court alleging illegitimate action taken by Israeli Forces in military operations.[347] Petitions were issued during combat, even petitions from suspected terrorists. Decisions had to be made in real time. Chief Justice Barak, President of the Supreme Court, wrote:

> Is it proper for judges to review the legality of the war on terrorism? On both extremes of the political spectrum there are many who argue that the Courts should not become involved in these matters. On one side, critics argue that judicial review undermines security; on the other side, critics argue that judicial review gives undeserved legitimacy to governments' actions against terrorism. Both arguments are unacceptable. Judicial review of the legality of the war on terrorism may make this war harder in the short term, but it also fortifies and strengthens the people in the long term. The rule of law is a central element in national security.[348]

721. In most of the cases brought before the Court, it stated that it would not intervene in operational military considerations. However, even when ruling that it would not intervene, the Court recognized, on the one hand the duty of the state to protects its citizens, and on the other hand, to give due attention to the need to ensure the constitutionality and legality of war.

722. Due to the unique nature of this subject in constitutional law, we will present some of the outstanding cases that have come before the Supreme Court, dealing with human rights and the war against terror.[349]

---

347. Among other matters, at the time, the Court was asked to order the IDF not to harm the civilian population in the Jenin refugee camp, to refrain from bombarding civilian targets, to order the IDF to refrain from the destruction of houses without pre-warning and to state whether the siege of the Church of the Nativity was legal. *See*, for example, HCJ 3022/02 *LAW v. Commander of the IDF in the West Bank*, 56(3) PD 9; HC 3451/02 *Alamdani v. Minister of Defence*, PD 56(3) 30; HCJ 3436/02 *Castodia Internationala de Tara Santa v. Government of Israel*, 56(3) PD 22.
348. Aharon Barak, *Foreword: A Judge on Judging: The Role of a Supreme Court in a Democracy*, 116 Harv. L. Rev. 16, at p. 158 (2002).
349. Most of these verdicts were published in English on the Supreme Court's official site, under 'Fighting Terrorism Within the Law'; see: http://elyon1.Court.gov.il/VerdictsSearch/EnglishStaticVerdicts.html.

A. *Targeted Pre-emptive Killings*

723. 'Targeted assassinations', or 'Targeted Pre-emptive Killings',[350] is the name given to a long-term activity undertaken by the Israeli Security Forces, aimed at terrorist leaders responsible for terrorist attacks directed against Israeli citizens.

724. In the 2000s, the Israeli security forces used tactics of pre-emptive assassinations against Palestinian militants, field commanders as well as infrastructure coordinators. This practice took place in the context of the Intifada, and served, on the one hand, as a central tool of Israeli security policy in response to 'the escalation of violence', and, on the other hand, as a trigger for this very escalation in the form of retaliatory actions by the Palestinians.

725. The legality of this policy was contested twice in the Supreme Court, when a petition seeking the cessation of a 'policy of execution without a trial' was presented before the Court.[351] It is important to note that in peacetime, Israeli law only permits capital punishment for those convicted of committing or assisting in genocide, and since Adolf Eichmann,[352] no criminal has been sentenced to death in Israel. Captured terrorists, convicted of murder by the Court, face life sentences.

726. In the first case, short judgment consisting of three sentences, the Court ruled that the petition was non-justiciable. The judgment reads: 'The choice of means of warfare, used by the Respondents to pre-empt murderous terrorist attacks, is not the kind of issue the Court would deal with.' The argument of 'unjusticiability', almost abandoned by the Supreme Court, was the key used to avoid dealing with the delicate and problematic issue. The absence of legal reasoning does not allow us to conclude whether a new border of judicial intervention in the military activity has been formed or whether the decision not to interfere was merely influenced by the violent conflict.

The second case was the last decision President Barak handed down before his retirement in 2006.[353] In it, the outgoing president quoted from a judgment he had

---

350. For further reading on the different views relating to this activity, *see*: O. Ben-Naftali & K. Michaeli, *We Must Not Make a Scarecrow of the Law': A Legal Analysis of The Israeli Policy of Targeted Killings*, 35(2) Cornell Int. Law J. (Spring 2003); E. Gross, *Thwarting Terrorist Acts by Attacking the Perpetrators or their Commanders as an Act of Self-Defence: Human Rights Versus the State's Right to Protect its Citizens*, 15 Temp. Int'l & Comp. L. J. 195 (2001); J.N. Kendall, *Israeli Counter-Terrorism: 'Targeted Killings' Under International Law*, 80 N.C.L. Rev. 1069 (2002); L. Rene Beres, *On Assassination as Anticipatory Self-Defence: The Case of Israel*, 20 Hofstra L. Rev. 321 (1991); M.N. Schmitt, 'State-Sponsored Assassination in International and Domestic Law, 17 *Yale J. Int'l L.* 609 (1992).

351. HC 5872/01 *Barakeh v. Prime Minister*, 56(3) PD 1.

352. The Nazi and Nazi Collaborators (Punishment) Law, 1950, 4 L.S.I. 154 (1949–1950), provides for capital punishment for criminals convicted under this law. The only case in the history of Israel in which a Nazi criminal was convicted and sentenced to death was the case of Adolf Eichmann. *See*: *Attorney General v. Eichmann*, 36 *Israel Law Review* 18 (1968) and *Eichmann v. Attorney General*, 36 *Israel Law Review* 277 (1968).

353. HCJ 769/02 *Public Committee against Torture v. the Government of Israel* (handed down on 14 Dec. 2006).

delivered several years earlier on GSS interrogation methods.[354] 'We are fully aware of the fact that this verdict does not make dealing with this reality any easier', he wrote. 'It is the fate of democracies that they may not approve of every means and cannot employ all the methods that their enemies use.'

The verdict examined the legality of the targeted assassinations policy and outlined some rules for its implementation, but the petition against the practice was rejected. The decision neither authorizes nor forbids the use of this tactic: 'It cannot be determined in advance that every targeted killing is prohibited according to customary international law.' The Court ordered that each case be examined in detail before the method is applied, and that the military commander further consider alternatives and the expected damage of each instance of the practice. Use of targeted assassinations must be proportional; that is, based on the balance between military benefits and the expected damage they might cause to innocent civilians. Practically, however, the security forces had followed similar considerations even before the verdict was handed down. Targeted assassinations were not practised daily, but now their preceding considerations appear in a legal document. This document was not written only for Israeli readers but is part of Israel's dialogue with the international community that closely monitors Israel's activities in the Occupied Territories.

B. The Assigned Residence Case

727. The wide scope of military operations and 'targeted pre-emptive killings' tactics did not put an end to terrorists' attacks in the early years of 2000s. Prevention and deterrence of suicide bombers became an urgent issue, and several measures were considered by the IDF. One of them was the decision to reassign the residences of terrorists' family members, and those of suicide bombers' families, from the West Bank to the Gaza Strip. Involvement of the relocated persons in terrorist activities was defined as a necessary condition for reassignment of their residences. The effect of the measure was to be twofold, namely, preventative and deterrent.

728. For the fulfilment of this new policy, the Security Provisions (Judea and Samaria) Order was amended, providing the military commander, if he is of the opinion that 'it is imperative for decisive security reasons', with the authority and discretion to place a person under special supervision. The amendment extended an original application of the Order, originally limited to Judea and Samaria, to the Gaza Strip as well. In accordance with the amendment, a person subject to special supervision could be required to live within the boundaries of a specific place in the West Bank or Gaza Strip.[355]

354. To be discussed further on HCJ 769/02 *Public Committee against Torture v. the Government of Israel* (handed down on 14 Dec. 2006).

355. Israeli military and civilians withdrew from the Gaza Strip in 2005.

729. In 2002, specific orders were signed assigning the place of residence of family members of three terrorists to Gaza, requiring each of them to live in the area for two years. According to the order, each of the persons to be relocated had been involved in assisting terrorist activities that resulted in human casualties. Petitions against the commander's order were submitted before the HCJ,[356] arguing that the Amendment Order was contrary to international law and therefore invalid.

730. The Court pointed out that the basic framework for examining the legality of the actions of the IDF Commander was to be found in the provisions of international law and the laws that apply to belligerent occupation. In the territories under IDF control, the international laws concerning belligerent occupation, such as the (Fourth) Hague Convention on the Laws of War and the Fourth Geneva Convention, are applicable. From a legal perspective, the areas of Judea, Samaria and Gaza comprise the same territory, and their formal status has not changed since the period of mandatory Palestine. Both districts are subject to belligerent occupation by Israel, and they are regarded and administered as one territorial unit by Israel and by the Palestinian side. Therefore, the case does not involve the transfer of a person outside the area subject to belligerent occupation, which would be an act prohibited by international law.

731. Furthermore, given that Judea, Samaria and the Gaza Strip are one territorial unit, the Order is in compliance with the Geneva Convention, and the decision of the Commander is an assignment of a place of residence, which is permitted under the Article 78 of the Convention.[357]

732. The Court ruled that the decision of assignment should be based on a 'balancing test' between human rights and the urgent needs of society. The existence of a reasonable possibility that the person himself presents a real danger must be proved. Deterring other terrorists should not be the only goal to be considered by the Commander. Prevention of danger is an essential condition for a relocation order.

733. It may be interesting to note that the justiciability 'barrier' was not mentioned in this case. President Barak raised the question of the judicial review of security issues, and referred to the role of the judge in times of war:

> We do not replace the military commander's security considerations with our own … . Our job is to maintain boundaries and to guarantee the existence of conditions that restrict the military commander's discretion.[358]

---

356. HCJ 7015/02 *Ajuri v. IDF Commander in the West Bank*, 56 PD 352.

357. Article 78 of the Fourth Geneva Convention begins: 'If the Occupying Power considers it necessary, for imperative reasons of security, to take safety measures concerning protected persons, it may, at the most, subject them to assigned residence or to internment.'

358. Convention against Torture and Other Cruel, Inhuman or Degrading Treatment or Punishment.

734. The judgment is concluded with two impressive closing remarks, dealing with the special conditions that exist presently in Israel. Justice Barak explains that a new reality, consisting of 'living bombs' and their collaborators, requires a dynamic approach to the Convention provisions. Furthermore, a democratic state respecting human rights faces a specific problem of normative restrictions in a time of war. The State of Israel has a right to self-defence; in its fight, it must act within the framework of the laws of war. As a result, not every effective measure is at the same time lawful. It is impossible, especially in these difficult times, to provide complete protection of human rights. Complete protection of state security, as if there were no human rights at all, is also not acceptable. A delicate balancing act is required.

735. Finally, the factual basis of the decisions was checked, and two petitions were rejected, allowing the residence assignment, while one petition was granted. The measure of assigned residence, sharply restricted by the Court, has not been exercised since. Since the withdrawal of Israeli forces and settlement in Gaza, this policy may well be irrelevant.

C. Methods for Interrogation of Suspects

736. A person's right not to be subjected to torture is one of the most basic human rights. It is a right occupying the same status as a person's right to life and the prohibition on slavery, and is an essential component of a person's right to the protection of his human dignity. In December 1984, the United Nations adopted a special convention for the purposes of its battle against torture. The Convention absolutely prohibits the use of torture under any circumstances (section 2(2)). The signatory states are required to adopt effective legislative, administrative, judicial or other measures to prevent acts of torture in any territory under their jurisdiction, including in the criminal realm, and to impose punishments that reflect the grave nature of the offences. Israel ratified the Convention in 1991. Furthermore, Israel's Basic Law: Human Dignity and Freedom provides a similar basis for the absolute proscription of torture of all kinds. In the same vein, the Penal Law forbids any person, including a public servant, from forcefully extorting another person, or threatening to use force, assaulting, grievously wounding or endangering human life.

737. Israel adopts a variety of strategies in its battle against terrorist organizations, including by way of the General Security Service (GSS), which is the key body involved in the frustration and prevention of hostile terrorist activities and the investigation of those suspected of such activities. The authority of the GSS to employ particular interrogation methods was examined by a Commission of Inquiry appointed by the government under the Commission of Inquiry Statute, 1968, which considered the legal status of the GSS. Following a prolonged deliberation, the Commission (the Landau Commission) approved 'the application of non-violent psychological pressure' and of 'a moderate degree of physical pressure'. The

Commission's recommendations were approved by the government.[359] However, between 1994 and 1999, several Palestinians and human rights groups filed petitions to the HCJ challenging the investigation methods of the GSS. The High Court's decision, delivered in September 1999 by nine judges, was unanimous: The GSS had the power to conduct interrogations, but the physical interrogation techniques were declared void and illegal.[360]

738. The petitioners argued that the physical means employed by GSS investigators not only infringed the human dignity of the suspect, but also constituted criminal offences. These methods are in violation of international law, as they constitute 'torture', which is expressly prohibited under international law. Furthermore, the 'necessity' defence, which is available to the investigators, constitutes an exceptional *post factum* defence, exclusively confined to criminal proceedings against investigators. It cannot provide GSS investigators with the pre-emptory authorization to conduct interrogations *ab initio.*

739. The Court ruled that a balancing test is required when dealing with interrogation rules. The balancing process results in the rules for a 'reasonable interrogation'. These rules are based, on the one hand, on preserving the 'human image' of the suspect, and on preserving the 'purity of arms' used during the interrogation. On the other hand, these rules take into consideration the need to fight the phenomenon of criminality and terrorist attacks. They reflect 'a degree of reasonableness, straight thinking (right mindedness) and fairness'. The rules pertaining to investigations are important to a democratic state. An illegal investigation harms not only the suspect's human dignity but also the fabric of society.

740. Therefore, a reasonable investigation is necessarily one free of torture, free of cruel, inhuman treatment of the subject and free of any degrading handling whatsoever. There is a prohibition on the use of 'brutal or inhuman means' in the course of an investigation. These prohibitions are absolute. There are no exceptions to them, and there is no room for balancing. The use of violence during investigations can potentially lead to the investigator being held criminally liable.

---

359. It is noted that this issue has been discussed in the past. In 1987, an official commission headed by former President of the Supreme Court, Justice Moshe Landau, published a report on the investigation methods of the GSS. The government, by virtue of the Commission of Inquiry Statute (1968), appointed this commission. It considered the legal status of the GSS (among other issues), and concluded that the GSS is authorized to investigate those suspected of hostile terrorist acts – even in the absence of express statutory regulation of its activities – in light of the powers granted to it by specific legislation and the government's residual powers. The commission concluded that in cases where the saving of human lives necessarily requires obtaining certain information, the investigator is entitled to apply both psychological pressure and 'a moderate degree of physical pressure'.

360. HCJ 5100/94 *Public Committee Against Torture v. the Government of Israel* 56(4) PD 56(4) 817. For further discussion of this particular case, *see* (Note) M.G. St. Amand, *Public Committee Against Torture in Israel, et al.: Landmark Human Rights Decision by the Israeli High Court of Justice or Status Quo Maintained?* 25 North Caroline J. Int'l Law & Com. Reg. 655 (2000).

741. Nevertheless, the Court assumed that if a GSS investigator who applied physical interrogation methods for the purpose of saving human life were to be criminally indicted, the 'necessity' defence would likely to be open to him in the appropriate circumstances. The 'necessity' exception is likely to arise in instances of 'ticking bombs', and the immediate need for the preservation of human life. The 'necessity' defence does not constitute a source of authority, allowing GSS investigators to make use of physical means during the course of interrogations.

742. In conclusion, the Court declared that Israeli law prohibits physical methods of interrogation. If the state wishes to enable GSS investigators to utilize physical means in interrogations, it must seek the enactment of legislation for this purpose. A warning was, however, included concerning such future legislation: It must be consistent with section 8 of the Basic Law: Human Dignity and Liberty.

743. In fact, the case law led to a significant change in interrogation practices. The HCJ banned the systematic resort to 'the vast majority of the physical methods of interrogation', that had been permitted by the Landau Commission, and these methods have disappeared almost entirely. In conclusion, the emergency situation in Israel brought the HCJ into the realms of the security networks. In these cases, too, its rulings are cautious. The HCJ is obliged to protect human rights and democratic values even during wartime. More than once, it has declared that the Israeli democracy fights with one hand tied behind its back, and that the state is unable to adopt all of the measures occasionally adopted by those fighting against it. Nonetheless, the protection of human rights during times of crises, and especially the degree of protection offered by the High Court to the Palestinian population in the territories, is necessarily restricted.

II. Conclusion

744. The judicial recognition and protection of human rights in Israel represents one of the most impressive achievements of the Israeli Supreme Court. In the absence of a constitution, and without any anchorage in formal Knesset legislation, the Supreme Court created 'ex nihilo', and applied the entire complex of human rights accepted in democratic, liberal states. Its consistent rulings curtailed and qualified sovereign authorities' ability to violate or otherwise abridge human rights, until the middle of the eighties of the previous century.

745. The Israeli legislature's contribution to human rights has been limited. The draft bill of Basic Law: Human Rights still awaits completion, and in fact is only in its initial stages. The enactment of the basic laws in 1992 also marks the discontinuation of the legislative process for completing the constitution. Israeli society is torn, and heterogeneous societal factors, which are reflected in the composition of the Knesset, at this stage continue to prevent the emergence of the consensus necessary for the completion of the constitution.

746. Today, as in the past, constitutional legislative vacuums, in which the legislature has yet to make a clear pronouncement, are filled by the Supreme Court. Its decisions bespeak its attempt to complete the Israeli 'bill of rights' even in the absence of an explicit legislative act on the Knesset's part. Basic rights such as equality, freedom of expression and freedom of religion, have been recognized by Supreme Court decisions since the establishment of the State, but still await constitutional anchorage and entrenchment in legislation, which would enable the Supreme Court to invalidate laws that unlawfully infringe them. Supreme Court decisions over recent years abound with statements that either allude to or explicitly recognize the possibility of entrenching anchoring unwritten constitutional rights by reading them into the concept of human dignity. Where there is no equality, there is no human dignity, and the absence of freedom of expression violates human dignity. This tendency to broaden the applicable scope of Basic Law: Human Dignity and Freedom was already anchored in various decisions at the Supreme Court, and will presumably be at the forefront of Supreme Court decisions on human rights issues in the coming years. The path, the foundations and the direction of the Supreme Court's decisions have been clearly delineated. If the legislature fails to complete its task of enacting a bill of rights, then the Supreme Court will do it instead, in a move resembling the constitutional revolution created by the *Mizrachi* judgment. This 'new revolution' explicitly recognizes the Supreme Court's power to invalidate laws that unlawfully violate rights that are not stipulated in the new Basic Laws, mainly the right to equality.

747. The narrative of human rights is really the narrative of Israeli society: a Jewish and democratic state that since its inception has found itself in a state of emergency; the need to establish a modus operandi for the harmonious coexistence of different nations and religions, and to strike a balance between a plethora of conflicting interests and needs; the need to balance between the fact of the State being the national state of the Jewish people, and its character as a democratic state; and the need to balance between the imperatives of human rights and the dictates of state security. As Israel enters the twenty-first century, it confronts a spectrum of national problems requiring in-depth comprehensive solutions, such as the definition of minorities and their rights, the termination of the state of war, and the internalization by all workstreams and ethnic groups of the need for compromise that will accommodate the preservation of civilized society. The solution to these problems is a precondition for completion of a Bill of Rights suited to Israel as a Jewish and democratic state at the start of the twenty-first century.

Chapter 3. Constitutional Problems of Minorities

§1. Introduction

748. Israel is a Jewish and democratic State. As the Jewish nation State, it realizes the right of the Jewish people to national independence and self-determination. However, this does not mean that the domestic law of the State of Israel confers extra privileges to Jews. The essence of the State as a democratic State dictates that the entire citizenry, Jews and non-Jews alike, enjoy equal political and civil rights. Concurrently, due to the definition of the State as a Jewish State, its Jewish population also enjoys, within the framework of the State, its collective right to self-determination. This is expressed, *inter alia*, in arrangements such as the Law of Return, which are intended to preserve the Jewish majority among the citizens of the State, and the innate right of all Jews to immigrate to Israel, as opposed to non-Jews who must go through a process of naturalization.[361] There are other arrangements, too, which are intended to retain the Jewish nature of public life in Israel.

749. In a formal sense, the Arab minority is not recognized as a national minority. Nonetheless, the arrangements applied in a number of contexts express recognition of the collective rights of the Arab public in Israel. At the same time, the process of recognition of the status of the Arab minority as a national minority, with all its implications, is still at an early stage and poses a number of difficult questions.[362]

750. The Arab minority in Israel is relatively large, constituting one-fifth of the State population, with a protracted historical connection to the country. The Arab minority is not a homogenous group, comprising a number of ethnic groups, characterized by important differences of religion, traditions and other factors. At the same time, the majority of those included in the group define themselves as belonging to a single national-cultural group – Palestinian Arabs – sharing many national features, such as language, common national aspirations, etc. The Israeli-Arab minority belongs to an even larger cultural-national unit, the Palestinian-Arab nation.

751. The Palestinian-Arab nation is engaged in a conflict with the State of Israel, which has persisted since the beginning of the Zionist enterprise. The Arab public actively and forcibly resisted the establishment of the Jewish State. A deep sense of affinity and brotherhood exists between the Arab minority in Israel and the Palestinian public outside of Israel, which is struggling to establish an independent Palestinian State, alongside the Jewish State. These features generate tremendous tension between the two communities in Israel. For many Jewish people, the Arab public, and particularly after the establishment of the State, was and continues to be

361. *See* discussion on Ch. 1 in this Part.
362. For further information on the legal status of the Arab minority, *see* D. Kretzmer, *The Legal Status of the Arabs in Israel* (1990); C. Klein, *Israel as a Nation-State and the Problem of the Arab Minority: in Search of a Status* (1987).

regarded as a mortal threat to the very existence of the State. However, relations between the two communities in Israel are not usually violent, and acts of violence between the Jews and the Israeli Arabs are the exception.

752. Israel's Declaration of Independence promised all of the state's citizens absolute equality in civil and political rights and rejected racial, religious or gender discrimination. The Declaration called on the Israeli Arabs to take part in building the state, and to assume representative positions in its institutions. Yet, while equality was promised, the newly founded state defined itself as 'a Jewish state in the Land of Israel', which hints at a distinction between the status of Jews and non-Jews in Israel. In practice, it is impossible to speak of equality when Israeli Palestinians are exempt from the military and national service duty, and do not enjoy all the same civil rights as are required by the rules of full equality. To date, the Arab minority has yet to merit explicit recognition as a national minority. However, de facto recognition is conferred upon the Arabs as a national minority, by reason of the application of a number of arrangements, primarily in the area of education, language, local government, personal status, provision of religious services, non-enlistment in the military, and others. The non-recognition of the Arab minority is also reflected in the case law of the Supreme Court.

753. In view of this, it appears that, despite the absence of explicit, formal recognition of the Arab community as a national minority that enjoys collective rights, on a practical level, it is indeed a minority group enjoying collective rights. Indeed, the main disputes in this context relate to the content of their collective rights.

§2. THE COLLECTIVE RIGHTS OF THE ARAB MINORITY (ISRAELI PALESTINIANS)

754. Recognition of the Arab or Israeli Palestinian minority's rights may be seen in five principal categories of arrangements:[363]

(1) Rights to self-government;
(2) The right to election of representatives in general government frameworks;
(3) Giving expression to Arab culture in public life and the status of Arabic as a language;
(4) Preservation of the culture of the Arab minority, and granting the Arab minority exemptions from certain general norms (e.g., the duty of military service); and
(5) The right to equality in the allocation of public resources.

I. Rights to Self-Government and Administration

755. The right to self-government relates to the community's ability to shape its governmental frameworks. The rights to self-government recognized in Israel for the Palestinian minority are based either on religious affiliation (primarily in the area

363. A. Rubinstein & B. Medina, *The Constitutional Law of the State of Israel* (6th ed. 2005, In Hebrew), pp. 428–449.

of personal status and religious matters), or on a territorial basis (in the realm of local government). These arrangements are not primarily intended to grant self-ruling rights to the Arab minority, but this is their result, insofar as the Israeli Palestinian minority consists of distinct minorities and insofar as most of the villages in which Arab citizens live are populated exclusively by Arabs.

756. In the realm of religious organization, the Arab public has certain rights of self-government.[364] Under Article 2 of the King's Order in Council (as amended in 1939), recognition was given to the eleven religious communities specified in the Schedule to the Kings Order. Article 83 of the Kings Order stipulates that a religious community enjoys autonomy in the management of its internal affairs. In practice, by force of the provisions of Article 83, the autonomy of the religious communities of the Arab minority is relatively limited. First, there has been a gradual reduction in the discretion granted to the religious Courts to rule in accordance with the religious law, by statutory provisions explicitly directed to them, by case law, and by force of the establishment of the Family Court. The underlying theme operating here – also directed against the Rabbinical Courts – is the desire to protect specific minorities within the religious groups (specifically women), and to entrench more liberal basic values.

757. Second, the appointment of position holders in the competent bodies of the religious communities and in the religious Courts is not exclusively under the control of the members of the sector itself. It is handled primarily by the representatives of the government and the Knesset. This is supplemented by the fact that the budgets for financing the provision of religious services are based almost exclusively on funds deriving from the central government.

758. An important area in which the Israeli Palestinian minority has self-government rights is local government. In that context, the Arab public enjoys a significant degree of self-government, primarily with respect to the manner of allocation of public resources (such as the determination of which activities will benefit from public funds), and the structuring of public communal life. This is, in fact, one of the main justifications for recognition of the minority's right to live in separate settlements (a right not conferred upon the Jewish majority, *inter alia*, by virtue of the fact that it benefits from self-determination in the State). It should be remembered that this policy has particularly grave social repercussions because it leads to the perpetuation and the deepening of serious disparities in the level of public services provided in Israel, in a manner prejudicial primarily to the Arab public.

II. Right to Suitable Representation in Governmental Institutions

759. The law in Israel provides structural arrangements ensuring that the decision-making process in society gives appropriate expression to the exceptional features of the Israeli Palestinian minority. The arrangements prescribed upon the

364. In this context, *see* I. Englard, *Law and Religion in Israel*, 33 Am J. Comp. Law, 185 (1987).

establishment of the State echo this notion. The Declaration of Independence includes the explicit call 'to the Arab inhabitants of the State of Israel to preserve peace and participate in the up building of the State on the basis of full and equal citizenship and due representation in all its provisional and permanent institutions'. Included among these arrangements are the amendments from the year 2000 in the State Service (Appointments) Law, 1959, and in the Government Companies Law, 1975, which were intended to ensure 'appropriate expression of Arab representation' in the State public service and in the directorates of government companies. These statutory provisions constitute the first statutory recognition, since the Declaration of Independence, of the Arab public's presence in Israel.

760. Mention should also be made of the Supreme Court ruling in the case of *The Citizen's Rights Association*, which recognized a general obligation to ensure appropriate representation for Arabs in government bodies, above and beyond explicit statutory provisions. The ruling was that 'the question of what constitutes appropriate representation in a particular body depends *inter alia* on the practical importance of that particular body in terms of the group entitled to appropriate representation'.[365] It was specifically ruled that 'the importance and intensity of the representation in the Israel Lands Administration is larger with respect to the Arab population ... [and therefore] the Government and the relevant Ministers must also take this consideration into account when appointing members to the Council'.

III. The Status of the Arabic Language

761. In a formal sense, based on Article 82 of the King's Order, the Arabic language is an official language, sharing the same status as the Hebrew language. This arrangement has not been changed since the establishment of the State, and has remained intact until today. The Hebrew language indeed enjoys clear preference over the Arabic language and in fact is the language of the State, as a result of the social reality:

> 2. Article 82 provides: All orders, official notifications and official forms of the government and all official notices of the local authorities and municipalities, in the regions determined in an Order of the High Commissioner, shall be published in English, in Arabic and in Hebrew. Having consideration for all such regulations as may be promulgated by the High Commissioner the three languages may be used in the government offices and in the Courts.

762. Despite the provision in Article 82, practically, it is not possible to apply to the authorities in Arabic, except for the branches in Arab settlements. The official notifications of the Government appear mostly in Hebrew, and until recently, the signposting on the roads was almost entirely and exclusively in Hebrew (and English).

---

365. HCJ 6924/98 *Citizens Rights Association v. Government of Israel*, 55(5) PD 15, 41.

763. Nonetheless, since the beginning of the nineties, the Courts have begun to require the authorities to discharge the duty of complying with various implications of the key status of the Arabic language. For example, the status of Arabic was at the heart of the *Re'em* case.[366] In this case, the Court dealt with the constitutionality of a municipal by-law. The by-law dictated that at least two-thirds of the inscriptions on notices published in the city must be in Hebrew. A commercial company wanted to publish a commercial notice in Arabic, addressed to the Arab population, on a notice board set up by the Upper Nazareth Municipality within the city limits. The Municipality opposed the publication in light of the above-mentioned city by-law. The company claimed, *inter alia*, that the city by-law violated the status of Arabic as an official language of Israel.

764. In their judgment, the Justices ruled that Arabic is an 'official' language of the State. However, in determining the principles that regulate the use of the official language, the Justices assumed that Hebrew is actually *the* official State language. For example, Justice Barak emphasized that 'the acts of government ... must be conducted in the official language of the State'. But in which official language? The question which must then be asked – is Arabic included in the definition of the 'official language'? On one hand, the Court stated that 'Arabic is also an official language'. However, on the other hand, the Court did not mandate the inscription, in Arabic, of traffic and warning signs, which reflect governmental actions, despite being referred to in Article 82.

765. In its decision, the Court used the term 'official language' in the singular tense and not in the plural. It appears that this 'technical' matter is of great significance. Justice Barak further stated that 'Israel respects the Arabic language' since 'an Arab minority whose language is Arabic lives in the State of Israel'. However, no legal explanation was given to the term 'respect' in relation to the Arabic language. Moreover, in his summarization in the judgment, Justice Barak emphasized that 'this judgment does not base itself on the official status of the language, but rather on the right of the individual to publish in the language of his choosing'. It is possible to conclude, therefore, that the Court chose not to conclusively determine the official status of the Arabic language. The right of the publisher to publish in Arabic was based on grounds of 'freedom of expression' and was not based on the right to publish in an official language.

766. According to this judgment, if, indeed, Arabic should receive official status in Israel, then this would be a secondary status, which would not oblige the government to print its publications in Arabic, despite the wording of Article 82 of the Order in Council. The Court held that the duty to publish official notices in Arabic depends only on 'the place and the matter'. It therefore appears that the judgment legally perpetuated the existing factual reality.

---

366. CA 105/92 *Re'em Engineers and Contractors Ltd. v. Upper Nazareth Municipality and others*, PD 47(5) 189 (hereinafter: 'the *Re'em* Case').

767. Furthermore, the Court also recognized the duty to give expression to the Arabic language in the public domain, by placing signs in Hebrew and Arabic on intercity highways, and in cities containing a significant Arab minority, even outside the Arab neighbourhoods. In the *Adalah*[367] case, the question adjudicated was whether the local authorities in which there was a significant Arab minority, bore an obligation to include Arabic captions on all of the municipal signposts. The respondents agreed that the duty to include Arab captions exists in those areas with an Arab minority, in the main thoroughfares, and in the signs to all the municipal institutions, as well as inside these institutions. The Court ruled, by majority, that the obligation is broader, also extending to all of the municipal signposts, including the names of streets that are not main roads, in all of the city's streets.

768. The judgments that determined these rules usually avoided relying on Article 82 of the Kings Order and on the status of Arabic as an 'official language'. Rather, they are based on the individual right to freedom of expression and the obligation on the State to have regard to the Arab public's right to express itself in its own language.

769. These judgments are especially important in view of their practical implications – the fashioning of the public domain in the State of Israel. The judgments are premised on the recognition that the standing of the Jewish culture in general, and specifically the standing of the Hebrew language, are sufficiently strong, and that accordingly, the basic character of the State as a Jewish State, can no longer justify the policy of granting exclusivity to Jewish culture in public life, at the expense of Arab culture in general, and specifically, the Arab language. Justice Barak dwelt on this point specifically, in the *Re'em* judgment:

> The weight attaching to the Hebrew language derives from the status of Hebrew as actually reflected in Israeli society. Many years ago … there was room for concern for the Hebrew language … there was an emphasis on the critical need to strengthen and encourage the language … [but today] the Hebrew language has struck broad and powerful roots … . We are a pluralistic society, aspiring to gather exiles, and to absorb them in a melting pot, while preserving their uniqueness, their customs, and origin. This is possible if on the one hand, they encounter a powerful Hebrew language that assists in their consolidation as one nation; and on the other hand, they should be given the freedom to express themselves in their homeland in accordance with their own customs and language … . Needless to say, should there be a change in the status of the Hebrew language and an erosion of the status of the Hebrew language, there would be room for considering a reassessment, and giving greater weight to the public interest in the Hebrew language.

---

367. HCJ 4112/99 *Adalah v. Tel-Aviv Yaffo Muncipality*, 56(5) PD 393.

IV. Preservation of Arab Culture

770. A number of arrangements are practised in Israel for the preservation of the culture of the Israeli Palestinian minority. This practice receives its primary expression in the State's general tendency to avoid imposing restrictions on members of the Arab minority in matters pertaining to education, culture and language, and in granting government funding for activities in these areas. The freedom granted to members of the Arab minority to preserve the main characteristics of their culture is recognized as a basic right in Israeli law. It was anchored in the Declaration of Independence, which declared that the State would ensure 'freedom of religion, conscience, language, education and culture', and it receives expression in many other areas.

771. For example, there are criminal prohibitions on damaging places or objects that are sacred to the votaries of a particular religion, disruption of religious ritual, giving offence to religious feelings, and there is also government assistance available for particular bodies involved in the provision of religious services.

772. Precisely the realm of public financing of religious services is an area which, for many years, has been subject to extensive discrimination, but since the 1990s, the Court has strictly enforced the obligation of acting on the basis of equality, and has consistently rejected claims to the effect that the definition of the State as a Jewish State entitles the Government to give greater financial assistance to Jewish religious activities than to the activities of other religions.

773. Nonetheless, it is clear that the status of the respective religions is not identical, and the allocation of public resources is not altogether equal. For example, the Jewish sector offers a religious State education, whereas in the Arab sector there is only one State system, the religious affiliation of which is not clearly defined. For the Jewish sector, significant assistance is given to those who study in Yeshivot (tertiary academies for Jewish religious studies), without similar assistance being provided for religious studies in other communities. Despite this, there is no doubt that the combination of non-interference in the freedom of activity in the realm of religious worship, and government assistance in the provision of religious services, ensures the right of the Israeli Palestinian minority to preserve its religious character, at a higher level than is conventional in the world at large, and higher than the minimum standard required under international conventions.

774. The Israeli Palestinian community's right to preserve its culture is also recognized in other spheres, unrelated to religion. This is seen primarily in the areas of freedom of language, education and culture. These freedoms are recognized as basic human rights in Israel, and as a rule, no restrictions are imposed on the Israeli-Arab citizens, curtailing their right to maintain an independent education system in the Arabic language, to give expression to Arabic culture, and to act in other ways which maintain and promote Arabic culture and language in Israel. As mentioned, the State enables the Arab public to live in separate communities, in the context of which the flavour of Arabic culture permeates public life.

775. The central area in which Israel takes steps in order to maintain and promote Arabic culture is the area of education. In a manner unprecedented in other democracies, Israel runs a publicly funded State school system, which is conducted in the language of the majority, and gives expression to its culture. In addition, there is also a private school system (for Christian schools), which receives partial public funding. This arrangement gives significant expression to the collective rights of the Arab minority, and also attests to the governmental recognition of the importance attached to the preservation of the minority culture.

776. The Israeli Palestinian public does have self-governing powers in its State school system. Nonetheless, these are somewhat limited, in acknowledgment of the need for State supervision of the syllabus, both to ensure the quality of instruction, and the inculcation of certain basic values.

V. Exemption from Military Service

777. In theory, the Defence Service [Consolidated Version], 1988 imposes a duty of military service on any person who is an Israeli citizen or permanent resident, without any distinction between Jews and non-Jews. Nonetheless, since the establishment of the State, the Arab-Israeli citizens have not been called up for service.[368] The exemption is not granted to the non-Jewish public in its entirety; since 1956, Druze and Circassian men have been enlisted for military service. Bedouin men, Muslim Arabs and Christian Arabs desiring to serve are permitted to do so.

778. The granting of this exemption is rooted in the State's unwillingness to force the Arab minority to fight Palestinian members of their nation, or other Arabs, and perhaps also a lack of faith in the trustworthiness of Arab citizens in a military context. The exemption from military service is regarded as an essential element in the preservation of the special status of the Arab minority in the complex web of relations between the State of Israel and the Palestinian nation.

§3. Conclusion

779. The character of the State of Israel as a Jewish and democratic State dictates both the importance attaching to the aspiration for equality between Jews and Arabs, and the complexity connected with the implementation of the principle of equality. It is precisely Israel's characterization as a Jewish State that may tip the

368. Under s. 13 of the Defence Service Law [Consolidated Version], 1986, the duty of reporting to service applies to any person called upon by the calling up officer. Since the establishment of the State, the calling up officer has avoided calling up Arab citizens of Israel for service, with the exception of Druze and Circassian.

scale in favour of the recognition of the Arab minority's collective rights. In fact, despite the absence of formal recognition of Israeli Palestinians as a national minority, the broad range of arrangements currently applied in Israel expressly recognize its status as a minority. This recognition is expressed *inter alia* in arrangements such as the exemption from military service, the status of the Arabic language and in the area of education.

780. The connection of the Arab minority to the Palestinian nation and the other Arab nations creates a situation in which the level of tension between the State of Israel and the Palestinian nation and the Arab world impacts directly on the standing of the Arab minority in Israel. Deterioration in the relationship between the two nations increases the tension between their people within Israel, to the extent of confronting the State of Israel with a danger that cannot be ignored. Currently, everyone has an equal right to social benefits that are not conditional upon completion of military service. By law, everyone is entitled to the same university tuition fees, housing provisions and child allowances. Nevertheless, the state's basic commitment to full equality, as expressed in the Declaration of Independence, has never been fully realized, and Israeli Palestinians still suffer from discrimination in many fields. They do realize their basic civil rights, but when it comes to sharing positions in, and benefits from, public establishments, or to the allocation of budgets for education, housing, settlement, social welfare, employment and local governments, there still are wide gaps between the positions of Jews and Arabs. Unequal resources are assigned to various public projects and government services, mainly for political and social reasons, as Israeli governments have consistently prioritized Jewish settlements.

781. In this context, mention should be made of the Or Enquiry Commission, which examined the violent confrontation between the Jews and the Arabs in October 2000 (which erupted in the wake of an escalation of the level of violence in the conflict between Israel and the Palestinian nation):

> That the Jewish and Arab populations are neighbours is a fact of life, leaving the parties with but one practical possibility – that of co-existence in an atmosphere of mutual respect. All other possibilities are sure recipes for the increasing of tension, exacerbation of existing hardships, and disruption of routine life. Coexistence is difficult to achieve ... the Arab citizens must remember that the State of Israel is the realization of the Jewish people's yearning for a State of its own, in which Jews constitute the majority; a State in which the gathering of exiles is a basic foundation, and which is the essence of the national ethos for its Jewish citizens ... the Jewish majority must remember that the State is not only Jewish, but also democratic ... it must understand that the events that turned the Arabs into a minority in this State constitute a national disaster for them, and that their integration into the State of Israel involves painful sacrifices from their perspective. The Jewish majority must

honour the identity, culture, and language of the Arab citizens ... it is appropriate to find ways of strengthening the Arab citizens' sense of belonging in the State, without prejudice to their culture and community.[369]

369. Report of the Commission of Enquiry into the Confrontations between the Security Forces and the Israeli Arabs beginning from 29 Sep. 2000 (2003) (*Or* Commission), Part 6 (ss 41–42), taken from Rubinstein & Medina, *ibid.*, p. 465.

Chapter 4. Judicial Control of Administrative Action

§1. Introduction: Preconditions for Judicial Review

782. The Israeli Courts are empowered to exercise judicial review of administrative actions if they are lawfully petitioned to do so for the purpose of settling a dispute. Until the 1980s, it was a precondition for the exercise of judicial review by the HCJ, that the petitioner possessed *locus standi*, i.e., that he had a real, personal interest in the subject matter of the dispute.

783. Gradually, exceptions were recognized to the demand for *locus standi*, and the capacity of a person to apply to the HCJ against an administrative decision underwent a process of 'liberalization'. The concept which developed was that in cases where the subject matter of the petition was of important public interest, judicial review would be exercised even if the petitioner did not have a personal stake in the matter. An acknowledged landmark decision in this context is that delivered by Justice Barak in the *Ressler* case,[370] in which he expressly rejected the approach whereby:

> the principal and fundamental objective of the judicial authority is to settle a dispute at the centre of which is a claim of injustice caused to one person by another. The source of this concept is private law, in which it is the litigant whose right has been infringed … Public law does not accept this approach at all.

784. In practice, since about the middle of the 1980s, the Court has exercised judicial review over every matter brought before it, without considering the existence of a defined 'dispute' or the nature of the personal interest of the petitioner. Today, the HCJ recognizes a 'public petitioner' as possessing *locus standi* to petition in respect of a breach of the law. The public nature of the petition serves as the basis for justifying the application of judicial review even if the petitioner cannot point to any real personal interest of his own. The dismissal *in limine* of petitions on the ground of lack of standing has become extremely rare.

785. The present trend is based on the perception that the purpose of judicial review is not solely to protect individual rights but also to 'preserve the rule of law and the legality of the regime'. The approach applied in Israel ensues from the view that other forms of review are not adequately efficient. Concurrently with the decrease in importance of the concept of the right of standing, new threshold conditions for the application of judicial review have become evident. Thus, in the past, unjustified delay in submitting a petition to the Court might have led to the petition

370. HCJ 910/86 *Ressler v. Minister of Defence*, 42(2) PD 441. For a broad discussion of the issue of *locus standi*, *see* by author, *Exemption from Military Service granted to Orthodox Students in Israel – a Case Study on Justicability, Equality and Judicial Review*, 6 European Public Law, 12 (2000).

being summarily dismissed on grounds of 'tardiness'. By contrast, under the current approach, the relevant factors considered relate to the actual consequences of the delay in applying judicial review.

786. Likewise, in general the Court has refrained from dismissing petitions *in limine* on grounds of the petitioner's lack of good faith, i.e., on grounds connected to the petitioner's conduct outside and within the context of the legal proceedings. The conduct of the petitioner may affect the outcome of the proceedings which touch him personally; however, in general, it is not a factor taken into account when examining the legality of the governmental act.

787. The character of the decision-making body influences the scope of judicial review. The view commonly held is that where the decision-making body is 'political' in nature, and represents the views of the public, the Court will be willing to limit the scope of judicial review. This is the case in relation to decisions of the Knesset as well as decisions of the government where judicial control is limited. It follows the idea that scrutiny of government decisions is the function of the Knesset and the public, and not the role of the Court.

788. One of the interesting questions relating to judicial review of the activities of governmental bodies concerns the degree of applicability of legal standards to the decision under consideration. The Court settles social dilemmas brought before it after assessing which interests are relevant, how much weight should be accorded to each of these interests and the outcome desired pursuant to the appropriate course of action. Obviously, this is not the only way in which social dilemmas may be resolved. The main alternative is to make a 'political' decision. A political decision does not, of course, guarantee that the different interests will be accorded a weight based on relevant factors. On occasion, a factor will be assigned weight on the basis of the organizational ability of various interest groups, their negotiating power and the like. Indeed, judicial review, which is based on standards of reasonableness and proportionality, will often mean that the discretion of political authorities will be replaced with that of the judiciary. In fact, it is the decision-making process influenced by the activities of 'interest groups' which is most likely to lead to social determinations that more truly reflect the entirety of the views accepted by the public, and therefore, express the true nature of the democratic regime.[371]

789. The approach taken by the former President of the Supreme Court of Israel, Justice Barak, is that it is always possible to examine the 'reasonableness' of governmental actions. Therefore, it would be wrong to dismiss a petition relating to 'political' matters on the ground of non-justiciability. However, the political nature of the petition influences the delineation of the 'zone of reasonable decisions' and consequently the scope of judicial review. A good example of this issue is the *Weiss*

371. For a view emphasizing the advantages of the political process as a decision-making device in relation to certain controversial public issues, *see* A.M. Bickel, *The Least Dangerous Branch – The Supreme Court at the Bar of Politics* (1962) 143–156. Y. Dotan, *Judicial Review and Political Accountability: The Case of the High Court of Justice in Israel*, 32 Israel Law Review 448 (1998).

case.[372] The Court considered a petition against Prime Minister Ehud Barak's government's continued negotiations with the Palestinian Authority, even though the Prime Minister's resignation meant that the government was operating as a 'transitional government'. President Barak held that the petition against negotiations during this period had to be dismissed, stating:

> Intervention in such cases will occur in exceptional cases … . The decision on this issue – the dominant components of which are political and at the core of the social conflict in Israel – must take place within the political discourse in Israel, through the organs of the Knesset or the public vote.

790. The practical outcome of recognizing such a broad sphere of reasonableness in relation to issues possessing a political character is, of course, a limitation of the scope of judicial review.

791. An additional example of judicial restraint may be seen in connection with the foreign relations of the state and the establishment of its permanent borders. The rule is that 'the issue of the manner in which the competent bodies conduct foreign policy is non-judiciable; it cannot be examined in accordance with legal standards and this Court will not intervene in such matters'.[373] It was for this reason that, in the past, in the *Reiner* case, a petition to prevent the entry into Israel of the German ambassador to Israel, on grounds of his service in the German army during the Second World War, was dismissed.[374] Also dismissed were all petitions against the release of Palestinian prisoners under agreements signed with the Palestinian Authority.[375]

792. It is worth recalling that the Court tends not to uphold petitions which seek 'all-inclusive relief', i.e., petitions which ask the Court to determine policy. Thus, for example, petitions asking the Court to establish a general policy on euthanasia – other than in relation to a specific case – have been dismissed.[376] The Court has also refrained from deciding petitions which are 'premature' in the sense that they concern administrative decisions which are not final (such as a decision by a Knesset committee to recommend to the plenum that it remove the immunity of a member of the Knesset).

---

372. HCJ 5167/00 *Weiss v. Prime Minister*, 55(2) PD 455.
373. HCJ 4354/92 *The Temple Mount and Land of Israel Faithful Movement v. Prime Minister*, 47(1) PD 37, 43.
374. HCJ 186/65 *Reiner v. Minister of Justice*, 19(2) PD 485.
375. For example, HCJ 9290/99 *Headquarters of Victims of Terrorism v. Government of Israel*, 54(1) PD 8, 14: 'The government's decision to release the prisoners is a political decision based on political factors, within the competence of the government, and it is well-known that this Court is not supposed to intervene, and does not intervene, in such considerations. Such a decision is within the purview of the government, and the place for reviewing it is the Knesset or in public opinion, and not in the Court.'
376. HCJ 945/87 *Nachyasi v. Israel Medical Association*, 42(1) PD 135, 136.

793. The scope of judicial review is also reflected in other ways. One of the most important of these is the choice of the remedy granted in circumstances where an administrative act has been found to be flawed. The Court has discretion to choose from among a range of remedies, starting with a declaration of the illegality of the act, which is unaccompanied by a binding order; through to remedies of 'relative voidability' or 'suspended voidability', which give limited effect to a decision regarding a defect in a governmental act; and finally a remedy which completely invalidates the consequences of the administrative act or imposes a duty of immediate performance.[377]

§2. Preventive Legal Protection

794. In proceedings before it, the HCJ has power to issue immediate interim orders (or *order nisi*, i.e., orders of specific performance or injunctions, in order to prevent, for example, irremediable damage). The Court may exercise broad discretion and make far-reaching orders. The objective in such cases is to preserve the status quo in order to ensure the effectiveness of the final remedy granted to the petitioner. It should be pointed out that the ordinary Courts too – not only the HCJ – are competent to issue temporary injunctions in cases where this relief is intended to safeguard the status quo. The Court recognizes the possibility of granting such relief even if the right has not yet been violated at the time of granting the interim order. An example of this would be an injunction preventing the publication of a book which prima facie contains defamation. This power is consistent with the principle of preventive relief – as the remedy pre-empts the harm. At the same time, the case law has held that such an injunction will only be given in very rare cases; when there is very near certainty of harm occurring. The issue of preliminary relief is, of course, dependent on considerations of fairness which are the source of this relief in the laws of equity.

795. One of the major principles guiding the rulings of the Court is that the grant of an interim order (or refusal to grant it) until the case has been heard on its merits, is weighed and decided according to the degree of convenience and inconvenience, and the degree of damage which will be caused to either side by the grant or refusal to grant the order. The Court seeks to draw a balance between the various interests of the parties (which in the natural course of things conflict with one another). The Court examines the potential damage to the two parties and weighs who will suffer the most damage. Where the right under consideration is a constitutional right, the Court indicates a greater tendency to grant the relief sought.

377. The choice of remedy reflects the need to take into account the anticipated consequences of the judicial remedy and any potential injury to the public interest in its entirety. For further discussion, *see* R.M. Levin, *'Vacation' at Sea: Judicial Remedies and Equitable Discretion in Administrative Law*, 53 Duke L. J., 291 (2003).

796. Another important factor is the nature of damage. It is necessary to show that the damage to the plaintiff will be irremediable if the temporary order is not granted.

797. An illustration of the exercise of judicial discretion may be seen in relation to the Knesset's internal procedures. The HCJ has decided that it has the power to supervise Knesset proceedings and examine decisions by the Knesset speaker and committees, and political coalition agreements, but whether it actually does this, and the extent of its intervention naturally depends on the body it audits. Dealing with the Knesset, for example, the Supreme Court exercises restraint. In the *Weiss* case, Supreme Court President Barak decided to reject a petition against the transitional government's right to continue negotiations with the Palestinian Authority. Among other things, Barak stated: 'intervention on such issues should be reserved to irregular situations … Such issues – whose primary components are political, and which are a major bone of contention for the Israeli society – should be addressed by political discourse, by the Knesset's organs, or by popular vote.'[378]

798. Another well-known, older example, particularly problematic in terms of the consequences of the interim order granted, is the case of the deportation in 1992 of about 400 Hamas and Islamic Jihad terrorists to Lebanon.[379] Following terrorist attacks and the killing of numerous Israeli citizens, the government decided to issue temporary deportation orders against members of the two organizations. This action drew massive attention in Israel and abroad. On the night when the deportation was due to take place, the families and attorneys of some of the deportees submitted petitions to the High Court seeking to delay the deportations in order to enable the deportees to appeal tribunals.

799. Justice Barak, who was the judge on duty that night, issued interim orders to stay the deportations until a hearing on the petitions, which was scheduled for 05:00 am. In the meantime, the 400 deportees waited on buses on the northern border of Israel for the Court to decide whether it would grant the temporary injunction. In the early morning hearing, the Court panel was increased to seven judges. The judges heard from witnesses, including the Chief of General Staff and representatives of the parties. The hearing lasted for many hours, and at about 19:00 the Court dismissed the petition for an interim order staying the deportation; and it did so without giving reasons. In the meantime, the advantage of deterrence sought by the planners of the deportation was lost; the waiting period in the buses on the border exposed Israel to international pressure, and the government of Lebanon decided to prevent the deportees from entering the country. In other words, even though the petition for the interim was dismissed, the judicial process disrupted the government's plan, and made it difficult to implement it.

---

378. HCJ 5167/00 *Weiss v. Israel's Prime Minister*, (2001) 55(2) PD 55(2) 455, 472 President Barak's verdict at [14].

379. HCJ 5972/92 *Association of Civil Rights v. Minister of Defence*, 47(1) PD 267.

§3. CURATIVE LEGAL PROTECTION

800. Naturally, the principal function of the HCJ in relation to judicial review of administrative decisions is 'corrective'. The powers of the HCJ are twofold: general and special. The general power is derived from section 15 of Basic Law: The Judiciary. The section empowers the Supreme Court to hear matters in which it deems it necessary to grant relief in the interests of justice and which are not within the jurisdiction of another Court. In other words, the Court is empowered to hear any matter which 'may' require its intervention in the interests of justice or any matter which the petitioner brings before the Court on the ground that he is entitled to relief in the interests of justice.

801. As noted, concurrently with its general power, the HCJ possesses a number of special powers which do not derogate from the generality of its competence. First, the Court has the power to make orders for the release of persons unlawfully detained or imprisoned. As noted, this power is 'corrective' and is in the nature of an order of 'mandamus'. This order is listed among the remedies which the High Court is empowered to make, and in effect was the first of the prerogative writs granted during the Middle Ages by the King of England preventing the unlawful arrest or detention of a person, and ensuring the freedom of all. An order of release is the fastest and most efficient remedy against an unjust denial of the freedom of movement of a person.

802. Second, the Court may make orders in respect of state and local authorities and the officials and bodies thereof, and other persons carrying out public functions under law. The orders may be divided into two classes – specific performance and prohibitions. These orders are addressed to state authorities only. They require the authorities to do or refrain from doing any act in the lawful exercise of their functions whereas the prohibitions require them – if they were improperly elected or appointed – to refrain from acting.

803. Third, the High Court may order Courts (*batei mishpat* and *batei din*) and bodies and persons having judicial or quasi-judicial powers under law, other than Courts dealt with by the Basic Law and other than religious Courts (*batei din*), to hear, refrain from hearing, or continue hearing a particular matter or to void a proceeding improperly taken or a decision improperly given. In practice, this provision empowers the High Court to ensure that the various Courts and tribunals will not exceed the jurisdiction granted to them by law. This provision does not apply to the District or Magistrate's Courts, which are governed by Basic Law: The Judiciary. Likewise, the provision does not apply to the religious Courts which are subject to a special parallel provision. In the event that a Magistrate's Court or District Court exceeds its jurisdiction, an appeal is of course available to the Supreme Court, which will then bring about the invalidation of the improper act.

804. The broad power conferred on the High Court, and its ability to make orders against all the administrative authorities in the state, have enabled the High Court to afford extensive protection to fundamental human rights even in the absence of a bill of rights. The High Court's willingness to make orders of performance against administrative authorities in effect imposed a duty on the authorities to preserve human rights, and thereby created a cause of action – an 'entry ticket' to the Court – which was made available to all those whose rights were infringed. Thus, for example, in the early days of the state, the Supreme Court recognized such rights as freedom of expression and freedom of occupation. One of the cases in which it did so was that of *Kol Ha'am*, which established the principle of freedom of expression.[380]

805. The lengthy judgment contained a broad theoretical discussion of freedom of expression and the test for limiting it. It adopted the test of 'near certainty' of real harm to public order in order to limit freedom of expression. The Court upheld the petition, invalidated the decision of the Minister of the Interior and established the rule according to which a person can obtain relief from the High Court in the event that his human rights have been infringed by an administrative authority.

806. The response of the administrative authorities to the HCJ's rulings regarding their decisions has led, on occasion, to changes to the law designed to validate the activities of the authorities. The interpretive rules of the High Court maintain that an administrative authority is not competent to infringe or restrict individual rights save if expressly empowered to do so. In recent years, there has been a growing tendency on the part of the High Court to intervene in decisions of an administrative authority when the latter deals with matters of principle or of decisive importance, on the ground that these matters ought to be regulated by 'primary legislation'.

807. Underlying this notion is the aspiration to ensure that it is the Knesset which represents the views of the public, and determines the primary arrangements according to which the governmental powers will be exercised. The concept holds that it is the law which is supposed to establish standards for making fateful, fundamental and substantive decisions regarding the life of the individual. In the past, the application of this rule could be seen in the restriction of individual freedoms in order to prevent the infringement of religious sensitivities and the promotion of the Jewish way of life in public. Therefore, one of the most important constitutional aspects of the administration's legality principle, as developed by Israeli adjudication, is the Knesset's assigned duty to set the principal arrangements by which the administrative authorities may act. For example, according to HCJ rulings, the Knesset may not settle for generally establishing a certain government authority, but

380. In 1953, the Minister of the Interior, exercising his powers under the Mandatory Newspaper Ordinance, ordered the cessation of the publication of the *Kol Ha'am* newspaper for a period of ten days, following the publication of editorials which sharply criticized the government and its policies. The *Kol Ha'am* newspaper applied to the High Court attacking the decision of the Minister of the Interior, but without a formal 'cause of action' founding its petition. At the time, freedom of expression was not a recognized right in Israel, in the absence of a constitution or a bill of rights. The only reference to it was found in the Declaration of Independence.

must outline the main arrangements that it must follow in legislation. This issue has been dubbed by the HCJ the 'primary arrangements'.[381]

808. Thus, for example, it was held that imposition of restrictions on the sale of pork was a 'general and national problem, which is not unique to a particular place, and the solution to which is subject to the exclusive jurisdiction of the national legislature, save if the national legislature saw fit to transfer the decision-making power to the local authorities'.[382] The Court held that with regard to:

> the various ideological disputes among sections of the public – such as religion, nationality, socialism and the like – their arena of battle is the Knesset or the central institutions of the government, and it is not the municipality or the local council which is responsible for regulating them or 'guilty' of their non-regulation.[383]

In response to this ruling, an 'empowering provision' was enacted, enabling local authorities to take into account 'grounds of religious tradition' when exercising their powers, without delineating clear legislative guidelines regarding the manner of exercising them.

809. In recent years, there has been an increasing tendency to extend the application of the rule regarding primary arrangements, in such a manner as to embrace considerable portions of the powers of the executive authority. The interpretive presumption applied is that the legislature does not intend to empower the executive authority to establish primary arrangements.

810. Likewise, it has often been held that administrative bodies are not entitled to make use of the governmental powers vested in them in a manner which takes the form of a decision of principle, particularly in the area of restrictions of individual freedoms for the purpose of advancing religious precepts.[384] This is also true, for example, in relation to the exercise of force in interrogations:

> The grant of power to GSS investigators to exercise physical force during the interrogation of suspects ... raises fundamental questions of law and society, morality and policy, the rule of law and security. These questions and the answers to them must be determined by the legislative authority.[385]

---

381. HCJ 11163/03 *The Supreme Monitoring Committee [of the Arab Citizens] v. Israel's Prime Minister* (published by Nevo on 27 Feb. 2006).
382. HCJ 122/54 *Aksel v. Mayor of Netanya*, 8 PD 1524, 1531.
383. HCJ 155/60 *Elazar v. Mayor of Bat-Yam*, 14 PD 1511, 1512. *See also* HCJ 3872/93 *Mitral Ltd. v. Prime Minister and Minister of Religious Affairs*, 47(5) PD 485, 497.
384. HCJ 98/54 *Lazarovitz v. Supervisor of Maintenance*, 10 PD 40. It was held that 'It is not the function of the Respondent to solve religious and national problems by administrative means given to it for completely different purposes and objectives. The problem is a national and not a local one, and its answer is in the hands of the legislature, which has the power – if it feels it necessary – to limit the freedom of the individual.'
385. HCJ 5100/94 *Public Committee Against Torture in Israel v. Government of Israel*, 53(4) PD 817.

Accordingly, it has been held that, in the absence of express statutory authorization, the security authorities are not entitled to take measures which inflict physical harm or impair the dignity of suspects. In this way, the HCJ has also afforded effective and corrective protection to residents of the territories, without having been vested with express statutory power to do so, but by virtue of the general power to provide relief in the interests of justice, and to make orders to the authorities of the state.

§4. Miscellaneous

I. Obligation to Give Reasons for Administrative Decisions[386]

811. In Israel, there is a statutory duty to set out the reasons for an administrative decision. The Administrative Procedures Amendment (Decisions and Statement of Reasons) Law, 1958 outlines two types of duties. The first is the duty to act. This duty requires a public servant to provide an answer to a citizen who applies to him as soon as possible and in any event, no later than forty-five days after receiving the application. The purpose of this duty is to promote efficiency. The second duty set out in the law is the duty to state reasons. When a public servant refuses a citizen's application, he must notify the applicant of the reasons for his refusal.

812. It is interesting that the legislature chose to enact an express law in relation to the duty to state reasons. The rationale for this duty is the fact that the public authority acts as a public trustee. The duty also ensues from the desire to prevent arbitrary decisions and to encourage uniformity by reiterating the same reasons in response to similar applications.

813. In order to give rise to the duties provided by law, the application must be made in writing to a public servant in an administrative authority. A verbal application is insufficient.

814. With respect to the scope of the duty to state reasons, it has been held that the broader the discretion of the administrative authority, the less detailed the statement of reasons which must be provided to the applicant, and vice versa. If the discretion of the authority is narrow, the greater the likelihood of a violation of authority, and the broader and more comprehensive the statement of reasons required. The statute also sets out exemptions from the duty of stating reasons. Among the exemptions are the following: if the law which vests the power provides that the public servant is authorized to exercise it without giving reasons; if the security of the state or its foreign relations require that the reasons for the decision not be disclosed; if the application refused by the public servant was for the appointment of the applicant to a particular post or the assignment to him of a particular task; if the disclosure of the reasons might unlawfully prejudice the rights of any

386. *See* Lydia Chokron, *Administrative Decisions: Statement of Reasons and Time Limit*, 7 Israel Law Rev. 127 (1972).

person; and if the disclosure of the reasons will involve the disclosure of a professional secret.

815. Breach of the duty to state reasons does not lead to the invalidation of the decision; rather, the law establishes a list of sanctions which may be imposed. In such a case, the Court may compel the authority to state reasons and even institute disciplinary proceedings against the public servant. In any event, the law confers a right of appeal against a decision of a public servant which is unaccompanied by reasons.

II. Free Access to Administrative Documents

816. In 1998, the Knesset adopted the recommendations of the public committee concerning freedom of information, and enacted the Freedom of Information Law, 1998, which came into force in 1999.

817. The law was intended to bring about a revolution in the area by entrenching in statute the civil right to obtain information from authorities both on the substantive level, by providing for the right in statute, and on the procedural level, by providing for time tables and the appointment of persons charged with ensuring compliance by the authorities with freedom of information obligations. The Freedom of Information Law has led to a revolution in the organizational culture of the bureaucracy and government in Israel and has introduced the principle of transparency into government.

818. Freedom of information is one of the primary tools for scrutinizing government, and provides an invaluable device for investigative journalists. The statute is not perfect, but it can provide the basis for a process of change which will ultimately lead to recognition and internalization on the part of governmental authorities of the right of every person to obtain information from the government. Today, the law applies to a large proportion of the public authorities operating within the state, but not to all. The public authorities to which the law applies are set out in section 2 of the law and include the following: the government and government ministries, including their departments and supporting agencies; the President's Office; the Knesset; the State Comptroller, except for information provided to him for the purposes of audits and inquiries into public complaints; Courts, religious Courts, bailiff offices and other agencies with legally derived judicial authority – except for information relating to the content of a legal proceeding; local authorities; a legally founded corporation, etc.

819. This list is not complete. The Minister of Justice and the Knesset Constitution, Law, and Justice Committee may add additional public bodies. Among others, the religious councils and sick funds have already been added to the list.

820. In order to satisfy the provisions of the law, the head of every public authority must appoint an employee of the authority to be responsible for providing information to the public, handling requests for information, and applying the instructions of this law. His function in general terms is to ensure that the written administrative regulations on the basis of which the authority operates are made available to the public; he must prepare and publish an annual report, which includes information about the authority's activities and responsibilities, and primarily he must handle requests for information addressed to the authority by citizens and residents of the state and supply the information sought in accordance with the provisions of the law. The person responsible for providing the information to the public must be a senior official of the organization who is capable of contending with the heads of the organization and compelling them to provide the information to the public, even when disclosure of that information might not prove favourable to the organization or its leaders.

821. The law and the regulations promulgated by virtue of it specify the precise manner of making an application for information. The most important principle introduced in this connection is that the applicant need not mention the reasons for wishing to obtain the information. Every citizen has the right to obtain information without giving an explanation. This concept, which emphasizes the right to obtain information, lies at the heart of the law. The latter is a human right and safeguards the principle of transparency of the activities of government, without the need to demonstrate motive or other practical reasons.

A. *Refusal to Provide Information*

822. The authority is not subject to a duty to provide information in every circumstance and under all conditions. It is possible to distinguish between two possible situations. The first is where the authority is prohibited by statute from disclosing the information sought. The second is where the authority is not required to disclose the information but may exercise its discretion to do so. In section 9(a), the statute sets out a number of situations in which the authority is prohibited from disclosing the information sought. In these circumstances, the authority does not have any discretion and it is under a duty to reject the application. These are situations in which the disclosure of the information may harm state security; the information constitutes an invasion of privacy; or disclosure of the information is barred by any law.

823. In all other situations, the authority has discretion whether or not to disclose the information. However, even in these cases, the premise should be one of freedom of information, and denial of the citizen's rights should occur in only extreme cases. The authority must exercise its discretion and take into account, among other things, the interest of the applicant in the information, if cited in the request, and the public interest in the disclosure of the information. Issues of discretion have been considered in recent years in Israeli case law and the interpretation preferred has been one of expanding the right to obtain information.

824. Section 8(1) of the law provides that a public authority is entitled to reject a request for information if fulfilling the request requires an unreasonable allocation of resources. The law does not define the term 'unreasonable allocation', which supersedes the right of the public to obtain information. The Court has yet to engage in a comprehensive analysis of what will be regarded as 'material difficulty' (in terms of locating the information) or 'reasonable efforts', for the purposes of the statute.

825. Likewise, the public authority is not required to disclose information if it concerns internal discussions; notes of internal consultations between public authority employees, members or advisors; words spoken in the course of an internal inquiry; opinions, drafts, advice and recommendations given for purposes of decision-making; information concerning internal management of the public authority, which does not concern the public, and is not of importance to it; and information, the disclosure of which is liable to disrupt the proper functioning of the public authority, or its ability to carry out its duties. This is a basket of categories, all of which concern the public authority's desire and practice of acting in secrecy. In this context, there are a number of cases which expose the aspirations of the authorities to continue pursuing their activities 'in the dark' and exclude the public from participating in the formulation of policy. The Courts have consistently criticized this tendency on the part of the authorities but have not always been sufficiently strong in supporting the principle of disclosure.

826. The statute further provides that the authority need not disclose information to which commercial or professional confidentiality applies, or which has economic value, when the publication of the information is liable to cause real harm to its value. An exception to this rule is information relating to the environment, which must always be disclosed to the public.

827. The Freedom of Information Law contains a special provision relating to the protection of third parties who may be harmed by the disclosure of information relating to them. Section 13 of the law provides for procedures whereby the authority must notify the third party in writing that such a request has been filed, and the third party's right to oppose the disclosure of the information. This section may frustrate the objective of the disclosure of information to the public in many cases and complicate the implementation of the law. It seems that in this context the Courts tend to restrict the rights of third parties and prevent them from imposing a veto on the disclosure of information to the public. The principle applied is that, where a person engages with a public authority, he is deemed to be aware that its activities and operations are transparent and that all the documents relating to his engagement may be exposed and supplied to the public.

B. Submitting a Petition to the Court

828. When a request for information under this law is rejected, the person making the request is entitled to file an appeal to the District Court within thirty days of being notified of the decision. The Court has the function of examining the authority's decision, and it is entitled to order the disclosure of the information if, in the opinion of the Court, there is a public interest in the disclosure of the information that takes precedence over the grounds for rejecting the request, provided that disclosure of the information is not forbidden by law (notwithstanding all the rationales stated in section 9 of the law).

C. Concluding Remarks

829. The Freedom of Information Law contains a variety of complex mechanisms for making information available to the public, for handling the transfer of information and for according broad discretion to the public authority concerning a wide range of issues. At the same time, the purpose of the law is to promote transparency and the right of the public to know how the authorities are spending public money and exercising the powers vested in them. The purpose of the law is to make a real change in the culture of the government and administration in Israel, and to eliminate previous practices of concealing information from the public.

830. The Courts have an essential role to play in shaping the law and implementing the principle of freedom of information in practice. This development is still in its infancy; however, there are already clear signs that the Courts are dissatisfied with the approach taken by the authorities and support, in general, the expansion of the principle of freedom of information and public access to information held by the authorities.

Chapter 5. Legal Position of Aliens

§1. Introduction

831. The phenomenon of employing huge numbers of foreign workers began in Israel in the aftermath of the Six Day War in 1967, with the entry of Palestinian workers into the labour market. At its peak, workers from the territories comprised 9% of the total number of employees in the economy. Almost half of the workers were employed in the construction and agricultural sectors.

832. The State of Israel began dealing with the issue of foreign workers about two decades ago. As a result of the events of the first Intifada (at the end of 1987) and the security closures, the entry of Palestinian workers into Israel was restricted. The result was damage to the economic sectors, primarily agriculture and construction, in which they worked. In order to meet the demand for labour, the government of Israel decided to give work permits to non-Palestinian labourers – foreign workers – and accordingly allocated permits to employers seeking labourers in the above sectors.

833. Israel, like the European states in the early years of this phenomenon, regarded the foreign workers as part of a transitory state of affairs – as a cheap, available and temporary workforce. The importation of foreign workers began without preliminary preparations on the part of either the bodies dealing with labour and employees, or on the part of those dealing with entry into Israel, and without the creation of an overall plan for dealing with the incomers. The primary objective of bringing in foreign workers was to create a very short-term foreign workforce; however, the real outcome was labour migration and a situation in which some of the foreign labourers created organizational structures.

834. At the beginning of 2003, after almost a decade, the population of legal and illegal foreign workers numbered about 240,000. The government decided to set up the Immigration Administration with the function of expelling illegal foreign workers from Israel. In 2003, the number of illegal foreign workers in Israel dropped, both because of the increase in the number of those leaving and because of strict restrictions imposed on the numbers of those entering. About 23,000 foreign workers were expelled. The effect was one of deterrence and 'voluntary departures'. The government adopted a policy of 'closed skies' and prevented the entry of new workers into Israel while potential workers were deterred from coming to the country by reason of the security situation.[387]

835. Furthermore, since 2009, large numbers (tens of thousands) of refugees and foreigners from Africa have entered Israel, a phenomenon which obliges the

387. *The Children of the Foreign Workers – Current Situation and Means of Coping in the Future* (The Knesset – Centre for Research and Information – June) (Hebrew) 2004. *See* Bar-Zuri (2003) *Foreign Workers Expelled from Israel* 2002, Information Sheets Relating to the Labour Market, the Human Resource Planning Authority (Hebrew).

Knesset to deal with this infiltration by law. The large scale of the phenomenon and its complexity, as well as the unique characteristics of the State of Israel in which immigration and naturalization laws are fairly strict, have forced Israel to turn its attention to the issue of foreign workers and to seek both short-term and long-term solutions. The arrival of refugees and asylum seekers also affects the composition of Israeli society.

§2. Government Policy towards Refugees, Asylum Seekers and Foreign Workers

836. As of 2012, about 60,000 refugees and asylum seekers reside in Israel, according to official figures. Most asylum seekers and refugees originate from various African states, mainly Eritrea and Sudan. The vast majority of asylum applications are denied.[388]

837. In order to stop the infiltration, Israel built a barrier along its southern border, but also dealt with this phenomenon in a legal manner. The Prevention of Infiltration Law, passed in the 1950s, to address Palestinian refugees who re-entered Israel after the establishment of the state of Israel, was 'adapted' in order to deal with the new infiltrators. Since 2008, the government of Israel began to apply this term to African asylum seekers. In 2011, the Knesset successfully passed an amendment to this law (Amendment 1). It allowed for administrative detention of individuals crossing the border with Egypt 'illegally' for up to three years and for those coming from 'enemy states' for up to seven years.

838. The HCJ struck down this amendment on the grounds of unconstitutionality.[389] The HCJ ordered the State to release all detainees (some 2,000 men women and children). The Knesset and Government did not fully comply with this decision, and subsequently passed a second amendment (amendment 2). This meant that after the first HCJ decision to strike down the law in September 2013, another amendment was passed that shortened the administrative detention period, and determined that only new asylum seekers would be detained there, while in a specific camp in the southern part of Israel – *Holot* – asylum seekers already living in Israel and who cannot be deported, could be held indefinitely. The State's explicit intention was to prevent asylum seekers from settling in Israeli cities. A new petition was presented to the HJC, claiming that amendment 2 was also unconstitutional. The HCJ declared amendment 2 void as well, by a majority of 6 to 3.[390]

839. Justice Uzi Vogelman, who wrote the majority ruling, termed conditions at *Holot* 'wretched', and said the Court was justified in striking down a law enacted by the Knesset for the second time because the legislation 'violates human rights in

388. Tally Kritzman-Amir Refugees and Asylum Seekers in the State of Israel (2012) http://www.clb.ac.il/AsylumSystem/Intro4.pdf.
389. HCJ 7146/12 *Adam v. the Knesset* (16/9/2012).
390. HCJ7385/13 *Eitan v. the Goernment and the Knesset* (22 Sep. 2014).

an essential, deep and fundamental way'. At *Holot*, Vogelman wrote in the majority ruling, the asylum seeker 'doesn't control his agenda; his daily routine is dictated by wardens, who have been granted powers of search and discipline; the infiltrator is vulnerable to being transferred into custody at the decision of an administrative body that isn't subject to judicial oversight to the requisite extent; his days are spent doing nothing, because he has no real possibility of leaving the center during the day; and his stay at the center has a beginning, but no foreseeable end'. 'All these cumulatively amount to an unbearable violation of his basic rights, first and foremost the right to freedom and the right to dignity.' 'A democratic society cannot deprive people of freedom for such a length of time when they don't pose any danger and aren't serving a sentence for a crime they committed, even if this deprivation of freedom has benefits', the majority ruling continued. 'Infiltrators don't lose their right to dignity, in the full sense of the term, just because they arrived in the country improperly,' wrote Vogelman. Thus, jailing them for a year when they have done nothing wrong, without their having the ability to do anything to advance their release, constitutes a severe violation of their rights.' ... Being held in custody exacts a heavy price from the detainee. There is virtually no right that isn't violated as a result,' Vogelman said, citing freedom, dignity, privacy, the ability to enjoy family life and personal autonomy as among these violated rights.

840. After amendment 2 was struck down in September 2014, the third amendment was passed in December 2014. This amendment shortens the period of incarceration even further, and limits detention in *Holot* to a period of twenty months. The new amendment also allows the asylum seekers to remain outside *Holot* the entire day. The third petition to the HCJ, was decided in August 2015.[391] The nine-justice panel ruled (by a majority of eight justices) that the maximum period asylum seekers could be held in *Holot* – twenty months – is too long, and gave the Knesset six months to amend the law and set a shorter maximum detention period. The Court declared that the maximum period set for residence at the facility is unconstitutional and has no parallel in comparative law:

> A person's freedom is the basic foundation of his life and existence, ' stated the Court. 'Depriving him of it, even if only for a day, substantially harms his rights. ... It must be remembered that these are infiltrators who can't be deported from Israel and who represent no concrete danger to the state's security or the lives of its citizens. Their only sin was entering our borders illegally, something for which the state as a rule isn't entitled to punish them.

841. In reality, it seems that no consistent, comprehensive policy has been formulated in relation to foreign workers. On one hand, the government makes decisions which have the effect of continuing the employment of foreign workers and issuing them with work permits, while on the other hand, the government makes

391. HCJ 8665/14 *Desete v. Minister of Interior et al* (11 Aug. 2015).

decisions limiting the numbers of migrants and expelling them from the country. The attitude of the authorities is reflected in legislation and regulations promulgated by the relevant minister, as well as in guidelines, instructions and circulars of the directors of the government ministries. These, however, must not be seen as part of a publicly declared governmental policy following from thorough debate of the issues but rather as individual solutions to specific problems.

842. Israeli law obliges an employer in the care-giving sector to arrange private medical insurance for his employees for as long as the employees work for him. The employer has to provide a copy of the insurance policy in a language the employee understands. The medical insurance should be paid by the employer, but he can deduct up to half of the sum paid from the employee's salary. Employees may also purchase health insurance, although many refrain from doing so for fear of being exposed and expelled. With regard to those who do purchase health insurance, the services to which they are entitled are less than those customarily given to citizens. Foreign workers receive treatment for medical emergencies but do not have cover for chronic illnesses.

843. In Israel, there are many NGOs dealing with the needs of foreign workers and asylum seekers, which struggle to implement the rights of foreigners, children and adults alike. The organizations operate in different ways: they assist foreigners by providing medical services, legal services and the like; they operate to raise awareness among decision-makers and the general public regarding the responsibilities of the state towards foreigners; and they file petitions in the HCJ.

§3. The Children of Foreign Workers and the Problem of Naturalization

844. One of the question arising in the public arena now and then is the issue of the status of the children of foreign workers, many of whom were born in Israel, have lived there for many years and consider themselves to be Israeli. Some of them even serve in the army. The civil status of children is the subject of Articles 7 and 8 of the Convention on the Rights of the Child.[392] These articles address the rights of the child to be registered after birth, the right to acquire a nationality and the need to assist children to re-establish their identity where they have been deprived of their identity.

845. As noted, Israel is one of the countries which confer nationality on the basis of the 'principle of blood'. Non-Jewish residents, including the children of foreign workers, are subject to other criteria which must be met before obtaining citizenship, including, in particular, the principle of citizenship by virtue of naturalization and the principle of citizenship by virtue of the powers vested in the Minister of the

392. The UN Convention on the Rights of the Child, 1989. Israel signed the Convention in 1990 and ratified it in 1991; *see also* International Convention of the Rights of All Migrant Workers and Members of Their Families, ILO, Geneva, 1990.

Interior. As noted, the principle of naturalization states that an adult may obtain citizenship if he has satisfied the conditions discussed in the previous chapter.

846. Likewise, the Minister of the Interior is entitled to grant Israeli nationality to a minor child who is a resident of Israel at the request of the child's parents, and to a resident of Israel who is present in Israel, on various grounds which are set in the Nationality Law. An additional law which regulates the status of persons present in Israel but who are not citizens of Israel or holders of immigration certificates or visas, including foreign workers, is the Entry into Israel Law, 1952. This law regulates different types of visas and residence permits in Israel. The law does not establish criteria for granting visas, and it vests the Minister of the Interior with complete freedom to extend, change or cancel a visa, at his discretion.

847. Another provision which refers to the status of the children of foreign workers is Regulation 12 of the Entry into Israel Regulations 1974 which states that 'a child, who was born in Israel and to whom Section 4 of the Law of Return, 1950 applies, will have the same status in Israel as his parents'. The purpose of this regulation is to preserve the integrity of the family unit and the safety of the child, so that a child whose parents hold permanent residence status is also entitled to this status, whereas a child whose parents are present in Israel illegally will also be regarded as an illegal alien and consequently will also be subject to detention and expulsion.

848. The absence of civil status affects the lives of the children of foreign workers from the date of their birth and continues until they reach adulthood. Failure to be able to obtain civil status prevents these children from being properly registered in the education system, and therefore denies them ancillary services; they are not given ID cards at the age of 16 and consequently they cannot obtain a driving license, register for matriculation exams and more. At the age of 18, lack of civil status limits their ability to apply for naturalization in accordance with the naturalization criteria applied in Israel or to receive the status of citizen under the Nationality Law.

849. In Israel, there is no law prohibiting the expulsion of illegally resident children; however, in practice the Ministry of the Interior and the Immigration Administration do not expel children, and often refrain from detaining families which include children. Accordingly, many children and their parents believe that the children provide immunity from expulsion. Yet, when they become adults, they do become subject to expulsion. At the same time, alongside the threat of expulsion, the children of the foreign workers are given an opportunity to institute proceedings to regulate their status.

850. From the moment they become adults, the applicants may obtain citizenship through naturalization. In order to commence this process, they must be entitled 'to reside permanently in Israel', i.e., to exchange their status as illegal aliens for that of temporary residents for a period of four and a half years. From that point, they may obtain the status of permanent resident, which is a precondition to naturalization. Notwithstanding the above, the adult children of foreigners generally do not apply to the branches of the Ministry of the Interior because of their fear of being expelled together with their families. They are trapped in a difficult situation: on one hand, they have reached an age at which they have lost the 'immunity' which protected them as children and have become subject to expulsion requiring them to hide from the authorities, whereas on the other hand, in order to regulate their civil status, they must apply to the authorities.

851. Today, efforts are being made to find an appropriate legal solution for all the children of foreign workers present in Israel, who currently number a few hundred. The government decided at the end of 2005 to grant nationality to some of the children of foreign workers in Israel, and a bill was tabled to amend the Nationality Law to provide for the naturalization of the children of immigrant families in a graduated procedure.

852. Meanwhile, the Minister of Interior decided in 2006 to grant Israeli citizenship to all children of foreign workers born in Israel, who have reached the age of 10 years, provided their parents entered Israel legally. I assume that in view of these developments, the status of the children of foreign workers in Israel will shortly attain final settlement.

Part V. Specific Problems

Chapter 1. War, Treaty and Foreign Affairs Powers

§1. War

853. The State of Israel has been in a state of war since its establishment, and this fact has significantly influenced Israeli law, especially with respect to the emergency powers vested in the executive branch. A state of emergency was declared in Israel at the time of the State's establishment, which has prevailed until today. Further to the perennial state of emergency, Israel has also been involved in numerous wars. Emergency powers, however, are limited. According to the HCJ, 'The maxim that "In time of war the laws are silent" (*Inter arma silentes leges*) … reflects neither existing, nor desirable law'.[393]

854. The topic of declaration of war is regulated by section 40 of Basic Law: The Government, which provides:

> Declaration of war
>
> 40. (a) The state may only begin a war pursuant to a Government decision.
> (b) Nothing in the provisions of this section will prevent the adoption of military actions necessary for the defence of the state and public security.
> (c) Notification of a Government decision to begin a war under the provision of subsection (a) will be submitted to the Knesset Foreign Affairs and Security Committee as soon as possible; the Prime Minister also will give notice to the Knesset plenum as soon as possible; notification regarding military actions as stated in subsection (b) will be given to the Knesset Foreign Affairs and Security Committee as soon as possible.

855. The authority to commence a war is thus vested in the government. Notably, the law distinguishes between a declaration of 'war', in accordance with the title appearing in section 40, and a declaration of an emergency situation pursuant to section 38. A state of emergency, declared upon the establishment of the State,

393. HCJ *Morcos v. Minister of Defence*, 45(1) PD 467, 470 'Even when cannons are firing, the military commander is obligated to obey the law. A society's strength in confronting its enemies is based on its recognition that it is fighting for values worthy of protection. The rule of law is one of those values.' *See also* A. Barak, *The Role of a Supreme Court in a Democracy, and the Fight Against Terrorism*, 58 U. Miami L. Rev. (2003) 125.

enables the executive branch to exercise an array of emergency powers, and as stated, the emergency situation in Israel has yet to be cancelled. The distinction between a state of emergency, pursuant to section 38, and the situation of being at war, pursuant to section 40, indicates the differentiation between various possible 'states of emergency'. The fact of Israel being at war is not normatively identical to a 'regular' state of emergency. Since 1992, the Knesset has renewed the state of emergency declaration annually. The fact that the state of emergency has not been withdrawn for more than sixty-seven years, since Israel was founded, has been the subject of severe criticism. In 1999, a petition was filed with the HCJ by the ACRI, requesting that the Court order that the state of emergency be terminated, arguing that this ongoing situation is both unjustifiable and harms the rule of the law, the separation of powers and basic laws. In a unanimous ruling delivered more than ten years later,[394] the Court held that the petition had 'run its course' because, since ACRI filed its petition, the State has slowly abolished several emergency laws. Justice Rubinstein said that, while 'much work remains to be done' on the issue, the government should be allowed to complete the legislative process. The threats to Israel's existence still remain, Rubinstein added. Still, it was only to be expected that emergency legislation should match the sixty-four year old democratic state, and this goal is achievable.

856. In terms of constitutional law, Israel does not recognize a special category of constitutional powers known as 'wartime powers', as distinct from powers conferred by virtue of the state of emergency. A salient characteristic of this situation is the HCJ's readiness to judicially review various aspects of military activities, even during a time of military conflicts.

857. Even though the war on terror may be distinguished from the war Israel had to contend with in 1967 (Six Day War) and 1973 (Yom Kippur War), the military activities in the areas of Judea and Samaria, and particularly those undertaken since the year 2000, shed light on the willingness of the Supreme Court to adjudicate petitions concerning the prosecution of the war, even during combat.

858. After the 1967 war, the HCJ became accessible to Palestinian residents of the Occupied Territories, who believe they were harmed by the military government's actions. Ever since the *Intifada* started, many Palestinians have filed appeals against allegedly illegitimate actions undertaken by Israeli forces as part of their military operations. Petitions were filed during combat, including by suspected terrorists, which meant that decisions had to be made in real time.

859. One interesting case dealt with the Evacuation of Bodies from Jenin Refugee Camp. In April 2002, the IDF conducted a massive operation against Palestinian militant infrastructure in the major cities of the West Bank. During the operation, the IDF entered the refugee camp adjacent to Jenin, and heavy fighting ensued. Following a few days of combat, the IDF took control of the camp at a cost of more than twenty of its own soldiers. The media was fast to report that a massacre had

394. HCJ 3091/99 *Association for Civil Rights v. the Knesset* (published by Nevo on 8 May 2012).

occurred and that many innocent civilians had been killed during the fighting. The petitioners asked the HCJ to order that the IDF refrain from evacuating the bodies, and that this task be assigned to medical teams and representatives of the Red Cross.

860. The ruling, made in accordance with the principles of international law, placed responsibility for the identification, evacuation and burial of the dead with the Commander of the IDF forces in the West Bank. Representatives of the Red Cross were ordered to be included in the teams. These activities were all to be carried out as quickly as possible, maintaining the necessary balance between respect for the dead and safeguarding the security of the forces. Both sides accepted this arrangement and in light of this compromise, the petition was formally rejected.

861. In the last lines of his judgment, Chief Justice Barak referred to rumours of a massacre in Jenin. He stated that the fact that the respondents (the Israeli army) had 'nothing to hide' clearly demonstrated that nothing akin to a massacre had taken place. It is interesting to note his words:

> It was claimed in the petitions that a massacre had been committed in the Jenin refugee camp. The Respondents disagree most strongly. In Jenin there was a battle – a battle in which many of our soldiers fell. The army fought from house to house, not by bombing from the air, in order to prevent, to the extent possible, civilians' casualties … . A massacre is one thing. A difficult battle is something else.[395]

862. Chief Justice Barak concluded his decision by saying that 'even in a time of combat, the law applying to combat must be upheld'. The military command practice of consulting the Chief Military Attorney on important anti-terrorism issues was emphasized. The Court reiterated that it would take no position regarding the way the combat was managed. This is a fascinating example of the degree to which the HCJ is willing to intervene in military activity, even during times of war. The petition itself was rejected, as were most of the petitions on these issues. However, it should be remembered that the petition was not rejected on the ground of it not being justiciable, as the Court actually evaluated the exercise of emergency powers and the military decisions on their merits.

863. Another case considered in 2006 dealt with a practice known as 'targeted killings'.[396] 'We are fully aware of the fact that this verdict does not make dealing with this reality any easier,' Chief Justice Barak wrote. 'It is the fate of democracies that they may not approve of every means and cannot employ all the methods that their enemies use.'

The verdict examined the legality of the targeted assassinations policy and outlined some rules for its implementation, but the petition against the practice was

395. HC 3114/02 *Barakeh v. The Minister of Defence and Others*, s. 11 (available in English at: <www-.Court.gov.il>).

396. HCJ 769/02 *Public Committee against Torture v. the Government of Israel* (handed down on 14 Dec. 2006).

rejected. The decision neither authorizes nor forbids the use of this tactic: 'It cannot be determined in advance that every targeted killing is prohibited according to customary international law.' The Court ordered that each case be examined in detail before the practice is applied, and that the military commander further consider alternatives and the expected damage. Use of targeted assassinations must be proportionate; that is, based on the balance between military benefits and the expected damage they might cause to innocent civilians. Practically, however, the security forces had followed similar processes even before that verdict was handed down. Targeted assassinations were not practised daily, but now their preceding considerations appear in a legal document. This document was not written only for Israeli readers. Essentially, the targeted assassinations case resembles the 'separation wall' case in nature, as the verdict on the former was also part of Israel's dialogue with the international community that closely monitors Israel's activities in the Territories. These 'security' verdicts explore the impossible situation faced by Israel when combating terrorists who attack it and then find refuge among innocent civilians.[397]

§2. Treaty and Foreign Affairs Power

864. Israel's powers in the area of foreign relations are not statutorily regulated. The traditional understanding is that these powers are conferred upon the government in recognition of its 'general powers of governance'. The Government is authorized to exercise powers with respect to foreign relations, even in the absence of explicit statutory authorization. Section 32 of Basic Law: The Government provides the formal basis for its exercise of these powers, providing:

> *The Government is authorized to perform in the name of the State and subject to any law, all actions which are not legally incumbent on another authority.*

865. This section empowers the government to recognize other states and foreign governments, to establish diplomatic relations with them, and to confer diplomatic status upon their representatives. In this area, there is almost no judicial review, and the Supreme Court displays extensive restraint in examining matters touching on the State's foreign relations. The rule is that 'the manner in which the competent authorities manage foreign affairs is "unjusticiable". It does not admit of examination in accordance with any legal criterion, and this Court eschews intervention in such matters'.[398]

866. The *Reiner* case dealt with a petition to prevent the entry into Israel of a person who had been appointed as German's ambassador to Israel, based on his service in the German Army during the Second World War. The petition was

397. For additional reading see: Amnon Rubinstein, Yaniv Roznai, *Human Shields in Modern Armed Conflicts: The Need for a Proportionate Proportionality*, 22(1) Stanford Law & Policy Review 93–127 (2011).

398. HCJ 4354/92 *Movement for the Temple Faithful v. The Prime Minister*, 47(1) PD 37.

rejected.[399] The Court similarly rejected petitions requesting it to order the Government to refrain from conducting negotiations with the Syrian Government, dealing with the Israeli sovereignty over the Golan Heights, and it also rejected all the petitions filed against the release of Palestinian prisoners pursuant to agreements signed with the Palestinian Authority. In this context, the Court ruled that:

> The Government's decision to release prisoners is a political decision adopted on the basis of political considerations, being within the government's competence, and as is well known, this Court is not supposed to intervene in such matters, and nor does it make a practice of intervening in its considerations. The decision resides with the government and is subject to the criticism of the Knesset or public opinion, and not of the Court.[400]

867. In the *Weiss* matter, the Court rejected a petition objecting to the pursuit of negotiations with the Palestinian Authority, during the service of a transitional government. Chief Justice Barak ruled that:

> the scope of intervention in such matters will be in extreme cases only … the resolution of this question, the dominant components of which are political, and which is the source of a dispute in Israeli society, must be in the arena of political discourse in Israel, by way of the organs of the Knesset or the national polls.[401]

Justice Zamir preferred to categorically deny the fundamental justiciability of these matters, stating: 'The Court … lacks the requisite qualifications for assessing the reasonability of any particular negotiations, or whether the responsibility involved in issuing an order prohibiting political negotiations.'

868. In this context, a distinction must be made between petitions contesting the constitutionality of the government's policy, and petitions claiming a breach of basic rights. This distinction receives expression in the petitions dealing with the policy of establishing settlements in the Occupied Territories. When it was claimed that the settlements violated rights conferred upon individuals – namely, expropriation of Palestinian owned land – the Court rejected claims of non-justiciability. It stated:

> Clearly, in matters of foreign policy … the decision belongs to the political branch and not the judicial branch. However, assuming that … a person's property was damaged or illegally denied him … it is difficult to believe that the Court would avert its eyes from that person, just because that person's right is also liable to the subject of political debate.[402]

399. HCJ *Reiner v. Minister of Justice*, 19(2) PD 485.
400. HCJ 9290/99 M.M.T. *Movement for Victims of Terrorism v. Government of Israel*, 54(1) PD 472.
401. HCJ 5167/00 *Weiss v. Prime Minister*, 55(2) PD 433, p. 472.
402. HCJ 606/78 *Oyev v. Minister of Defence*, 33(2) PD 113, 123.

869. As for the recognition of a foreign state, such recognition is an act of government, and only a state recognized by a government is granted immunity. In this context, the Court ruled that, 'the government is entitled to determine what the factual situation is in matters pertaining to the State's foreign relations, such as whether a particular person has diplomatic immunity, which is a matter for the determination of the Foreign Ministry'. This ruling was implemented with respect to the actions against the Palestinian Authority (for its liability for damages caused as a result of terrorist acts). It was ruled that the question of whether to recognize the Authority as a sovereign body for the purposes of applying the immunity principle to a 'foreign sovereign' belonged to the category of 'acts of state': 'In deciding the question in the legal dispute regarding the application of immunity, the criteria for defining a state are not legal criteria, but are determined in accordance with the Government's position in relation to the political body concerned.'[403]

870. The power to sign an international convention is similarly a power of the Israeli government, as a part of the general powers of governance referred to above. Becoming a party to an international convention comprises two stages: The first is the signing of the convention by a representative of the government; the second is the 'ratification' of the convention. The convention is only obligatory upon the state after its ratification (and in many cases – only after having being ratified by a number of states). In Israel – as in England – the accepted understanding is that the convention only binds the state in terms of international law, but does not become part of the domestic law unless explicitly enacted in Knesset legislation.

871. The Court has made it clear that the establishment and maintenance of international relations in general, and specifically – the concluding of international agreements – belong to the domain of the executive branch, and not the legislative branch. In this sense, our constitutional position differs from the constitutional position of those states in which international conventions have the status, or effect, of law, and even of a law with special status. In those states, the act of signing an international convention is *ipso facto* an act of legislation. This is not the case in Israel, where an international instrument only receives its legislative status by force of explicit Knesset legislation.

872. The rule that international conventions have no force in domestic law is largely based on the assumption that ratifying power is vested in the Government and not in the Knesset. In other words, its lack of domestic legal force is the result of granting ratifying power to the Government. All the same, in certain cases, signing an international convention compels the state to adjust its domestic law, even without formally amending the domestic law to conform with the provisions of the convention. Hence, while the actual duty only exists in terms of international law, from a practical perspective it severely curtails the Knesset's legislative ability.

---

403. CF (Jer.) 2538/00 *Noritz v. The Palestinian Authority* (decision given 30 Mar. 2003). For elaboration, *see* Rubinstein & Medina '*The Constitutional Law of the State of Israel*' (2005 In Hebrew) pp. 914–915.

873. In Israel, it was claimed that there was room for revising the conception that ratification of conventions belongs to the realm of foreign relations, and is, therefore, an authority residing with the Government. The argument is that the Knesset should be granted the power of ratification. In fact, the practice in Israel is for the government to table conventions in the Knesset prior to their ratification, but this is more a matter of 'constitutional custom' than of binding law. However, it is understood that the mere act of giving notice does not ensure appropriate Knesset oversight of conventions entered into by the Government on the State's behalf.

874. Rubinstein and Medina assert that there is a basis for the claim that, during the last decades, a binding constitutional custom has emerged, by which the ratification of singularly important treaties including treaties involved the transfer of territories under state sovereignty to the possession of a foreign sovereign, must be completed by the Knesset. In fact, by force of that constitutional custom, treaties and agreements of exceptional importance, such as political-military agreements, are presented for Knesset approval before commencing effect. Since the Yom Kippur War, all of the important political-military agreements have been accompanied by Knesset debate and approval. These have included the Disengagement of Troops Agreement signed after the Yom Kippur war; the disagreement of Israel's settlement from the Gaza strip; the Peace Agreement with Egypt; the Peace Agreement with Lebanon in 1983; agreements for Palestinian Self-Rule (Oslo Accords I); and the Peace Agreement with Jordan, which included the conceding of territories and which was accompanied by the enactment of legislation known as the Treaty of Peace Between the State of Israel and the Hashemite Kingdom Law, 1995. In all of these cases, the government's position was that it did not require Knesset approval for ratification of the international agreements that it had signed, but it preferred to present them for Knesset approval for essentially political and public reasons.

875. Nonetheless, as yet there is no unequivocal ruling on whether the Knesset is the authorized body, in terms of Israeli constitutional law, to ratify treaties of exceptional public importance. To date, the Court has refused to rule on the matter. The *Weiss* case, for example, dealt with the negotiations with the Palestinian Authority during the incumbency of the transitional government. The Court ruled that it was sufficient for the Government to declare that: 'Any agreement concluded in this matter will be presented for the ratification of the Knesset', without ruling on the question of whether the Government was obliged to do so.[404]

---

404. HCJ 5167/00 *Weiss v. Prime Minister*, 55(2) PD 455.

Chapter 2. Taxation and Spending Power

§1. General

876. Israel resembles other democracies in that it too is governed by the doctrine of 'no taxation without representation'. In other words, the decision to levy taxes must be adopted by a body that represents the public, namely the legislature. The requirement that the imposition of tax be effected by or under law is expressed in Basic Law: State Economy, section 1 of which provides that: 'Taxes, compulsory loans and other compulsory payments shall not be imposed, and their amounts shall not be varied, save by or under Law.' The section further provides that:

> Where the amounts of any taxes, compulsory loans or other compulsory payments, or fees, payable to the Treasury are not prescribed in the Law itself, the amounts prescribed therefore by regulations shall require approval – in advance or within the period prescribed by the Law – by a decision of the Knesset or of a committee of the Knesset empowered by it in that respect.

877. However, despite these provisions, section 39(c) of Basic Law: The Government enables the government to 'impose or increase taxes or other compulsory payments' by virtue of Emergency Regulations.

878. Recognition of the importance attaching to Knesset oversight of secondary legislation, on the basis of which taxes are imposed, led to the rule that the Knesset is entitled to order the retroactive annulment of this kind of secondary legislation, if it came into force prior to deliberation by the Knesset.

879. The central question raised by the wording of section 1 of Basic Law: The State Economy is the nature of 'compulsory payments', the imposition of which requires statutory authorization. A basic distinction is drawn between three categories of payments: tax, fee and price. The distinction is based on the essence of the payment. In essence, a tax is a compulsory payment, for which there is no direct consideration. A fee is a payment imposed for a particular service provided by the authorities, but the purchase of the service is basically compulsory, either in theory or in practice. A price is a payment collected by the authorities for a service provided in accordance with the expense (or value) of the service, the purchase of which is not compulsory.

880. By way of example, the law provides that where payment is a precondition to receiving a license, such as a construction license, driver's license, license for a vehicle, etc., it is regarded as a compulsory payment, the imposition of which requires statutory authorization. These are situations in which the payment is a condition for the removal of a restriction placed by the authority on the individual's freedom of action, and the payment is therefore regarded as a compulsory payment within the meaning of section 1 of Basic Law: The State Economy.

881. The authority's power to collect a 'price' for services it provides may be restricted where a statutory provision compels the authority to provide a particular product or service, but does not explicitly empower the authority to collect payment for providing that product or service. These cases require legislative interpretation. For example, with respect to the statutory duty imposed on a local authority to provide a life-saving service on the beaches within its jurisdiction, it was ruled that the authority is entitled to collect payment in consideration for bathing in the sea, to enable it to provide the life-saving services.[405] In relation to the integration of children from special education into the mainstream education system, it was ruled in the *Yated*[406] case that the provisions of the Special Education Law should be interpreted as imposing an obligation on the State to provide special needs children with free education not only in the educational institutions for special education (as specifically mandated by law) but also where the children are integrated within the institutions of general education.

882. The power to collect payment may also be restricted with respect to services that the state is obliged to provide. For example, a special statutory authorization is required for the Fire Fighting Services to collect payment for their services.

883. The position of the Israeli Supreme Court is that the government has a wide discretion as to the manner of allocating the public budget. The Court has stated:

> The factoring-in of all the considerations that go into the Budget Law – including the establishment of a scale of priorities – is a role that fundamentally belongs to the Knesset and the Government within the ambit of general policy, and inevitably restricting the scope for Supreme Court intervention.[407]

§2. State Expenditure: The Budget Law

884. Under section 3 of Basic Law: The State Economy, Government expenditure for each year is determined in a special law, known as the Budget Law. The Government submits its proposal for the budgetary framework to the Knesset and the Knesset approves the Government's proposal in the Budget Law. The Knesset's deliberations over the Budget Law differ from its deliberations with respect to other draft bills.

885. Section 3(a)(1) of Basic Law: The State Economy states that 'The State Budget shall be prescribed by law. The budget shall be for one year and shall set out the expected and planned expenditure of the Government'. The Budget should include an itemization of all the Government's expenses, and the Finance Minister must submit the Knesset with an annual report regarding the implementation of the

---

405. HCJ 464/84 *Ezra v. Tel-Aviv-Jaffa Mayor*, 39(1) PD 745.
406. HCJ 2599/00 *Yated – Non-Profit Organization for Parents of Children with Down Syndrome v. Ministry of Education*, 56(5) PD 834.
407. HCJ 240/98 *Adalah – Legal Centre for Rights of Arab Israeli Minority v. Minister for Religious Affairs*, 52(5) PD 167, 190.

State Budget. One of the essential conditions for realizing the goal of the Budget Law – namely, Knesset oversight of the Government's activities – is a high degree of budgetary specification, and the budgetary allocations to well-defined activities. Section 3(b)(2) of Basic Law: The State Economy contains a general requirement: 'The Budgetary draft bill shall be detailed.'

886. Section 2(c) of the Budgetary Principles Law states that: 'the Budget shall indicate the amounts of expenditure … divided into budget items, fields of operations and schemes'. One of the main problems that arise in this area has come to be known as 'special funds', which are allocations of sums of money for particular areas of activity, in the framework of the Government's coalition commitments. In such cases, the funds can be allocated to various bodies, in accordance with the discretion of the Minister responsible for that particular area. Severe public criticism of these arrangements lead to the amendment of the Budgetary Principles Law, and a provision was enacted mandating consideration of the principle of equality when allocating budgets. All the same, the Minister has the authority to determine the criteria for allocation, subject to his obligation to fix 'equality based' criteria. In this context, the Supreme Court ruled[408] that the provisions of the Budget Law cannot violate the obligation to allocate the budget according to equality-based criteria, and where the Annual Budget Law includes provisions or criteria for budgetary allocation that violate this obligation, the Court may compel the minister concerned to ignore that provision and act on the basis of equality.

887. The annual governmental expenditure is therefore regulated by two laws: The Budgetary Principles Law, which prescribes the manner of enacting the budgetary laws, and which includes provisions which enable the enforcement of the specific Annual Budget Law, enacted on a yearly basis, determining the particular expenditures for the coming year. The parallel existence of these two laws raises the question of their respective normative status, i.e., the relationship between the Budgetary Principles Law, and the Annual Budget Law. This issue was referred to in an obiter dictum of the Court in the case of *HaTenua HaMesoratit*. The Court stated that section 3A of the Budgetary Principles Law, prescribing the budgetary allocation according to principles of equality, has a normatively superior status to the Annual Budgetary Law, and that as such, 'the Court is competent to annul a provision of the Annual Budgetary Law that violates a provision of the Budgetary Principles Law'. The conceptual basis of this ruling is that, in accordance with its essence, the Budgetary Principles Law purports to establish *les cogens provisions*, applicable specifically to the Annual Budgetary Laws, and determining normative, binding ground rules for the formulation and enforcement of Governmental budgetary policy. These provisions are rendered futile if they are not binding for the purposes of the Annual Budgetary Laws. Indeed, Justice Cheshin took the view that section 3A of the Budgetary Principles Law is normatively equivalent to the provisions of a Basic Law or constitution.

408. HCJ 1438/98 *HaTenua HaMesoratit v. Minister for Religious Affairs*, 53(5) PD 337.

888. Section 3B of the Basic Law: The State Economy addresses the situation which arises when the Budget Law has not been adopted before the beginning of the financial year. It states that:

> Where the Annual Budget Law has not been adopted before the beginning of the financial year, in each month the Government is entitled to spend a sum equivalent to one twelfth of the previous annual budget with the addition of linkage in accordance with the consumer price index … (b) funds according to subsection (a) will first be designated for defrayal of the State's obligations under law, contracts, and treaties; the remaining sums shall be used by the Government exclusively for the provision of essential services and for actions included in the previous annual budget.

889. An amendment to Basic Law: The State Economy resulted in an interesting case dealt with by the HCJ. In the *Bar-On* case of 2011, the HCJ was asked to rule on a petition against an ad hoc, provisional instruction that amended Basic Law: The State Economy so that the state budget is determined biennially. Ruling on the issue, the HCJ stated that the annual approval of the Budget Law is a cornerstone of democratic regimes and is the main tool at the disposal of the legislature to supervise the government's budgetary activities and priorities. Thus, it found that the provisional instruction impeded the Knesset's supervisory powers and was actually intended to weaken the Knesset and strengthen the government.

The Court further argued that the introduction of a biennial budget law conflicts with a long trend of tightening the Knesset supervision of the Executive through, among other means, establishing specific dates by which the government must present the budget bill to the Knesset. The petitioners in this case argued that the amendment impairs the Knesset's ability to disband and thus overthrow the government if the budget law is rejected. They argued that this powerful instrument, with which the parliament can attempt to replace one Cabinet with another, is given to the Knesset only once a year. The provisional amendment restricts it, allowing that tool to be applied only every other year, which further disrupts the balance of power and alters the relationship between the government and the Knesset.

The HCJ ultimately rejected the petition because it felt that the harm caused by this specific amendment was not so grave as to necessitate the Court's intervention in the law-making process. In this case, the HCJ was asked to nullify an amendment to a basic law – a product of the constituent authority – when the legal power to judicially review even ordinary laws has not yet been anchored in a basic law or a solid constitution.

890. The Budgetary Principles Law establishes a number of arrangements that enable the government to attain financial resources for financing its activities during the financial year, where it transpires that the authorized budgetary outlay is insufficient. Upon receiving a governmental proposal, the Finance Committee in the Knesset may authorize the expenditure of revenues received in excess of forecasted revenues for a particular financial year to cover, reduce or prevent price increases in existing plans. The government is entitled to update the budget during the year, in view of the amount of revenues and having regard for inflation. During the financial year, the Government is also entitled to submit an additional budget with specification of additional expenditures. The Finance Minister may instruct that expenditure sums prescribed in one scheme be transferred to another scheme.

891. A particularly interesting subject in this context concerns the normative status of the provisions of the Budget Law. The Budget Law does not impose a duty of action upon the State, and its provisions are nothing more than a permit for the government to spend money for particular purposes. Usually, it cannot be regarded as a substitute for the requirement for substantive authorization for the exercise of any governmental power. Nevertheless, the Court was ready to recognize the budgetary authorization as providing the basis for governmental authority to act in a particular area. One example of this was in the *Gross* case, in which government financial assistance granted to released soldiers exceeded the amounts prescribed in the Discharged Soldiers (Adjustment Grant) Law 1988. The Court recognized the Government's authority to do so, not on the basis of 'general governmental authority' but rather on the basis of its authorization in the Annual Budget Law.[409]

§3. The Budget Law and the 'Arrangements' (Omnibus) Law

892. In the wake of the profound economic crisis that struck Israel in 1985, and in the context of the emergency plan that was crystallized in an attempt to stabilize the economy, the State Economy Arrangements (State of Emergency) Law 1985, (hereinafter 'the Arrangements Law') was enacted. The goal of this law was to establish arrangements for the state of emergency, and therefore the government compiled a collection of laws and amendments of laws, all of which were presented for Knesset approval in a single instrument. In 1985, this was an essential factor in the implementation of the Economic Plan, but it subsequently became a regular feature of economic legislation in Israel. Since that time, the Arrangements Law has been presented to the Knesset annually, as a supplement to the Annual Budget Law. Similarly, since then, the Arrangements Law has included a broad range of legislative amendments pertaining to different subjects. These legislative amendments are unified by the Government's perception of their importance in the realization of its economic policy. As a result, over the last decade, the Arrangements Law has become part of standard procedure in Israeli economic legislation.

893. In 2005, the Supreme Court dealt at length with one of the Arrangements Laws, and gave the following description (per Justice Beinish) of the development and proliferation of the Arrangements Law:

> Over the years the use of the legislative mechanism of the Arrangements Law has developed and expanded, and a number of 'Arrangements Laws' were passed not as an ancillary supplement to the State Budget, but rather as an element of the government's economic policy. The Arrangements Law and its

409. HCJ 381/91 *Gross v. Ministry of Education*, 46(1) PD 53.

cognates, such as the Economic Program law forming the subject of the petitions before us, have grown into massive legislative projects that deal with an ever larger agglomeration of subjects covering a broad range of areas, even extending to areas bearing no overt and necessary connection to the budget itself. Furthermore, over the years, the Arrangements Law has increasingly been utilized not only for necessary legislative amendments required to adjust the existing legislation to the Budget Law, but also as a 'platform' for substantive and far reaching legislation. In that capacity, they operate as a tool for effecting structural changes in the economy and the society, including with respect to publicly disputed topics, which the government would have had difficulty in passing by a regular legislative procedure.[410]

894. Recent years have seen a decline in the number of legislative amendments compiled within the Arrangements Law, but at the same time, recent economic reforms have been accompanied by legislation resembling the Arrangements Law, which has not been passed as an appendix to the Budget Law.

895. In the *Poultry Growers Association* case, the Supreme Court considered substantive flaws in the Arrangements Law, but ruled that these flaws were insufficient to invalidate the law. The judgment was a testimony to judicial restraint and moderation with respect to judicial intervention occasioned by a flaw in the legislative process of a law. However, the judicial restraint and moderation that characterize the Court's relationship to the Knesset should not be underestimated. The constitutional case law of the HCJ is replete with innovative rulings and criteria for judicial intervention that were established in cases in which the petitions themselves were rejected. This format was adopted both regarding judicial review of internal Knesset proceedings and judicial review of legislation. The Court establishes a new law, or lays new conceptual groundwork for intervention, without actually implementing them in the case at hand. This method was adopted by the Supreme Court in the monumental *Mizrachi Bank* case, which recognized the Supreme Court's power of judicial review of Knesset legislation, but refrained from striking down the law petitioned against in the instant case. Occasionally these innovations are even the product of 'incidental remarks'. At the next stage, all that remains is to apply the new criteria.

896. The petition in the *Poultry Growers' Association* case challenged the legislative process of the chapter on agriculture in the Economic Program Law, 2003 and 2004. The legislation preceding the enactment of the agricultural section in the Economic Program Law granted the poultry growers and their organizations a dominant position in relation to the activity of the agricultural councils, and wide autonomy in relation to the management and regulation of the agricultural branches. In an accelerated, 'lightning' procedure, the Knesset adopted the Economic Program Law, consisting of extensive reforms for the agricultural sector, and a transfer

410. HCJ 4885/03 *Poultry Growers Association et al. v. The Government of Israel*, 59(2) PD Similar laws are also passed in other states, as for example the 'Ley de Acompañamiento' in Spain.

of powers from the agricultural councils to the Minister of Agriculture. The petitioners claimed that the legislative process of the Economic Program Law was similar to procedures that generally accompany the Arrangements Laws, which are adopted together with the Annual Budget Law. The Finance Committee devoted less than one meeting to the debate on the agricultural section, the second reading of the law was conducted almost immediately thereafter and the voting on each section of the law took place from the afternoon of that same day until the wee hours of the early morning the next day.

897. The Court rejected the petition. According to Justice Beinish, a resort to the mechanism of the Arrangements Law raises a number of problems in terms of appropriate democratic procedure. Such legislation is characterized by a perfunctory legislative procedure that thwarts deep and serious discussion, and inhibits the law makers' ability to formulate a position on the contents of the bill. A procedure of this kind precludes any serious and proper discussion of the bill, and does not allow for an objective inspection and examination of the legislative process, primarily by the Knesset.

898. This judgment's innovation concerns the Court's ability to invalidate a law due to a defect in the legislative process, when the flaw is such that it goes to the very root of the procedure, harming its fundamental principles. The judgment provides four examples of such defects: the principle of participation, the principle of majority decision, the principle of publicity and the principle of formal equality. In discussion of the petition's merits, the Court ruled that the instant case did not evince extreme impropriety or irregularity to such a degree that warranted the Court's intervention, and therefore recommended that the Knesset consider its continued reliance on the problematic mechanism of the Arrangements Law. It is incumbent upon the Knesset, quite simply, to change the rules of the game in respect. Since then, the Arrangements Law passed every year along with the annual budget has been much shorter than it was previously, and important reforms have been withdrawn from this law and passed through regular legislation.

Chapter 3. Emergency Laws

§1. Introduction

899. From a legal perspective, Israel has been in a 'state of emergency' since its establishment. The declaration of a state of emergency enables emergency legislation; in other words, the executive authority is empowered to enact regulations that deviate from regular parliamentary legislative procedures. As such, they may be enacted expeditiously, and may also be changed or amended with flexibility in order to adjust them to a dynamic, changing reality. Emergency legislation enables the Government to arrogate to itself extensive powers, normally vested in the Knesset. Given that these powers are exercised exclusively during times of emergency, they are characterized not only by granting power to impose far-reaching restrictions on individual freedoms, but also by their deviation from, and even the violation of, fundamental principles of law (in the substantive sense), and the separation of powers. For example, the power to enact emergency regulations provides the basis on which the Government is permitted to suspend or abrogate laws, and provides the authority to detain a person in 'administrative detention' without the need for a judicial procedure to prove his guilt.

900. The subject of exercising governmental powers during a national emergency is one of the most difficult issues confronted by a democratic state. It epitomizes the dilemma involved in striking a balance between the State's duty to protect its citizens' lives – a duty which receives its most profound expression in times of emergency – and its duty to avoid the infringement of the basic rights of its citizens and of people in general, even if they number among the State's enemies.

901. Any discussion of emergency legislation in the Israeli context cannot ignore the unique situation in which Israel finds itself. 'Israel is the only state in the twentieth century that has succeeded in preserving its democratic institutions and a reasonable level of human rights for its citizens, despite the perpetual external threat.'[411]

§2. Declaration of a State of Emergency

902. The Israeli Government has been vested with extraordinary powers, which it may exercise when the competent authorities have declared a state of emergency. A state of emergency was declared at the time of the establishment of the State, and until today, it has not been cancelled. As such, for the purposes of implementing the laws and regulations specified below, Israel is in a 'permanent state of emergency'.

411. M. Hoffnung, *Israel–State Security Versus the Rule of Law (1948–1991)* (1991), p. 346; *see also* A. Dershowitz, *Preventative Detention of Citizens During a National Emergency – A Comparison Between Israel and the United States*, 1 Israel Yearbook on Human Rights 295 (1971).

903. Israel's system of emergency legislation comprises three central mechanisms:

(1) The power to promulgate emergency legislation pursuant to sections 38 and 39 of Basic Law: The Government;
(2) The power granted to the Minister of Defence to detain a person by way of administrative detention, under the Emergency Powers (Detention) Law, 1979;
(3) Existing restrictions on freedom of association and freedom of expression by force of the government's power to declare a group of a people as a 'terrorist organization' under the Prevention of Terror Ordinance, 1948.[412]

904. According to Basic Law: The Government, as amended in 1992, the Knesset may declare a state of emergency, which may remain in force for one year, after which the Knesset can renew its declaration if it sees fit. Since 1992, the Knesset has renewed the state of emergency declaration annually. The fact that the state of emergency has not been withdrawn for more than sixty years since Israel was founded has been the subject of severe criticism. In 1999, a petition was filed with the HCJ by the ACRI, requesting that the Court order that the state of emergency be terminated, arguing that this ongoing situation is both unjustifiable and damaging to the rule of the law, the separation of powers and basic laws. In an unanimous ruling delivered more than ten years later,[413] the Court held that the petition had 'run its course' because since ACRI filed its petition, the state had slowly abolished several emergency laws. Justice Rubinstein said that while 'much work remains to be done' on the issue, the government should be allowed to complete the legislative process. The threats to Israel's existence still remain, Justice Rubinstein added. Still, it was only to be expected that emergency legislation should match the sixty-four year old democratic state, and this goal is achievable.

905. Section 38 of the Basic Law: The Government deals with the declaration of a state of emergency. It does not enumerate the circumstances that may justify the declaration of a state of emergency, and to date, the Court has refrained from addressing the relevant considerations and assessing their reasonableness.

§3. Emergency Regulations

906. Once a state of emergency has been declared, the Government is authorized to promulgate emergency regulations that may alter any law, temporarily suspend its effect or introduce conditions, and may also impose or increase taxes or other compulsory payments unless there is another relevant legislative provision dealing with this issue. The authority to enact regulations in a state of emergency

412. M. Hoffnung, *Israel–State Security Versus the Rule of Law (1948–1991)* (1991), p. 346; *see also* A. Dershowitz, *Preventative Detention of Citizens During a National Emergency – A Comparison Between Israel and the United States*, 1 Israel Yearbook on Human Rights, 295 (1971).
413. HCJ 3091/99 *Association for Civil Rights v. the Knesset* (published by Nevo on 8 May 2012).

vests in the Government legislative powers that are equivalent to primary legislation, in circumvention of the Knesset's legislative power. This situation, in which the Executive effectively usurps the Legislature's power, violates the principle of the separation of powers, raising the question of supervision of the Government's exercise of the Knesset's legislative powers. In this context, the Government's 'extra-legislative powers' are subject to the following two restrictions:

(1.) *The Requirement of Parliamentary Supervision* – Basic Law: The Government empowers the Government to enact regulations. The intention is that this refers to the Government in its entirety, even though Section 39(b) states that 'Should the Prime Minister deem it impossible to convene the Government, given the existence of an immediate and critical need to make emergency regulations, he may make such regulations or empower a Minister to make them'.

907. In view of the above, the Executive's power to enact regulations is conditional upon the Knesset (i.e., Legislature) having declared that a state of emergency exists. The Basic Law further provides that the emergency regulations must be tabled with the Foreign Affairs and Security Committee at the earliest possible date after their enactment. The section does not stipulate this requirement as a condition for the regulations' validity.

908. The validity of the emergency regulations is limited to three months, and only the Knesset is entitled to extend their validity, by legislative means. This restriction has existed since the establishment of the State, and is intended to ensure that any long-term arrangement is effected exclusively by way of Knesset legislation, in independent, self-sustaining legislation. As such, even if the law was only adopted after the passage of three months, this does not impair its validity.[414]

909. (2). *'It is necessary to defend the State, public security and the maintenance of supplies and essential services.'* The Basic Law: The Government provides that 'During a state of emergency the government is entitled to make emergency regulations to defend the State, public security and the maintenance of supplies and essential services'. This section effectively establishes substantive parameters determining the contents of these regulations. Case law has tended to interpret these conditions particularly broadly, and the ambit of 'legitimate goals' is interpreted as covering not only the need to confront threats to the existence of the State, but also as including crisis situations compelling the adoption of special measures for the maintenance of essential services. For example, the Court recognized in principle that the determination of special arrangements in the area of planning

414. HCJ 243/52 *Bialer v. Minister of Finance*, 7 PD 429, where it stated that 'Where the Knesset, by its own legislation, extends the 'validity' of national emergency regulations enacted by a particular minister, it effectively expresses its affirmative view of the regulations, and furthermore that for the duration of the extended period it vests them with a stamp of approval in the form of primary legislation. What this means is that at least from the date of the extension, the regulations are legal in every sense'.

and construction, for the rapid construction of apartments occasioned by the need to absorb immigration, can be regarded as an essential measure.[415]

910. The High Court has also added to the statutory conditions, the requirement that there be a substantial impediment preventing the regulation of the matter in regular legislation. In the *Paritzky* case, the Court explicitly ruled that:

> Emergency regulations cannot be enacted unless the emergency situation prevents the legislation of a law ... the requirement is that the impossibility of legislating the law be caused by the state of emergency prevailing in the State, in other words, emergency legislation may only be enacted if the Knesset is unable to conduct regular legislative proceedings as a result of the state of emergency.[416]

911. An outstanding example of this case law requirement is the *Poraz* case. In this case, the HCJ struck down emergency regulations from 1990, which had established an expedited procedure for the approval of building plans, by suspending the validity of the provisions of the Planning and Construction Laws. During the very period in which the regulations were enacted, the Knesset was conducting deliberations pertaining to a similar legislative proposal, likewise intended to expedite legislative proceedings. The Court ruled that in view of the fact that the Knesset was in any event conducting an expedited legislative process, it was appropriate to wait until the completion of its legislative process, and there were no grounds for exercising the power to make emergency regulations: 'Where the possibility exists for organized and prompt legislation by the Knesset, the power of the executive branch to make emergency regulations must be subordinate to it.'[417]

912. The contents of emergency regulations are similarly demarcated, both in legislature and in case law. Basic Law: The Government subjects the contents of the emergency regulations to specific restrictions: 'Emergency regulations may not prevent recourse to legal action, or prescribe retroactive punishment or allow infringement of human dignity.' Similarly, a restriction appears in a number of laws, and especially in basic laws, according to which emergency regulations cannot alter the arrangements specified in them, temporarily suspend them or make them subject to conditions. These restrictions are supplemented by other restrictions grounded in case law, which are intended to secure the inviolability of individual rights or of the fundamental principles of the system, except to the extent necessitated by the state of emergency. The Supreme Court may exercise judicial review over regulations, and for that purpose, their status is equivalent to that of secondary legislation. As such, judicial review is not limited to cases in which there is a contradiction of provisions in other basic laws, and also includes the grounds of unreasonableness and disproportionateness.

---

415. HCJ 2994/00 *Poraz v. Government of Israel*, 43(3) PD 317.
416. HCJ 6971/98 *Pritzky v. Minister of the Interior*, 53(1) PD 763.
417. *Poraz, ibid.*, p. 322.

§4. The Prevention of Terror Ordinance

913. The Prevention of Terror Ordinance prevents the creation, and activities, of terrorist organizations, and its application is restricted to periods declared to be times of emergency. A group of people is considered to be a terrorist organization if 'it resorts in its activities to acts of violence calculated to cause death or injury to a person or to threats of such acts of violence'.

914. The Ordinance establishes a prohibition on the activities of a terrorist organization, including membership thereof, and delivering propaganda speeches at a public meeting or over the radio on behalf of the organization. Moreover, the Ordinance also prohibits support for a terrorist organization, in the form of publishing 'words of praise or sympathy for or support of a terrorist organization'. The goal of the Prevention of Terror Ordinance is to prevent all activity of terrorist organizations. Defining a group as a terrorist organization does not require a formal declaration, and for purposes of any proceeding pursuant to the Ordinance, it may be proven that a particular organization is a terrorist organization. At the same time, the Government may declare that a certain body is a terrorist organization independently of any measure being taken against its members. 'If the Government, by notice in the Official Gazette, declares that a particular body of persons is a terrorist organization, the notice shall serve, in any legal proceeding, as proof that that body of persons is a terrorist organization, unless the contrary is proved.' Indeed, over the years a number of organizations have been declared to be terrorist organizations.

§5. Administrative Detention

915. Administrative detention is detention without trial, the aim of which is not to punish a person for past misdeeds, but rather to prevent any danger posed by his future actions to national and public security. As such, administrative detention is not contingent upon the commission of an offence, or even on suspicion to that effect. A person can only be placed in administrative detention when there is no less grave method of preventing the danger posed by his actions. Resort to the extraordinary method of administrative detention within Israel has been sporadic, but it is used more frequently in relation to the activists of terrorist organizations in the areas of Judea and Samaria.

916. Section 2 of the Emergency Powers (Detention) Law, 1979, empowers the Minister of Defence to detain a person for a period of six months, and to periodically extend his detention for additional periods of six months, without limitation, if he believes that reasons of national and public security still compel his detention. The detention must be confirmed by the President of the District Court within forty-eight hours of the arrest, and the decision can be appealed before a justice of the Supreme Court.

917. The Courts have emphasized the extreme nature of administrative detention, and that it must therefore be limited to extraordinary cases and circumstances.

'The power granted to the Minister of Defence is far reaching and exceptional, because it enables him to deny a person's freedom without regular legal process, and as such must be exercised with tremendous caution and only in cases where the danger to national and public security is grave, and there is no other way of avoiding the danger.'[418]

918. The exercise of the power of administrative detention seriously infringes basic principles such as the rule of law and the notion according to which it is forbidden to negate a person's freedom other than by a legal process in which his guilt is proved. The granting of this power is grounded in the perception that certain circumstances compel the adoption of deterrent measures against a person liable to commit actions that may prejudice public security, where the person considered to be dangerous is not indictable under the conventional criminal law. The rule is that the power to order administrative detention cannot be used as a penal measure. In keeping with this rule, the Supreme Court ruled that 'Since the administrative detention order is intended to prevent an anticipated danger, the reasonability test must be used. In other words, there must be an evaluation of the actions and words of the detainee as evidenced by the material – which usually includes confidential material – in order to determine the degree of danger than can be expected from him in the future ... another factor to be considered as part of the evaluation is the nature of the activity ... [it must pertain to particularly heinous offences that may damage national or public security]'.[419] The test accepted in the case law is that of 'near certainty'. The Court may only approve administrative detention if persuaded that 'it is almost certain that the detainee will commit grave crimes unless his freedom is limited by way of detention'.

919. In fact, the power of administrative detention should only be used if proved that there is no possibility of conducting regular criminal proceedings:

> Where it is possible to adequately ensure national and state security, where necessary, by an arrest detention order anchored in the regular criminal proceedings, there is no justification for resorting to special emergency powers, intended for exceptional circumstances, in which national or public security necessitate a person's detention without there being any other legal possibility of achieving that result.

920. One of the most difficult subjects discussed to date in Israel, before a nine-justice bench, was the issue of whether administrative detention can be ordered when the detainee does not pose any immediate danger to state security, but rather, serves as a 'bargaining chip' for the purposes of negotiations for the release of, or information regarding, Israeli prisoners and soldiers missing in action.

921. The petitioners, ten Lebanese citizens, were brought to Israel between 1986 and 1987 by the security forces. They were prosecuted for being members of hostile

418. AAD 1/82 *Kawassma v. Minister of Defence*, 36(1) PD 666, 669.
419. AAD 8788/03 *Federman v. Minister of Defence*, 58(1) PD 176.

terrorist groups, found guilty and imprisoned. Despite serving their full sentence, they were not released. Legally, they were held in 'administrative detention', ordered by the Minister of Defence under Article 2 of the Emergency Powers (Detentions) Act. The objective of this imprisonment, however, had nothing to do with their conduct or acts. They were held in an Israeli prison for the sole purpose of being used as 'bargaining chips' for negotiations with Islamic groups. Israel believed that Islamic groups (mainly Hezballah) held one or more Israeli soldiers missing in action.[420]

922. The Lebanese hostages appealed to the Supreme Court on a number of occasions. In November 1997, the Supreme Court determined (by a majority vote of 2:1) that the Lebanese hostages' administrative detention for the sole purpose of being used as 'bargaining chips' was valid. In 1998, the Court decided to hold a further hearing on the case. The decision following this additional deliberation was handed down in April 2000, reversing (by a majority of 6:3) the decision of 1997. Therefore, the Lebanese hostages were released and returned to Lebanon. The judgment of the majority was based on an analysis of the detention powers and whether the motive for holding the hostages – the possibility of exchanging prisoners – was legally justified.

923. The Court stated that in a democratic state, a person posing danger to state security can be placed under administrative detention, yet this power cannot be extended to a person who himself does not pose such a danger and is held only as a 'bargaining chip'. Such detention infringes the principles of human dignity and liberty in such a deep and profound way that it cannot be tolerated in a state that aspires to the values of liberty and dignity, even for reasons of state security. The Court determined that the goal of administrative detention is the prevention of danger to state or public security as posed by the detainee himself, and may be used provided that there are no other means of attaining that goal by having resort to the criminal law.

924. This ruling led to the enactment of the Imprisonment of Illegal Fighters Law, 2002, which authorized the Chief of the General Staff to order the imprisonment of person who participated in hostile activities, but who were not entitled to the status of 'prisoner-of-war' in accordance with international law (instead, falling into the category of 'illegal combatants'), in the event that the Chief of Staff had reasonable grounds to believe that … [the prisoner] was an illegal fighter, and that his release would prejudice state security.

§6. Restrictions on Human Rights by Force of the Defence (Emergency) Regulations 1945

925. The Defence (Emergency) Regulations, 1945 originated in the Mandate period, and were promulgated by the High Commissioner pursuant to the King's

420. AAD 7048/97 *Anonymous v. Minister of Defence*, 53(1) PD 721.

Order in Council. They have the status of primary legislation, despite their appellation as 'regulations'. Over the years, the Knesset has revoked some of the Defence Regulations but to date has rejected all proposals to repeal the regulations in their entirety.

926. The Defence Regulations confer far-reaching powers upon the security authorities, including the Military Censor, and military commanders appointed under Regulation 6 of the Military Tribunals Law. *Inter alia*, the Regulations provide the legal basis for establishing the Military Courts, whose judges are appointed by the Chief of Staff. These Military Courts are competent to adjudicate all of the offences enumerated in the Defence Regulations, even in deviation from the regular rules of evidence and procedure. Although they are empowered to impose the death penalty, in practice, the Military Courts do not exercise this power to sentence offenders to death. There are also prohibitions relating to the use of firearms and disturbance of the public order. The security authorities also have a number of problematic powers of deterrence and even of punishment, including powers of seizure and confiscation, entry and searching of premises, declaration of unlawful associations, censorship, declaration of closed areas and house detention, demolition of houses, curfew, closures and others.

927. The Court practises judicial review of the exercise of powers conferred under the Defence Regulations. Although the Court does not have the authority to declare the regulations void, since the enactment of Basic Law: Human Dignity and Freedom in 1992, the Court has been guided by the notion that the Defence Regulations are today part of the legislation of a democratic state. They must be interpreted according to the basic principles of Israeli law.

928. An example of judicial review exercised in relation to the Defence Regulations is the case of the demolition of the homes of terrorists and those who send them. In a series of judgments, the Court ruled that by force of the Defence Regulations the power to demolish houses (in the Territories and within the State of Israel) could be exercised exclusively for military-operational purposes or as a deterrent measure, for the prevention of future acts of violence. Specifically, the Court ruled that the military commander is not permitted to order the demolition of the houses of suicide terrorists and their senders as a punitive measure; the administrative nature of the authority precludes its utilization for punitive means, which are the domain of the judicial authorities.

929. The Court ruled that the exercise of this power involved punishing the innocent, and therefore bore traces of collective punishment. However, despite this ruling, the Court rejected almost all of the petitions filed on this matter, while accepting the declarations of the security authorities that this was a preventative measure aimed at deterring potential terrorists.[421] The Court also rejected the claim

---

421. *See* the case of *Abu Fareh*, HCJ 2006/97, 51(2) PD 651. For elaboration on this subject *see*: D. Kretzmer, *The Occupation of Justice – The Supreme Court of Israel and the Occupied Territories* (2002) 69.

that exercising the power to demolish houses contradicted the provision of Basic Law: Human Freedom and Dignity. In actual fact, this method is rarely used by the security forces, although in 2015 several houses of terrorists in the Territories have been demolished, following HCJ decisions that rejected petitions against this power.

930. The Court has generally dismissed claims concerning the non-justiciability of the choice of military means, even where petitions are filed during the course of battle. However, the examination itself is conducted having regard for the relatively broad range of reasonable decisions that may be adopted by the security authorities, and almost absolute reliance on military assessments regarding the effectiveness of the measures adopted, their necessity and their proportionality. The nature of the war against terror has generated increasing readiness on the Court's part to conduct an in-depth, substantive examination of the methods utilized by the army.

931. Both on the public and parliamentary levels, judicial intervention in security-military related matters has been criticized. For example, the judicial intervention in the *Plonim* case, concerning the illegality of the continued holding of detainees as 'bargaining chips' for attaining information on IDF prisoners and absentees, incensed their families as well as the security authorities. In this context, it bears mentioning that the criticism of the Court's principled decision to recognize the justiciability of the matter may have been correct. However, it is clear that there was a need for a ruling of the Supreme Court on the substance of the matter – the restriction of illegal actions – even if motivated by security considerations.

Chapter 4. The Power of the Military

932. Israel is not only a civil society, but also a society in which the army plays a crucial role in the national life and culture. Like all other security branches, the Israeli army is under government supervision. Since the creation of the State, and particularly in view of the ongoing state of emergency, the IDF has been a key player in everyday life. The IDF's centrality in Israeli life has dictated the need to clearly institutionalize its powers, and primarily, its subordination to the civil echelons of power. Israeli does not live under a serious spectre of a military *coup d'état*, but civil supervision of the IDF's activities is of particular importance, especially when having regard for its agglomeration of powers, and its ability to infringe numerous basic human rights.

§1. Subordination to the Government

933. The government is the authorized body responsible for all matters pertaining to national security, and the subordination of the various branches of the security regime to governmental authority is a core principle of the democratic regime. This principle receives explicit expression in section 2(a) of the Basic Law: The Army, which states that '(a) The Army is subject to the authority of the Government'; and in section 3(b) under which the Chief of the General Staff, who serves as 'the supreme command level in the army', is stated as being 'subject to the authority of the Government and subordinate to the Minister of Defence'.[422]

934. The Minister of Defence is the minister charged by the government with oversight and supervision of the IDF, and the Basic Law: The Army contains a number of explicit provisions in this regard. Section 2(b) states that 'The Minister in charge of the Army on behalf of the Government is the Minister of Defence' and section 3(c) stipulates that 'The Chief of the General Staff shall be appointed by the Government upon the recommendation of the Minister of Defence. By force of this section, the government is also authorized to remove the Chief of Staff from office, upon the recommendation of the Minister of Defence.'

935. As stated, the Army is subject to the authority of the government and subordinate to the Minister of Defence. This means that in the event of conflict between the guidelines of the government and the guidelines of the Minister, the Army must comply with position established by the Government. Hence, in the case of *Duikat*, it transpired that the position of the Minister of Defence differed from that of the government over the question of there being a military need to establish settlements in the Territories. In accordance with the above rule, the Supreme Court determined that 'the Government decision is binding on the Chief of the General Staff', even if that decision runs contrary to the position of the Minister of Defence.[423]

422. Due to the importance of Basic Law: The Army, it is cited here in its entirety.
423. HCJ 390/79 *Duikat v. Government of Israel*, 34(1) PD 1, 10.

936. The scope of the Defence Minister's authority (and that of the government) to give orders to the Chief of General Staff, and by extension, to the army as a whole, is fiercely disputed. Obviously, the Minister is authorized to prescribe guidelines for the army concerning its general policies and fundamental goals or strategy. The question is whether this authority also extends to the means of achieving those goals, that is, tactics. In the Israeli political reality, the Ministers of Defence are quite frequently retired military men, and even past Chiefs of Staff. The reality created is therefore one in which the Minister of Defence is in effect a 'supra-Chief of Staff'.

937. It would appear that, like the division of powers between ministers and other position holders in the public administration serving by virtue of their professional expertise, in a formal sense, the Minister of Defence is authorized to instruct the army in relation to both its strategic goals, and the manner in which it accomplishes specific tasks. Nonetheless, practical considerations compel judicious and careful use of the power of the civil authority to interfere with 'tactical decisions' of the army.[424]

938. The Minister of Defence also bears ministerial responsibility for the army's actions. His responsibility is expressed first and foremost in the determination of the strategic goals that constitute and guide defence policy. However, with respect to operational decisions during battle, his responsibility for specific decisions of the defence authorities is more limited. The distinction between the responsibility of the military authorities and that of the civil authorities has been examined in a number of Commissions of Enquiry, the most important of which were the Agranat Commission, established in the aftermath of the failures of the Yom Kippur War, for the purpose of examining the responsibility of the civil authorities, and the Kahn Commission, which dealt with the massacre in the Sabra and Shatilla refugee camps in Lebanon.

939. The Agranat Commission exempted the political echelon from responsibility and blame for the failures leading to the military's unpreparedness for the Yom Kippur War. The ruling derived from the notion that the civil branches had not been granted the authority to intervene in specific military activities, and hence were blameless for its failures. The Commission found that 'it was never determined that the Minister of Defence is a "supra-Chief of Staff"'. As such, the Commission exonerated the political authorities, and ruled that the military branch, namely, the Chief of Staff and other key officers, bore responsibility for the army's failure to adequately prepare for the war. The Agranat Commission's conclusions and recommendations dealt *inter alia* with the need to explicitly define the division of responsibility between the Government, the Minister of Defence, and the Chief of General Staff. The result was that in 1976, Basic Law: The Army was enacted. However, the basic law did not implement the Commission's recommendations in their entirety.

424. A. Rubinstein & B. Medina, *The Constitutional Law of the State of Israel* (6th ed. 2005, In Hebrew) pp. 979–989, and references in n. 16, *ibid.*

The Commission further recommended the establishment of an independent evaluative body by the government, which would ensure pluralism in intelligence assessments, and this recommendation has only been implemented over the last few years, with the establishment of the National Security Council in 1999. The Council's primary purpose is to serve as a national security staff, and as a senior advisory forum for the political level on matters of national security. In this context, it centralizes the assessment of expected trends and processes as they relate to all levels of national security, makes recommendations on national security policy to the Cabinet, and engages in the long-range planning of national security.

940. The Kahn Commission dealt with the issue of responsibility for the massacre in the Sabra and Shatilla refugee camps. In contrast to the Agranat Commission, the Kahn Commission found that the political authorities were personally responsible for supervising the manner in which the IDF carried out its activities. The Commission found serious flaws in the conduct of the Prime Minister and the Foreign Minister, but its criticism was directed primarily at the Minister of Defence, who, at the time, was Ariel Sharon. The Commission determined that Sharon was personally responsible for having failed to take the requisite measures to eliminate or reduce the danger of a massacre, as a condition of the Falangists' entry into the camp. This constituted a failure to properly perform the duty imposed upon him as the Minister of Defence, as a result of which the Committee recommended his dismissal from office, as indeed occurred.

§2. Military Powers

941. Like any other administrative authority, the activities of the Army are also governed by law, but the problem is that there is no clear statutory definition of the army's powers. For example, there is no statutory enumeration of the duties that the Government may impose on the Army, and to what extent the army can be used for goals that are not directly related to the protection of state security, including national and social goals, such as the evacuation of citizens, or the replacement of striking workers.

942. Under the Law and Administration Ordinance (as amended in 1995), the Government's authority to utilize the army for the protection of the State's security was supplemented by its authority to use the army 'for the attainment of its national security goals'. In this context, one of the most interesting constitutional questions raised recently, during the Israeli withdrawal (disengagement) from the Gaza Strip, was the question of whether the soldiers of the IDF are permitted to take part in the implementation of the Disengagement Plan within the borders of the State of Israel.[425] Since the evacuees are Israeli citizens, it was unclear whether use of the army to evacuate citizens is legal.[426]

---

425. HC 7455/05 *The Legal Forum for the Land of Israel, 'Advocates Section, 2005' v. The Government of Israel* (handed down on 22 Aug. 2005).
426. The withdrawal of Israeli settlers, including the dismantling of Jewish settlements and evacuation of Jewish settlers, took plan in August 2005, and was implemented by Prime Minister Ariel Sharon.

943. The petitioners sought to differentiate between law enforcement actions performed within the State's borders, directed at Israeli citizens, and the preservation of state security directed against external enemies. Actions falling within the first category are the exclusive responsibility of the Israeli Police. Unleashing the IDF against the civilian population for the preservation of public order contradicts the very essence of the army's role.

944. Chief Justice Barak, who wrote the Court's decision, emphasized that, like any other administrative authority, the IDF is subordinate to the principle of legality, and that all of its actions must be anchored in the law, foremost among them, the Basic Law: The Army. Section 25 of the Disengagement Implementation Law explicitly empowers IDF soldiers to operate in the evacuated area to prevent illegal entry and to remove those illegally remaining within the areas. Moreover, there is also a general empowerment provision. Under section 18 of the law, and under the Administration Ordinance (as amended in 1995), the IDF's general authority to operate for the protection of the State is supplemented by its empowerment to take all measures required for the attainment of its national security objectives. The Evacuation Compensation Law purports to implement a policy determined by the Knesset and the government as a national security goal. It follows that IDF soldiers are permitted to perform all the requisite actions for the attainment of this goal. The use of the army for the enforcement of the Law therefore falls within the ambit of actions that the army is permitted to perform.

945. Having established the legal basis for the government's power to use IDF soldiers, the Court proceeded to examine the reasonability of its decision to use army soldiers. Chief Justice Barak ruled that the government's exercise of discretion was reasonable in the circumstances. The Evacuation Compensation Law necessitated a number of actions for its implementation, among them the prevention of mass disturbances of public order, and the prevention of illegal entry into the Gaza Strip. The declared purpose of the mass disturbances and illegal infiltration was to prevent the execution of the Law. Under the circumstances, these tasks exceeded the capacity of the Police and there was, therefore, an urgent need to use the army for the realization of these goals. Therefore, the petition was rejected.

§3. The Duty to Enlist in the Army

946. Service in the Israeli army is mandatory, both in the context of regular service, and in reserve duty, for men and women. Section 4 of Basic Law: The Army

---

The plan was legally based on the Disengagement Plan (Implementation) Law, (otherwise known as the 'Evacuation Compensation Law'), which prescribed the guidelines for the evacuees' compensation. Those opposed to the disengagement concurrently waged a legal battle in the chambers of the Supreme Court. They petitioned the High Court of Justice in relation to almost every governmental decision dealing with the disengagement, perhaps in a last ditch, desperate attempt to forestall what they regarded as the 'evil decree'. The High Court thus became an active partner in the movement at all its various stages. For a discussion on this matter *see*, by author, S. Navot, *The Israeli withdrawal from Gaza-a Constitutional Perspective*, 12(1) European Public Law, 17 (March 2006).

is limited to the imposition of a general duty, according to which the duty of serving in the army and recruitment for the army 'shall be as prescribed by or by virtue of Law'. The duty to serve in the army was originally regulated by the Defence Service Law. This law prescribed a period of thirty months' service for men and twenty-four months' service for women. The Defence Service Law was amended in 1995, to expressly provide that the duration of service for men would be thirty-six months. The force of this amendment was for a limited period, which is extended from time to time. Since 2015, the length of basic military service is thirty-two months for men and twenty-four months for women.

947. The existing arrangement regarding military service indicates glaring inequality, given that the duration of service is actually a year longer for men than for women. Similarly, a number of grounds for exemption relate specifically to women, such as, *inter alia*, being the mother of a young child, pregnancy, or reasons related to her family and religious environment that prevent her service in the army. A few years ago, an amendment implementing the Court's ruling in the *Miller* case was introduced into the Woman's Equal Rights Law, 1951. This amendment provided that 'all women who are candidates for, or currently in, the army shall have a right equal to that of a man, to serve in any position, or to be posted in any position; a distinction between men and women shall not be regarded as violating this right where it flows from the essence, or character of the role'.

948. The Defence Service Law also empowers the Minister of Defence to grant an exemption or deferral of service for the various reasons enumerated by the law. The discretion to exempt certain persons from the obligation of mandatory military service has constituted the basis for deferring military service for many years. Effectively, this discretion has been used to exempt from service male ultra-Orthodox Jews who have reached the age of recruitment but are full time students at a religious institution (a Yeshiva). The first Prime Minister of Israel, David Ben-Gurion, compromised with the ultraorthodox Jews, exempting Yeshiva students from serving in the Army.[427] As a result of this agreement, this ultra-religious portion of the population is, in effect, exempt from any military duty.

949. This exemption has been at the core of a continuous struggle between secular and orthodox Jews for over fifty years. Its importance lies not only in the fact that it breaches the basic principle of equality, but also, and primarily, due to the security problems in Israel. Due to the protracted Arab-Israeli conflict, thousands of soldiers have lost their lives in combat since 1948. Exemption from military service is, therefore, a real advantage, since it means, essentially, exemption from mortal danger and from a basic social responsibility. The main reason for the fact that the exemption policy has lasted so long is the Israeli political structure. Religious parties supporting the exemption have played a crucial role in every government. In many, if not all cases, the governing coalition has depended upon the support of the

427. It is of note that the word 'exemption' is not used, and formally the enlistment of Yeshiva students is 'postponed' as long as they keep studying in the Yeshiva.

religious parties for its survival. Therefore, the religious parties have regarded the exemption policy as a legitimate political demand during coalition negotiations.

950. Over the years, there have been numerous attempts at cancelling the exemption granted to Yeshiva students, by way of petitions to the HCJ. In 1998, in the *Rubinstein* case, the Supreme Court ruled that the decision on the deferral of service for Yeshiva students 'must be adopted in the framework of a national decision made by the Knesset regarding the position of the State of Israel on a controversial national-social issue'.[428] The Court therefore ruled that the Minister of Defence was not empowered to grant a sweeping deferral to full time Yeshiva students, in the absence of a substantive arrangement, addressing the entire matter, in primary legislation. However, the Court did not actually cancel the exemptions that had already been granted, and it suspended the effect of its decision, pending a substantive legislative solution. Following protracted deliberations within the framework of the Tal Commission, and subsequently in the Knesset, the enlistment deferral was anchored in law, which was struck down by the HTC in 2012, as it disproportionately impaired the equality principle. A new law granting again a deferral to full time Yeshiva students was passed in 2015 and a petition against it is still pending, before an expanded panel of nine judges.

951. The Minister of Defence is also authorized to grant an exemption from service on the grounds of conscience, based on the authority conferred by the Defence Service Law. Here, the exemption is granted to a person who opposes military service on an ideological or principled basis.[429] A special committee is charged with dealing with this kind exemption.

952. In conclusion, in Israel the actions of the army are subject to ongoing supervision, both by the Government and the Knesset, and by the Supreme Court. However, Israel is a State that has been fighting for survival since its establishment, having fought a number of wars, and having been a victim of countless, ongoing heinous terrorist attacks. The resultant ongoing state of national emergency on the security front involves a plethora of extraordinary rights and powers being granted to the security authorities. This, in turn, has necessitated exceptionally tight and broad supervision of the manifold activities of the security authorities.

---

428. HCJ 3267/97 *Rubinstein v. Minister of Defence*, 52(5) PD 481.
429. HCJ 1380/02 *Ben Artzi v. Minister of Defence*, PD 56(4) 476; *see also* HCJ *Zonshein v. Judge Advocate General* (2003) 57(1) PD 726, in which the Israeli Supreme Court recently distinguished between an objection in principle to military service, for which an exemption may be given, and 'selective conscientious objection', based on an objection to a particular form of service, based on opposition to a particular Government policy (such as service in the Territories, or Lebanon), which the Supreme Court was not prepared to recognize as an acceptable form of conscientious objection.

Chapter 5. The Constitutional Relationship Between Religion and State

§1. Introduction

953. The State of Israel is variously defined as the Jewish State, the State of the Jews, or the State of the Jewish People. The 'Jewish' component of the definition is a constitutive component of its statehood, and was recognized as such by the international community in the framework of the Partition Decision adopted by the General Assembly of the United Nations on 29 November 1947, even before the establishment of the State. Indeed, this component finds profound expression in the Declaration of the Establishment of the State of Israel, and primarily, it finds expression in a series of arrangements actually practised in the State of Israel.

954. Israel is the political framework in which the Jewish people realizes its rights to self-determination, and was established as the state of the Jewish people, serving as its nation state. However, the phenomenon known as 'Judaism' comprises 'national' as well as 'religious' elements, and Judaism does not distinguish between elements normally classified as 'national' and components normally classified as religious or theological. The political framework that realizes Jewish national self-determination – Israel – has never accepted a principled separation between the state and religion. However, while rejecting the principle of separation of state and religion, the desirable combination of these elements has been, and continues to be, disputed. This dispute is manifested in a plethora of important, substantive questions that affect practical issues on the national agenda. Accordingly, the question of 'who is a Jew' affects the interpretation of the Law of Return, and the question of what is Judaism affects the interpretation of the directive in Basic Law: Human Dignity and Freedom, to entrench the 'values of Israel as a Jewish and Democratic State'.

955. The characterization of Israel as a Jewish state does not necessarily confer extra privileges upon Jewish citizens or establish the Jewish religion as state law. The Jewish character of the State receives its expression in the Declaration of the Establishment of the State. The Supreme Court recognized that the Jewish character of the State underlies the basic principles and values of the State. Today, this recognition of the Jewish character of the State finds expression in the basic law dealing with human rights, which states that human rights 'shall be upheld in the spirit of the principles set forth in the Declaration of the Establishment of the State of Israel'.

956. The recognition of the legitimacy of the existence of the State of Israel as a Jewish State is premised on three basic foundations:[430] (a) the international resolution of 1947 accepting the Partition Plan, under which a Jewish State would be

430. A. Rubinstein & B. Medina, *The Constitutional Law of the State of Israel*, 322–335 (6th ed. 2005, In Hebrew).

established in the State of Israel; (b) the moral recognition of the Jewish people's right to self-determination in a national framework. Under international law, a nation's right to 'self-determination' is defined as follows: 'All peoples have the right of self-determination. By virtue of that right they freely determine their political status and freely pursue their economic, social and cultural development';[431] and (c) the practice in other democratic nation states around the world, which refutes the claim that the democratic system necessitates 'state neutrality' from a national perspective.

957. The accepted view in Israel today is that in order to ensure that the Jewish people is able to actually realize its right to self-determination, it is necessary to ensure the continued existence of a decisive Jewish majority in the State. The Jewish public in Israel is plagued by a real fear that loss of a national majority in the State of Israel would not only result in the negation of the possibility of realizing significant aspects of the Jewish people's right to self-determination within the framework of a state; it would also pose an existential danger for the Jewish citizens, as a result of the Jewish-Palestinian dispute, which is the conflict between the Israeli Jews and the Palestinian nation, of which some of the Israeli Arabs feel ethno-culturally a part.

958. At the same time, the State of Israel is also a democratic state, in the sense of the sovereignty of the state's citizens as a whole, irrespective of their ethnic, national origins. The definition of the State of Israel as a Jewish state does not, therefore, contradict its parallel definition as the democratic state of all its citizens. The State is a Jewish state in the sense of providing a framework for the realization of particular interests of the Jewish people. However, sovereignty in the State is vested in its entire citizenry, which includes the non-Jewish public. The State is a Jewish state in the sense of constituting a framework for the realization of the interests of the Jewish people as a national-cultural group. These interests receive their expression in a number of principal dimensions, including the preference for Jews in terms of entry into Israel – the definition of the state as a Jewish State legitimizes arrangements such as the Law of Return; the adoption of special measures to ensure the preservation of a Jewish majority within the Israeli citizenry; the application of particular measures intended to maintain the 'Jewish character' of public life; extensive state provision of religious services, primarily to the Jewish public; the application of Jewish religious law as the personal status law of Jews in Israel; the preservation and promotion of strong ties to the Jews of the Diaspora; and granting national state standing to the institutions of the Jewish people.

959. The relationship between the Jewish religion and the state is a complex one. On the one hand, the distinction between religion and state is preserved, in the sense that state mechanisms are not used to enforce individual performance of religious precepts. Apart from the specific law of personal status, religious law lacks the status of judicially enforceable state law. On the other hand, there is considerable

431. Article 1(1) of the International Covenant on Civil and Political Rights, and Arts 1(2) and 55 of the UN Charter.

readiness to legitimate the utilization of state power in enforcing norms originating in religious commandments. This form of coercion is exercised, *inter alia*, to infuse Israeli public life with a Jewish character, to promote general societal goals (such as ensuring weekly rest for workers), and to prevent offending religious sensibilities. The State's involvement in these areas is supplemented by its extensive involvement in the provision of religious services and the organization of ritual activities (such as, *inter alia*, the provision of prayer books at holy sites, the maintenance of holy sites, and ritual baths).This involvement often necessitates the use of State power to enforce religious precepts, to the extent required for the provision of religious services.

§2. The Legal Framework for the Regulation of Religious Affairs

960. In Israel, the State may be involved in the provision of religious services and in the regulation of activities connected with religious ritual, and in this context 'religious' considerations are legitimate considerations in the government's activities. For example, the Court ruled that the State may take into account the needs of the religious public when determining the dates for implementing 'summer time' (prior to this matter being statutorily regulated),[432] in the provision of special protective gas masks for men with beards,[433] and in exempting women from the obligation of military service based on religious conviction. The Israeli HCJ ruled that:

> considerations pertaining to the observance of *commandments*, as such, cannot be countenanced in the actions of the administration, except to the extent permitted by law; however considerations of the *person*, as such, and when appropriately balanced, are certainly acceptable ... the underlying foundation of the balance lies in the rule that it is possible, and even obligatory, to take account of the person, or the interests of a certain sector of the population, provided that it does not lead to the imposition of commandments on another person.[434]

I. The Council of the Chief Rabbinate and the Chief Rabbis

961. Several statutory bodies were established and vested with state powers for the purpose of providing religious services to the Jews in Israel: the Council of the Chief Rabbinate of Israel, and the Chief Rabbis (pursuant to the Chief Rabbinate of Israel Law, 1980), 'town rabbis' (i.e., local rabbis) and religious councils, under the Jewish Religious Services Law, 1971.

---

432. HCJ 217/80 *Segel v. Minister of the Interior*, 34(4) PD 429.

433. HCJ 4919/90 *Miller v. Minister of Defence*, 45(2) PD 293. This ruling recognized the duty of the Minister of Defence to provide special protective kits for those who grow beards for religious reasons. Later on, the Court ruled that in this respect there were no grounds for discriminating against those who grow a beard for other reasons, unrelated to religion: HCJ 205/94 *Nof.* v. *Minister of Defence*, 50(5) PD 449.

434. HCJ 3872/93 *Mitral v. Prime Minister and Minister of Religion*, 47(5) PD 485, p. 50ff.

962. According to the Chief Rabbinate of Israel Law, the Council of the Chief Rabbinate of Israel consists of the two Chief Rabbis of Israel (one of them a Sepharadi and the other Ashkenazi), four town rabbis, and ten rabbis elected by the 'Electoral Assembly', consisting of eighty rabbis and seventy representatives of the public, among them, the heads of local councils, members of Knesset, and representatives of the public appointed by the Government. The Assembly also appoints the two Chief Rabbis, each of whom serves for a period of ten years. During the first five years of their tenure, one of them serves as President of the Council and the other as the President of the Rabbinical Court of Appeals; in the second five years they switch positions.

963. The Council of the Chief Rabbinate provides religious services to the religious public. By force of law, the Council is authorized to give answers and expert opinions in halakhic matters, to give Kashrut certificates, and to determine competency for the position of a town rabbi. The Council also advises the governmental authorities on halakhic questions, and their advice is subject to judicial review, despite its halakhic content.

964. Thus in the *Shakdiel* case, the Supreme Court overturned the Rabbinate's determination regarding the *halakhic* position on the competence of women to serve on the religious councils. The Court ruled that the services provided by the religious councils are indeed religious, but that the council's role is limited to the provision of the services only, and does not require any religious-halakhic decision regarding the services themselves. As such, there is no impediment, even according to religious law, to appointing a woman as a member of the council.[435] With respect to the Rabbinate's claim that, according to the Jewish religious law, women cannot be appointed to public positions, the Court ruled that this was an inaccurate (or at least incomplete) presentation of the *halakhic* position, given that there were a number of leading contemporary *halakhic* authorities which permitted the appointment of women to public positions. The ruling also rejected the Rabbinate's position that people espousing a non-orthodox world view cannot be appointed as members of the religious council. The rule in this respect is that in appointing its representatives to the religious council, the local authority must consider two factors: the principle of representation, meaning that the composition of the candidates of the local authority in the religious council must, as far as possible, reflect the balance of powers in the council of local authority; and the 'test of personal suitability', according to which it is sufficient that a person has a positive attitude towards religious matters. Specifically, it ruled that a candidate was not to be disqualified because of his world view: 'The disqualification of a candidate for reasons relating to his world view, such as his affiliation with a non-orthodox stream, constitutes illegal discrimination and will be rejected.'[436]

965. However, despite these rulings, the actual situation is not always satisfactory, and occasionally, the Rabbinate refuses to accept the authority of the HCJ.

435. HCJ 153/87 *Shakdiel v. Minister for Religious Affairs*, 42(2) PD 221, 238.
436. HCJ 4733/94 *Naot v. Haifa Municipal Council*, 49(5) PD 111.

II. Rabbinical Courts

966. The Rabbinical Courts operate by virtue of the Rabbinical Court Jurisdiction (Marriages and Divorce) Law. The Rabbinical Courts have exclusive jurisdiction in all matters of marriage and divorce of Jews in Israel, and concurrent jurisdiction in 'any matter connected with the divorce suit' including maintenance and jurisdiction for any other matter agreed upon by the parties, related to personal status and succession. The Rabbinical Courts adjudicate in accordance with *Din Torah* (Jewish religious law). The HCJ has quite frequently interfered with the decisions of the Rabbinical Court on the basis of general substantive principles, such as the best interests of the child or equality of rights for women, or even on the basis of procedural flaws, such as a violation of the principles of natural justice. As stated above, with respect to the Chief Rabbinate of Israel, the Rabbinical Courts too have often been unwilling to accept the authority, or the substantive decisions, of the HCJ.

III. Legal Religious Considerations

967. Because of the special status of religion in Israel, there a number of substantive legal arrangements intended to give expression to the Jewish culture and character of public life in Israel, which infringe individual rights such as the freedom of religion, freedom from religion, freedom of occupation, and freedom of movement, among others. The system of arrangements in numerous areas in which a balance is struck between the Jewish character of the State and individual rights is referred to as the status quo, and in the context of preserving the status quo, the authorities are empowered to operate in accordance with religious considerations.

968. The status quo was created as a form of political compromise, without legal validity, that was agreed upon in 1947, in anticipation of the establishment of the State. It covered areas such as the observance of the Sabbath in public, government funded offices and institutions, the observance of *Kashrut* in governmental offices, institutions, the army, etc., the application of religious law with respect to marriage and divorce, ensuring educational autonomy for the various streams, and others. Over the years however, these arrangements have changed considerably, and in accordance with political developments, the status quo has declined considerably in recent years. Attempts to anchor the status quo in legislation and even within the framework of a basic law have thus far been unsuccessful, and the Court does not recognize the status quo as bearing any binding character.

969. The law provides that a governmental authority is only permitted to restrict individual freedom in order to enhance the Jewish character of public aspects of Israeli life, if it is explicitly authorized by law to take those considerations into account. Consequently, there are numerous 'enabling provisions' which empower local authorities to take into account 'considerations of religious tradition' in their regulative capacity, for example regarding the opening hours of businesses, and the prohibition on opening businesses on the *Sabbath*. The Pig-Raising Prohibition

Law, which imposes a state-wide prohibition on the raising and keeping of pigs, empowers the local authorities to enact by-laws that restrict or prohibit the raising or keeping of pigs, and the selling of pork and pork products intended for eating. Another important law in this context is the Matzot (Prohibition of Leaven) Law, 1986, which prohibits the owner of a business to publicly display any leavened product for sale or consumption during the Passover period.

970. These provisions are subject to judicial review by force of Basic Law: Freedom of Occupation, and with respect to legislation enacted after 1992, by Basic Law: Human Dignity and Liberty. To date, the Court has refrained from invalidating any such statutory provision. In this context, however, provisions of this kind are given a narrow interpretation. For example, in addressing the by-law that prohibited the opening of businesses of the Sabbath, the Court ruled:

> This is a coercively formulated statutory provision, which … to protect the interests of the religious public, to prevent damage to the character and spirit of the day of rest … when any statute is intended to restrict or impair individual rights, its interpretation must be appropriately narrow.[437]

971. An outstanding example of judicial review of provisions restricting human rights on the basis of religious considerations is the *Solodkin* judgment. This case dealt with the powers of the local authorities to prohibit the sale of pork within their borders, i.e., to prohibit the opening of stores that sell un-kosher meat. The unanimous verdict of the Court was that it is essential to balance between the aspiration to protect religious and national feelings that are wounded by the sale of pork, and the protection of the freedom of conscience and freedom of occupation of individuals wishing to purchase and to sell pork. The arrangement prescribed in the Local Authorities (Special Enablement) Law was intended to ensure the striking of an appropriate balance between interests, against the background of the 'specific local characteristics' of each particular township, and even of every specific area within a township or a regional council, to the extent that such a separation is possible.[438] The Court ruled, in its decision on the matter, that the local authority had to consider two primary factors: the appropriate protection of the feelings of the offended residents, which was a function of the proximity of their dwellings to the place where the pork was being sold, and their relative numbers in terms of the overall population; and the need to ensure the potential for purchasing pork in a near and accessible location. In this context, the Court ruled that:

> in a mixed settlement, in which there is even a minority whose freedom would be abridged if the sale of pork and its products is prohibited, it is imperative to ensure that the violation of their freedom is proportional. This condition is

437. HCJ 5073/91 *Israel Theatres Ltd. v. Nethanya Municipality*, 47(3) PD 192, 210.
438. *See* HCJ 953/01 *Solodkin v. Beit Shemesh Municipality* (as yet unpublished, delivered in July 2004). This concept is based on s. 2 of the Local Authorities (Special Enablement) Law, according to which 'A local authority may impose a limitation or prohibition [on the sale of pork] on the whole of its area of jurisdiction or on a particular part thereof; but in the latter case it shall apply to the whole population of such area or part.'

satisfied if there are arrangements to ensure that there is a place in the settlement (even on its outskirts) – or nearby, in which one can purchase and sell pork and its products. It must ensure that the selling point is accessible and that it is actually possible to maintain a location for the sale and purchase of pork products in that place.

972. Accordingly, the local authority must examine the character of the territorial unit. It must evaluate the degree of social consensus within that unit, and the degree of readiness for reciprocal tolerance in that unit. The Court recognized that, in principle, a local authority can prohibit the sale of pork within particular boundaries, and that it has discretion, but that this discretion is not unlimited, and must have consideration for certain factors such as the population composition of specific place, its habits, its lifestyle, and the character of that particular place.

IV. The 'Holy Places'

973. An additional area requiring State involvement in the provision of religious services, which requires religious considerations, is the Government's regulation of accepted forms of behaviour within the Holy Places. The accepted position in Israel is that the large numbers of holy sites for different groups necessitates the governmental regulation of religious activities in these places.

974. Under section 1 of the Protection of Holy Places Law, 1967 the governmental authority must make arrangements to ensure that the Holy Places are 'protected from desecration and any other violation, and from anything likely to violate the freedom of access of members of different religions to the places sacred to them or their feelings with regard to those places'. As such, where diverse groups wish to use the Holy Places in different ways, arrangements must be made that reflect consideration for the feelings of all.

975. One of the interesting questions in this context relates to the regulation of permitted forms of prayer in the Holy Places. In the *Hofman* case, the Court discussed the right of a women's prayer group to pray at the Western Wall according to their own custom, involving carrying Torah scrolls, wearing *tallitot*, and reading out loud from the Torah. This was considered to be unacceptable in the eyes of the authorities in charge of prayer arrangements at the Wall, and aroused the fierce objection of the overwhelming majority of those praying at the Wall – both men and women – and was accompanied by disturbances, and physical and verbal violence. The 'Women of the Wall' claimed that their form of prayer did not in essence differ from the 'custom of the place', apart from the fact that this form of prayer was exclusive for men. They did not request the removal of the partition between men and women, or to conduct themselves in a manner that deviated from what was accepted in the prayer service. They claimed that the offence to religious feelings caused by their form of prayer was the product of the majority's perception, in accordance with 'Orthodox' Jewish religious law, that men and women were not equal (or at least that women are forbidden from playing an active role in prayer services). As such, the dispute focused on the appropriate degree of consideration to be given to the intolerant attitudes of a group within society, and in addition, to whether the local custom should be interpreted as being identical to the 'status quo' and the traditional local custom, or whether it admitted of changes.

976. The petitioner's claim was that this was not a case of a group requesting the State to leave it alone and refrain from interfering with its discriminatory practices. The issue concerned a group requesting state assistance in imposing its own discriminatory practices upon others. The adjudication of the case stretched out over a decade, consisting of a number of judgments.

977. In the first judgment,[439] as a matter of principle, there was a majority for the view (per Justices Shamgar and Levin, against the dissenting view of Justice Elon) that the petitioners had a basic right to pray at the Western Wall, according to their own custom. However, on a practical level, Justice Shamgar joined Justice Elon in deferring the petitions (though not for the same reason), and recommended that the Government determine the appropriate arrangements and conditions in the framework of which the petitioners would be able to realize their right to pray at the Western Wall according to their custom. This led to the submission of recommendations, proposing that the women be allowed to realize their right to pray at a site adjacent to the Western Wall. This proposal was rejected by the Women of the Wall, and their position was accepted by Justice Mazza,[440] who ruled that the Government's recommendation contradicted the aforementioned guideline laid down by Justice Shamgar, and that accordingly, the Government must make arrangements that would enable the women to pray according to their custom, at the Western Wall. However, in a further hearing, this result was partially overturned, and the majority ruled that the appropriate balance between the conflicting interests dictated conducting the women's prayers at a location adjacent to the Western Wall, having consideration for the grave offence given by their prayers to the other worshippers at the Western Wall, and provided that a proper place of prayer be prepared for them within one year.[441]

978. With respect to the scope of judicial review regarding this matter, the judgments evince diverse approaches. Justice Englard expressed the view that the matter was not appropriate for judicial review. A second approach called for the preservation of the status quo in the location, which meant adopting a position that reflected the feelings of the majority, which was expressed by the status quo. The third approach, which was adopted by the majority of the justices who gave opinions in the *Hoffman* case, was based on a balance between the different interests, without giving *a priori* preference to 'local custom'. An attempt must be made to

---

439. HCJ 257/89 *Hoffman v. Appointee of the Western Wall*, 48(2) PD 265.

440. HCJ 3358/95 *Hoffman v. Director General of Prime Minister's Office*, 54(2) PD 345, 358 (Justice Mazza). Nonetheless, in practice, after one case which culminated in a violent outburst, the prayers of the women's group according to the Reform version, have been forbidden.

441. FHC 4128/00 *Director General of Prime Minister's Office v. Hoffman*, 57(3) PD 289.

enable the appropriate realization of each one of the conflicting interests. Accordingly, the legitimacy of the prohibition on prayers at the Wall in deviation from the local custom must be dependent on the existence of a reasonable alternative for those wishing to pray in a manner that diverges from the local custom. Needless to say, whether or not a place adjacent to the plaza of the Western Wall constitutes a reasonable alternative is a matter of opinion.

§3. The Legal Status of the Institutions of the Jewish People in the Diaspora

979. As stated above, the definition of the State of Israel as a Jewish state expresses its essence as a political framework which gives expression to the Jewish people's right to self-determination. In that capacity, the State of Israel maintains a special link to the Jewish people in the Diaspora. Among other things, this connection manifests itself in the allocation of funds and various other forms of assistance to Jewish communities all over the world, and in the assumption of jurisdiction over offences committed abroad against 'the life, bodily welfare, health, freedom or property of a Jew, as a Jew, or the property of a Jewish institution, because it is such'.[442] Furthermore, the State grants special standing to the 'National Institutions' of the Jewish people, whose declared and official *raison d'être* is the promotion of Jewish interests. For example, section 5 of the World Zionist Organization – Jewish Agency (Status) Law, 1953 states that:

> The mission of gathering in the exiles, which is the central task of the State of Israel and the Zionist movement in our days, requires constant efforts by the Jewish people in the Diaspora; the State of Israel, therefore, expects the cooperation of all Jews, as individuals and groups, in building up the State and assisting the immigration to it of the masses of the people, and with respect to the unity of all sections of Jewry as necessary for this purpose.

980. The national institutions operate in Israel to promote the interests of Jews. For example, the settlement department of the Jewish Agency creates settlements for the settling of Jews; and the Jewish National Fund deals with the settling of Jews in lands under its ownership. Although these organizations are basically private, and do not receive State funding, they nonetheless express the Jewish character of the State. The essence of the Agency Status Law is in the expression it gives to the historical connection between the Jewish people and the State of Israel.

981. The question that arose in case law was to what extent the national institutions can adopt discriminatory policies based on national ethnic considerations. According to the *Kaadan* ruling, the Jewish Agency cannot adopt discriminatory policies (e.g., the establishment of a 'Jews only' settlement), when establishing a settlement on land that it has received from the State. The state and those acting on

442. Section 13(b)(2) of the Penal Code, 1977.

its behalf are not permitted to discriminate in the allocation of state resources, on the basis of religion and nation.

982. In conclusion, the State of Israel was designated as the national home of the Jewish people. Its renaissance was accompanied by international recognition of the Jewish state, by force of an explicit United Nations resolution. Nonetheless, while Israel is the national home of the Jews, by force of its founders' intentions and yearnings, and by force of its laws, it is also, equally, the home of all its resident citizens, including its Arab citizens. As a Jewish and democratic state, it fulfils this function despite the unabated hostility and the war with the Arab world and terrorist actions against it. As a Jewish and democratic state it confronts the ongoing need and challenge of balancing between the values of a 'Jewish' state and those of a 'democratic' state, and of ameliorating the tension created by the need to confront the exigencies of a state of war, and of granting equal civil rights to the Arab minority.

Selected Bibliography

§1. On the Israeli legal system:

Barak, A. 'Constitutionalization of the Israeli Legal System as a Result of the Basic Laws and Its Effect on Procedural and Substantive Criminal Law'. 31 *Israel Law Review* (1997): 3.

Barak, Aharon. 'A Constitutional Revolution: Israel's Basic Laws'. (1993) *Faculty Scholarship Series*. Paper 3697. Available at: http://digitalcommons.law.yale.edu/fss_papers/3697.

Barak-Erez, D. 'From an Unwritten to a Written Constitution: The Israeli Challenge in American Perspective'. 26 *Colum. Human Rights L. Rev* (1995) 309.

Brichta. *Political Reform in Israel – The Quest for a Stable and Effective Government* (2001).

Gavison, R. 'Forty Years of Israeli Law: Constitutional Law (in response to Prof. S. Shetreet)'. 24(3–4) *Israel Law Review* (1990) 431.

Gavison, Ruth. 'Constitutions and Political Reconstruction?: Israel's Quest for a Constitution'. in Saïd Amir Arjomand (ed) *Constitutionalism and Political Reconstruction* 69 (Leiden, BRILL, 2007).

Harris, Ron, Kedar, Alexandre (Sandy), Lahav, Pnina and Likhovski, Assaf. *Israeli Legal History: Past and Present: The History of Law in a Multi-Cultural Society: Israel, 1917–1967* (Aldershot: Ashgate Publishing, 2002).

Hirschl, R. 'Israel's Constitutional Revolution: The Legal Interpretation of Entrenched Civil Liberties in an Emerging Neo-liberal Economic Order'. 46 *American Journal of Comparative Law* (1998): 427.

Friedmann, D. 'The Effect of Foreign Law on the Law of Israel: Remnants of the Ottoman Period'. 10 *Israel Law Review* (1975): 92.

Friedmann, D. 'Infusion of the Common Law into the Legal System of Israel'. 10 *Israel Law Review* (1975): 324.

Friedmann, D. 'Independent Development of Israeli Law'. 10 *Israel Law Review* (1975): 515.

Hofnung, M. 'Unintended Consequences of Unplanned Constitutional Reform: Constitutional Politics in Israel'. 44 *American Journal of Comparative Law* (1996): 585.

Klein, C. *Le Système Politique d'Israel* (Collection Thémis, PUF Paris 1983).

Klein, C. *Le Droit Israélien* (Collection Que sais-je, PUF 1990).

Kretzmer, D. 'The New Basic Laws on Human Rights: A Mini Revolution in Israeli Constitutional Law'. 26 *Israel Law Review* (1992): 238.

Selected Bibliography

Mandel, M. 'How We Changed Everything so That Everything Would Remain the Same' 32 *Israel Law Review* (1998): 250.

Mandel, M. 'Democracy and the New Constitutionalism in Israel'. 33 *Israel Law Review* (1999): 259.

Navot, S. The Constitution of Israel- a Contextual Analysis (Hart, 2014).

Table of Cases

Table of Cases

Civil case (CC)

Civil File Jerusalem (CF (Jer.))

Civil Leave to Appeal (CLA)

Criminal Appeal (Cr. A)

Further Hearing (FH or FHC)

Criminal request to appeal (Cr. Req. A.)

Election Appeal (EA)

High Court of Justice (HCJ)

Table of Cases

51/68 *Azur Local Municipality v. Minister of the Interior*, 507 – 22(2) PD 226
316/03 *Bakri v. Israel Film Council,* 704 58(1) 849
5872/01 *Barakeh v. Prime Minister,* 725 – 56(3) PD 1
3114/02 *Barakeh v. The Minister of Defence and Others*, 861- 56(3) PD 11
4908/10 *Bar-On, MK v. The Knesset*, 58, 70, 213, 443 -(rendered on April 2011)
1000/92 *Bavli v. Rabbinical Court of Appeals*, 667 – 48(2) PD 221
40/70 *Becker v. Minister of Defence,* 404, 408 – 24(1) PD 238
1380/02 *Ben Artzi v. Minister of Defence*, 951 – PD 56(4) 476
98/69 *Bergman v. Minister of Finance,* 38, 420, 622 – 23(1) PD 693
1/49 *Bezerano v. Minister of Police*, 136, 577 – 2 PD 80
243/52 *Bialer v. Minister of Finance*, 908 – 7 PD 429
296/80 *Bokovza v. State of Israel,* 544 – 35(1) 492
3436/02 *Castodia Internationala de Tara Santa v. Government of Israel*, 720 – 56(3) PD 22,
7111/95 *Centre for Local Government v. Knesset*, 440 – 50(2) PD 485
36/51 *Chet v. Haifa Municipality,* 503 – 5 PD 1553
6924/98 *Citizens Rights Association v. Government of Israel*, 41, 760 – 55(5) PD 15
86652/96 *Citizens rights Association v. Minister of Interior*, 446 – PD (3) 117
6111/94 *Committee for Traditionalists v. Council of the Chief Rabbinate of Israel*, 608 – 49(5) PD 94
2481/93 *Dayan v. Jerusalem District Commander*, 691 – 48(2) PD 456
8665/14 *Desete v. Minister of Interior et al*, 840 – (11 Aug. 2015)
3434/96 *Dr. Menachem Hoffnung v. Knesset Chairman*, 57 – 50(3) 70
390/79 *Duikat v. Government of Israel,* 10, 935 – 34(1) PD 1
7385/13 *Eitan v. the Government and the Knesset*, 838 – (22 Sep. 2014)
721/94 *El-Al Airlines v. Danilowitz,* 680 – 58(5) PD 749
39/82 *Elazar Hanpling et al. v. Tzvi Tzikler et al*, 110 – 36(2) PD 537
155/60 *Elazar v. Mayor of Bat-Yam,* 808 – 14 PD 1511
152/82 *Elon v. Israeli Government,* 486 – 36(4) PD 449
5537/91 *Ephrati v. Ostfeld,* 146 – 46(3) PD 501
464/84 *Ezra v. Tel-Aviv-Jaffa Mayor,* 881 – 39(1) PD 745
6579/99 *Filber v. Israeli Government*, 461 – (unpublished)
953/89 *Ganor v. Attorney General,* 463 – 44(2) PD 485
253/64 *G'eris v. Official in Charge of the Haifa District*, 231 – 18(4) PD 673
381/91 *Gross v. Ministry of Education,* 891 – 46(1) PD 53
3166/14 *Gutmann v. Attorney General,* 57- (March 12, 2015)
1438/98 *HaTenua HaMesoratit v. Minister for Religious Affairs*, 886 – 53(5) 337
9290/99 *Headquarters of Victims of Terrorism v. Government of Israel*, 791 – 54(1) PD 8
257/89 *Hoffman v. Appointee of the Western Wall*, 977 – 48(2) PD 265
3358/95 *Hoffman v. Director General of Prime Minister's Office*, 977 – 54(2) PD 345
453/94 *Israeli Women's Network v. Government of Israel*, 661 – 48(5) PD 529
5073/91 *Israel Theatres Ltd. v. Nethanya Municipality*, 970 – 47(3) PD 192
428/86 *Itzhak Barzilai v. Government of Israel and 52 others*, 206 – 40(3) PD 505
1635/90 *Joseph Jerecezwski v. Prime Minister*, 133 – 45(1) PD 749
6698/95 *Kaadan v. Israel Lands Administration*, 652 – 54(1) PD 258

Table of Cases

Severe Criminal case (SCC)

Index

The numbers here refer to paragraph numbers.

Index

www.ingramcontent.com/pod-product-compliance
Lightning Source LLC
Chambersburg PA
CBHW071422230926
51846CB00001B/111
9789041169433